FIXED IDEAS OF MONEY

Most European countries are rather small, yet we know little about their monetary history. This book analyzes for the first time the experience of seven small states (Austria, Belgium, Denmark, the Netherlands, Norway, Sweden, and Switzerland) during the last hundred years, starting with the restoration of the gold standard after World War I and ending with Sweden's rejection of the Euro in 2003. The comparative analysis shows that, for most of the twentieth century, the options of policy makers were seriously constrained by a distinct fear of floating exchange rates. Only with the crisis of the European Monetary System (EMS) in 1992–1993 did the idea that a flexible exchange rate regime was suited for a small open economy gain currency. The book also analyzes the differences among small states and concludes that economic structures or foreign policy orientations were far more important for the timing of regime changes than domestic institutions and policies.

Tobias Straumann is Lecturer in the History Department of the University of Zurich and the Economics Department of the University of Basel. He studied at the Universities of Bielefeld and Zurich and the Ecole des Hautes Etudes en Sciences Sociales in Paris. After a career in economic journalism, he was a visiting scholar at the University of California at Berkeley and lecturer at the University of Lausanne. Dr. Straumann has worked in the fields of Swiss economic history and European financial and monetary history. He has published articles in the *Journal of Contemporary History*, the *European Review of Economic History*, and the *Historische Zeitschrift*.

STUDIES IN MACROECONOMIC HISTORY

SERIES EDITOR
Michael D. Bordo, *Rutgers University*

EDITORS
Marc Flandreau, *Institut d'Etudes Politiques de Paris*
Chris Meissner, *University of California, Davis*
François Velde, *Federal Reserve Bank of Chicago*
David C. Wheelock, *Federal Reserve Bank of St. Louis*

The titles in this series investigate themes of interest to economists and economic historians in the rapidly developing field of macroeconomic history. The four areas covered include the application of monetary and finance theory, international economics, and quantitative methods to historical problems; the historical application of growth and development theory and theories of business fluctuations; the history of domestic and international monetary, financial, and other macroeconomic institutions; and the history of international monetary and financial systems. The series amalgamates the former Cambridge University Press series Studies in Monetary and Financial History and Studies in Quantitative Economic History.

OTHER BOOKS IN THE SERIES

Howard Bodenhorn, A History of Banking in Antebellum America [9780521662857, 9780521669993]

Michael D. Bordo, The Gold Standard and Related Regimes [9780521550062, 9780521022941]

Michael D. Bordo and Forrest Capie (eds.), Monetary Regimes in Transition [9780521419062]

Michael D. Bordo and Roberto Cortés-Conde (eds.), Transferring Wealth and Power from the Old to the New World [9780521773058, 9780511664793]

Claudio Borio, Gianni Toniolo, and Piet Clement (eds.), Past and Future of Central Bank Cooperation [9780521877794, 9780511510779]

Richard Burdekin and Pierre Siklos (eds.), Deflation: Current and Historical Perspectives [9780521837996, 9780511607004]

Trevor J. O. Dick and John E. Floyd, Canada and the Gold Standard [9780521404082, 9780521617062]

Barry Eichengreen, Elusive Stability [9780521365383, 9780521448475, 9780511664397]

Barry Eichengreen (ed.), Europe's Postwar Recovery [9780521482790, 9780521030786]

Caroline Fohlin, Finance Capitalism and Germany's Rise to Industrial Power [9780521810203, 9780511510908]

Michele Fratianni and Franco Spinelli, A Monetary History of Italy [9780521443159, 9780521023450, 9780511559686]

Continued after the Index

Fixed Ideas of Money

*Small States and Exchange Rate Regimes
in Twentieth-Century Europe*

TOBIAS STRAUMANN

University of Zurich

CAMBRIDGE UNIVERSITY PRESS
Cambridge, New York, Melbourne, Madrid, Cape Town,
Singapore, São Paulo, Delhi, Tokyo, Mexico City

Cambridge University Press
32 Avenue of the Americas, New York, NY 10013-2473, USA

www.cambridge.org
Information on this title: www.cambridge.org/9780521112710

First published 2010
Reprinted 2011

A catalog record for this publication is available from the British Library.

Library of Congress Cataloging in Publication Data

Straumann, Tobias.
Fixed ideas of money : small states and exchange rate regimes in twentiethcentury
Europe / Tobias Straumann.
  p. cm. – (Studies in macroeconomic history)
Includes bibliographical references and index.
ISBN 978-0-521-11271-0
1. Foreign exchange – Europe. 2. Monetary policy – Europe.
3. States, Small. I. Title. II. Series.
HG3942.S78 2010
332.4´56094–dc22   2010011779

ISBN 978-0-521-11271-0 Hardback

To Manuela, Emil, and Jakob

Content

Figures

Tables

Preface

Few topics have been more popular among economic historians and political scientists than the monetary history of Western Europe, and the industry is still alive and well. Yet, as with any industry, some paths of discovery have been followed more frequently than others. Most important, scholars usually have focused on the large European countries because, obviously, France, Germany, and the United Kingdom have been the driving forces in Europe's monetary history, and therefore, the experiences of small European states have been neglected. This blind spot is the main reason for this study. It attempts to make a first step toward a more comprehensive understanding of the monetary history of seven small, economically developed countries: Austria, Belgium, Denmark, the Netherlands, Norway, Sweden, and Switzerland.

Given that almost every small state has its own language and has produced a bulk of literature on its monetary history, I decided to restrict the study in two ways. First, I focused on the question of exchange-rate regime changes, and second, I confined the period under study to the interwar years and the decades after the end of Bretton Woods because the regime changes were particularly frequent during these two periods. This restrictive approach enabled me to cope with the huge amounts of primary and public sources and to tell a coherent story. My main finding is that for most of the twentieth century, small European states preferred having their exchange rates fixed or pegged and that the reason for this preference was not institutional or economic in nature but rather the result of a deeply rooted fear that a floating exchange rate would hamper trade and complicate monetary policy.

Because of this strong preference for fixed rates, I have chosen to call this study *Fixed Ideas of Money*. The expression is not meant in negative terms, however, although these fixed ideas sometimes proved counterproductive, especially during the Great Depression of the 1930s. As I try to show, the fear of floating was based on considerations about possible risks of foreign exchange markets. In retrospect, this fear may seem exaggerated, yet it was entirely rational at the time, given that the goals of policy makers were to make controlled adjustments and to avoid short-term fluctuations. The corporatist ideal of keeping the power of markets within clearly defined limits was reflected directly in the way small European states chose their exchange-rate regimes during the twentieth century.

During the current crisis, there are signs that the trend toward floating exchange may become less popular among small states. In particular, Iceland, once overwhelmingly sceptical toward Brussels, is now considering adoption of the euro. Such a move would not question the basic argument of this study, however. First of all, Iceland is a very small country, counting only 320,000 inhabitants, and therefore hardly comparable with Belgium, Sweden, or Switzerland. Second, Iceland is not considering a return to the traditional monetary order by introducing fixed exchange rates. Policy makers know well enough that the old regime of the twentieth century would not have shielded them from the recent turbulence. On the contrary, it is very likely that a fixed-exchange-rate regime would have harmed the economy even more, similar to what happened in Argentina in the final phase of the currency board period. The "fixed ideas" of the twentieth century are not experiencing a comeback.

Needless to say, all this research could not have been done without the help of others. First of all, I would like to thank Albrecht Ritschl, through whom I discovered the monetary history of Europe, and Brad DeLong, Barry Eichengreen, and Tim Hatton, who introduced me to Europe's economic history during the twentieth century. Without the encouragement of all these inspiring teachers, I hardly would have approached this complicated topic. I am very thankful to Harold James for his great support. He read the manuscript, helped me to improve the basic argument, and endorsed the publication. I also profited from critical comments made by members of the scientific committee of the University of Zurich who reviewed my thesis: Volker Bornschier, Jörg Fisch, Dieter Ruloff, Jakob Tanner, and Ulrich Woitek. Last but not least, I would like to thank the editors of the series, in particular Michael Bordo and Scott Parris, for their interest and encouragement.

I am heavily indebted to a number of colleagues who have read parts of the manuscript: Nicolas Cuche, Luciano Ferrari, Klas Fregert, Patrick Halbeisen, Per Hansen, Lars Hörngren, Erik Jones, Drew Keeling, Hein Klemann, Sverre Knutsen, Daniel Lampart, Claude Million, Jonathon

Moses, Markus Stierli, Oliver Zimmer, and Mathias Zurlinden. And I have profited from conversations and exchanges with Elisabeth Allgoewer, Jan Baumann, Felix Butschek, Thomas David, Gerald Feldman, Serge Gaillard, Sébastien Guex, Eduard Hochreiter, Håkan Lindgren, Johannes Lindvall, Håkan Lobell, Ivo Maes, Margrit Müller, Philipp Müller, Tom Notermans, Kurt Schiltknecht, Peter Scholliers, Hansjörg Siegenthaler, Lars Svensson (Lund), Brigitte Unger, Anders Vredin, Herman van der Wee, and Jan Luiten van Zanden.

Finally, I thank all the people who helped me find the archival sources and publications I was looking for: Walter Antonowicz and Bernhard Mussak (Österreichische Nationalbank), Daisy Dillens (Nationale Bank van België/ Banque Nationale de Belgique), Aase Skjødt (Danmarks Nationalbank), Joke Mooji and Joke van der Hulst (Nederlandsche Bank), the personnel of the National Archives in Oslo (Riksarkiv), Inger Kindgren and Mira Barkå (Sveriges Riksbank), Patrick Halbeisen (Swiss National Bank), and Edward Atkinson and Chris Bennett (BIS Archives and Library). I am also grateful to Chris Young, who put in a lot of time and effort providing many helpful comments on style and clarity.

This research project was funded in part by the Swiss National Science Foundation (application number 1115–61633.00). In particular, this financial support enabled me to spend the academic year 2000–2001 at the University of California at Berkeley.

Introduction

This entire ... episode is a fascinating example of how important what people think
about money can sometimes be.
  – M. Friedman and A. Schwartz, *A Monetary History of the United States,
  1867–1960*, p. 133.

When in September 2003 a sound majority of Swedish voters rejected the
euro, many Scandinavian analysts highlighted the fact that all major parties
had campaigned for a "yes" but obviously had failed to convince their constituencies.[1] For example, the liberal Swedish newspaper *Dagens Nyheter*
concluded "that the 'no' outcome in the recent referendum on Sweden's
joining the European Monetary Union is a protest against the political
establishment." Similarly, the Norwegian conservative daily *Aftenposten*
wrote, "Not even a massive bunch of well-meaning threats could compete
with voter skepticism in a situation where fundamental values are at stake.
The Swedes have said no to their leaders – an alliance of politicians, union
heads, business people, and media figures."[2]

The protest against the political establishment was in fact remarkable,
especially in a country where government institutions enjoy a high degree of
acceptance among the population. Nevertheless, it would be wrong to interpret the referendum in negative terms. By casting a no vote, most Swedes
not only rejected the euro but also expressed surprisingly strong support
for the flexible-exchange-rate regime Sweden had adopted only 10 years
prior to the referendum. Before that date, from the introduction of the gold

---

[1] The referendum took place on 14 September 2003. Voters rejected the euro by a 14-point
margin, 56 to 42 percent, with 2 percent of ballots ruled invalid.

[2] *Dagens Nyheter,* Stockholm (Sweden), 15 September 2003, and *Aftenposten,* Oslo
(Norway), 16 September 2003. Both articles were translated by *World Press Review* 50(12).
The referendum is analyzed by Jonung (2007) and Miles (2005, pp. 219–259).

standard in the 1870s to the early 1990s, when the Swedish currency began to float, there had been an overwhelming consensus that a small European country such as Sweden needed a fixed exchange rate. "Before the 1990s," a Swedish central bank governor explained, "the predominant view was that a floating exchange rate regime was not suitable for a small open economy."[3] Thus, from a long-term perspective, the real surprise of the referendum was how readily a majority of Swedish voters accepted an exchange-rate regime that had been considered dangerous for more than a century. Moreover, the fact that the current regime has not been questioned ever since, despite tremendous international financial instability, shows that rejection of the euro was more than an accidental decision.[4]

The main purpose of this study is to highlight Sweden's historical verdict in greater detail by making a general argument about how small Western European states chose their exchange-rate regime during the twentieth century. It tries to explain why they displayed such a strong preference for fixed exchange rates, how this preference was conditioned by the small size of these countries, and why there has been such a complete reversal of these "fixed ideas" in the last 20 years. The remainder of this chapter will provide an outline of the major arguments and results. The first section discusses the relevance of the topic and provides a survey of the major exchange-rate-regime changes during the twentieth century. The second section presents the scale and scope of the study. The third and fourth sections summarize the major results. The last section briefly explains the structure of the study.

CHOICE OF THE EXCHANGE-RATE REGIME

Which exchange-rate regime is best for a country? To outsiders, this question may appear arcane, overly technical, or even aberrant. To economists and economic historians, however, the debates about exchange-rate regimes are "perennially lively."[5] One reason for this is that reality has constantly come up with new surprises. A notable example is the introduction of the euro in the 1990s. Another reason is that there is much at stake. As Argentina's crisis in the early twenty-first century has shown, a country having an inappropriate exchange-rate regime can suffer from tremendous losses in the short run. The currency board guaranteed a fixed exchange rate against the

---

[3]   Bäckström (2000, p. 1).
[4]   "Sweden PM: No Euro for Now," Associated Press, 30 January 2009.
[5]   Rogoff et al. (2003), p. 4. For an introduction, see Broz and Frieden (2006).

dollar, but such a regime proved disastrous under the conditions of rising interest rates, an appreciating dollar, and a deepening recession.[6] Even today, large parts of Argentina's society have not yet recovered from the severe economic crisis.

This study also addresses the question of which exchange-rate regime is best for a country. It does not focus on the economic costs and benefits, however, but on the actual choices small European countries made throughout the twentieth century. Whether or not these choices can be considered economically sound from today's viewpoint is irrelevant because the perspective is exclusively on what *policymakers at the time* considered the optimal regime to be.[7] This selective approach is motivated by the lack of research. As Rose (2007) correctly observes, "we do not have a good understanding of how countries choose their monetary regime in practice."[8] This study tries to make a contribution to a more systematic understanding of this problem.

These regime choices were made within a clearly defined international monetary system that has undergone fundamental changes in the last 140 years.[9] As for Western Europe, we can distinguish four major periods. From the 1870s to World War I, the prevalent regime was the *classic gold standard*. All prices of currencies were fixed in terms of a specified weight of gold, and the primary responsibility of central banks was to preserve the official parity between its currency and gold and to guarantee the convertibility of the currency. To fulfill this function, central banks were required to keep an adequate stock of gold reserves. The interwar years were marked by the protracted construction of the *gold exchange standard* and its rapid dissolution in the 1930s. The gold exchange standard was very similar to the prewar gold standard. The major difference was that not only gold but also a number of currencies were accepted as central bank reserves, in particular the British pound, the US dollar, and the French franc. This extension was adopted because policymakers feared that gold reserves were not adequate to meet the demand for international reserves.

The postwar era was the time of the *Bretton Woods* system. Like the gold standard, it was based on fixed exchange rates, but only the US dollar

---

6   On Argentina, see, for example, Edwards (2002) for the subsequent debate on exchange-rate regimes and Blustein (2005) for a narrative account.

7   This narrative approach owes much to the seminal papers by DeLong (1997), Romer and Romer (2004), and Nelson (2005).

8   Rose (2007, p. 673).

9   For a long-term view, see Eichengreen (1996b), Aldcroft and Oliver (1998), Bordo and Schwartz (1999), and Bordo (2003). On the interwar years, see Brown (1940) and

continued to be fixed to gold, whereas all other currencies were pegged to the dollar. It thus was a sort of "gold dollar standard," as central banks held gold and dollars as international reserves and had the right to sell dollars to the Federal Reserve for gold at the official price. After the collapse of the Bretton Woods system, Western European countries either adopted floating exchange rates or joined the two monetary arrangements of the European Community (EC): the *Snake* (1972–1979) and the *European Monetary System* (EMS) (1979–1999). At the end of the century, most Western European countries abandoned their national currency and introduced the *euro*. All other countries have a flexible-exchange-rate system.

The dynamics behind these four phases can best be described in terms of the *impossible trinity* or the *trilemma*. It states that it is impossible for a country to have all three of the following at the same time: capital mobility, an independent monetary policy, and a pegged exchange rate.[10] The classic gold standard was a system with pegged exchange rates and open financial markets. It was relatively stable because the participating countries abstained from pursuing an independent monetary policy.[11] Accordingly, the main reason why the gold exchange standard collapsed in the 1930s was the fact that governments wanted to have it all: fixed exchange rates, capital mobility, and an independent monetary policy, the latter in order to cope with the negative consequences of the war and the rising demands resulting from mass politics. During the better part of the Bretton Woods system, capital movements were tightly controlled, which allowed a relatively independent monetary policy and the maintenance of fixed but adjustable exchange rates. Finally, in the fourth phase – which was characterized by a high degree of capital mobility, such as during the eras of the classic gold standard and the gold exchange standard – two paths were chosen. Western European countries either completely abandoned their monetary independence by adopting the euro, or they shifted to a floating regime.

In sum, one can identify two long-term trends depending on the choices made during the last phase. Countries that participated in the fixed-exchange-rate systems of the EC and subsequently adopted the euro have completed a sort of circular movement because they started from and have returned to a world in which there is no room for monetary independence.

Eichengreen (1992); on the postwar years, see Ludlow (1982), Solomon (1982), James (1996), Gros and Thygesen (1998), and Dyson and Featherstone (1999).

[10] The trilemma is the major theme of Eichengreen (1996b).

[11] Recently, Bordo and Flandreau (2003) have tried to show that the autonomy was greater than traditionally assumed. Their view remains disputed, however. See the comment of Schwartz (2003).

In retrospect, their experiences with floating exchange rates during the interwar years appear to be isolated episodes. In contrast, countries that have adopted a floating regime pursued a more linear path throughout the twentieth century from a regime precluding monetary independence toward a regime allowing a high degree of monetary independence. Accordingly, the interwar experiences with flexible exchange rates were not isolated episodes but appear to be a first step toward the present situation. The main topic of this study is the path small Western European states followed during the twentieth century.

SCALE AND SCOPE OF THIS BOOK

Reconstructing the motivation behind the regime choices required the analysis of a variety of evidence: archival material, published sources, descriptive statistics, and, of course, secondary literature. In fact, the amount of written documents to be considered was so abundant that the scale and scope had to be narrowed. In particular, two restrictions needed to be imposed. First, only the experience of economically advanced small states of Western Europe is considered. This group consists of Austria, the Benelux countries (Belgium-Luxembourg[12] and the Netherlands), three Scandinavian countries (Denmark, Norway, and Sweden), and Switzerland. Smallness is defined by the population figure, the gross domestic product (GDP), the degree of trade openness, and the self-perception of small states. Small states are primarily small because their inhabitants are convinced that they are small and therefore enjoy only limited power in international relations.[13] Today, the Netherlands is the largest of the small countries, with 16.5 million inhabitants and a GDP of US$766 billion, and Norway is the smallest of the group, with 4.8 million inhabitants and a GDP of US$388 billion.[14] Trade openness ranges from roughly 150 percent (Belgium) to

[12] In 1922, Belgium and Luxembourg formed an economic union, the first step toward monetary cooperation. Parity was established between the Luxembourg franc and the Belgian franc. In 1935, Belgium and Luxembourg formed a currency union: Belgian coins and banknotes became legal tender in Luxembourg, and from then on until 1999, the Belgian National Bank was in charge of monetary policy for both countries. Because of the dominance of Belgium in this currency union, this study does not deal with Luxembourg.

[13] Hey (2003) highlights the crucial importance of self-perception. See Alesina and Spolaore (2003) for an economic approach to the size of nations. Because I take the size of nations as exogenous, their perspective goes beyond the main question of this study. I also do not address the question of whether or not small European states are more successful in economic terms than large states.

[14] GDPs in US dollars are calculated on the basis of official exchange rates and do not express purchasing-power parities. The GDP figures are World Bank estimates for 2007.

75 percent (Norway). By contrast, the big four – France, Germany, Italy, and the United Kingdom – have population figures ranging from 60 to 82 million inhabitants, GDP figures between US\$2,100 and US\$3,300 billion, and degrees of trade openness that lie within the range of 50 to 70 percent.

Admittedly, this selection of countries is rather small, given that there are presently more than 30 small and very small European states. However, because no scholar has ever studied the monetary history of more than four small states at a time, the restriction appears to be legitimate.[15] In addition, three other considerations are relevant. First, throughout the twentieth century, these seven small European states belonged to a group of economically advanced European economies. This similar level of development makes it possible to compare them with one another as well as with large European states and allows us to focus on the importance of country size. Otherwise, if the small states being studied were too different regarding their trade structure, their degree of trade openness, or their financial maturity, the analysis would be strongly biased by the differences between countries in the core and those in the periphery. Second, Katzenstein, in his seminal work on small states in world markets (1985), has dealt with the same country group, which makes it easier to see the implications of the exchange-rate-regime choices for overall economic policymaking. And third, because the analysis is based largely on narrative evidence, it was necessary to learn several languages, which proved to be time consuming.[16]

The second restriction is that the study does not encompass the whole of the twentieth century but is focused on two periods in which exchange-rate-regime changes were particularly frequent: the interwar years and the decades from the end of the Bretton Woods system until the Swedish referendum on the euro in September 2003. Accordingly, not every country gets the same attention at every point of the analysis. The study will focus on crucial episodes in which one or a group of small states changed the exchange-rate regime. Altogether, the argument is based on eight such episodes – four during each of the two periods. The following two sections will outline the major results of this comparative analysis.

---

[15] See, for example, Scharpf (1991), Kurzer (1993), Moses (1995), Notermans (2000), and Jones (2008).

[16] For a German-speaking Swiss historian, it is feasible to learn Dutch-Flemish and the Scandinavian languages within a reasonable period of time. Learning Finnish, however, as well as the Eastern European languages, simply was beyond my intellectual capacity.

SMALL VERSUS LARGE STATES

According to official classifications of exchange-rate regimes, during the twentieth century, small European states made roughly the same choices as large European states.[17] After World War I, they let their currencies float and introduced the gold exchange standard, with the small neutral states fixing the exchange rate at the old parity (like the United Kingdom), and the small war-stricken states devaluing (like France) or even replacing their currency (like Germany). In the 1930s, some small states left the gold exchange standard (like the United Kingdom) or abandoned it by introducing capital controls (like Germany), whereas other small states joined the gold bloc and devalued (like France). After Bretton Woods, we find both small and large states pursuing the paths toward the euro and a floating-exchange-rate regime. Today, Austria, Belgium, and the Netherlands have the euro (like France, Germany, and Italy), whereas Norway, Sweden, and Switzerland have a flexible exchange rate (like the United Kingdom). In addition, Denmark has tied its currency to the euro.

There is also narrative evidence suggesting that small states enjoyed as much room to maneuver as large states. In fact, the differences between small states appear to have been bigger than those between small and large states. Under the regime of floating exchange rates during the early 1920s, Sweden and Switzerland are said to have pursued a hard-currency policy, whereas Danish historians have pointed out that their central bank took an accommodating stance.[18] As for the 1930s, Sweden is known to have been the first European central bank to adopt price-level targeting as its official monetary policy framework.[19] By contrast, Belgium, the Netherlands, and Switzerland maintained the gold standard until 1935 and 1936, respectively.[20] And in early 1973, Switzerland abandoned the fixed exchange rate against the US dollar earlier than France, Germany, or Italy, while the other small European states maintained a fixed exchange rate.[21]

Finally, there is statistical evidence showing that country size was secondary. According to this research, only small states with a very open economy and one major trading partner have always preferred to have a fixed

---

[17] Until 1996, the International Monetary Fund (IMF) Annual Report on Exchange Rate Arrangements and Exchange Restrictions reflected only the regimes as reported by the IMF members themselves.
[18] See Chapter One.
[19] See Chapter Three.
[20] See Chapter Four.
[21] See Chapters Five and Seven.

exchange rate.[22] In all other cases, the evidence is not conclusive. Economists have explained this result by the fact that the type of exchange-rate regime does not affect long-run macroeconomic performance.[23] The argument is that importers and exporters can hedge their exchange-rate risks.[24] Thus, in sum, the choice of the exchange-rate regime seems to be more or less accidental. Whether small or large, Western European countries had the same options.

Yet, despite this considerable evidence, the view that country size was of minor importance is flawed because it neglects the fact that official classifications are often misleading.[25] It is true that after World War I Swedish and Swiss central bank and government officials declared that they wanted to bring the currency back to the prewar parity as soon as possible, but because the authorities of every European country made such a statement at the time, these declarations are not particularly revealing. Conversely, Danish central bank officials wanted to facilitate the difficult change from a war to a peacetime economy by pursuing a policy of cheap money, but again, every other European central bank had the same policy goal. It is correct that the Swedish finance minister explained in 1931 that monetary policy would be aimed at stabilizing the internal price level, but in reality, the Swedish central bank continued to target the exchange rate.[26] And finally, Switzerland shifted to a floating exchange rate earlier than some large European states, but the regime change was not really completed until the late 1970s, and since the early 1980s, the floating of the Swiss franc has been rather "dirty." Therefore, it would be completely wrong to consider the Swiss case representative.

More generally, if the analysis of exchange-rate-regime choices is based on actual policies, country size becomes highly relevant. During the interwar years, this factor determined the timing of regime change, that is, when countries introduced and abandoned the gold exchange standard and which exchange-rate regime they adopted before and after the operation of the gold exchange standard. Small European states always reacted to the regime changes of large states and hardly pursued an independent

[22] Honkapohja and Pikkarainen (1994). Seminal papers are Heller (1978) and Melvin (1985). For a comprehensive summary of this literature, see Edison and Melvin (1990).

[23] Influential papers are Baxter and Stockman (1989), Flood and Rose (1995), and Ghosh et al. (2003). For a survey of the literature, see Goldstein (1995) and Begg et al. (2003).

[24] Recently, this finding has been questioned. See Begg et al. (2003) on the new literature. See also Klein and Shambaugh (2004) on the positive effects of fixed exchange rates on trade.

[25] Until about 10 years ago, economists, including Honkapohja and Pikkarainen (1994), based their calculations on the official classifications of the IMF.

[26] Lester (1939), Jonung (1979, 1992), and Berg and Jonung (1999).

monetary policy. They were forced to change course when large states made a regime shift. After World War I, all five small neutral countries were looking to London when they returned to the gold standard at the prewar parity. Even Sweden, which made the *de jure* restoration one year earlier than the United Kingdom, tried to be in synchronization with the policy of the Bank of England. Only Austria and Belgium followed their own path when returning to the gold standard, but for obvious reasons: The negative consequences of the war were so profound that appreciation to the prewar parity proved impossible – just as for France and Germany.[27]

In the early 1930s, the policy of the United Kingdom continued to play a crucial role. Denmark, Norway, and Sweden abandoned the gold standard a few days after the British government took this step. And after suspension of the gold standard, Denmark, Norway, and Sweden maintained a stable exchange rate against sterling informally from autumn 1931 to summer 1933 and officially from summer 1933 onward. Belgium, the Netherlands, and Switzerland followed France and formed the gold bloc during the London Economic Conference in 1933. The Netherlands and Switzerland did not devalue until France took this decision. Only the Belgian franc was devalued somewhat earlier, but only because of an imminent collapse of the financial sector.

After 1971, country size was even more relevant. First, small European states needed more time than large states to accept the idea that a floating exchange rate was a viable option for them. With the exception of Switzerland, all small states either participated in the Snake and the EMS or shifted to a basket peg after leaving the Snake, whereas all large European states abandoned their fixed exchange rates during the 1970s: the United Kingdom in 1972, Italy in 1973, and France in 1974 and again, after a short interlude, in 1976; Germany, although still participating in the Snake, adopted monetary targeting in early 1975. Thus, contrary to the view based on official classifications, small states in fact displayed some "fear of floating" during the 1970s and 1980s. Only in the early 1990s, when Norway and Sweden abandoned the fixed-exchange-rate regime, did it become normal for the currencies of small European states to float. Switzerland ceased to be an exception confirming the rule.

Second, country size also mattered with respect to the causes of the regime shift from fixed to floating. In the case of the small states, the combination of open financial markets and the lack of EC membership proved

---

[27] For this reason, the monetary history of Austria and Belgium during the 1920s will not be discussed in detail.

crucial. In January 1973, Switzerland had no choice but to let the franc float when massive capital inflows put enormous upward pressure on the Swiss franc. Had it been a member of the EC, it would have joined the Snake, the first monetary regime of the EC, and revalued within the Snake. Similarly, Norway and Sweden were forced to let their currencies float in the course of the 1992 crisis of the EMS, which was the successor regime of the Snake. If the countries had been EC members, they would have either defended or devalued their currencies within the EMS – just as the small EC member states Denmark or Portugal did. But, owing to the lack of EC membership and the concomitant weak credibility of the currency peg in a world of high capital mobility, Swedish policymakers opted for a temporary float and finally decided to remain outside because the floating regime proved viable. Norway took this step some years later after a failed attempt to maintain a stable exchange rate vis-à-vis the EMS currencies without officially fixing it. Large states, by contrast, were all EC members at the time they left the Snake or the EMS. Accordingly, the causes of their regime shifts were different.

Why did small European states closely follow large states during the interwar years, and why did it take longer for them to adopt a floating regime? The main thesis of this study, as expressed by its title, is that neither economic interests nor specific institutions but rather the macroeconomic models of policymakers ("fixed ideas") determined their actions.[28] Until the early 1990s, there was a widespread consensus that small, open economies needed a fixed exchange rate. It was argued that under a regime of floating exchange rates, trade and investment would be hampered by the volatility of the foreign exchange markets. Because, during the interwar years, policymakers in large states shared the same view, the resulting exchange-rate policies of small and large states were quite similar. Policymakers across Europe considered the years before the return to the gold standard and after its dissolution as periods of transition. Accordingly, the main difference was, as noted, the timing of regime changes.

Of course, the early 1920s and 1930s differed from the time when the gold exchange standard operated. In those two periods, central banks were able to function as lenders of last resort in case of a banking crisis or could be forced more easily to continue printing money in order to finance the

---

[28] In recent times, several economists and political scientists have highlighted the importance of ideas for the choice of exchange-rate regimes, especially with respect to the interwar gold standard and the making of the European Monetary Union (EMU). As for the interwar years, see Eichengreen and Temin (2000), Mouré (2002), and Balderston (2003); on the EMU, see McNamara (1998) and Maes (2002).

rising fiscal deficits after the war.[29] Thus, returning to and going off the gold standard have to be regarded as regime changes. Yet the crucial point is that even during these periods, policymakers continued to think in the categories of the gold standard. There was a large gap between how exchange rates moved and what the monetary authorities were trying to do.[30] Or to put it differently, the interwar years were a period with flexible exchange rates but without flexible-exchange-rate regimes.

After the end of Bretton Woods, as large states shifted to floating exchange rates, the preference for fixed exchange rates became confined to the group of small European states. As during the interwar years, policymakers were convinced that volatile exchange-rate movements would hamper trade and investment and complicate the control of inflation and wage negotiations. In other words, the old view of Nurkse (1944) was still influential during the 1970s.[31] For this reason, a floating exchange rate was never considered a viable option. This conviction became particularly visible when Swedish policymakers left the Snake and adopted the currency basket in 1977. Government and central bank officials believed that a floating exchange rate was "almost immoral" and therefore preferred keeping an exchange-rate target.[32] Only when Sweden adopted inflation targeting after the 1992 currency crisis and the new monetary policy framework proved to work well did this aversion to flexible exchange rates become more and more outdated. In Norway, the fear of floating persisted even longer than in Sweden. Even after abandoning the fixed-exchange-rate regime in late 1992, the Norwegian government obliged the central bank to maintain a stable krone. Only when oil prices began to fluctuate in the late 1990s did the strategy become obsolete. In 2001, Norway officially adopted inflation targeting.

The same reluctance to adopt flexible exchange rates can be observed in the case of Switzerland in the early 1970s. All major policymakers as well as bankers and executives of manufacturers were convinced that the

---

[29] This is one of the main points made by Eichengreen (1992).

[30] See the current debate on official declarations and actual country practice: Calvo and Reinhardt (2002), Masson (2001), Reinhart and Rogoff (2002), Levy-Yeyati and Sturzenegger (2005), Genberg and Swoboda (2004), and Klein and Shambaugh (2006).

[31] On the views of Nurkse and Haberler, who advocated flexible exchange rates, see Bordo and James (2001). Krugman (1989, p. 63) mentions that the view of Nurkse "remains a popular argument among practical men." Cf. Frankel (1999, p. 10): "Twenty or thirty years ago, the argument most often made against floating currencies was that higher exchange rate variability would create uncertainty; this risk would in turn discourage international trade and investment... Most academic economists tend to downplay this argument today... Nevertheless, this argument still carries some weight. It looms large in the minds of European policymakers and businesspeople."

[32] Lindvall (2004, p. 125).

Swiss economy was too open to allow the franc to float.[33] Accordingly, most observers, except for a few academic economists and journalists, did not welcome the end of fixed exchange rates in 1973. They considered this move to be a mistake and were hoping that there would be a swift return to a fixed regime. In 1975, following a steep appreciation of the Swiss franc, the national bank sought participation in the Snake because it considered a fixed exchange rate more appropriate for a small, open economy. Only when France definitely blocked the Swiss initiative and later signaled that it would oppose participation of the Swiss franc in the European Monetary System did Switzerland make the regime shift toward floating permanent.

To be sure, the title "fixed ideas" is not used in a pejorative sense. On the contrary, the preference for a fixed exchange rate is quite understandable, although it did not always lead to optimal results, especially during the interwar years. World War I had brought a traumatic inflationary experience not only in the belligerent countries but also in the neutral countries. All governments had suspended convertibility in the summer of 1914 and financed the rising public debt by printing money. In addition, interest rates had been kept at a low level until 1920 in order to avoid a further increase in the debt burden. All this caused a surge of inflation unheard of since the Napoleonic wars. It thus was only natural that policymakers became convinced that suspension of the gold standard would automatically lead to inflation and that a swift return to the prewar monetary regime was vital. The question of how a flexible-exchange-rate regime could be combined with an independent central bank and a price-level target was brought up as an idea but never seriously discussed. The aversion to floating exchange rates was deeply anchored, and it survived the crisis of the 1930s and shaped the formation of the Bretton Woods regime in 1944.[34]

It is also understandable that small European states continued to prefer fixed exchange rates when in the 1970s the international monetary scene became extremely unstable and exchange-rate movements were unpredictable. In small European states, policymakers were determined to avoid sudden changes and to reduce price differentials by wage negotiations and, only if absolutely necessary, by devaluations and revaluations. The goal was not to eliminate the market but to stretch the period of adjustment and to control the terms of adjustment. In other words, the preference for fixed exchange rates was based on the same sense of vulnerability that inspired

---

[33] Ferrari (1990).
[34] Bordo (1993).

the forming of corporatist institutions.[35] Thus "fixed ideas" were based not on irrational beliefs but rather on considerations that even from today's viewpoint are comprehensible.

SMALL VERSUS SMALL

Of course, country size was not the only determinant of how small European states chose their exchange-rate regime during the twentieth century. Differences between them were just as salient. As for the interwar years, not all these differences deserve a thorough discussion, however. As noted, the fact that Austria and Belgium, suffering from inflation during the 1920s, failed to restore the prewar parity, whereas the Scandinavian countries as well as the Netherlands and Switzerland succeeded can be explained easily by the differing degrees of war involvement.[36] The same is true for the early end of the gold standard in Austria in 1931. The newly formed state and the economy were still struggling with the negative consequences of war defeat – just like Germany.[37]

There are three other episodes worth discussing. The first one concerns the five neutral countries and their return to gold. The Dutch guilder, the Swedish krona, and the Swiss franc returned to the gold standard at the prewar parity in 1924–1925, whereas the Danish and Norwegian currencies needed more time for this process. The second episode is related to the currency crisis of 1931. The Scandinavian countries devalued their currencies in late 1931, whereas Belgium, the Netherlands, and Switzerland maintained their currencies. And the last episode has to do with the dissolution of the gold bloc. The Belgian franc was devalued in the spring of 1935, and the Dutch guilder and Swiss franc followed in autumn of 1936 after France took this step.

Some scholars, notably Simmons (1994), have suggested that not only economic factors but also institutional features and political power relations played a crucial role. In particular, the strength of the Left, government instability, and central bank independence are said to have been important.[38] This study, by contrast, has not found any empirical evidence that domestic factors were the crucial determinants of regime choice. For

---

[35] Katzenstein (1985, 2003) has argued that the sense of vulnerability was the key factor for the emergence of "democratic corporatism" in small European states. For a somewhat longer discussion of this point, see the Conclusion of this study.

[36] Baudhuin (1946a, 1946b), Van der Wee and Tavernier (1975), and Cassiers (1989).

[37] On Austria, see Schubert (1991) and Stiefel (1988).

[38] Simmons (1994, p. 280).

example, the relatively smooth return of the Swedish krona to prewar parity in the early 1920s cannot be explained by the strength of the Right, government stability, or central bank independence. On the contrary, Swedish governments after World War I were particularly instable, the Left gained in power, and the Riksbank was less independent than other central banks. The same is true for the fall of the Belgian franc in the spring of 1935. As noted, it was mainly due to a persistent banking crisis, not to the agitation of the Belgian labor movement under Hendrik de Man. It is true that this movement gained in strength in the course of the crisis, but we can observe a parallel course of events in the Netherlands and Switzerland, and yet the Dutch guilder and the Swiss franc remained on the gold standard.[39] Obviously, the statistical approach as applied by Simmons appears to be unable to detect the underlying causal linkages and to catch the historical conditions under which policymakers had to make decisions. It can only observe general tendencies and probabilities.

Furthermore, there is no evidence that the interests of banks, insurers, or multinationals were responsible for the disastrous hard-currency policy. If that had been the case, it would be impossible to explain the zeal with which the Danish and Norwegian governments were trying to return to prewar parity in the 1920s because neither Denmark nor Norway had any multinational manufacturers, and the banking sector was hit particularly hard by the tightening of monetary policy. This view is also misleading in the case of the gold bloc countries. They delayed the devaluation of their currencies mainly because they were convinced that such a step would bring more harm than good, in particular a surge of inflation, and not because the banking sector and the multinational manufacturers were profiting from the strong currency.[40] The causality ran differently. Because devaluation was not an option, multinational manufacturers were looking for strategies enabling them to survive. And the financial sector was increasingly agnostic about the official exchange-rate policy. Its main goal was to anticipate the devaluation in order to be on the winner's side, not to help avoid it.[41]

Rather, the crucial factors were economic and financial.[42] First, Denmark and Norway had more problems restoring the gold standard at prewar

---

[39] Curiously, Simmons does not even mention Belgium's banking crisis in her case study, in contrast to Belgian economic historians, for example, Van der Wee and Tavernier (1975) and to Eichengreen (1992).

[40] Hogg (1987) and Allgoewer (2003).

[41] Baumann and Halbeisen (1999).

[42] Wandschneider (2008) and Wolf (2008) also emphasize the importance of trade, banking, and the creditor status of a country.

parity mainly because they suffered from large trade deficits in 1919–1920, and their banking systems proved less able to deal with the depression of the early 1920 than those of the Netherlands, Sweden, and Switzerland. Second, the devaluations of the Scandinavian currencies in 1931 can be explained by close trade relations with the United Kingdom, the importance of sterling for shipping contracts, and – especially in the case of the Swedish krona – the high amount of net short-term foreign debt in combination with the contagious effect of the sterling crisis. Third, the main reason why Belgium, the Netherlands, and Switzerland were not forced to follow sterling was that they disposed of large gold reserves, enabling them to defend themselves against speculative attacks.[43] And fourth, devaluation of the Belgian franc in the spring of 1935 was caused by a banking crisis, whereas in the Netherlands, there was no such crisis at all, and in Switzerland, the crisis was confined to a few banks and thus relatively easy to contain. Summarizing, it was basically a story about advanced countries (Benelux and Switzerland) and various types of emerging markets (Scandinavia).[44]

As for the period after Bretton Woods, the question why in 1973 Switzerland and in 1992 Norway and Sweden were forced to abandon their fixed-exchange-rate regime has already been addressed. It was the combination of open financial markets and the lack of EC membership that made their currencies more vulnerable than those of other small European states and excluded the option of revaluation or devaluation. Yet the fact that some small states adopted floating exchange rates whereas others maintained fixed exchange rates and ultimately introduced the euro was not the only striking difference among small states. During the 1970s and 1980s, small European states also differed with respect to the exchange rates to which they were pegging their currencies as well as to the strength of their pegs. There were three groups. The Austrian schilling and the Dutch guilder maintained a hard peg against the Deutsche mark, the Belgian franc and the Danish krone shifted from a hard peg to a soft peg and then back to a hard peg, and the Swedish and Norwegian currencies were first tied to the Deutsche mark and then to a currency basket.

The conventional model highlights differences in policy preferences and domestic institutions.[45] The starting point of the argument is that in the

---

[43] Cf. van Zanden (1998, p. 106): "In a way it was just bad luck that the Netherlands was not thrust off gold in 1931 and that its gold reserves were so ample that a forced devaluation was out of the question."

[44] On the importance of financial maturity for the choice of the exchange-rate regime, see Bordo and Flandreau (2003).

[45] See Chapter Six.

difficult world after Bretton Woods, almost all small states were forced to make a choice between price stability and full employment because they lacked the consensus on how to combine the hard peg against the Deutsche mark with wage restraint – supposedly only Austria managed to find the right policy mix. The Benelux countries preferred price and exchange-rate stability because of the strong position of the central bank and because the goal of full employment was less deeply rooted in the political culture. Norway and Sweden, two countries with a strong Social Democratic tradition, strong labor unions, and weak central banks, considered full employment to be the top priority. Consequently, they decided to leave the Snake, to devalue their currencies, and to accept high inflation rates when it became obvious that the restrictive course of Germany threatened the goals of their economic policy. Denmark was an unfortunate mix of both cases because it suffered from the fact that there was no clear majority for either full employment or price stability. The currency became weak, the unemployment rate soared, and the inflation rate remained high.

However, for all its elegance, this explanation is not convincing for two reasons. First, the indices used to classify the institutions are based on formal criteria, not on the actual state of the institutions.[46] With respect to the 1970s, this methodology is particularly unfortunate because the gap between these two categories was never bigger than during that decade owing to the breakdown of the postwar consensus on which the smooth functioning of these institutions depended. Only in Austria was the so-called social partnership still in good shape, but even there, labor unions failed to sufficiently moderate their wage claims in order to avoid a steep appreciation of the real exchange rate. Second, the conventional explanation ignores the external constraints with which small states and small economies were confronted. As Moses (2000) puts it, "[c]losed-economy and closed-state models may still maintain some utility in the United States, but they are increasingly problematic in the world west of Los Angeles."[47]

However, though indispensable for a more realistic assessment of history, including these external constraints makes the analysis much more complicated because the comparison shows that small European states differed not only with respect to their domestic institutions and policy preferences but also with respect to their external political and economic structures. We are therefore confronted with what can be called the *problem of double difference*. In the 1970s and 1980s, Austria, Norway, and Sweden not only

---

[46] See Chapter Five.
[47] Moses (2000, p. 203).

had dependent central banks, a highly centralized wage bargaining system, and a strong Left, but they also were outside the EC and controlled international capital movements. By contrast, Belgium, Denmark, and the Netherlands were EC members with open financial markets and had relatively independent central banks, less centralized wage bargaining systems, and a weaker Left.

This problem of double difference can hardly be solved by regression analysis. A more promising approach is to analyze the motivations behind the decisions taken by governments and central banks. The comparison shows that altogether four external factors determined whether a small state maintained the peg to the Deutsche mark or shifted to a currency basket and whether the peg to the Deutsche mark was hard or soft: EC membership or nonmembership, the trade structure, the degree of financial openness, and the dependence on oil and natural gas. Domestic policy preferences or institutions may have played a role as well, but owing to the very different constraints small states were confronted with, it is more plausible to assume that they were of secondary importance. Of course, it is conceivable that, for example, the Netherlands would have pursued a hard-currency policy regardless of the circumstances because the Dutch central bank had a powerful position. Conversely, it is possible that Sweden would have left the Snake to maintain full employment even if it had been an EC member. But there is no way to prove this claim because of the "double difference." But it seems fair to conclude that any explanation based exclusively on domestic differences is condemned to fail. Arguing with external constraints, by contrast, has a solid empirical basis.

EC membership determined whether a small country could leave the Snake or not. The Benelux countries and Denmark were EC members and therefore remained loyal; Norway and Sweden were not and therefore had the freedom to leave the Snake. The trade structure explains whether it made sense to leave the Snake or not. The Benelux countries had close trade relations with Germany and with each other, so shifting to a currency basket would not have made a great difference. This was even truer in the case of Austria. The Scandinavian countries, by contrast, traded less with Germany but more with the United Kingdom, which made shifting to a currency basket a reasonable move. When economic integration conflicted with political integration, the latter factor proved to be more important: Denmark remained in the Snake despite its unfavorable trade structure.

The degree of financial openness was linked to two aspects. First, it determined whether it was possible to adopt a currency basket or not because having a stable exchange rate against the currencies of the major trading partners required tight capital controls. Thus, even if they had wanted to leave the Snake, the Benelux countries and Denmark could not have shifted to a currency basket because of their open financial markets. They would have been forced to let their currencies float. Second, the degree of capital mobility determined whether a small state was forced to follow the monetary policy of Germany or not. The Benelux countries and Denmark had relatively open financial markets and thus could not shield themselves against the rise of German interest rates. As a result of this monetary link, growth slowed down in 1974–1975, unemployment rose, the increase in real wages decelerated, and inflation rates were gradually reduced.

In Norway and Sweden, by contrast, interest rates could be kept low, thanks to tight capital controls. Consequently, growth rates remained high, maintaining full employment and encouraging labor unions to demand substantial real wage increases, thus damaging the competitiveness of the export sectors. By 1977, Norway and Sweden had gotten completely out of step with Germany. Especially Sweden had put itself in an untenable situation and therefore demanded a devaluation by 10 percent. The Snake members, however, were not ready to accept such a sudden change of exchange rates and proposed a smaller devaluation. This, in turn, was not acceptable to Sweden, which then left the Snake. Norway followed little more than a year later. Austria could have pursued the same policy of low interest rates as the two Scandinavian countries, but owing to its close economic and political ties to Germany, the Austrian central bank took account of the rise in German interest rates and thus pursued a moderately restrictive monetary policy.

The dependence on oil and natural gas was the main factor explaining whether a currency was stable, regardless of the kind of peg. Thanks to the revenues from the export of natural gas, the Netherlands had a persistent current account surplus from 1973 to 1982 (with the exception of 1978), allowing the central bank to defend the guilder against almost any speculative attacks. By contrast, Belgium and particularly Denmark were confronted with increasing current account deficits, especially during the second oil crisis, forcing them to shift from a hard to a soft Deutsche mark peg. Norway began to exploit its oil reserves during the 1970s and enjoyed a strong current account surplus from 1980 on. Accordingly, the krone was stable after the shift to a currency basket. The Swedish krona, by contrast, had to be devalued even after the regime shift owing to the big current account deficit following the second oil crisis. Just as Belgium and Denmark did, Sweden devalued its currency by little less than 20 percent altogether. Finally, Austria also should have had a weak currency owing to the heavy dependence on the import of oil and natural gas. The reason why the schilling remained strong despite this dependence was that the authorities had found a way to improve the current account that was only possible in Austria: They generously subsidized exports to Eastern European countries – a strategy for which they were to pay a high price in the 1980s. It thus was an exception confirming the rule.

From a long-term view, the interwar years and the period after Bretton Woods share striking similarities. Most important, the trade structure was a major factor in both periods. Also, the financial sector played a crucial role in most of the episodes. But the differences are more telling. To begin with the latter, the dominant influence of the financial sector changed across the twentieth century. In the interwar years, the resilience of the banking sector determined when the gold standard was restored and abandoned. This resilience was conditioned by many factors, in particular by the maturity of the economy, the international experience of the big commercial banks, and the country's inflationary record. The degree of financial openness, by contrast, was secondary because the gold standard, by definition, required capital mobility. Only when countries abandoned the gold standard did the question of capital controls emerge, but most small states maintained open financial markets. In the world after the end of Bretton Woods, however, the degree of financial openness and the timing of liberalization were central for the regime choice. In addition, two new factors emerged: EC membership/nonmembership and the existence of oil and gas reserves. Thus, while the regime choices during the interwar years were a function of economic and financial maturity, the choices after Bretton Woods depended on the specific combination of economic, financial, and political integration.

STRUCTURE OF THE STUDY

The story of how small European states chose exchange-rate regimes during the twentieth century is told in two parts and eight chapters. The first part deals with the interwar years; the second part, with the period from the end of the Bretton Woods regime to the rejection of the euro by Swedish voters in autumn 2003. Part One has four chapters and proceeds chronologically. Chapters One and Two deal with the period from the end of World War I to restoration of the gold exchange standard. Chapters Three and Four focus on the dissolution of the gold exchange standard. Part Two also has four chapters but is organized analytically. Chapter Five highlights the differences between small and large European states in the period after Bretton Woods, whereas Chapter Six tries to explain the divergence between small

European states maintaining a peg during this period. Chapters Seven and Eight discuss why in 1973 Switzerland and in 1992 Norway and Sweden abandoned their fixed-exchange-rate regime and how they managed their currencies after the regime change. The study ends with a short chapter that summarizes the results and draws a conclusion.

PART ONE

THE INTERWAR YEARS

The outbreak of World War I in August 1914 marked the beginning of a new era of monetary instability that Europe had not experienced since the Napoleonic wars.[1] Each European country, whether belligerent or not, suspended convertibility, introduced exchange controls, and experienced high inflation resulting from the unsound financing of public debt. When the war ended, policymakers thought that a rapid return to the gold standard would bring back the prewar prosperity, but as is well known, this plan failed. Not only did it take longer than anticipated to restore the old monetary order, but the newly created gold exchange standard only aggravated the economic and political problems stemming from the war and the peace settlements. In the early 1930s, the international monetary system began to collapse. Austria and Germany experienced a severe banking crisis and introduced exchange controls, and the British government suspended convertibility and let the pound fall. In April 1933, the Roosevelt administration devalued the dollar, and in september 1936, France put the last nail in the coffin by devaluing its currency as well.

However, the interwar years not only were a period of disaster and instability, but they also opened up new opportunities for monetary experiments. Since the gold standard was not restored until the mid-1920s, central banks were free of the obligation to maintain a stable exchange rate and therefore enjoyed the potential to adjust their monetary policies to the business cycle. The same is true for the time after suspension of the gold standard in the 1930s. Thus the times of crisis also were, as has often been the case in history, a period of unprecedented opportunities for innovation.

---

[1] The literature on monetary history during the interwar years is abundant. See, for example, Brown (1940), Eichengreen (1992, 1996b), Feinstein et al. (1997), Aldcroft and Oliver (1998), James (1996, 2001), Toniolo (2005), and Fior (2008).

Did small European countries seize these opportunities? Did policy-makers sometimes neglect the exchange-rate stability in order to promote economic growth? There is reason to assume a certain flexibility. Some Danish economic historians have claimed that in the wake of the war, the Danish National Bank focused on the domestic economy and accepted a depreciation of the currency. And there is a widely shared belief that Sweden shifted to price-level targeting after abandoning the gold standard in September 1931. From a comparative perspective as undertaken in the following four chapters, these conventional views appear to exaggerate the flexibility of monetary policy during the interwar years. There is strong evidence that policymakers were reluctant to try out the new freedom in monetary policy. Neither did the Danish National Bank neglect the exchange rate after the war, nor did Sweden replace exchange-rate targeting with price-level targeting. On the contrary, a strong and stable currency remained the main goal of macroeconomic management throughout the whole period. In the 1920s, small European states tried to restore the gold standard at prewar parity, with the former neutral countries succeeding and the small states struck by the war failing. In the 1930s, small states devalued only when they were forced to by a financial crisis or the devaluation of their main trading partner, and they continued to maintain a stable exchange rate in the 1930s either by fixing a new gold parity or by tying the currency to sterling. In late 1932, the Swedish central bank even tried to make the krona appreciate to the old parity against sterling, although this move had strong deflationary effects. The only innovation we can observe is the competitive devaluation of the Danish krone in the early 1930s in reaction to devaluation of the currency of New Zealand, whose farmers were competing directly with Danish farmers on the British market.

It is true that these new pegs were less rigid than the gold standard and marked an important progress. Yet it would be wrong to claim that the 1930s were a decade of great innovations in monetary policy. Policymakers continued to be very skeptical toward "manipulation of the currency," as they named the more modern exchange-rate management. And it is also true that fixing the exchange rate was not always a bad strategy. By tying their currencies to sterling after the devaluation, the Scandinavian countries recovered more rapidly from the depression than the Benelux countries and Switzerland. But the crucial point is that the positive consequences were rather the result of mere luck, not of a more modern understanding of the role of monetary policy. Policymakers adhered to fixed ideas in every respect because they showed little flexibility and preferred a system of fixed exchange rates. Understandably, they adjusted their thinking only gradually to the new economic and monetary realities.

My conclusion is based on the analysis of four episodes. Chapter One tries to show why the claim that the Danish National Bank pursued an independent monetary policy after the war is flawed. Chapter Two answers the question why Denmark and Norway decided to restore the gold standard at prewar parity even though their currencies had depreciated after the war by 40 and 50 percent, respectively. Chapter Three discusses the devaluation of the Scandinavian currencies in 1931 and tries to demonstrate how policymakers continued to act according to the rules of the gold standard framework even after they had suspended convertibility. And finally, Chapter Four explains why Belgium devalued earlier than the Netherlands and Switzerland and how these three small states, in a way similar to the Scandinavian countries, abstained from major changes after the devaluation.

Of course, focusing on these four episodes requires a selection that excludes other important episodes. Notably, Austria, Finland, Ireland, Portugal, and the small Eastern and Central European countries are missing on this list. Yet, as explained in the Introduction, my main interest is in the developed small European states because only in these cases it is reasonable to ask for monetary experiments. By contrast, Finland, Ireland, Portugal, and most Eastern European countries were at the periphery or semiperiphery, and Austria and the more advanced Central European countries were completely absorbed by the difficult postwar transition. For the same reason, I also have excluded the monetary history of Belgium during the 1920s because the devaluation of the Belgian franc is largely a result of the wartime occupation and the struggle for reparations. In addition, the Belgian experience has been treated in numerous excellent studies.[2] The following four chapters thus try not only to expose the patterns of exchange-rate policies pursued by small advanced states but are also limited to those episodes that have been partially neglected by financial historians.

---

[2] Shepherd (1936), Chlepner (1943), Baudhuin (1946a, 1946b), van der Wee and Tavernier (1975), Cassiers (1989), and Eichengreen (1992).

ONE

Early Divergence

It is well known that after World War I only a small number of countries succeeded in restoring the gold standard at prewar parity,[3] namely, the United Kingdom and the five small neutral countries. It is also well established that within this group the time of restoration differed considerably. Sweden completed the process shortly before and the Netherlands and Switzerland shortly after the United Kingdom, whereas Denmark and Norway needed another two to three years (Table 1.1). As Chapter Two will show, the main reason for this unwanted delay was that their banking systems suffered from a particularly severe crisis in the early 1920s.

What is less known, by contrast, is that the Danish krone and the Norwegian krone had been weaker even before the outbreak of these banking crises. As Figure 1.1 illustrates, both currencies depreciated by 50 percent from the end of the war until October 1920, whereas the Dutch guilder, the Swedish krona, and the Swiss franc lost only 20 to 30 percent of their prewar parity and remained just as strong as or even stronger than the British pound. The figure also shows that the Danish and Norwegian currencies never fully recovered from this plunge. In 1922, the Danish krone reached only 80 percent and the Norwegian krone only 70 percent of prewar parity, whereas the other currencies were near or even above the prewar parity.

What was the reason for this striking divergence? Was it because Denmark and Norway made more use of the monetary freedom resulting from suspension of the gold standard? If this were the case, it would be remarkable

---

[3] Restoring the gold standard at prewar parity meant restoring the prewar dollar rate because the United States was the only country having maintained the gold standard during the war. Yet, since US consumer prices increased by roughly 50 percent from 1913 to the mid-1920s when most European countries returned to the gold standard, prewar parity was lower than the term implies.

Table 1.1. *Chronology of the Gold Standard*

| | Return to Gold | | Off Gold |
	de facto	*de jure*	
France	1926	1928	1936
Germany	1923	1924	1931
United Kingdom	1925	1925	1931
Austria	1922	1923	1931
Belgium	1926	1926	1935
Netherlands	1924	1925	1936
Switzerland	1924	1925	1936
Denmark	1926	1927	1931
Norway	1928	1928	1931
Sweden	1922	1924	1931

Source: Aldcroft and Oliver (1998, p. 5), date of *de jure* stabilization corrected for Austria, Denmark, and Sweden on the basis of Bachinger et al. (2001), Johansen (1987), and Östlind (1945).

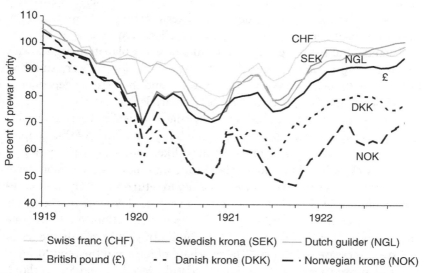

Figure 1.1. British pound and currencies of five small neutral countries (percentage of prewar parity). (*Commission of Gold and Silver Inquiry, 1925.*)

because it would have been the first time in the twentieth century that a small European state pursued an independent monetary policy. Since there has been a lack of comparative studies covering all five neutral countries, there is no structured literature from which to start the discussion. However, drawing from studies on the monetary history of individual small states or of selected small state groups, we can distinguish three explanations. The first one suggests that policy differences in fact played a crucial role. The starting point of the argument is the theory of purchasing power parity (PPP), stating that exchange rates reflected the fact that from 1914 to 1920 Danish and Norwegian prices increased faster than those in the Netherlands, Sweden, and Switzerland. Given that at the time there were lively public debates on inflation and monetary policy, several scholars conclude that there must have been a strong link between policies, prices, and exchange rates. Especially Swedish economic historians have liked the idea that the krona's early return to the gold standard was strongly influenced by the intellectual and moral power of liberal economists – just as for the early 1930s when Sweden supposedly became a pioneer in price-level targeting. The second explanation highlights institutional and political factors and their consequences for the credibility of monetary policy. Denmark and Norway were politically more unstable, and their central banks were weaker than elsewhere, so currency traders and investors began to doubt the determination and capacity of the authorities to implement the deflationary policies required to restore the gold standard at prewar parity. The third and last explanation argues with the short-term trade problems that Denmark and Norway were suffering from owing to their one-sided trade structure and their strong dependence on the British market, policy differences were irrelevant.

In short, the crucial question is whether the divergence of exchange rates was caused by differences of policy, credibility, or trade. As this chapter will show, the last explanation is the most likely one. The depreciation of the Danish krone and the Norwegian krone was mainly due to short-term trade problems resulting from the difficulty to return smoothly to a peacetime economy. Denmark's main problem was the slow growth of exports as the United Kingdom maintained its import restrictions for some time after the war. Norway's big trade deficit, by contrast, was mainly the result of a steep increase in imports. The purchase of food and the rebuilding of the fleet proved very costly. The Netherlands, Sweden, and Switzerland, by contrast, had less difficulty coping with the turbulent economic situation immediately after the war. In fact, the Netherlands and Switzerland were on the winning side as the guilder and the franc began to function as reserve currencies and international media of exchange.

In contrast, differences in policies and prices, as highlighted by the first explanation, appear to have been secondary. Everywhere, the monetary authorities were quite cautious, waiting for better times that would allow a return to the gold standard, and they raised discount rates only when the gold cover ratio decreased rapidly or an important trading partner, in particular the United Kingdom, led the way. Thus, not only were central banks across Scandinavia pursuing more or less the same policies, but growth rates of money and prices also were very similar. A comparison of Denmark with Sweden in particular reveals that monetary forces could not have been the main determinant of exchange rates. The same conclusion holds for the second explanation focusing on credibility issues: Differences were too small to matter. Sweden, for example, went through a particularly unstable phase after the war, yet the krona never depreciated as much as the currencies of its Scandinavian neighbors. In sum, the weakness of the Danish krone and the Norwegian krone resulted from inherited economic structures, not from specific national ideologies and policies.

This chapter will develop the argument in four steps. The first section presents the conventional view claiming that divergent growth rates of money and prices, caused by different monetary policies, explain the divergence in exchange rates. The second section tries to show that this view is inconsistent from a comparative perspective. The third section is devoted to the credibility argument suggesting that institutional and political factors were crucial. Since this argument also appears to be flawed, the last section discusses the third and most plausible explanation, which highlights differences in the trade balance in 1919 and 1920.

PURCHASING POWER PARITY AND DISCOUNT RATES

Why were the Danish krone and the Norwegian krone so much weaker after the war than the Dutch guilder, the Swedish krona, and the Swiss franc? As for the Scandinavian countries, the most popular answer has been that divergent growth rates of money and prices from 1915 to 1920 were the main cause. Furthermore, some Swedish and other Scandinavian economic historians have linked these divergent growth rates to different monetary policy stances. We can find similar explanations in the case of the Netherlands and Switzerland. This section will give a survey of the monetary approach.

A good starting point is the paper by Bergman, Gerlach, and Jonung (1993) on the rise and fall of the Scandinavian Currency Union (1873–1920). They have suggested that monetary growth was higher in Denmark and

Norway than in Sweden because the former did not experience the same sharp rise in foreign exports after the outbreak of the war. One important measure is the annual growth rate of notes in circulation. Before 1914, this rate was almost identical across the three Scandinavian countries, but from 1914 onward, they diverged, with Norway registering the highest increase and Sweden the lowest. The other important measure is the inflation rate, which also started to diverge at the beginning of the war. The paper concludes: "Divergent growth rates of money and prices in the three member countries during the period 1915–1920 caused eventually the dissolution of the Scandinavian Currency Union."[4]

Bergman, Gerlach, and Jonung (1993) do not link the divergent growth rates of money and prices to different monetary policy stances. Yet several other Swedish and Scandinavian scholars have highlighted the role of discount-rate policy. Klovland (1998) has made the most convincing case. He claims that Denmark's and Norway's policymakers failed to stem the rising inflationary pressure during the war and its immediate aftermath by a more restrictive monetary policy. Their Swedish colleagues, by contrast, were more determined and succeeded in stopping inflation, "perhaps due to the influence of eminent Swedish economists at the time."[5] Östlind (1945) has given a very detailed account of how the influence of these economists determined the course of events.[6] His narrative begins with the legendary parliamentary debate in mid-March 1920. Both chambers discussed the urgent request of the Riksbank to suspend the convertibility of notes into gold. Unlike most other European countries, Sweden had only prohibited the export of gold during the war, but not the right to exchange notes for gold at prewar parity. Because the krona had been depreciating against the dollar for some time, it became profitable to make arbitrage transactions. Swedish residents could bring their kronor to the central bank and exchange them for gold and realize the profit as soon as the ban on gold exports was lifted. When the famous Swedish economist Eli Heckscher recommended this transaction to the broad public by publishing an article in the daily newspaper *Stockholms Dagblad* (11 March 1920), a minor run

---

[4] Bergman, Gerlach, and Jonung (1993, pp. 514–515). On the Scandinavian Currency Union from 1875 to 1914, see Henriksen and Kaergård (1995) and Bordo and Jonung (1999). Jack (1927, p. 72) also claims that Denmark and Norway had experienced more inflation than Sweden.

[5] Klovland (1998, p. 336). Fregert and Jonung (2004, pp. 97–99) also highlight the importance of Swedish economists for policymaking.

[6] The article by Montgomery (1955) also has been influential. For a short overview of the crisis of the early 1920s, see Schön (2000, pp. 287ff).

on the Riksbank took place. The Riksbank immediately sent the urgent request to suspend convertibility.[7]

The Social Democratic government and the Banking Committee discussed and adopted the request in record time.[8] But the Riksdag was more skeptical and agreed only after several days of intense debate.[9] In the First Chamber, whose members were elected indirectly through the county councils and town councils of the larger cities so that the upper classes dominated, the vote was overwhelmingly in favor of the proposal. In the Second Chamber, whose members were elected by the people, the votes were evenly divided, with the Speaker of the Chamber casting the final ballot.[10] In the course of the debate, prominent politicians of all parties criticized the Riksbank for its unwillingness to raise the discount rate in the face of rising inflation rates. On the basis of articles and speeches by liberal economists, a radical change of course was demanded.[11] Immediately after the debate, the Riksbank raised the discount rate from 6 to 7 percent and three weeks later the rediscount rate.

The Swedish parliament did not content itself to criticize the government and the Riksbank. It also urged the government to set up a committee that would deal with fiscal policy.[12] The government complied a few weeks later so that a committee of financial experts (*finanssakkunniga*) could begin their work in May and deliver their report a few months later.[13] According to Östlind (1945), the recommendations expressed in this report were an important basis for the deflationary policies leading to appreciation of the krona.[14] Consequently, only six weeks later, the Riksbank raised the discount

---

[7] Parts of Heckscher's article are printed in Östlind (1945, pp. 344–345).

[8] Kongl. Maj: Proposition Nr. 221 (den 12 mars 1920). The Banking Committee of the Riksdag discussed the proposal on Sunday morning, 14 March: Bankoutskottets utlåtande, nr 23 (den 14 mars 1920). The first debate began on Sunday evening, 14 March. The Riksdag complained about the tight schedule adopted by the government.

[9] First Chamber, 14 March and 16–17 March (FK: 23–25), Second Chamber, 16 March (AK: 29).

[10] First Chamber: Yes 115, No 23; Second Chamber: Yes 88, No 88.

[11] In the First Chamber, the most prominent opponents were Social Democrats: Örne (FK 23, pp. 80–84; FK 24, pp. 31–36; FK 25, pp. 23–25), Wigforss (FK 23, pp. 86–89; FK 24, pp. 5–10; FK 25, pp. 19–23). Notermans (2000, pp. 68–71) highlights the role of Swedish Social Democrats in restoration of the gold standard. In the Second Chamber, the most outspoken critics were Sommelius (AK 29, pp. 10–13) and Wikström (AK 29, pp. 3–10, 35–38).

[12] The Riksdag sent the request on 27 April 1920.

[13] The documents of the *finanssakkunniga* are at the Riksarkiv in Stockholm, among them the illustrative responses to the questionnaire sent to all major associations and firms. Riksarkiv: 1920 Års Finanssakkunnigas: Protokoll och Handlingar. The final report also can be found in the archives of the Riksbank.

[14] Östlind (1945, pp. 352–353). He also points out that the Social Democrat Örne who criticized his own government in March became under-secretary in the newly formed

rate to a record-high 7.5 percent. The krona became stronger and, in the summer of 1921, reached 90 percent of its prewar parity. In short, the article by Eli Heckscher, the pressure of other liberal economists, the debate of the Riksdag, and the recommendations of the Committee on Public Finance – all these factors forced the Swedish authorities to conduct a more restrictive policy in order to bring the krona back to prewar parity.[15]

As for the other small neutral countries, the established view is not as coherent as in the Swedish case, but we can find similar arguments. Like Klovland (1998) in his comparative article, Danish historians have highlighted the benign neglect the authorities displayed vis-à-vis the exchange rate after the war.[16] Carl Ussing, the managing director of the Danish National Bank, explained that "protection of production" was more important than "protection of bank notes." To Johansen (1987), "a manifestation of the 'production policy' was that the bank rate in 1919 and 1920 was kept at a lower level than in many other European countries."[17] The central bank first wanted to facilitate the transition from war to peace and then to restore the gold standard at prewar parity.

Hoffmeyer and Olsen (1968) identify three motives behind this benign neglect. The first one was the fear of social and political unrest. As elsewhere, the decrease of real wages during the war radicalized workers so that after the war the labor unions had no difficulty in organizing a series of strikes. Moreover, Denmark was close to countries with strong revolutionary movements: Russia, Finland, and Germany. In particular, Hamburg and Kiel, the two German seaports, where the German revolt started in November 1918, were very close to the Danish border. The second motive was Ussing's solidarity with the government under Prime Minister Carl Theodor Zahle, a progressive liberal. He thought that the central bank was a political institution bound to cooperate with other political institutions.

finance ministry in the summer of 1920, still under the Social Democratic government of Hjalmar Branting (until October 1920). Notermans (2000, p. 70) also highlights the role played by this committee: "The committee proposed that energetic measures be taken to stop inflation, followed by measures to depress the price level, and that the krona be linked to gold again."

[15] Cf. Haavisto and Jonung (1995, p. 252): "The policy of deflation was designed in terms of exchange-rate targets, and the price level was subordinated to this target. In Sweden, the domestic currency was kept overvalued as long as was needed to restore the prewar parity."

[16] See the seminal study of Olsen (1968, pp. 62–65), reproduced in Johansen (1987, pp. 25–27) and Hansen (1996, pp. 89–90). For a short summary of Danish exchange-rate policy, see Abildgren (2004a).

[17] Johansen (1987, p. 27).

He also was aware of the fact that in order to keep the Social Democrats inside the government, the central bank had to be cautious about reducing inflation. The third motive was the will to strengthen the Danish economy before the integration of northern Schleswig. Following the defeat of Germany, the Versailles powers offered Denmark the return of Schleswig-Holstein. Fearing German irredentism Denmark, however, refused to consider the return of Holstein and insisted on a plebiscite concerning the return of Schleswig. In 1920, following the plebiscite, northern Schleswig was recovered by Denmark.

Unlike Klovland (1998), however, most Norwegian historians have argued that Norges Bank was too restrictive in 1920, not too expansionary, although the krone was weak, not strong. They have reckoned that the central bank, willing to bring the krone back to prewar parity by raising the discount rate to 7 percent in June 1920, contributed to the deflationary slump starting in 1921.[18] Besides Klovland, Knutsen (2000) also has challenged the conventional view, pointing out that Norway's policy was less restrictive than Sweden's, although inflation had been higher, and that Norges Bank pursued a rather expansionary policy during the banking crisis from 1921 to 1924. Accordingly, he explains the steep fall of prices from September 1920 to December 1922 mainly by the international downturn starting in the United States and the United Kingdom.[19]

As for the Netherlands and Switzerland, we find several scholars highlighting monetary forces and monetary policy. Van Zanden (1998) observes that unlike the British and the Scandinavians, the Dutch government "did not have to deflate the economy": "During the 1910s prices had increased much less in the Netherlands than in Britain (or Denmark, Sweden, and Norway), which made possible a very smooth return to gold."[20] The Nederlandsche Bank in fact left the discount rate unchanged from July 1915 to July 1922 and only increased the Lombard rate from 4.5 to 5.5

---

[18] The seminal paper is Hanisch (1979). For a newer version of the argument, see Hanisch, Søilen, and Ecklund (1999). Hodne (1983, p. 31) and Nordvik (1995, p. 440) follow Hanisch. On the relation between purchasing price parity (PPP) and the exchange rate of the krone, see Edison and Klovland (1987). They conclude that the period from 1914 to 1928 cannot be explained by a PPP model.

[19] Knutsen (2000, pp. 10–11). His criticism of the book of Hanisch, Søilen, and Ecklund (1999) opened up a debate in the journal *Sosialøkonomen 2000*. See the replies by Ola Honningdal Grytten (no. 3) and Jan Tore Klovland (no. 5), as well as the concluding contribution by Knutsen (no. 6). As for Norway's banking crisis in the 1920s, see Chapter Two.

[20] Van Zanden (1998, S. 103). On the macroeconomic development of the Netherlands during the interwar years see the seminal study by Keesing (1947) as well as Central Bureau voor de Statistiek (1987) and Bie (1995).

percent in October 1920.[21] However, we find the same controversy between liberal economists and central bankers as elsewhere, as de Vries (1989) has shown.[22]

Swiss economic historians have pointed out that the Swiss National Bank was the first European central bank to raise the discount rate in the late 1910s, even before the Bank of England, and thus succeeded in curbing inflation earlier than elsewhere. The narrative begins in early 1918, when Eduard Kellenberger, a young economist, newspaper editor, and lecturer at the University of Berne, published a series of articles in which he held the Swiss National Bank responsible for the onset of inflation.[23] In April, the *Neue Zürcher Zeitung,* the most influential business newspaper of Switzerland, published an op-ed article by the Secretary of the Chamber of Commerce of Zurich in which Kellenberger's criticism was repeated. In May and June, the two largest private banks (Schweizerischer Bankverein and Schweizerische Kreditanstalt) criticized the Swiss National Bank in their monthly newsletter, and in June, the Swiss parliament debated monetary policy for the first time since the outbreak of the war, thereby casting some doubt on the generous financing of public debt. A few weeks after Kellenberger's articles in early 1918, the Swiss National Bank started to discuss the matter, and in the summer, it decided to take measures against the expansion of notes in circulation. In July, it raised the Lombard rate and the rate for treasury bills, and in October, it decided to increase the discount rate and the Lombard rate.[24]

Guex (1993) claims that the increase in the discount rate has to be considered "an anti-inflationary turning point" and "a true change of opinion by the authorities."[25] The Swiss National Bank was in fact the only European central bank to take such a step just before the end of the war,

---

[21] The increase in the Lombard rate from 4.5 to 5.5 percent concerned only domestic securities. Regarding foreign securities, the Lombard rate was raised from 5 to 6 percent. In addition, as for banks' current account deposits at the central bank, the rate was increased from 5.5 to 6 percent. See the Annual Report of De Nederlandsche Bank for the Year 1920–1921, p. 31, de Vries (1989, pp. 230–233), and Van Zanden (1997, p. 143).

[22] De Vries (1989, pp. 320–338): In 1920, fourteen Dutch economists called for a more restrictive monetary policy. Shortly afterward, 17 bankers and businessmen warned against such a policy turn, thus endorsing the Nederlandsche Bank. On the position of the business sector, see also Notermans (2000, p. 73).

[23] This short version is based on the two main Swiss studies on the monetary policy of Switzerland during and after the war: Ruoss (1992) and Guex (1993).

[24] Guex (1993, pp. 265–276) was the first to highlight these articles.

[25] Guex (1993, p. 264) observes *"un véritable changement dans l'attitude des autorités fédérales."* He also points out (p. 291) that Switzerland was particularly restrictive. Ruoss (1992, p. 118) also concludes that the rate increase came early in comparison with other European countries.

thus having a higher discount rate from October 1918 to November 1919 than, for example, the Bank of England. According to Ruoss (1992), this early tightening dampened the postwar boom and decelerated inflation – Switzerland in fact registered lower inflation rates in 1919 and 1920 than most other European countries.[26] The great slump, however, is not attributed to the discount-rate policy but to international developments that lay outside the influence of the Swiss National Bank.[27]

Furthermore, Guex (1993) argues that there were three reasons why the Swiss elites decided to reduce inflation by increasing the discount rate in October 1918. First, they feared that the labor movement would become more radical if inflation was not halted.[28] Second, they were dissatisfied with price controls and the economic consequences of inflation. Finally, they were concerned about the decreasing gold cover ratio, but this concern is rated as a reason of minor importance by economic historians. In short, the forces critical of high inflation rates were much stronger in Switzerland than elsewhere in Europe, and accordingly, the Swiss National Bank acted earlier than other European central banks.

DISCOUNT RATES, EXCHANGE RATES, AND THE MAKING OF MONETARY POLICY

Is the PPP explanation the most appropriate one? Two arguments contradict such a view. First, recent research on exchange-rate movements since the end of Bretton Woods system has shown that it is impossible to detect a significant correlation between PPP and the exchange rate in the short run.[29] Second, Figures 1.2 and 1.3, which plot the exchange rate as a percentage of the PPP rate, suggest that the same is true for the years after World War I. Particularly in 1920, the differences in nominal exchange rates were mainly due to differences in real exchange rates and not to divergent price levels. Similarly, the strength of the Swiss franc in nominal terms in 1921 resulted from a strong real appreciation.

---

[26] Ruoss (1992, pp. 135–136). Bordo and James (2007, pp. 48–51) share their view about the discount-rate increase of 1918. Cf. Guex (1993, p. 316), who agrees but is more cautious in his judgment. Bucher (1943, pp. 157–159) is convinced that the rate increase improved the balance sheet of the National Bank.

[27] Ruoss (1992, p. 150).

[28] Accordingly, the title of this chapter (pp. 263ff) is *"combattre l'inflation pour combattre le socialisme."*

[29] See the seminal paper by Meese and Rogoff (1983) and the May 2003 volume of the *Journal of International Economics*, which is devoted to the twentieth anniversary of this paper.

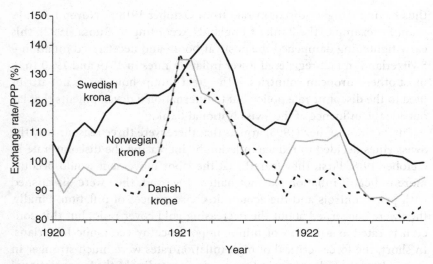

Figure 1.2. Denmark, Norway, and Sweden: exchange rates as a percentage of PPP. (*Commission of Gold and Silver Inquiry, 1925.*)

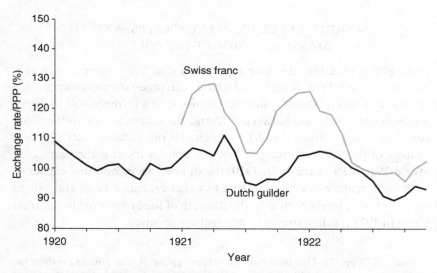

Figure 1.3. The Netherlands and Switzerland: exchange rates as a percentage of PPP. (*Commission of Gold and Silver Inquiry, 1925.*)

We can make the same observation with respect to consumer prices and notes in circulation (Tables 1.2 and 1.3). Consumer prices in Denmark and Sweden increased at a similar pace from 1918 to 1922, and the volume of notes in circulation was roughly at the same level in 1920 when exchange

Table 1.2. *Consumer Prices of Small European Neutrals (1914 = 100)*

	Denmark	Netherlands	Norway	Sweden	Switzerland
1918	182	162	253	219	204
1919	211	176	275	257	222
1920	261	194	300	269	224
1921	232	169	277	247	200
1922	200	149	231	198	164

Source: Maddison (1991), appendix E, pp. 293 ff.

Table 1.3. *Notes in Circulation of Small European Neutrals (First Semester 1914 = 100)*

	Denmark	Netherlands	Norway	Sweden	Switzerland
1918	219	281	283	235	239
1919	287	340	380	323	333
1920	316	335	379	302	358
1921	348	346	388	301	354
1922	300	328	347	252	336

Source: Commission of Gold and Silver Inquiry (1925).

rates started to diverge. Furthermore, in Switzerland, notes in circulation had increased considerably more from 1914 to 1920 than in Denmark, but the Swiss franc was much stronger than the Danish krone. Only the cases of the Netherlands and Norway can be reconciled with the claim that differences in money growth rates and price levels caused divergent nominal exchange rates.

Likewise, it is problematic to make a direct link between discount rates and exchange-rate movements.[30] The Swedish Riksbank may have pursued a more restrictive monetary policy, but obviously, it failed to materialize. Yet not even this claim is true. A closer look at the movements of discount rates reveals that differences were rather small (Figures 1.4 and 1.5). In particular, the Scandinavian rates differed only slightly. In the first quarter of 1919 and in the last quarter of 1920, Sweden had somewhat higher discount rates than Denmark and Norway, but convergence, not divergence, was the central feature of Scandinavian monetary policy from 1919 to

[30] Fregert (1994, p. 281).

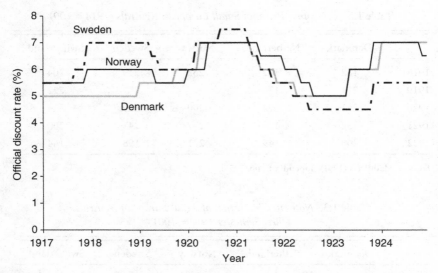

Figure 1.4. Discount rates of Denmark, Norway, and Sweden, 1917–1924. (*Commission of Gold and Silver Inquiry, 1925.*)

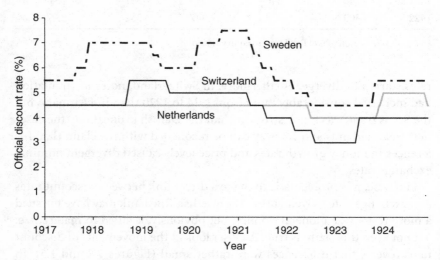

Figure 1.5. Discount rates of the Netherlands, Sweden, and Switzerland, 1917–1924. (*Commission of Gold and Silver Inquiry, 1925.*)

1922. In spring of 1920, Denmark followed Sweden only a few weeks later, on 16 April, one day after the Bank of England had increased the rate on treasury bills to 7 percent.[31] The same is true for Norway: The discount rate was raised to 7 percent as well, although somewhat later.[32]

If we include the Netherlands and Switzerland in the comparison, the explanation focused on discount rates is even harder to maintain. As noted, the Nederlandsche Bank kept the rate at a low level throughout the postwar period until mid-1922, and the Swiss National Bank lowered the rate to 5 percent in August of 1919 and did not change it until early 1921. Nevertheless, the Dutch guilder and the Swiss franc were the two strongest European currencies in 1920.

Finally, the figures show that in 1920 discount-rate increases could not have a great effect because they were made in a highly inflationary environment (see Table 1.2). In all three Scandinavian countries, real interest rates remained negative from January to October 1920 when the peak of the restocking boom was reached.[33] It is true that prices were rising faster in Denmark and Norway than in Sweden, but it is hard to believe that this divergence was caused by a temporary and small discount-rate difference in the spring of 1920. Thus Knutsen and Ecklund (2000) have been right in pointing out that central banks of small states hardly had the power to slow down economic growth by raising interest rates by a few percentage points and to cause the steep fall in prices in the early 1920s.

Accordingly, it is fair to conclude that economic historians have overestimated the effect of the discount-rate increase by the Swedish Riksbank to a record high of 7.5 percent in September of 1920. Of course, it was an unusual step because the new rate was higher than the British one. For chronological reasons, though, it cannot explain why the Swedish krona was stronger than the Danish krone and the Norwegian krone. First, the Danish and Norwegian currencies had depreciated *before* September 1920. And second, they were in fact catching up vis-à-vis the Swedish krona only a few weeks *after* the increase of the Swedish rate to 7.5 percent.

[31] *The Economist*, 1 May 1920, country report Denmark, p. 911: "The Danish National Bank has followed the trend of other countries in raising its rate of discount from 6 per cent, at which is has stood since October 7th, to 7 per cent."

[32] Cf. Knutsen (2001, p. 12): "On June 25 1920, the central bank's discount rate had been raised to 7 percent. This decision was, however, rather reluctant and was made several months after Sweden and Denmark, in spite of a particularly strong inflation in Norway."

[33] From January to October 1920, consumer prices in Sweden rose by 8.5 percent when the peak of the postwar inflation was reached.

Furthermore, all Scandinavian central banks reduced their discount rates in several successive steps from spring 1921 until summer 1922, but strikingly, the rapid climb of the Swedish krona toward prewar parity occurred precisely during this period of monetary relaxation.

Finally, the same statistical arguments also show that the traditional interpretation by Swiss economic historians overstates the effects of monetary policy. Raising the discount rate by only 1 to 5.5 percent in October 1918 was hardly enough to fight inflation successfully and to dampen the postwar boom. If the Swiss National Bank had been serious about fighting inflation, it would have raised the rate again during the restocking boom that started in the middle of 1919. Instead, the Swiss National Bank lowered the rate to 5 percent in August 1919, where it remained until April 1921 when the postwar slump reached the Swiss economy. The striking deceleration of Switzerland's consumer prices from 1918 to 1920 must have had other causes.

In sum, the monetary approach is incomplete. It explains the exchange-rate movements of the Dutch guilder and the Norwegian krone but not those of the other currencies. This conclusion suggests that the second part of the conventional view, namely, that central banks raised interest rates in response to public pressure, is flawed as well. To prove this point, it is necessary to take a closer look at the minutes of central bank boards. They reveal that policymakers increased discount rates only when they were forced to, namely, when their gold and foreign-exchange reserves fell dramatically or when the Bank of England raised the rate. In other words, the actions of central bankers were still inspired by the prewar gold standard, although it remained suspended until the mid-1920s. Of course, when the reserve ratio deteriorated, it was mainly due to inflation that stirred public criticism. The crucial point, however, is that central banks, alarmed by the low level of reserves, raised interest rates anyway, regardless of whether a few professors and lawyers were complaining about monetary policy or not.

The reason for the cautious approach was the conviction of policymakers that the reversal of inflation would have required such a tight monetary policy that the transition from the wartime to the peacetime economy would be seriously endangered. Thus Danish historians have been correct in pointing out that their central bank officials were concerned about the social consequences of a tight monetary policy, but they failed to mention that this attitude was very normal across Europe. Everywhere, central bankers refused to follow the advice of liberal economists because they knew that they would have to bear the blame for the resulting increase in unemployment. This careful approach led to a kind of schizophrenic monetary policy. On the one hand, central bankers still followed the rules of the prewar gold standard; on the other hand, they believed that these rules were inadequate during the reconstruction period. On the one hand, discount rates were raised in order to stop the deterioration of the gold cover or to follow the British monetary policy; on the other hand, they did not make any significant difference as long as inflation rates were higher than nominal interest rates. Not surprisingly, the timing of such a monetary policy was far from optimal: Rate increases were not realized in the beginning or in the middle of a boom but at a very late stage.

As for Switzerland's early rate increase in October 1918, the limited role of public pressure and the lack of anti-inflationary rhetoric are particularly evident. First of all, the board of the Swiss National Bank never declared publicly nor stated in internal memos that it had increased the discount rate with the purpose of fighting inflation. In the public statement explaining the rate increase in October, it wrote that the rising private discount rate and the dramatic decline in the reserve ratio had caused the monetary authorities to act. In the internal memo, it explicitly ruled out that the fight against inflation had been the main motive.[34] Second, in the crucial period from December 1917 to October 1918, public criticism was mentioned only twice in internal meetings – in April and June. Yet, in these two meetings, the board considered this criticism unfounded. Besides, the metallic cover ratio was rising at the time[35] (Figure 1.6). Only in August, when the ratio dropped dramatically, did the board begin to discuss a rate increase, but without any reference to public criticism.

Possibly, this silence was due to the fact that the governing board tried to avoid the impression that the critics had been right and that the Swiss National Bank should have reacted earlier. The internal records do not support this view, however. The Swiss National Bank had considered a discount-rate increase as early as December 1917, several months before public criticism became fierce. The reserve ratio deteriorated at a fast pace, but bank officials abstained from a rate increase for two reasons. First, the federal government was planning to place a war loan (*Mobilisationsanleihe*) within the next weeks, and second, they did not believe that a higher discount rate would halt the expansion of notes in circulation. The economic

[34] Archives Swiss National Bank, *Beilage Direktionsprotokoll*, No. 41, 4 Oktober 1918, pp. 192–193: "*An die Direktionen der Zweiganstalten: Motive zur Erhöhung des Diskontosatzes auf 5.5 percent und des Lombardsatzes auf 6 percent.*".

[35] Archives Swiss National Bank, *Protokoll des Direktoriums*, 25 April 1918, p. 14; *Protokoll des Direktoriums*, 17 June 1918, pp. 5–8.

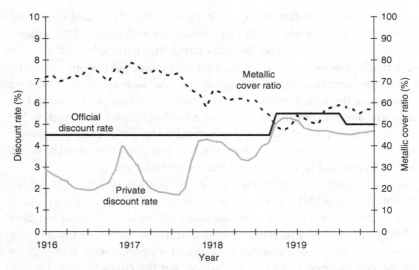

Figure 1.6. Switzerland: discount rates and metallic cover ratio. (*Commission of Gold and Silver Inquiry, 1925.*)

situation was "abnormal," the president of the governing board explained. The traditional tools were considered worthless.[36]

The passive attitude of Swiss National Bank officials was rewarded by relaxation of the money market in the first months of 1918. Yet, as noted, the governing board discussed a rate increase at its meeting on 22 August and concluded that a discount-rate increase was inevitable. At the same time, it remained skeptical about the effectiveness of this measure and was hesitating to take this step before another war loan (*Mobilisationsanleihe*) raised by the federal government was issued.[37] By a slim majority (4 to 3), the Bank Council Committee decided in its meeting on 10 September 1918 to postpone the increase of the discount rate.[38] Yet, as soon as the war loan (*Mobilisationsanleihe*) was issued, the governing board demanded action and was determined to pursue a more restrictive monetary policy because the situation had become alarming. Interestingly, the board still remained skeptical about the effectiveness of such a measure.[39] Nevertheless, the

---

[36] Archives Swiss National Bank, *Bankausschuss*, 8 February 1918, p. 23.
[37] Archives Swiss National Bank, *Beilage zum Direktionsprotokoll*, 22 August 1918, p. 156.
[38] Close board decisions have been quite rare in the history of the Swiss National Bank. Archives Swiss National Bank, *Bankausschuss*, 10 September 1918, p. 211.
[39] Archives Swiss National Bank. *Beilage zum Direktionsprotokoll*, 26 September 1918, p. 187.

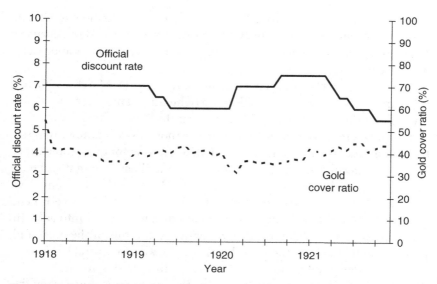

Figure 1.7. Sweden: official discount rate and gold cover ratio. (*Commission of Gold and Silver Inquiry, 1925.*)

decision was made to increase the discount rate by 1 percent and the Lombard rate by 0.5 percent. The Bank Council Committee agreed on 3 October.[40] The skepticism was fully justified: The tightening of monetary policy was without any lasting effect (see Figure 1.6). Notes in circulation continued to increase, and the reserve ratio remained low. Only thanks to the short postwar recession in 1919 did the situation improve.

Swedish monetary policy was motivated by similar considerations. When the board of the Riksbank discussed discount-rate increases, neither Governor Victor Moll nor other board members ever mentioned the fight against inflation or the appreciation of the krona as the primary goal of their policy. Like their colleagues in Switzerland, they felt that discount rates did not have the same effect as before the war and would only harm business if raised vigorously. Accordingly, events unfolded in the same manner as in Switzerland because the Riksbank officials were focusing on the declining reserve ratio. Figure 1.7 shows that the reserve ratio had been dropping continuously since late summer of 1919 so that already in December 1919 rumors of an imminent discount-rate increase to 7 percent

---

[40] Archives Swiss National Bank, *Bankausschuss*, 3 October 1918, p. 223.

were spreading through Europe.[41] In January 1920, the situation improved, but this was due to seasonal fluctuations, so that by the end of February 1920, the situation had become alarming: The reserve ratio was approaching the legal limit of 40 percent.

Thus, when Heckscher published his article on 11 March 1920, the Riksbank had already been considering a tightening of monetary policy for several months. The minutes of the meeting (18 March) at which the discount-rate increase was decided quote Governor Moll explaining that the balance sheet of the Riksbank had been deteriorating for quite some time. He spoke of record-high amounts of lending and illustrated in detail how the reserve ratio had declined.[42] Accordingly, Heckscher's article only had the effect that the Riksbank immediately sent a request to the government to be exempted from the duty to redeem Swedish bank notes into gold. In this request, the Riksbank explicitly mentioned the role of the press and pointed out that neither the Danish nor the Norwegian central bank were bound to redeem notes into gold.[43] However, the decision to increase the discount rate would have come anyway, at the latest in mid-April when the Bank of England increased its rate from 6 to 7 percent.

Furthermore, the debate in the Swedish Riksdag did not exert the big influence that has been ascribed to it by some economic historians. True, the Riksbank minutes of the crucial meeting of 18 March 1920 mention that a discount-rate increase had been intensely discussed lately, which certainly was an allusion to the recent debate in the government and in the press.[44] As noted, though, the government and a clear majority of the parliament supported the policy of the Riksbank wholeheartedly.[45] The minutes also reveal how Governor Moll was doing everything to avoid the impression of a regime change, which is another proof that the Riksbank refused to follow the advice of its critics. He explained that he only wanted to raise the discount rate, not the rediscount rate, which was

---

[41] Archives Swiss National Bank, *Beilage zum Direktionsprotokoll*, 24 December 1919, p. 281.

[42] Archives Sveriges Riksbank, *Särskilt protokoll*, 18 March 1920, p. 63: "*Utlåningen den 13 dennes 576 mill. Kr. är den största som någansin förekommit.*" On gold movements, see pp. 65–66.

[43] The request is quoted in the proposal of the government to the parliament (1920: 25, Bihang till Riksdagens protokoll 1920, 13. Band, Kongl. Maj: proposition Nr. 221) and in the report of the Banking Committee (1920: 53, Bihang till Riksdagens protokoll, åttonde samlingen, Bankoutskottets utlåtande Nr. 23).

[44] Archives Sveriges Riksbank, *Särskilt protokoll*, 18 March 1920, p. 66.

[45] As reported, the approval by the Second Chamber was in fact very close, but the First Chamber consented by 115 to 23 votes.

the central rate for private banks, although he knew that the Riksbank might be forced to increase this rate in the near future as well owing to the tightening of the money market.[46] On 8 April 1920, the Riksbank felt forced to take this step, but again, Governor Moll emphasized that this decision should not be interpreted as a first step toward a further raise of the discount rate.[47] Thus, although it raised interest rates, the Riksbank did not change course. It just applied the old rules, and the board itself did not expect any great effect.[48]

Even Eli Heckscher himself later pointed out that the root of the problems of the Riksbank was the convertibility of the bank note, which he dubbed "an anomalous situation," because it caused a decline in gold reserves. He merely used this situation "to put pressure upon the Riksbank," but he had not created the dilemma itself.[49] Heckscher also contradicts the view that the Committee on Public Finance had a great influence on the course of events. A closer look at the report confirms this view. The recommendations made in the final report were ambivalent and contradictory, and there was no timetable beyond the general statement that these goals should be realized "as soon as possible." The Riksbank was expected to stop inflation but not to hamper industrial production. Private commercial banks should curb lending but also without causing any problems for industry. And foreign lending was to be limited.[50] It is hard to interpret these proposals as a coherent deflationary scheme that was designed to restore the gold standard at prewar parity. It was rather a compromise that left many questions open. The reason why the committee was careful in proposing a far-reaching deflation is not hard to discover: Most employers' associations were against the increase in interest rates.[51]

Whatever the committee explained, it did not prevent the balance sheet of the Riksbank from further deteriorating. The discount-rate and rediscount-rate increases had no effect, as the board had expected. The reserve ratio remained low throughout the summer and began to approach the

---

[46] Archives Sveriges Riksbank, *Särskilt protokoll*, 18 March 1920, pp. 66–67.

[47] Archives Sveriges Riksbank, *Särskilt protokoll*, 8 April 1920, pp. 83–85.

[48] The Riksbank focused on demand of business, calculated as loans, discounts, and advances minus deposits (because deposits in Sweden were mainly money of the state). See Archives Sveriges Riksbank, *Särskilt protokoll*, 18 March 1920, p. 64.

[49] Heckscher (1930, pp. 243–245).

[50] 1920 *Års Finanssakkunniga: Utlåtande angående frågan huruvida och i vad mån ett program för den närmaste framtiden för svensk finanspolitik må kunna åstadkommas. Avgivet den 6 Augusti 1920 av särskilda sakkunniga*, Stockholm 1920, pp. 37–38.

[51] The results of this survey are summarized on the first 20 pages of the report. Among these documents, there is a detailed overview of the answers given by Swedish firms.

legal minimum of 40 percent again. This time, the main reason for the decrease in the ratio was not that the Riksbank was losing gold but that the number of notes in circulation increased from 708 million kroner in May to 742 millions kroner in August 1920. The unused note issue was approaching the zero point. In the meeting of 16 September, the Riksbank considered two measures: the import of gold or a discount-rate increase. The first option was dismissed because it proved too costly and too diffi- cult, so that the board preferred the second option. As in March, the min- utes do not contain any hint of an active exchange-rate policy.[52] Heckscher points out that the Riksbank would have asked the parliament for an extraordinary extension of the right to issue notes if it had not been for the strong criticism in the sessions of March 1920. This is a possible interpreta- tion, but Heckscher cannot provide any evidence for his thesis. Subsequent parliamentary debates suggest otherwise: In April 1921, both chambers approved the Riksbank's request to increase the right to issue notes.

In sum, in Switzerland and Sweden, central banks were not conducting an active exchange-rate policy or adopting a strong anti-inflationary stance owing to public pressure, as some historians have suggested. They increased their discount rates only when the gold and foreign-exchange reserves were shrinking. Accordingly, we cannot find any discount-rate increases in the Netherlands because the Nederlandsche Bank had sufficient gold reserves and because the Dutch money market was not as dependent on the British money market as those of the Scandinavian countries. Like anywhere else in Europe, there was no lack of criticism of how the Nederlandsche Bank conducted its monetary policy. Some economists publicly demanded a restrictive stance. But bank officials refused to change course and kept the discount rate at 4.5 percent, which had been its level since July 1915. They could afford to ignore the criticism because the balance sheet of the Nederlandsche Bank was in a very healthy condition.[53]

Similarly, in the case of Denmark and Norway, the discount-rate increases in 1920 were not motivated by public pressure or a sort of mon- etarist turn. The Danish National Bank and Norges Bank simply followed the Swedish Riksbank. The Danish authorities decided to raise the rate to 7 percent on 17 April 1920, only one month after Sweden. The delay was caused by the decision of the Danish government to give loans to some

---

[52] Archives Sveriges Riksbank, *Särskilt protokoll*, 16 September 1920, pp. 244–248.
[53] Vissering et Holstijn (1928, pp. 69–72, 98–101). When the Swiss National Bank discussed the increase in the discount rate in the course of 1918, it often referred to the more favor- able situation of the Netherlands that had been able to import more gold during the war. See, for example, Archives Swiss National Bank, Bankausschuss, 14–15 May 1918, p. 36.

municipalities in the near future. At a meeting with the governing board of the Danish National Bank on 17 March 1920, Finance Minister Brandes and Trade Minister Hage convinced the board to wait.[54] The board, just informed by the Swedish Riksbank of the discount-rate increase on the next day to 7 percent, wanted to follow immediately.[55] When it met again on 16 April, this time with the new government, the board decided to raise the discount rate because the loans had been granted to the municipalities. Moreover, the Bank of England had just raised its discount rate.[56] Norway delayed the rate increase until June because the government issued a bond in March 1920. The *Economist* observed in early April that "but for the Government loans, no doubt the Bank rate, at present 6 per cent, would have followed that of Stockholm, where, on the 18th inst., the discount was raised to 7 per cent."[57] Not surprisingly, the Norges Bank in its annual report, as well as the so-called Foreign Exchange Council (*valutarådet*) in its final report, highlighted this anomaly.[58] In any case, once the bond issue was concluded successfully, the board decided to raise the rate to 7 percent, although by a slim majority: Three were for the rate increase; two, against it. The minutes cite Klingenberg, a lawyer, explaining that his opposition was based on three reasons. First, a rate increase would slow down the economy; second, it was not guaranteed that it would strengthen the rate of the krone; and third, a discount-rate increase would not stop inflation because private banks still would have enough incentives to expand their credit volumes.[59] In short, the discussion led within the board of the Norges Bank was very similar to the one in Switzerland and Sweden: The discount rate was raised, but policymakers were aware that it would not reverse inflation.

THE CREDIBILITY ARGUMENT

A second possible explanation of why exchange-rate movements diverged after the war is that the Danish and Norwegian authorities suffered from a credibility problem. There are several possibilities to measure such an

---

[54] Archives National Bank of Denmark, *Direktionsprotokol,* 17 March 1920, p. 175.
[55] Cf. the annual reports of the National Bank: Denmark is always compared with Norway and Sweden.
[56] Archives National Bank of Denmark, *Direktionsprotokol,* 16 April 1920, p. 176.
[57] *The Economist,* 10 April 1920, p. 782.
[58] Norges Bank, Annual Report 1920, p. 4; *Beretning om valutarådets virksomhet, 13 de februar 1920–31 te august 1921,* p. 11.
[59] Riksarkivet, Arkiv: Norges Bank, *Direksjonsarkivet I, Arkivskaper: Serie: A – Forhandlingsprotokoll for Direksjonen,* 30.03.1918–28.01.1921, A 0047, p. 549.

effect. Simmons (1994), who has undertaken the most comprehensive study on the credibility issue during the interwar years, used four variables: central bank independence, the stability of the government, the strength of the Left, and the number of strikes. She concludes that foreign-exchange markets had more trust in countries with stable governments, independent central banks, and weak leftist parties and labor unions. These results also hold when economic control variables such as the exchange rates of the most important trading partners are included.[60] Another important indicator may have been the size of public debts, in particular of floating debts. Possibly, since Danish and Norwegian authorities failed to signal their determination to reduce their floating debts, foreign-exchange markets were running out of patience and punished these governments.[61] Part of this signaling process could have been the timing of discount-rate increases: Sweden's early tightening in March 1920 may have made an important difference.[62]

Yet, like the PPP explanation, the credibility argument has some weaknesses. First of all, the institutional and political variables used by Simmons are only weakly correlated with the strength of currencies (Table 1.4). As for central bank independence, Sweden's central bank, owned and controlled by the Riksdag, was only slightly more independent than Norway's and clearly less independent than Denmark's, yet the Swedish krona was much stronger than the Danish krone and the Norwegian krone. According to Simmons, the Danish central bank was also more independent than the Swiss National Bank, which again does not correspond with the strength of the currencies.

Furthermore, Denmark's and Norway's political situation after World War I was not more turbulent than Sweden's. On the contrary, starting in 1912, the high ranks of the Swedish Social Democratic Party were confronted with strong internal opposition against following a moderate path and reaching out for a coalition with liberals. When, after the elections of October 1917, four leading Social Democrats, including the party's head, Hjalmar Branting, formed the coalition government with the liberals, headed by Nils Edén, the radicals gained more importance. In the Lower House of the Riksdag, they formed a new party, the Social Democratic Leftist Party, consisting of 15 seats, and pressed the socialization issue. Scared by the rising popularity of the new party, the Social Democrats themselves began to introduce proposals for socialization of the sugar and coal industries. After

[60] See also Eichengreen and Simmons (1995).
[61] Cf. James (1992, p. 5960).
[62] Fregert and Jonung (2004, p. 106).

Table 1.4. *Political and Institutional Differences*

	Percentage of Left in Parliament	Number of Governments	Central Bank Independence	Number of Workers Involved in Strikes (Percentage of Population)
	1917–1925	1918–1922		1918–1922
Denmark	31	4	7	1.0
Norway	27	3	4	
Sweden	43	4	5	1.4
Netherlands	23	2	6	0.8
Switzerland	25	2	5	0.4

Percentage of Left: including Left-Socialists and Communists (Anti-Comintern, Pro USSR); figures for Sweden only for the Second Chamber (Andra kammeren).
Central bank independence: The index is based on two criteria: 1. Central Bank Appointments, 2. Central Bank Supervision/Policy Control. For each criterion scale from 1 to 4, 8 is the maximum.
Population figures: census of 1920.
Sources: Caramani (2000), Simmons (1994), and Mitchell (2003).

the war, governing with the liberals became even more difficult. In March 1920, a government crisis broke out, with the consequence that a purely Social Democratic government under Hjalmar Branting was formed, for the first time in Swedish history. The basis for the new breakthrough of the Left was very thin, however, because the Social Democrats only formed the largest party but were still a minority in the Riksdag.

As explained earlier, in March 1920, the Riksbank was fighting against the loss of gold reserves, and the Scandinavian currencies were following sterling in its steep rise toward the US dollar. Unlike the Danish krone and the Norwegian krone, the Swedish krona was able to maintain its level in the second quarter of 1920. Obviously, foreign-exchange markets were not impressed by Sweden's political problems. They did not react either when the Social Democrats began to press the socialization issue more than ever by setting up a commission on industrial democracy and one on socialization in June 1920. The suggestions of the latter commission were not revolutionary, but nevertheless, they included the gradual socialization of all necessary natural resources, industrial enterprises, credit institutions, transport, and communication routes.[63] The

[63] Hamilton (1989, p. 161).

commission also envisioned curtailment of the properties and fortunes of the upper class. Yet the Social Democratic government did not have the time to implement its program: In the elections in October 1920, the Social Democrats experienced a setback, and since the liberals refused to renew their coalition with the Social Democrats, the king appointed a government of nonpolitical experts. 1920 also was a year that witnessed numerous strikes, especially in the first months of the year. The main issue was introduction of the eight-hour-day that had become law on 29 September 1919 but had to be implemented on the firm-level. It was the year with the greatest strike participation by workers since 1909, the year of the great general strike.[64]

In the comparative literature on the Scandinavian Left, it has become popular to portray the Norwegian Left as by far the most radical among them.[65] This claim has been based on the fact that the Norwegian Labor Party joined the Comintern in 1920, whereas the Danish and Swedish sister parties never considered this step seriously. Accordingly, the rhetoric was much more extreme than elsewhere. This may have influenced foreign-exchange markets, but it is hard to see through which channels because the success of the radicalized Labor Party was very limited. Obviously, the violent rhetoric was rather counterproductive to the political goals of the party.[66] Comparative strike statistics confirm this picture: Norwegian workers were by no means more militant than Danish or Swedish workers. On the contrary, in 1920, the Swedish labor unions were the most active.[67] Furthermore, Norwegian workers were not more successful in raising their real wages than their colleagues in Denmark and Sweden. From 1918 to 1920, real wages increased by 56 percent in Denmark, by 39 percent in Norway, and by 44 percent in Sweden.[68]

Even if there had been a relationship between labor radicalism and currency depreciation, the Danish story still would remain a puzzle. In contrast to Norway, there is a strong consensus among historians that the Danish Left and labor movement were the most moderate of all three

---

[64] Jonung and Wadensjö (1979, pp. 65–66): "… unrest on the labor market increased considerably, reaching a record level by 1920, as measured in terms of the number of strikes and the number of work days lost."

[65] They all refer to Galenson (1952, p. 149). I follow the argument of Lafferty (1971).

[66] Lafferty (1971, p. 185).

[67] Mikkelsen (1992, pp. 433, 444, and 446). Even if we use the more optimistic figures given by the Norwegian Industrial Union (*Landsorganizationen*), Norwegian strike activity per capita was clearly lower than the Swedish one.

[68] Calculations based on Johansen (1987, p. 295), Hodne (1983, pp. 25–27), and Bagge, Lundberg and Svennilson (1933, p. 255).

Scandinavian cases.[69] True, there were riots and strikes in the spring of 1920 when King Christian X decided to dissolve the government,[70] but the crisis was resolved after a few weeks. The king had deposed the government on 29 March, new elections that eased the situation were held on 26 April. The political situation had become stable before the Danish krone plunged.

As for the Netherlands and Switzerland, one could make the case that the political stability contributed to the strengthening of the currency. But the stability was only relative. In the Netherlands, 1919 and 1920 were record years in terms of number of strikes and days lost through strikes. From 1910 to 1920, membership in Dutch labor unions increased from 16 to 30 percent, and the movement gained momentum.[71] In Switzerland, a general strike broke out in November 1918. Although the unions failed to achieve their goals and were defeated after a few days, the event proved a traumatic experience for the economic and political elites of the country.[72]

As for the growth rate and level of floating debt, it is equally difficult to tell a story covering all five small neutral countries. Norway may in fact have suffered from a credibility problem as floating debt per capita was increasing in 1919 and 1920, whereas the Swedish government reduced floating debt considerably in 1919 (Table 1.5). Also, as noted, the Norwegian authorities repeatedly delayed discount-rate increases owing to debt considerations. In May 1919, they surprised markets with their decision to lower the discount rate from 6 to 5.5 percent because, a few weeks later, the government was to issue a new loan.[73] In 1920, they waited until June to increase the rate to 7 percent, whereas Sweden, the United Kingdom, and Denmark had done so in March and April, respectively. Yet again, this

---

[69] Lafferty (1971, p. 176): "Danish voters at no time during the period of interest expressed a strong preference for radical labor parties even though the Danish Communist Party competed in every election after 1919. They began with 0.7 percent of the votes in 1920, and by 1935 they had raised this to 1.6 percent."

[70] Christiansen, Lammers, and Nissen (1988, pp. 125–131).

[71] Van Zanden (1998, p. 74).

[72] The standard study on the Swiss general strike of November 1918 is Gautschi (1988).

[73] *Economist*, June 28, 1919, p. 1178: "The lowering of the official discount rate by the Bank of Norway on May 9th to 5.5 per cent took most people by surprise. There did not seem to be much in the general aspect of the money market to presage such a step on the part of the bank, and, indeed, very recent utterances by men in leading position led to the anticipation that the rate would remain unaltered for a good while yet. Intimations of a forthcoming application of the Government for a rather large public loan shortly after the reduction of the discount-rate seemed, however, to explain the reduction which was taken as serving to pave the way for the loan."

Table 1.5. *Public Finances*

	Surplus/ Deficit	Unfunded Debt	Total Debt	Unfunded debt in Percentage of Total Debt	Total Debt per Head (1913 US$)
	[1]	[2]	[3]	[4]	[5]
Denmark (Million Kroner)					
1913	−66				
1914	3				
1915	−35	20	413	5	37
1916	−69	16	477	3	47
1917	102	2	591	0	59
1918	−47	44	647	7	69
1919	−185	82	862	10	70
1920	8	28	954	3	54
1921	−252	61	1136	5	66

Norway (Million Kroner)

	Surplus/ Deficit	Unfunded Debt	Total Debt	Unfunded Debt in Percentage of Total Debt	Total Debt per Head (1913 US$)
	[1]	[2]	[3]	[4]	[5]
1913	7.1	5	363	1	39
1914	5.5	5	357	1	38
1915	−20.3	27	421	6	43
1916	14	16	423	4	48
1917	76.2	11	456	2	55
1918	51.4	246	737	33	90
1919	10.4	425	1008	42	98
1920	−157	402	1130	36	73
1921	−143	346	1191	29	70

Sweden (Million Kronor)

	Surplus/ Deficit	Unfunded Debt	Total Debt	Unfunded Debt in Percentage of Total Debt	Total Debt per Head (1913 US$)
	[1]	[2]	[3]	[4]	[5]
1913	59	20	648	3	31
1914	46	43	745	6	35
1915	86	36	855	4	39
1916	52	57	993	6	50
1917	240	140	1149	12	65
1918	−87	559	1656	34	94
1919	198	285	1567	18	69
1920	112	215	1497	14	53
1921	132	77	1511	5	59

Netherlands (Million Guilders)

	Surplus/ Deficit	Unfunded Debt	Total Debt	Unfunded debt in Percentage of Total Debt	Total Debt per Head (1913 US$)
	[1]	[2]	[3]	[4]	[5]
1913	−11	13	1159	1	74
1914	−114	174	1161	15	74
1915	−241	168	1314	13	85
1916	−223	251	1574	16	105
1917	−154	335	1759	19	116
1918	−490	614	1944	32	144
1919	−116	643	2465	26	153
1920	−100	514	2826	18	151
1921	−281	839	3083	27	165

(continued)

Table 1.5 *(continued)*

Switzerland (Million Francs)

	Surplus/ Deficit	Unfunded Debt	Total Debt	Unfunded Debt in Percentage of Total Debt	Total Debt per Head (1913 US$)
	[1]	[2]	[3]	[4]	[5]
1913	−5.4	1	147	1	8
1914	−22.5	58	283	20	14
1915	−21.6	110	516	21	26
1916	−16.6	227	804	28	41
1917	−50.7	346	1091	32	60
1918	−61.9	371	1449	26	87
1919	−95.7	400	1782	22	89
1920	−99.5	270	1876	14	83
1921	−127.6	200	1958	10	89

Population of 1915 (except Denmark 1916, Norway: mean of 1920 and 1920; Sweden 1915; Netherlands: mean of 1909 and 1920; Switzerland: mean of 1920 and 1920) for the calculation of debt per head.
Denmark: Debt: end of June, unfunded debt: end of July (Cohn, 1926, p. 306);
Switzerland: National debt (without railways, etc.).
Exchange rate data:
Switzerland: Swiss National Bank (1944): spot (yearly average), Denmark: Johansen (1985)
Source: Commission of Gold and Silver Inquiry (1925).

assessment is not true at all with respect to Denmark. On the contrary, the Danish authorities had done a rather good job in containing floating debt during the war, even a better than Sweden, and therefore were not forced to reduce such debt drastically after the armistice. Furthermore, if debt management had played a role, it would be hard to explain why Denmark and Norway were punished by the markets, whereas the Netherlands and Switzerland, two countries with a fair amount of floating debt, were not. Total debt and floating debt per capita were even higher in the Netherlands and Switzerland than in the three Scandinavian countries. In sum, it is hard to make the case that domestic institutional and political factors as well as the management of floating debt caused the divergence of exchange-rate movements in 1920. On the contrary, Sweden especially went through difficult times, but foreign-exchange markets appear not to have been impressed by internal power struggles: The Swedish krona remained stronger than the Danish krone and the Norwegian krone.[74]

THE LOGIC OF RECONSTRUCTION

The third and last explanation is less sophisticated than those based on monetary factors or credibility problems. It states that the Danish krone and the Norwegian krone were weak simply because of big trade deficits in 1919 and 1920. Nevertheless, this explanation appears to be the most plausible one. Again, the comparison of Denmark and Norway with Sweden is the best method to test whether the argument is convincing or not. Table 1.6 shows how much better the Swedish economy performed after the war. Expressed in US dollars per capita, Denmark's and Norway's trade deficits in 1919 and 1920 were two or three times higher than the Swedish trade deficit. Given such large deficits, it is hardly surprising that the Danish and Norwegian currencies depreciated vis-à-vis the British pound, whereas the Dutch guilder, the Swedish krona, and the Swiss franc continued to be just as strong as or even stronger than the British pound.

Yet how can we be sure that trade deficits were in fact the main determinant of exchange rates in 1919 and 1920? Lacking daily reports on the

Table 1.6. *Trade Balances of Denmark, Norway, and Sweden*

	Denmark		Norway		Sweden	
	Trade Balance (in Danish kr)	Per Capita (in US$)	Trade balance (in Norwegian kr)	Per Capita (in US$)	Trade Balance (in Swedish kr)	Per Capita (in US$)
1913	−140	−13	−160	−16	−50	−2
1918	−200	−21	−488	−55	−13	−1
1919	−1654	−134	−793	−71	−958	−42
1920	−1352	−76	−1772	−106	−1038	−37
1921	−139	−8	−818	−44	−161	−6
1922	−280	−20	−519	−34	40	2

Sources: Mitchell (2003) and author's calculations.

---

[74] The strikes did not even have a negative effect on tradings at the Stockholm Stock Exchange, as the German weekly *Wirtschaftsdienst* observed with great astonishment. *Wirtschaftsdienst*, 4 June 1920, p. 335.

foreign-exchange market, I undertook a systematic analysis of articles in the *Economist* because this weekly magazine was particularly close to the City of London, where the bulk of exchange-rate trade was taking place after World War I. Two kinds of articles were analyzed: the weekly money report and the country reports written by the correspondents in Copenhagen, Oslo, and Stockholm. These texts do not provide us with an abundance of information on Scandinavian exchange rates, but the comments are consistent.

There are several instances in which the *Economist* directly identified the trade deficit as the main factor causing the fall of the Danish krone and the Norwegian krone. In late February 1920, the correspondent in Copenhagen wrote: "It is hardly surprising that the Danish krone is faring somewhat badly at present, when one sees that the country's imports during 1919 exceeded 2,500,000,000 kr, against exports amounting to approximately 735,000,000 kr for Danish products and 179,000,000 for foreign goods." But the correspondent remained optimistic: "The unusually heavy imports during 1919 are, of course, not exceptional in Europe today; Denmark has that in common with a number of other countries, stocks being almost entirely exhausted everywhere. No doubt, the matter by degrees will right itself, when the production and export of Denmark's staple products become more normal."[75]

In the beginning of May, the correspondent in Denmark wrote that a temporary stop of exports was causing a further decline of the krone: "The continued strike amongst the seamen, stokers, and transport hands is becoming a serious matter, putting a stop to all export of some of the country's chief products – butter, bacon, and eggs. ... As a natural consequence of the entire stoppage of export the value of the Danish kr is declining."[76] This assessment was again mentioned at the beginning of June.[77] Interestingly, the strike was not seen as a political event causing credibility problems but as a purely economic factor hampering exports.

In July, when the decoupling of the Danish krone and the Norwegian krone became fully apparent, the money report contained an unusually long assessment of the situation in Scandinavia: "The quotation for our

---

[75] *Ibid.*

[76] *Ibid.*

[77] *Economist*, Country report, 5 June 1920, p. 1250: "Whilst the Copenhagen Stock Exchange remains exceedingly dull and quiet, exchanges have been having an exciting time. £ at 23.68, $ at 617.00, Dutch gulden at 224.25, and Stockholm at 129.25 are very stiff quotations. The country's exports are seriously hampered by the continued strike of seamen, stokers, and transport hands. Voluntary labor has done its best to remedy transport matters."

currency in Sweden has been weak for some days, and at 17k 58 is about half a krone below parity. Sweden just now is a highly productive country, her nationals are specially encouraged to save, the export trade is very satisfactory, and imports have been kept down. Norway, on the other hand, has considerable amounts to pay us on account of ship-building contracts, and this causes a demand for sterling bills; the quotation is equal to about 23k 15 for £1."[78] This comment is perhaps the best illustration for the thesis that foreign-exchange markets were reacting to trade deficits and economic performance, not discount rates, PPP, or political events.

When the Danish krone and the Norwegian krone began to recover at the end of the year, the money report of the *Economist* states three times that this recovery happened because of decreasing trade deficits. On 4 December: "The three Scandinavian exchanges have improved considerably, Stockholm having fallen to 18.00, and Christiania and Copenhagen more than half a kroner each. It is probable that this recovery is due rather to the falling off of imports rather than to any improvement in the export position in any of the three countries."[79] On 11 December: "The Scandinavian exchanges show a marked movement against London, due largely to the gradual operation of the decrease in imports, and somewhat to the relief afforded by money raised in the United States."[80] And on 18 December: "... the Scandinavian centres, ... with the exception of Christiania, have moved against us, being the progressive effect of a growing restriction of imports."[81]

As a result of the conviction that trade deficits were the main determinant of the exchange rate, the *Economist* always considered the weakness of the Danish krone and the Norwegian krone temporary. For example, in May 1920, the money market report stated: "The Scandinavian exchanges all continue in favour of London, but the general opinion is that rates have about reached their limit, and the market now looks for an appreciation in the currencies of Norway and Denmark."[82] When the Danish krone and the Norwegian krone were in fact appreciating in December 1920 and January 1921, the *Economist* was still regarding it as a long-awaited correction of a temporary deviation and not as a new, unexpected movement. In mid-January 1921, the *Economist* wrote in the country report on Denmark: "It really looks as if the Danish kr at last is about to right itself."[83]

---

[78] *Ibid.*
[79] *Ibid.*
[80] *Ibid.*
[81] *Ibid.*
[82] *Ibid.* The expectation that a reappreciation was near was repeated on 19 June (p. 1332).
[83] *Ibid.*

Two weeks later, the country report stated that a rapid return to parity with the pound sterling was expected: "The £ and $ and Swedish kr are almost tumbling down, Saturday's quotations being, respectively, 19.50, 515.00, and 112.00, whilst £ and $ as recently as November, 1920, were at 25.86 and 768.00. There appears to be no demand for foreign money, and the opinion is expressed that it would cause no surprise to see £ and Swedish kr below par before long, although there may, of course, be temporary breaks in the downward move."[84]

There are only two instances in which the *Economist* did not focus exclusively on trade deficits, both times in the weekly money report and both times with regard to Norway. In the first instance, in August 1920, the report also mentioned the financial situation[85]; in the second instance, in October 1920, a failed loan was considered the main determinant for exchange-rate fluctuations.[86] Yet, as shown, the overwhelming majority of the reports singles out the trade deficit as the main cause for the weakness of the Danish krone and the Norwegian krone. Thus the third explanation seems to be the most plausible one.

Why did Denmark and Norway register larger trade deficits than Sweden? Table 1.7 shows the reason: Denmark was suffering from export problems and Norway from import problems. The Danish exporters were blocked because the United Kingdom, their main market, kept many wartime regulations in place until several months or even years after the war. The British war strategy had been to rely on imports from countries that were outside German influence. New Zealand, as a member of Commonwealth, could take over the share of Denmark. In 1913, Denmark had sent two-thirds of its exports to the United Kingdom (410 million kronor of a total of 637 million kronor went to the United Kingdom), mostly cattle and

---

[84] *Ibid.*

[85] *Ibid.*, 14 August 1920, p. 254: "In the Scandinavian exchanges the most striking movement is that of Norwegian kroner, which have moved up from 23.58 to 24.13–17, partly on account of the continued uncertainty as to the financial situation in Norway, and partly, it is said, through transactions by Norwegian shipowners."

[86] *Ibid.*, Money market report, October 2, 1920, p. 498: "Considerable business has been done in exchange, and somewhat violent fluctuations have been experienced in certain markets, notably in the case of Norway. The abandonment of the proposed loan in London lifted the Norwegian rate to 26.75 at one time last week, but on the announcement that negotiations had been successfully concluded to raise the money in New York the rate rapidly relapsed to under 25 on Tuesday, and was quoted yesterday about 24.25. The understanding that a portion of the funds borrowed in New York would be applied in payment of the ships contracted for by Norway in this country had a steadying effect on New York rate, which gradually rose from 3.48 1/4 on Saturday to 3.50 3/4 on Tuesday." More details on the loan: *Ibid.*, 2 October 1920, p. 503.

Table 1.7. *Trade Figures of Denmark, Norway, and Sweden,*
1918–1922 (1913 = 100, Current Prices)

Imports	Denmark	Norway	Sweden
1918	117	231	146
1919	308	464	299
1920	379	550	391
1921	199	271	149
1922	187	243	132
Exports	Denmark	Norway	Sweden
1918	111	192	165
1919	116	199	193
1920	250	317	279
1921	221	162	134
1922	185	200	141

Sources: Mitchell (2003) and author's calculations.

products for the English breakfast table: bacon, butter, and eggs. By 1919 and 1920, overall sales were low, especially of cattle; only the export of eggs was taking off again in 1920. Danish exporters tried to raise the sales of fish and agricultural products such as potatoes and cabbage, but the quantities were too small to compensate for the losses.[87] The British only gradually relaxed import barriers. In February 1920, the cabinet finally allowed the free import of Danish bacon; New Zealand was losing the privileges it had acquired during the war.[88]

Some Danish officials also claimed that import prices were higher than export prices in 1920.[89] But this was rather a consequence than a cause of the depreciation – wholesale prices rose in Denmark in the second half of 1920, peaking in November 1920, whereas in Sweden the peak had been reached in June 1920. The same is true for Norwegian prices: In June, prices were at the same level as in Sweden (115), but then they took off by roughly another 10 percent, reaching their peak in September (128). Not

[87] Olsen (1968, p. 69). Cf. *Wirtschaftsdienst*, 10 October 1919, pp. 764–766.
[88] Beveridge (1928, p. 306): "The issues raised before the Cabinet Committee of February 1920 were settled more in favour of the Ministry than had at one time seemed possible... The buying of Australian butter and Danish bacon was allowed." *Economist*, 21 May 1921, pp. 1019–1020: "Our imports of breakfast table foods."
[89] League of Nations (1920, Vol. 3, pp. 140–142). The delegate of Denmark was R. Gluckstadt.

all this increase can be attributed to the falling exchange rates, but certainly a considerable part can.

The huge trade deficit and the falling krone caused growing concerns.[90] In December 1919, the five major banks urged the government to act. The driving force was the director of the Landmandsbank, Denmark's largest bank. He proposed to form a Foreign Exchange Board, called *valutafælles-rådet*.[91] The board was formed and composed of representatives of all the major federations and the five leading banks of Copenhagen, including the Danish National Bank. The idea was to stabilize the krone by restricting the use of foreign exchange by a voluntary regulation of imports. Technically, a committee of five men, consisting of the representatives of the central bank and the four major banks (Privatbanken, Landmansbanken, Handelsbanken, and Diskont- and Revisionsbanken), should meet daily to approve or turn down the requests by Danish import firms. The guidelines for their daily work should be set up by a board under the chairmanship of the trade minister, consisting of all five major banks and all federations. From the beginning, there was a serious problem: The whole system depended on honest reporting to the committee, but the incentives to look for other means to obtain foreign exchange were too strong. The committee was asking for more authorities and competences.[92] In March 1920, the *Folketing,* the Danish parliament, discussed the proposal but turned it down after a long debate mainly because representatives of agricultural interests and the liberal parties were against regulating imports. With this negative verdict, the *valutafællesrådet* had no reason to continue with its work and was dissolved.

After this dramatic failure and a renewed fall of the Danish krone starting in May 1920, the government set up the Foreign Exchange Committee, called *valutakommissionen,* under the auspice of Trade Minister Rothe. Unlike the board, the committee was not given any administrative power but was supposed to advise the government on how to stop the fall of the krone.[93] The committee started its work in September and presented a report on 10 November, of which some passages were published. The main finding was that the depreciation of the Danish krone had been caused mainly by the balance of payments. To correct this imbalance, domestic consumption should be curbed. The committee could, however, not agree

---

[90] *Wirtschaftsdienst,* 10 October 1919, p. 765.
[91] Olsen (1968, pp. 79–80). Cf. *Wirtschaftsdienst,* 2 January 1920, p. 13, and 9 January 1920, p. 31.
[92] *Economist,* 13 March 1920, p. 609.
[93] *Wirtschaftsdienst,* 10 September 1920, p. 517.

on how this proposal was to be implemented, so nothing happened.[94] By November 1920, the international economic situation had changed dramatically anyway. The end of the restocking boom had arrived, prices plunged, and imports receded. The Danish krone, just as the Norwegian currency, appreciated by 40 percent from December 1920 to February 1921.

In Norway, the basic problem was not exports but imports.[95] The main export goods, accounting for more than 50 percent (54.83 percent) of all exports in 1913, were fish and wood products, including paper. Although fish products were not selling well in 1919 and 1920 (with the exception of salted herring), the sales of wood products flourished. The main problem was the import situation. The purchase of food and the rebuilding of the fleet were very costly. In 1913, the latter item was important, but accounted only for 5 percent of total imports. In 1920, it was the second most important item, accounting for 12.6 percent. As noted, compared with Denmark and Sweden, the index numbers for imports (1913 = 100) were roughly 40 percent higher in 1919 and 1920 (see Table 1.7).

As in Denmark, the Norwegian government set up a Foreign Exchange Council, called *valutarådet*, to study the situation and to propose measures. The council recommended import restrictions, and in contrast to Denmark, the government and the parliament followed this recommendation. As in Denmark, though, the trade and foreign-exchange issue became irrelevant as the restocking boom came to an end and made room for a sharp fall in commodity prices. Of greater relevance was another import restriction. Just as in the United States, a strong Protestant movement was campaigning successfully for prohibition. In 1919, a majority of 60 percent voted in favor of it. As a result, Portugal and Spain, the main buyers of Norwegian fish, could not export their wine and alcohol to Norway anymore and therefore restricted imports of Norwegian products. In 1926, a majority voted for the removal of prohibition.[96]

Sweden faced the same problems as Denmark and Norway but could handle them much better. The strong demand for wood, wood pulp, and paper was the main reason why exports increased in 1919 and 1920. And because Sweden had developed its agricultural sector during the war, the population was less dependent on food imports than Norway. The

---

[94] *Valutakommissionen 1920*; Hoffmeyer and Olsen (1968, pp. 84–85).
[95] *Economist*, May 14, 1921, p. 962: "Although Norway has radically restricted imports, she is in the position of having to purchase abroad large proportions of her foodstuffs and other necessaries, and as the market for her wood and wood products has fallen away, the proposed loan, though not for large figures, will afford a certain measure of relief."
[96] *Weltwirtschaftliches Archiv* (1924), p. 46.

Netherlands and Switzerland also experienced smaller trade deficits than Denmark and Norway. In addition, both countries played a crucial role in the financial reconstruction of postwar Europe. Amsterdam and Zurich became major European financial centers, and the Dutch guilder and Swiss franc became international currencies, which put upward pressure on their exchange rates.[97] In 1929, Denmark and Norway still had export structures with a big share of agricultural products and raw materials. Only 12 of Denmark's and only 22 percent of Norway's total merchandise exports were manufactured goods. The corresponding figures for the Netherlands, Sweden, and Switzerland were 37, 41, and 80 percent, respectively.[98]

In sum, there is strong evidence that not monetary forces but different degrees of trade deficits caused the divergence of exchange-rate movements in the immediate aftermath of the war. Owing to the uneven process of reconstruction, Denmark and Norway had to accept higher trade deficits during the postwar boom than the other small neutral countries. In 1920, their exchange rates became weaker vis-à-vis the British pound and did not recover fully before the banking crises broke out, which initiated another period of depreciation. It was all about trade, not policy and politics.

---

[97] Einzig (1932), appendices, compares Amsterdam, Switzerland, and Sweden. On Switzerland's financial relations to the large European countries and the United States, see Guex (1999).

[98] Feinstein, Temin, and Toniolo (1997, p. 59).

TWO

The Return to Prewar Parity

Another piece of evidence proving that policymakers in small neutral states failed to grasp the policy options opened up by suspension of the gold standard is Denmark's and Norway's determination to bring their currencies back to the prewar level.[1] Owing to a particularly severe banking crisis that prompted central banks to stop the deflationary course required to appreciate the currency, the Danish krone and the Norwegian krone fell to a level 40 to 50 percent below the dollar in 1924. And yet, despite this renewed weakness, Denmark and Norway restored the gold standard at prewar parity – Denmark in January 1927 and Norway in May 1928 (Figure 2.1).

What were the deeper reasons behind this policy that from today's viewpoint contradicts any sound economic reasoning? There is a strong consensus among economic historians that the overwhelming majority of policymakers and voters sincerely believed that economic stability could be achieved only by restoring the old monetary order. Deflation was not seen as an unnecessary burden for the economy but as an appropriate way to correct previous distortions. Going back to the prewar parity was seen as the final step in overcoming the chaotic postwar period and reinstalling the favorable conditions of the gold era before World War I. Moral arguments played an important part in this reasoning because most politicians wanted their "old, honest crown" back. In many ways, it is the same reasoning that inspired the senseless battle fought by the gold bloc countries during the first half of the 1930s that will be described in Chapter Four. Belgian, Dutch, and Swiss

---

[1] Restoring the gold standard at prewar parity meant restoring the prewar dollar rate because the United States was the only country having maintained the gold standard during the war. Yet, since US consumer prices increased by roughly 50 percent from 1913 to the second half of the 1920s when Denmark and Norway returned to the gold standard, prewar parity was lower than the term implies.

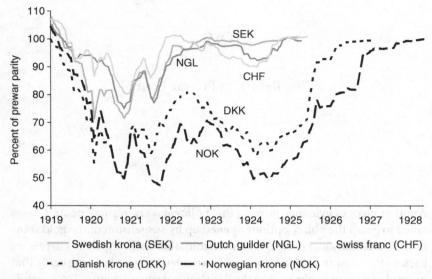

Figure 2.1. Exchange rates of currencies of small neutral states until restoration of gold standard (percentage of prewar parity). (*League of Nations.*)

policymakers argued that a devaluation would only deteriorate the situation and failed to understand the negative consequences of deflation.

Yet, although the lack of macroeconomic understanding was the main reason behind this policy, it would be wrong to draw a direct line from this conviction to the policies pursued in practice and the movements of the exchange rate. The process was rather protracted and inconsistent. There was never a plan of how to proceed but only a general agreement that ultimately the currency was to return to prewar parity. The only measure that was taken was a tightening of monetary policy, yet the resulting reduction in prices was too small to make the currency appreciate to the desired level. In the end, international speculators decided the issue. Knowing that policymakers were reluctant to fix the krone below prewar parity, they could be sure that a speculative attack would not be addressed seriously by the central bank. Accordingly, they bought Danish and Norwegian assets in great amounts, making the currencies literally jump by roughly 30 percent.

This chapter has three parts and tries to add some new observations gained from a comparative perspective that have not been mentioned in the well-developed literature on restoration of the gold standard. The first section discusses the banking crises in the five neutral states, including the crisis in Switzerland, which has been largely ignored by non-Swiss economic historians. The second section compares the different roads to the gold standard completed by Sweden, which was the first to take this step, and by the Netherlands and Switzerland. Again, although the basic facts are known, the comparison has never been made. Finally, the third section tries to provide a more systematic description of Denmark's and Norway's return to prewar parity than has been given so far.

THE BANKING CRISES, THEIR CAUSES, AND THEIR CONSEQUENCES

The courses and causes of the banking crises of the early 1920s have been explored extensively, so the basic mechanism is well understood.[2] The standard explanation begins with the observation that during the inflationary boom from 1914 to 1920, commercial and savings banks engaged in excessive lending and speculating. Two mechanisms led them to do so. First, as nominal assets depreciated, commercial banks needed to switch to "real" assets, in particular shares. Second, as their cash reserves increased rapidly owing to the creation of excess liquidity by the government and the central bank, commercial banks were forced to lend more extensively and rapidly in order to maintain their profits. This led to more intense competition among banks, weakened their position toward their clients, deteriorated the quality of lending, and increased overall debt. As a result of the speculative boom, the banking system became increasingly vulnerable to external shocks.

This shock arrived in the autumn of 1920 when postwar deflation began to work its way through Western Europe and pushed up real interest rates. Commercial banks were facing a deterioration of their position on both sides of the balance sheet. On the one hand, their deposits shrank because the demand for cash increased during the crisis. On the other hand, assets depreciated because share prices declined, and the number of nonperforming loans increased because firms had to cope with a drop in demand and at the same time rising real interest rates. James (1991) describes the process as follows: "higher interest rate or restricted credit puts pressure on businesses to reduce inventories by lowering prices; falling prices reduce the value of securities against loans; banks at first demand additional securities

---

[2]   The literature on individual banking crises in Europe during the 1920s is abundant and will be cited below. For a comparative view of the interwar banking crises, see Bernanke and James (1991), James, Lindgren, and Teichova (1991), Grossman (1994), Jonker and van Zanden (1995), and Feinstein, Temin, and Toniolo (1997).

to cover the loans, but when none are any longer forthcoming, they start to call in loans; borrowers are forced further to liquidate stocks; and prices fall still further in consequence. Banks call yet more loans, and the familiar vicious circle of 'debt deflation' described by Irving Fisher sets in."[3]

However, although the basic mechanism was the same across all five small neutral states, the intensity and duration of the banking crises varied greatly. The Swiss banking crisis was relatively weak and confined to a few banks, whereas the Danish and Norwegian banking systems almost collapsed. The crises in Denmark and Norway also lasted much longer than elsewhere. The first wave of bank failures that began in 1921 and reached its peak in 1922–1923 hit commercial banks in all five neutral states, but the second wave, starting in the mid-1920s, concerned only Danish and Norwegian banks.

As a first approximation to understanding the scope of the crises, we can use the yield on capital of commercial banks (Figures 2.2 and 2.3). The differences are striking. Norway experienced by far the worst banking crisis because commercial banks suffered losses in seven consecutive years.[4] Denmark's commercial banks also underwent a severe crisis, but losses were at least confined to only three years (1922, 1925, and 1928). On the other side of the spectrum, Swiss commercial banks performed rather well and registered profits in every year. The Swedish and Dutch commercial banks were in between the two extremes: They registered losses in 1922 and 1924, respectively.

A brief review of each individual crisis confirms the first impression gained from the yield data. In Norway, the crisis was particularly severe. A total of 85 commercial and 45 savings banks failed during the 1920s. Of these, 41 commercial banks and 15 savings banks eventually were liquidated, some of them after a failed rescue operation by the government and the central bank.[5] Among the failed banks were three of the six largest banks. The first victim was *Foreningsbanken*, the product of the 1920 merger between *Andresens Bank* and *Bergens Kreditbank*. By October 1922, the losses had reached a total of more than 75 million kroner. The central

---

[3] James (1991, p. 6). He refers to Fisher (1933). See also Kindleberger's anatomy of a typical crisis developed from the writings of Hyman Minsky: Kindleberger (1989, pp. 15–24).

[4] In the case of Norway, the figures based on official statistics are imprecise because they exaggerate the losses in the second half of the 1920s. On the basis of archival sources, Knutsen and Ecklund (2000, pp. 89–94) and Knutsen (2001, pp. 15–17) have shown that the Norwegian banking crisis peaked in the early 1920s, as elsewhere. But since Figures 2.2 and 2.3 are meant only to be a first approximation for the sake of comparison, the official figures nevertheless are used.

[5] On the Norwegian banking crisis, see Jacobsen (1924), Rygg (1950), Knutsen (1991, 1995, 2001), Nordvik (1995), Knutsen and Ecklund (2000), and Gerdrup (2004).

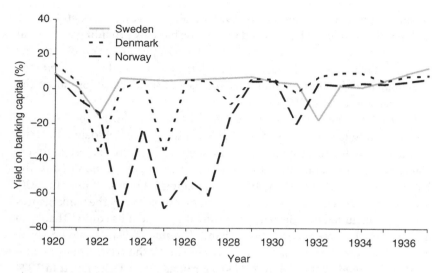

Figure 2.2. Yield on banking capital in Denmark, Norway, and Sweden, 1920–1937 (net profit or loss as a percentage of capital and reserves). (*Jonker and van Zanden, 1995.*)

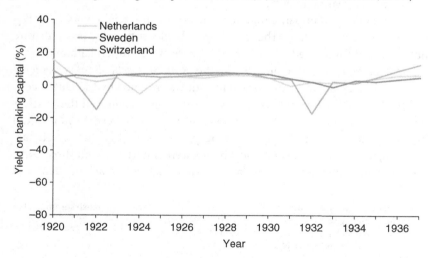

Figure 2.3. Yield on banking capital in the Netherlands, Switzerland, and Sweden, 1920–1937 (net profit or loss as a percentage of capital and reserves). (*Jonker and van Zanden, 1995.*)

bank, the government, and major stockholders tried to avoid the collapse by granting a 50 million kroner loan, but in April 1923, *Foreningsbanken* was put under public administration. The second victim, the *Centralbanken for Norge,* was the largest Norwegian commercial bank in 1920. Problems began to appear in the autumn of 1921. Again, the Norwegian authorities and major commercial banks tried to save the bank by providing additional loans, but in April 1923, *Centralbanken* also was put under public administration. Finally, in 1924, another of the large commercial banks, *Den norske Handelsbank*, had to suspend payments and seek protection under the Administration Act of 1923.

In Denmark, nearly 80 banks were hit by the crisis during the 1920s. Of these, 18 were taken over by other banks, and 35 were liquidated, in some cases after a failed reconstruction by the state.[6] Of the nine largest commercial banks, the most prominent victim was the *Danske Landmandsbank*, the largest bank in Scandinavia, with assets totalling 1.4 billion kroner in 1920. The event that triggered the failure was an investigation by the bank inspector, who concluded that the bank had lost 70 percent of its equity. Thanks to a bailout by the state and the central bank, *Landmandsbank* could be saved. Two other large commercial banks also were hit by the crisis. The *Disconto- og Revisionsbank*, with 418 million kroner of assets in 1920, failed in 1924 and was soon liquidated. The *Andelbank*, with 171 million kroner of assets in 1920, disappeared in 1925.

In Sweden, by contrast, altogether only 14 commercial banks were liquidated during the 1920s. The four largest banks suffered losses but were not seriously threatened.[7] In the Netherlands, 11 commercial banks were liquidated, and only 1 major bank, the *Rotterdamsche Bankvereeniging (Robaver)*, was facing serious problems but was rescued by the Dutch central bank.[8] Finally, commercial banks in Switzerland managed the postwar deflation even better than Dutch and Swedish banks. Nevertheless, it would be wrong to assume that there were no problems at all, as some scholars have suggested.[9] Several small local banks were liquidated, and three commercial banks threatened to collapse.[10] The most important of them was

---

[6] The standard study is Hansen (1996), written in Danish, but with an English summary. For English-language articles, see Hansen (1991, 1994, 1995).

[7] On the Swedish banking crisis, see Larsson (1991, 1993).

[8] On the Dutch banking crisis, see de Vries (1989), Jonker (1996), and van Zanden (1997, 1998).

[9] Jonker and van Zanden (1995, pp. 80–81): "Switzerland followed an altogether different path, explained by the banking system's particular course of development... No banking crisis occurred, however, since the wheat had already been separated from the chaff just before the war during seven years of profound restructuring."

[10] League of Nations (1931, p. 263) on the Swiss banking crisis: "The drop in the number of banks between 1910 and 1913 was due mainly to failures among the small local banks. New local banks, however, were established at the beginning of and immediately after the war. As a result of the post-war crisis the number of banks was again reduced through liquidations of smaller banks between 1920 and 1925. On the whole, the Swiss

the *Bank Leu,* the oldest of the eight large commercial banks, which had invested large sums in Germany. Only after several waves of restructuring could the bank be saved from liquidation.[11] The second largest commercial bank, the *Schweizerische Kreditanstalt,* also suffered great losses resulting from its large investments in Germany, but thanks to the liquidation of a part of hidden assets, a crisis could be avoided.[12]

The reasons why Norway experienced the most severe banking crisis are not hard to detect. First, as was shown in Chapter One, the growth rate of money and prices from 1914 to 1920 had been higher than in other small European states. Second, bank lending increased by a larger amount than elsewhere.[13] Third, there was no banking supervision. And fourth, the economic structure was one-sided. All these factors together made Norwegian banks highly vulnerable. Some local or regional banks were heavily dependent on a few businesses of the same sector, as a contemporary economist observed.[14] Perhaps the highly decentralized structure of the Norwegian banking system also was an important cause, but this finding is controversial.[15]

By contrast, the question of why the banking crisis in Denmark was deeper than in the Netherlands, Sweden, and Switzerland is harder to answer.[16] There are three points that complicate the problem. First, as Chapter One showed, growth rates of money and prices in Denmark and Sweden were quite similar from 1914 to 1920. It is thus hard to argue that monetary factors had made the Danish banking system more vulnerable to the deflationary shock. Second, while it is true that the degree of centralization was much lower in Denmark than in Sweden, it also clearly was higher than in Norway. There were several commercial banks with branches across the country and in close cooperation with provincial banks. By 1913, the three largest banks held more than half the total balances of the commercial banks. As noted, the crisis was serious not only because many small

---

banking system endured the post-war crisis remarkably well. In 1926 and 1927 few new local banks were established, and the number of banks in 1929 was almost as high as in 1906."
[11] See Keller (1955, pp. 173–202).
[12] Jöhr (1956, pp. 329–331).
[13] Knutsen (2001, p. 18): The 1920 index figures (1913 = 100) are 451 (Norway), 316 (Denmark), and 242 (Sweden).
[14] Jacobsen (1924, p. 55*).
[15] Knutsen (2001), for example, has found only little evidence after initially highlighting the banking structure in Knutsen (1991).
[16] Accordingly, many scholars making comparative observations prefer to focus on the comparison of Norway and Sweden, thus leaving aside the complicated Danish case. See, for example, Olsson (1991), Larsson (1993), and Nordvik (1995).

and medium-sized provincial unit banks failed but also because two large Copenhagen banks, in particular, *Landmandsbank*, almost collapsed in the early 1920s. Hansen (1995) therefore concludes that "there is no evidence that banking structure mattered much" in Denmark.[17]

Third, it is not clear whether the lack of banking supervision made a crucial difference. In the case of Sweden, it may have been important that the government had enacted a first banking law in the 1880s, in reaction to the banking crisis of 1878–1879, and that banking supervision was further strengthened in 1911. The latter certainly curtailed the emergence of new banks during the inflationary period – the number of banks even decreased from 1913 to 1920 from 75 (with 555 branches) to 41 (with 1,369 branches).[18] In Denmark, by contrast, the number of commercial banks increased by 50 percent, from 139 to 202.[19] Yet, if we compare Denmark with the Netherlands and Switzerland, the role of banking supervision becomes less obvious. In the latter cases, the banking sectors still were poorly regulated until the 1930s. Switzerland passed the first Federal Banking Act in 1934, and the Netherlands established a state committee for the banking sector as late as 1937.[20]

The Dutch and Swiss banking sectors also were quite decentralized. From 1900 to 1920, the number of independent commercial banks in the Netherlands increased from 242 to 330. In 1920, the five largest commercial banks had no more than a quarter of the total assets of the banking sector.[21] The Swiss National Bank classified 179 commercial banks as independent in 1920. If we include mortgage banks and savings banks, the number rises to 314.[22] Moreover, the League of Nations observed that "[i]n consequence

[17] Hansen (1995, p. 32). In this respect, the American discussion is interesting. Since the studies by Bernanke and James (1991) and Calomiris (2000), it has become conventional wisdom that unit banking was more crisis-prone than branch banking. But more recent studies, for instance, by Carlson and Mitchener (2006), have shown that the focus on unit versus branch banking is not sufficient to explain the American banking crises during the Great Depression. Rather, the competitive environment seems to have been of crucial importance.

[18] League of Nations (1931, pp. 246–247). Knutsen (1991, p. 65) mentions 1,410 branch offices.

[19] Hansen (1996, p. 77). The figures of the League of Nations, Commercial banks (1913–1929, pp. 202–203) and Johansen (1987, pp. 264–265) are not entirely correct.

[20] On Swiss banking supervision, see Bänziger (1985, 1986), Halbeisen (1998), and Baumann (2004); on Dutch banking supervision, see de Vries (1994), Jonker (1996), and Mooij and Prast (2002).

[21] De Vries (1989, pp. 208–209), van Zanden (1997, pp. 124–127).

[22] *Schweizerische Nationalbank, Schweizerisches Bankwesen im Jahre* (1920, p. 79); Cassis (1994, p. 1018): "Swiss banking has remained, throughout its history, comparatively little concentrated."

of the great number of small banks in existence, the big banks have comparatively few branches and agencies."[23] In sum, from the perspective of a majority of small Europeans states, Sweden's highly concentrated and well-supervised banking structure was rather the exception than the rule.

Thus neither inflation differentials nor differences in banking structure and legislation seem to grasp the essence of the Danish banking crisis. This leaves us with the structure of financial networks, as Feldman (1998) argues.[24] This approach is in fact more promising because one major reason why the *Landmandsbank* failed was its tight link with the *Transatlantik Kompagni*. This holding company was founded in 1916 by a Danish merchant and the *Landmandsbank* itself and controlled no less than 150 subsidiaries, mainly in the trading sector. By the end of 1920, the *Landmandsbank* had invested almost 200 million kroner, corresponding to more than 10 percent of the bank's total assets.[25] The *Transatlantik Kompagni* was a typical product of the exuberant optimism during the war boom, but it also was an expression of crony capitalism that seems to be typical for banking systems in emerging markets. The alliance between the *Landmandsbank* and the *Transatlantik Kompagni*, built on the personal relationship between the bank's managing director Emil Glückstadt and the Danish merchant Harald Plum, reminds of the alliance between Oscar Rydbeck, the managing director of the *Skandinaviska Banken*, and Ivar Kreuger that brought down the Swedish currency and the banking sector in 1931–1932.[26]

Whatever the exact causes of the banking crises, there is no doubt about their consequences. In Denmark and Norway, central banks had to provide the banking sector with additional liquidity, which reversed the downward movement of prices and ultimately weakened their currencies (Figure 2.4). By contrast, in the Netherlands, Sweden, and Switzerland, prices kept falling, and the exchange rate joined in the appreciation of sterling starting in the summer of 1921. By the beginning of the following year, all three currencies were near or even at prewar parity, and from then on, it was only a matter of time until the countries would restore the gold standard. Sweden took this step in April 1924, the Netherlands and Switzerland waited until the British government had made its decision. On 28 April 1925, Chancellor of the Exchequer Winston Churchill gave a speech in the House of Commons announcing the return to the gold standard at prewar parity. One day later, Dutch Finance Minister Hendrik Colijn made the same statement in Den

---

[23] League of Nations (1931, p. 263).
[24] Feldman (1998, p. 56).
[25] Hansen (1996, pp. 186–187).
[26] See Chapter Three.

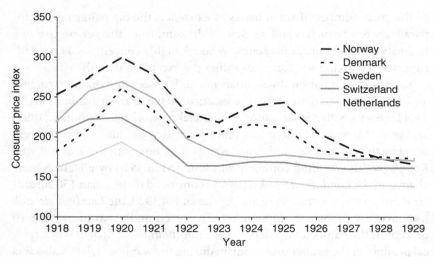

Figure 2.4. Consumer prices of five small neutral states, 1918–1929. (*Maddison, 1991.*)

Haag, and the Swiss National Bank issued a press release on 17 June stating that the bank would keep the franc within the gold points of the dollar rate.[27]

In conclusion, exchange rates diverged in 1922–1923 mainly because the degree of vulnerability of the banking systems varied greatly across small neutral states. This leaves us with two other questions. First, how did it come about that despite their renewed weakness the Danish and Norwegian currencies appreciated to the prewar level in 1926–1927? And second, why did Sweden restore the gold standard before the United Kingdom did, whereas the Netherlands and Switzerland waited until London made an official statement? The remainder of this chapter will deal with these two issues. The next section discusses Sweden's early return to gold, the subsequent and last section treats Denmark's and Norway's painful road to prewar parity.

EARLY RETURN TO THE OLD PARITY

Until late 1922 when the Swedish krona reached prewar parity, Sweden's path to the gold standard was almost identical to the one completed by the Netherlands and Switzerland. In 1921–1922, their currencies joined in the general upward movement led by the British pound and caused by the convergence of price movements. Most important, all three central banks

---

[27] *Schweizerische Nationalbank* (1932, p. 286); De Vries (1989, pp. 340–345).

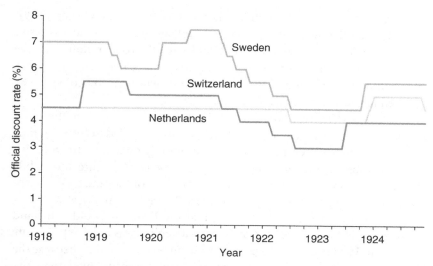

Figure 2.5. Official discount rates of the Netherlands, Sweden, and Switzerland, 1918–1924. (*League of Nations.*)

pursued the same discount-rate policy during 1921–1922 aimed at relaxing monetary conditions when prices literally plunged and businesses suffered from a severe depression (Figure 2.5). They did not welcome the strengthening of their currencies at all because it only accelerated the fall of prices and deepened the economic crisis. At the same time, however, just as during the depreciation period in 1919–1920, they also were reluctant to take measures that would curb the appreciation. Convinced that they could not make any difference, they continued to wait and see until conditions became normal. In other words, the return to prewar parity was to a large extent accidental. Managing the exchange rate was not embraced by central bankers, although the suspension of the gold standard gave them great room for discretion.

Yet, once the krona reached prewar parity in late 1922, Sweden began to take another path from the Netherlands and Switzerland, leading to an early reintroduction of the gold standard in April 1924. It also was a policy that was quite unusual for a small European country. London had been the center of European and world finance, and most observers expected it to take this role again after the war. It was therefore unheard of that a small European state would go ahead of the United Kingdom. Accordingly, Gerard Vissering, governor of the *Nederlandsche Bank* and a true believer in international cooperation, commented: "We follow with interest the experiments which are being undertaken in this direction elsewhere, but it is our opinion that none of the smaller countries can achieve such a result alone. To that end consultation and subsequently cooperation with the strong central banks of Europe's large countries will be necessary. Therefore we are afraid that it is bound to take some time before this outcome can be achieved for our currency as well."[28]

Why Sweden? There is only one plausible answer: It was due to the peculiar institutional position of the Swedish *Riksbank,* founded in 1668 and thus the oldest European central bank.[29] It was entirely owned by the Swedish state: The cabinet appointed the chairman of the court of directors, while the parliament elected the remaining six directors of the court. Obviously, such a strong dependence made it more vulnerable to political pressure. It is true, as Chapter One has shown, that the *Riksbank* could withstand this pressure as long as only the discount-rate policy was involved. The rate increases in 1920 from 6 to 7.5 percent were undertaken mainly because the gold cover ratio was deteriorating, not because of pressure by parliament. Yet, when it came to regime changes, the government and the *Riksdag* were able to overrule the *Riksbank,* in particular, its Governor Victor Moll.

The dependence on the government and the parliament made itself felt in early 1923.[30] When the *Riksbank* asked for the usual prolongation of the provision suspending convertibility (until 15 May), it met strong opposition. No less than 5 of the 12 ministers of the Social Democratic government under Prime Minister Hjalmar Branting rejected the request of the central bank. Finance Minister Fredrik Vilhelm Thorsson, a former member of the board of the *Riksbank,* called for an immediate restoration of the gold standard. The main reason why Social Democrats showed a strong preference for a return to prewar order was their fear of another wave of inflation that would reduce real wages.[31]

In the end, the *Riksbank* prevailed with its standard argument that it would be too risky to introduce convertibility ahead of all other European states, in particular, the United Kingdom, the Netherlands, and Switzerland. However, since at the end of April the *Riksbank* had to renew its request

[28] *Wirtschaftsdienst,* 1 August 1924, p. 1006.
[29] The Bank of England was founded in 1694.
[30] The following narrative is based on the English version of Eli Heckscher's account: Heckscher (1930, pp. 253–267). Yet, for some parts, I also used the more detailed original Swedish version: Heckscher (1926, pp. 137–148).
[31] Notermans (2000, pp. 71–73). During a US Senate hearing in 1925, Oscar Rydbeck, president of one of the largest commercial banks in Stockholm (*Skandinaviska Kreditaktiebolaget*), also highlighted the fear of real wage losses. See Commission of Gold and Silver Inquiry (1925, p. 209).

for a prolongation of the provision suspending convertibility, the debate was far from over. Now, the newly elected Conservative government under Prime Minister Ernst Trygger had to deal with the issue, and this time, the *Riksbank* did not prevail without any reservation. Backed by the cabinet, Finance Minister Jacob Beskow declared that the suspension of convertibility would be maintained only if the *Riksbank* agreed to stabilize the krona at the current gold parity, even under the condition of a high fluctuation in gold prices. Despite strong opposition, a majority of the *Riksdag* followed the arguments of Beskow and approved the proposal.[32]

With hindsight, this decision turned out to be the prelude to the final act leading to early restoration of the gold standard because, in late 1923, stabilization of the krona became very difficult as the dollar began to rise against the British pound and all other European currencies because of divergent price movements and a general capital flight from Europe caused by occupation of the Ruhr by Belgian and French troops in January 1923.[33] Initially, the *Riksbank*, like some other central banks, tried to stop the depreciation of the krona by increasing the discount rate – from 4.5 to 5.5 percent on 9 November 1923 (Figure 2.6). Then, as it became clear that this measure proved insufficient to keep the krona from falling below gold parity, the *Riksbank* introduced a sort of dual market for dollars. It sold dollars to importers at the prewar parity, thus upholding the impression that the krona rate had remained stable. The rationale behind this strategy was to prevent a run on its foreign exchanges because if the *Riksbank* had officially acknowledged that it was depreciating, many investors would have exchanged their Swedish assets for dollar assets.

In any case, by taking this measure, the *Riksbank* directors were convinced that they had succeeded in maintaining the agreement with the *Riksdag*. The Swedish government, however, strongly objected. On 7 March 1924, when the central bank again asked for a continuation of the suspension of convertibility, Finance Minister Beskow, who had set up the agreement a year earlier, explained that the *Riksbank* had violated the rules and called for an immediate return to the gold standard. He was only ready to give the *Riksbank* a little more than three months of preparation so that the gold standard would be restored at the beginning of July. This period also was considered to be necessary in order to dissolute the Scandinavian Currency Union. It was the first time since 1914 that the Swedish government declined to follow the directors of the *Riksbank*. Accordingly, this

---

[32] See the Report of the *Riksdag*, 12 May 1923.
[33] Brown (1940, pp. 308–310).

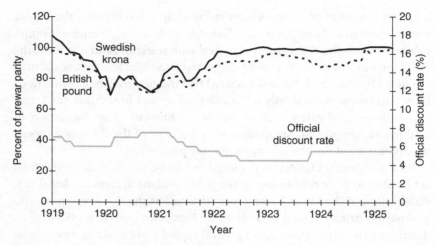

Figure 2.6. Swedish krona and British pound (percentage of prewar parity) and Swedish discount rate. (*Commission of Gold and Silver Inquiry, 1925.*)

caused a great stir in the *Riksbank*. Yet, at the same time, Beskow's statement also made the difference between the official rate and the market rate of the krona disappear immediately. Obviously, markets understood immediately that the gold standard was about to be restored.

Surprisingly, the Standing Committee on Banking of the *Riksdag* went even further. On 22 March 1924, it proposed unanimously that convertibility was to be reintroduced three months earlier than the finance minister had suggested, thus on 1 April instead of 1 July. The argument of the committee was that by advancing the date of restoration, unnecessary debates and irritations could be avoided. In exchange for this demanding schedule, the committee proposed that gold imports continued to be prohibited except when ordered by the bank in order to avoid a "flood of gold," as it was called. In addition, the ban on gold exports was not lifted yet. The *Riksbank* agreed to this compromise without any major objections, although it had warned of an early restoration of the gold standard for years. On 29 March, both chambers of the *Riksdag* approved the proposal of the committee with a sweeping majority. On 1 April, Sweden was the first European country to be back on gold at prewar parity.

According to the German weekly *Wirtschaftsdienst*, published by the Hamburg Institute of International Economics, the return to prewar parity was not the only option that was discussed in early 1924.[34] Some exporters, such as the "Match King" Ivar Kreuger, proposed that the krona be tied

[34] *Wirtschaftsdienst*, 7 March 1924, pp. 269–270.

to the British pound. Already in 1921–1922 when the krona climbed to prewar parity, Kreuger had called for such a solution.[35] In addition, some economists favored the idea of price-level targeting, inspired by the writings of Knut Wicksell and Irving Fisher. Of course, both proposals suffered from the problem that they required a change of policy, whereas the return to prewar parity was only a matter of formally confirming a de facto state of affairs. Nevertheless, it is striking that both proposals were adopted a few years later after the krona went off gold in September 1931. The *Riksbank* adopted price-level targeting as its new policy framework, although only officially, as we will see in Chapter Six, and in 1933, the krona was tied to the British pound.

In sum, the *Riksbank* pursued a policy that it had rejected but was forced to accept owing to its strong dependence on the government and the *Riksdag*. In the Netherlands and Switzerland, by contrast, the central banks were powerful and independent enough to define the time of restoration of the gold standard, namely, not before the British pound was back on gold. It would be wrong, however, to assume that because of the higher degree of central bank independence, the return to the gold standard was completed without any major conflicts with the government or difficulties in management of the exchange rate.

To begin with the latter issue, both the *Nederlandsche Bank* and the Swiss National Bank were struggling with exchange-rate fluctuations during two phases[36] (Figure 2.7). In 1921–1922, the guilder and the franc appreciated against the dollar at a time when the economy was in a deep recession, and the German *Reichsmark* was plunging, and in late 1923, both currencies suffered from the strength of the dollar and the pessimistic mood in Europe. In the first phase, both central banks abstained from taking measures, although there was much talk about the negative consequences of "*valuta*-dumping" from Germany.[37] In the second phase, both central banks intervened in order to prevent the exchange rate from falling below gold parity, although not fully successfully.

As Figure 2.7 shows, the return of the Swiss currency to the gold standard was somewhat bumpier than that of the Dutch guilder. In 1921, the Swiss franc appreciated by 25 percent against the dollar and reached prewar parity in December, the Dutch guilder by only 15 percent. The latter did not climb to prewar parity until December 1923. The fact that the Swiss

---

[35] Heckscher (1930, p. 255).
[36] For a brief overview of the movements of the Dutch guilder and the Swiss franc, see Jack (1927), pp. 79–87, and Aliber (1962), pp. 229–238.
[37] Keesing (1947, p. 51); *Schweizerische Nationalbank* (1932, p. 237).

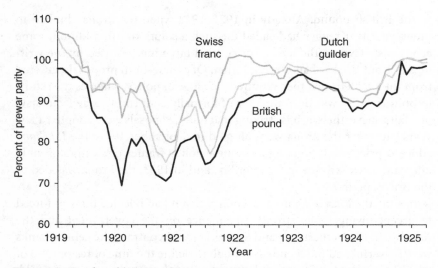

Figure 2.7. Dutch guilder, Swiss franc, and British pound (percentage of prewar parity). (*Commission of Gold and Silver Inquiry, 1925*.)

franc appreciated to prewar parity so early despite a negative trade balance and high unemployment was a great mystery to many observers. The *Nederlandsche Bank* wrote in its annual report of 1921–1922 that the example of the Swiss currency showed "how complicated the problems" were.[38] The Swiss National Bank also was perplexed. In October 1921, it asked a London correspondent for an explanation, but the correspondent felt incapable of making sense of the rise of the Swiss franc. The foreign-exchange market, he wrote, had remained "very obscure."[39] In January 1922, the Swiss franc had climbed above prewar parity, and the Swiss National Bank asked for an explanation from the International Acceptance Bank in New York. The answer it got was not better than the one it had gotten from London. At least it was pointed out that capital flight from Germany might have caused the appreciation. The board of the Swiss National Bank dryly concluded that there was neither in New York nor in Europe "a fully satisfactory explanation."[40] However, in the annual report of 1921, the board argued that there had been a very simple reason, namely, that Europe's demand for dollars had very much decreased since the depression had set in.[41]

[38] Annual Report of *De Nederlandsche Bank* for the year 1921–1922, p. 9.
[39] Archives Swiss National Bank, *Protokoll des Direktoriums*, 13 October 1920, p. 247.
[40] Archives Swiss National Bank, *Protokoll des Direktoriums*, 19 January 1922, pp. 18–19.
[41] Ruoss (1992, p. 155); *Schweizerische Nationalbank* (1932, p. 229).

Unlike in Sweden a year later, there was no question of maintaining dollar parity in order to be capable of restoring the gold standard more easily.[42] And as the exchange rate of the Swiss currency slowly depreciated until the summer of 1922, to the great relief of the Swiss National Bank, the question answered itself. But then, in September 1922, the movement of the Swiss franc again was more volatile than that of the Dutch guilder, which continued to appreciate toward prewar parity without any disturbance. This time, however, the reason for the sudden fall of the Swiss franc was very clear. In January 1922, the Social Democratic Party had submitted an initiative calling for a one-time capital levy to narrow the fiscal deficit. The Swiss government, which strongly objected to such a measure, set the date for the referendum to 2 December 1922 so that the campaigns were started after the summer break, which unsettled international and domestic investors. As a result, the volume of notes in circulation increased rapidly, sight deposits were reduced, and the private discount rate rose by more than 1 to 2.5 percent.[43] At the meeting of the Committee of the Bank Council in November 1922, the president of the governing board explained that the impending referendum on the capital levy had prompted "our capitalists to shift their investments abroad, in particular to Holland, London and New York."[44]

Yet although Swiss voters rejected the idea of a one-time capital levy by a very large margin (87 percent), the Swiss franc recovered only temporarily. In the spring of 1923, the depreciation movement started again owing to further capital outflows, leading the Swiss National Bank to abandon its aversion to market interventions and to begin to play a more active role. In the time from April to July, it took three measures.[45] First, it drove the private discount rate upward by selling treasury bills (*Reskriptionen*). Second, it sold dollars to the foreign-exchange market. And third, on 14 July it raised the discount and Lombard rates by 1 to 4 percent and 5 percent, respectively. These measures had only a short-term effect, however. After a short stop in August, the Swiss franc continued to depreciate until March 1924. Then, with the sudden recovery of the British pound, the Swiss franc appreciated by almost 10 percent and reached prewar parity in November 1924.[46] From

---

[42] Archives Swiss National Bank, *Protokoll des Direktoriums*, 12 January 1922, p. 22.

[43] Ruoss (1992, pp. 156–157).

[44] Archives Swiss National Bank, *Bankausschuss*, 1 November 1922, p. 234.

[45] Ruoss (1922, pp. 160–161).

[46] See Cottrell (1995, pp. 91–92) on the British situation. In the summer of 1924, the Chamberlain-Bradbury Committee began its work dealing with how to reduce floating debt and to return to prewar parity, and in November, a new Conservative government came to power. These two factors made investors more optimistic about the outlook of the British economy and sterling.

then on, the Swiss National Bank stabilized the exchange rate, announcing in a press release in June 1925 that it would keep the franc within the gold points of the dollar rate. The formal *de jure* restoration of the gold standard did not take place until 1930, however, when a new amendment to the National Bank Law became effective.[47]

The Dutch guilder also joined in the upward movement of the British pound, reached prewar parity in November 1924, and then was stabilized at that level. The depreciation preceding this rapid recovery had been different from that experienced by the Swiss franc. Until autumn 1923, the rate of the guilder had been stable and remained only a little below prewar parity. Unlike in Switzerland, investors were not scared off by an impending referendum on capital levy, as Keesing (1947) pointed out.[48] Thus the sudden depreciation in late 1923 must have been caused by other factors. According to the *Wirtschaftsdienst,* the main reasons were the general mistrust in Europe and the falling prices in the United States resulting from a short but steep recession.[49] In other words, the guilder fell victim to the same forces as the Swedish krona. Not surprisingly, therefore, the *Nederlandsche Bank* in December 1923 resorted to the same measure to stop the depreciation as the Swedish *Riksbank* had taken a month earlier, namely, to raise the discount rate by 1 percent. The success was modest in both cases. Only when the outlooks on Europe became more optimistic was the trend reversed.

In conclusion, managing the exchange rate and bringing it back to prewar parity were not much easier for the *Nederlandsche Bank* and the Swiss National Bank, although both central banks had more room to maneuver than the Swedish *Riksbank*. By the same token, both central banks were repeatedly involved in conflicts with the government, especially when dealing with the issue of floating debt. And interestingly, Sweden was able to solve this problem much better than the Netherlands and Switzerland (Table 2.1). In 1921, Swedish floating debt was reduced by two-thirds, whereas Dutch and Swiss floating debt kept rising.

In the Netherlands, the central bank pressed the government to reduce the volume of floating debt once the war was over. However, the process took longer than the *Nederlandsche Bank* had wished.[50] One reason was that the government was divided on this issue so that the struggle eventually culminated in the summer of 1923. Finance Minister de Geer, who had entered the cabinet in 1921 and had begun to put the state finances back

[47] *Schweizerische Nationalbank* (1932, p. 286).
[48] Keesing (1947, p. 63).
[49] *Wirtschaftsdienst,* 14 December 1923, p. 1137.
[50] De Vries (1989, pp. 371–372).

Table 2.1. *Floating and Total Debt*

Year (End of)	Netherlands		Sweden		Switzerland		
	Floating Federal	Total Debt	Floating Federal	Total Debt	Floating Federal	Railways	Total Debt
1913	13	1,157	20	648	1	70	1,711
1918	614	2,459	559	1,656	371	176	3,262
1919	643	2,691	285	1,567	400	216	3,740
1920	514	2,760	215	1,496	270	352	4,018
1921	859	2,872	77	1,511	200	275	4,242
1922	838	2,981	86	1,551	118	230	4,405
1923	666	2,975	46	1,643	154	150	4,642
1924	360	2,959			36	76	4,721
1925	306	2,899			85	48	4,772
1926	235	2,800			22	72	4,748

Sweden: Floating debt 1920–1922: Figures include loan from state pension institution.
Switzerland: Only national debt (without cantons and towns), including debts of national railways.
Sources: Keesing (1947, pp. 57, 86); SNB (1944, p. 199); Commission of Gold and Silver Inquiry (1925).

into balance in 1922, resigned over the draft for the so-called Fleet Law designed to provide the Dutch Navy with additional funding. The absolute amount was not very considerable, but the fact that an increase in spending was imminent annoyed de Geer. In addition, the fact that the military was supposed to get more funds while in other areas the government was cutting its expenses met strong popular opposition. In September 1923, 80,000 protesters marched through Amsterdam, and in the end, the Second Chamber of the Parliament rejected the bill by a wafer-thin majority (50 to 49).[51]

Once this issue was resolved, de Geer's successor, Colijn, was able to balance the budget and reduce floating debt. As Table 2.1 shows, the year 1924 brought considerable progress, helped by the upswing in the Dutch economy. Floating debt was reduced by almost 50 percent, and total debt began to decrease, although slowly.[52] The measures were dire. Colijn cut the

[51] Keesing (1947, pp. 60–61).
[52] A detailed account of the development of floating debt has been given by de Jong (1957).

funding for education and the military, the salaries of public servants were lowered, and some parts of the payments to disability funds were slashed. In addition, the government reduced its contribution to the construction of cheap housing.[53] By his determined method of solving fiscal problems, Colijn set the stage for an excellent career in public life, and he became probably the most prominent Dutch politician during the interwar years. He was Prime Minister from 1925 to 1926 and again from 1933 to 1939, when he made himself known as a particularly staunch defender of the old parity of the guilder.[54]

In Switzerland, the development was quite similar.[55] Once the war was over, the Swiss National Bank saw no reason to continue financing the deficits of the federal government and the national railways. In February 1921, the governing board decided to reduce the advances, arguing that the independence of the central bank was endangered if this financing did not end soon.[56] As in the Netherlands, 1924 was the year when the issue was resolved (see Table 2.1). Moreover, Swiss Finance Minister Jean-Marie Musy adopted a similarly tough stance to eliminate the Swiss federal fiscal deficit, and he also played an important role in the defense of prewar parity of the Swiss franc in the 1930s. In 1934, he resigned when he failed to pass his austerity plan.[57]

In contrast to the Netherlands, however, the conflict between the central bank and the government appears to have been more virulent. In spring of 1923, when the Swiss franc continued to weaken even after the referendum on the one-time capital levy had been rejected by a sweeping majority of Swiss voters, Finance Minister Musy urged the Swiss National Bank to sell dollars in the market. The bank reacted indignantly, insisting on its independence in management of the exchange rate.[58] A year later, the same conflict broke out again. In April 1924, Musy wanted the Swiss National Bank to sell US$5 million in the market in order to push the franc upward. The bank repeated its reluctance to take orders from the finance minister and added that such an operation would not be successful anyway. After a meeting with the governing board, Musy accepted the approach of the Swiss National Bank.[59]

---

[53] Keesing (1947, p. 61).
[54] See Chapter Four.
[55] *Schweizerische Nationalbank* (1932, pp. 191–199); Ruoss (1992, pp. 127–128).
[56] Archives Swiss National Bank, *Protokoll des Direktoriums*, 17 February 1921, p. 9.
[57] See Chapter Four.
[58] Ruoss (1992, p. 158).
[59] Ruoss (1992, pp. 163–164).

In sum, the return to prewar parity was no case of plain sailing for the Netherlands, Sweden, or Switzerland. Nor was it identical across the three small states. In Sweden, the *Riksbank* was forced to restore the gold standard a year before the United Kingdom, the Netherlands, and Switzerland owing to the strong dependence of the central bank on the government and the *Riksdag*. On the other hand, the Swiss franc proved to have the most volatile exchange rate of the three. In the Netherlands, finally, reduction of the debt led to a serious cabinet crisis. Yet, of course, in comparison with Denmark and Norway, these differences pale into insignificance. The next section will discuss these two cases in more detail.

LATE RETURN OF DENMARK AND NORWAY

In mid-1924, the rates of the Danish krone and the Norwegian krone were quoted well below the old parity with the dollar, at 60 and 50 percent, respectively. Yet only a few years later both countries restored the gold standard at prewar parity, Denmark in early 1927 and Norway in the spring of 1928. It was a very painful process and pushed both economies back into a deep recession, whereas most other European countries enjoyed an upswing lasting until the end of the decade[60] (Table 2.2). And the banking sector, hardly recovered from the deflation of the early 1920s, went through another severe crisis. From an economic point of view, the exchange-rate policies of Denmark and Norway after 1923 were disastrous.

Given these foreseeable consequences, how could this happen? Economic historians agree that most policymakers and voters regarded prewar parity as the natural equilibrium and therefore were not able to imagine a viable alternative.[61] Even business leaders, bank managers, and farmers who knew that a deflation would be costly never unanimously rejected restoration of the old monetary order. Denmark and Norway were not at all special in this approach. As Heckscher (1930) pointed out, the international comparison shows that "no country that has kept its currency at a level at all comparable to its old value has been able to bring itself to a definite devaluation."[62] Princeton economist Richard Lester made the same observation: "Failure to return to the pre-war parity was depicted as dishonest and a national

---

[60] For the economic consequences, see Broadberry (1984) and Klovland (1998).

[61] For a comparative view, see Lester (1939), Broadberry (1984), and Klovland (1998). On the return of the Danish krone to parity, see Olsen (1968, pp. 86–106). As for the Norwegian krone, see Rygg (1950, pp. 171–423), Keilhau (1952, pp. 158–199), Hanisch (1979), and Hodne (1983, pp. 37–39).

[62] Heckscher (1930, p. 247).

Table 2.2. *Economic Indicators of Denmark, Norway, and Sweden (1922–1929)*

	Denmark			Norway			Sweden		
	Wholesale Prices	Industrial Production	Unemployment Rate (%)	Wholesale Prices	Industrial Production	Unemployment Rate (%)	Wholesale Prices	Industrial Production	Unemployment Rate (%)
1922	100	100	9.6	100	100	6.9	100	100	9.4
1923	109	121	6.3	100	111	5.1	94	110	5.2
1924	86	136	5.3	114	119	3.9	94	125	4.2
1925	96	130	7.3	110	130	5.2	93	128	4.5
1926	74	126	10.3	86	115	8.0	85	140	5.0
1927	69	129	11.2	72	119	8.1	84	145	5.0
1928	69	140	9.2	68	130	7.3	85	158	4.4
1929	68	150	7.7	64	145	6.4	81	165	4.2

Sources: Grytten (1995), Mitchell (2003), Pedersen (1931).

disgrace in view of the fact that Sweden had returned to pre-war parity and that no country whose currency had depreciated less than 50 per cent had until then dared to devalue."[63]

It would be wrong, however, to assume that there was a clear plan designed to bring the Danish and Norwegian currencies back to the prewar level. Norwegian economist Wilhelm Keilhau, an early advocate of devaluation, wrote in retrospect that "by and large one can say that there was no Norwegian exchange-rate policy during the 1920s."[64] The same is true for the Danish exchange-rate policy. There was enormous uncertainty on how to proceed. Policymakers agreed only that a devaluation would be premature, not least because the press and the public were overwhelmingly in favor of a return to the old parity. There also was a consensus that the exchange rate was to appreciate in a controlled manner, but the question of how long the appreciation was supposed to last remained unanswered. In the end, international speculators decided the issue as Swedish economist Gustav Cassel observed in 1928: "Once international speculation came to believe that a restoration of the old gold standard was to be expected, it took the currency into its own hands, and the authorities lost all control over developments."[65] In the second quarter of 1925, after the United Kingdom, the Netherlands, and Switzerland had restored the gold standard, they turned their attention to Denmark and Norway and drove the exchange rate upward at a fast pace, doing no more than taking Danish and Norwegian officials at their word. These, by contrast, were alarmed by the speed of the appreciation, but because they had always declined to devalue, no serious attempt to stop the process was made. The speculators won the game, and the gold standard was restored at prewar parity much earlier than planned.

Of the two countries, Denmark was the first to reestablish the old monetary order thanks to the fact the Danish krone had been roughly 10 percent stronger than the Norwegian currency when the appreciation process had started in late 1924 (Figure 2.8). The distance to be completed to prewar parity was considerably smaller. The two main reasons for this relative

---

[63] Lester (1939, p. 195). Lester travelled to Scandinavia and wrote his book in the late 1930s. Page 190, footnote 5: "Some of the author's conclusions and interpretations are based upon interviews with Danish and Norwegian economists, bankers, and businessmen during the summer of 1936."

[64] Keilhau (1938, p. 10): "*Im grossen und ganzen kann man wohl sagen, dass in den 1920er Jahren keinerlei norwegische Währungspolitik betrieben wurde. Gewiss wurden von Zeit zu Zeit Einzelmassnahmen vorgenommen im Hinblick auf die augenblickliche Situation, aber irgendein Plan auf lange Sicht wurde nicht verfolgt. Das Parlament nahm nicht ein einziges Mal Stellung zu den Richtlinien für eine künftige Währungspolitik.*"

[65] Cassel (1928, p. 19).

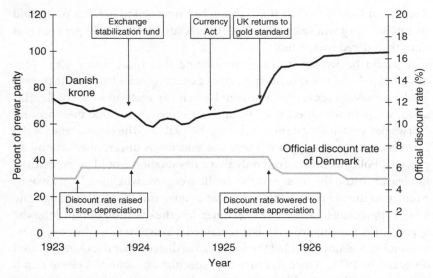

Figure 2.8. Danish krone (percentage of prewar parity) and official discount rate. (*Wirtschaftsdienst; Lester, 1939; and Hoffmeyer and Olsen, 1968.*)

difference were that Denmark had experienced less inflation from 1914 to 1920 and that Denmark's banking crisis had been less severe. To understand the interplay between the longing for the old monetary order and market speculation that ultimately led to the strong appreciation of the krone, it is necessary to distinguish among three phases.[66]

The first phase, starting in the spring of 1923 and lasting until March 1924, was characterized by failure to stabilize the exchange rate through market intervention and by the tightening of monetary policy. Shortly after the end of the banking crisis, the Danish National Bank tried to fight depreciation by raising the discount rate from 5 to 6 percent at the beginning of May 1923 and by sending a shipment of gold to the United States in July 1923.[67] Yet, because the effect of these measures was negligible, the board of directors approached Prime Minister Neergaard with the proposal

[66] Olsen (1968, pp. 104–106) also suggests three phases: from the end of the war until the appointment of the Foreign Exchange Conference (appointed in August 1923); from the conference until autumn 1925, when the krone had come near to prewar parity; and the time until the restoration of the gold standard. Christiansen, Lammers, and Nissen (1988, pp. 170–172) also use this chronology. See also Jack (1927, pp. 74–76) for a brief description of the Danish case.

[67] The discount rate was increased at the beginning of May 1923. The shipment of gold to the United States was done in July. Gold and silver commission, Serial 9, Vol. II, p. 95: "Import

to appoint a committee that would study the causes of the fall of the krone and work out measures to reverse the depreciation.[68] The government, led by the Farmers' Party (*Venstre*) and supported by the Conservative Party, agreed.

The Foreign Exchange Conference (*valutakonferencen*), as the committee was called, was appointed in August 1923 and consisted of representatives of all important economic sectors as well as independent experts.[69] The opinions were strongly divided on whether the krone should be brought back to prewar parity or not. At the first meeting, an economics professor, a business director, and the president of the stock exchange favored a stabilization at roughly 75 percent of prewar parity, arguing that a steep appreciation of the krone would reduce employment.[70] In the second meeting, the chairman of the conference and one of the directors of the Danish National Bank, Theodor Ussing, strongly objected on legal, moral, and practical reasons. By legal and moral reasons, Ussing meant that Denmark had the obligation to comply with international agreements and to guarantee the rights of foreign and domestic creditors. And by practical reasons, he meant that a devaluation of the krone would bring stability only vis-à-vis the dollar but not vis-à-vis the British pound, the currency of the most important trading partner that was still floating but which was expected to return to prewar parity in the following years. Ussing was endorsed by two influential economics professors, Axel Nielsen and Harald Westergaard, and by employers and labor unions. The latter were represented by Carl Valdemar Bramsnæs, who became finance minister in Denmark's first Social Democratic government appointed a few months later (April 1924).

Yet, although the advocates of an eventual return to prewar parity held a clear majority, a compromise was reached. The final statement, published on 23 October 1923, only mentioned that an "improvement of the krone's value" was to be aimed for and that, given the uncertain conditions in Europe, "the conference saw little use in dealing with the possible movements of

---

of Danish gold to the United States amounted to US$3,600 for that month. In September 1923, the bank gave some further support to exchange by selling some of its own foreign holdings."

[68] Olsen (1968, p. 87).

[69] *Valutakonferencens forhandlinger* (1923). The publication is a very valuable source because it contains not only the final statement by the conference but also a summary of each session and a useful statistical annex and various economic comments. The list of the members is on pp. 5–6. A short and useful review of the conference is given by Olsen (1968, pp. 87–92).

[70] The economics professor was Laurits Vilhelm Birck, the director was Jakob Kristian Lindberg, who joined the board of the National Bank in 1924, and Julius Schovelin.

the krone in a distant time."[71] To reach the goal of a slow appreciation of the krone, the conference proposed creation of an exchange-rate stabilization fund (*kursegaliseringsfond*) financed by a foreign loan and a series of measures to ensure the success of the active exchange-rate management, namely, a balanced budget, a reduction of the trade deficit, and a general lowering of prices.[72] Not all members of the conference agreed to the compromise, however. In a separate statement, two farmer representatives and the director of the trade companies had several reservations. In particular, they objected to any import duties and regulations and cautioned against a rapid appreciation of the krone and discount-rate increases.[73]

The government under Prime Minister Neergard, who also was finance minister, swiftly adopted the idea of an exchange-rate stabilization fund and obtained a loan of £5 million. But Neergard was not willing to find a majority for the accompanying measures because his base, the Farmer's Party, was strongly opposed to a protectionist trade policy. Accordingly, the *Valutazentrale* that was appointed to stabilize the krone failed in its task. After an initial appreciation in November, the fall of the krone continued as if nothing had happened. At the end of the year, the initial enthusiasm had quickly evaporated, and the whole experiment was buried a few months later.

In reaction to this failure, the Danish National Bank raised the discount rate from 6 to 7 percent on 16 January 1924. Prime Minister Neergard had tried to prevent such a step because he feared that it would hurt businesses and farmers – clear proof that there was no plan on how to restore prewar parity.[74] But the directors of the Danish National Bank saw no other possibility to stabilize the krone after the negative experience with the fund.[75] Furthermore, in March 1924, the central bank, this time urged by the government, admonished private banks to restrict their credits, threatening a closer monitoring of all security for future advances.[76] Finally, Prime Minister Neergard tried to raise taxes in order to curb consumption, but since he did not find a majority, he saw no other way than to dissolve parliament and call for new elections.[77] The winners of these elections, held

[71] *Valutakonferencens forhandlinger* (1923), p. 7.
[72] *Ibid.*, pp. 8–9.
[73] *Ibid.*, p. 10.
[74] Olsen (1968, p. 95).
[75] Archives National Bank of Denmark, *Direktionsprotokol*, 16 January 1924, p. 221.
[76] The circular letter advising a more restrictive lending policy (*kredibegrænsingscirkularet*) is printed in the Annual Report of the National Bank (*Nationalbankens årsberetning*) for the year 1923–1924, p. 405.
[77] *Wirtschaftsdienst*, 9 May 1924, p. 571; Lester (1939, p. 193).

on 11 April 1924, were the Social Democrats, which formed a minority government for the first time in Denmark's history (from 23 April 1924 until 14 December 1926).

With the Neergard government gone, the second phase began. In July 1924, Social Democratic Prime Minister Stauning asked parliament to convene a Foreign Exchange Council (*valutaråd*) that, like its predecessor in 1923, was to consist of the representatives of the major economic sectors and the Danish National Bank and to come up with ideas of how to make the krone stronger. Stauning needed the endorsement of all parties because his minority government controlled only the *Folketing* (by way of toleration by the Social Liberal Party) but not the *Landsting*.[78] The Foreign Exchange Council, chaired by the prime minister himself, began its deliberations in mid-July and delivered its report in early November.[79] Its main proposal was to oblige the Danish National Bank to gradually improve the exchange rate of the krone against the dollar. The exchange rate was not to depreciate below 65 percent of prewar parity and to be appreciated to roughly 70 percent until the end of 1926. What would happen afterward was left open.

It is not entirely clear how this compromise proposal came about. In the German weekly *Wirtschaftsdienst*, which also was one of the major sources used by Lester (1939), it is claimed that Stauning had aimed for a stabilization of the krone at the current level, that is at roughly 65 percent of the prewar parity. Yet, owing to the enormous public pressure that was put on him once his intentions had become known, he backed off. The report cites a Danish National Bank official saying at a conference that the proposal of a devaluation was so destructive that it would not be discussed in that circle. He added: "We want a honest krone, a krone at the old parity."[80] Olsen (1968), by contrast, suggests that the Stauning government was determined to bring the krone back to prewar parity.[81] Finance Minister Bramsnæs, for example, had advocated a gradual appreciation of the krone to prewar parity when he participated in deliberations of the Foreign Exchange Conference in 1923. Furthermore, labor unions knew that their members would profit from a deflation in terms of higher real wages. In any case, on 20 December both chambers of parliament passed the Currency Act, based

---

[78] The Social Democratic Stauning government could count on the regular support by the radicals (*Venstre*) in the *Folketing*.

[79] The report of the council is printed as a supplement to the foreign exchange bill that was discussed in the *Folketing* on 17 November 1924: *Rigsdagstidende* 1924–1925, *tillæg A, spalte* 2907–2915.

[80] *Wirtschaftsdienst*, 7 November 1924, pp. 1542–1543, and 9 January 1925, p. 61.

[81] Olsen (1968, pp. 98–99).

on the recommendations of the Foreign Exchange Council to be effective on 1 February 1925. Only the Conservative Party was against the plan and asked for higher import duties.

Although not intended, the bill was like an invitation to investors to speculate with the krone, and they readily accepted this offer. Thus adoption of the Currency Act introduced the third phase of the drama. The krone had already started to appreciate before December, ironically only a few weeks after the council that was supposed to strengthen the krone had begun its deliberations. The main reason for the upward movement was the conclusion of the Dawes Plan in August 1924 and the successful floatation of the German loan in October. But the improving outlook of the Danish economy and the tightening of monetary conditions also seem to have mattered.[82] Yet the run on the krone did not begin until spring 1925 right after the United Kingdom, the Netherlands, and Switzerland restored the gold standard at prewar parity, and international investors were looking for other opportunities to make money in the foreign-exchange market.

From June to September, the krone appreciated by almost 30 percent, reaching more than 90 percent of prewar parity. Not surprisingly, the Danish National Bank observed this alarming development with increasing nervousness. Most of the directors had always wished to return to prewar parity, but not at such a fast pace. Jakob Lindberg, who had been appointed to the Danish National Bank by Stauning and who had always favored a devaluation,[83] proposed a lowering of the discount rate on 3 July, but the majority of the directors objected, and nothing happened.[84] Accordingly, the krone continued to shoot upward. Only after the *Industrirådet*, the organization of Danish industries, sent a resolution on 10 July and the Currency Committee of parliament unanimously called for a rate decrease on 23 July did the opinion begin to shift in favor of Lindberg.[85] A month later, the Danish National Bank lowered the discount rate from 7 to 6 percent and on 8 September from 6 to 5.5 percent.[86] From September to December, the exchange rate remained stable.

Of course, the rapid rise of the krone required an amendment to the Currency Act. The question was whether to restore the gold standard at

---

[82] See Brown (1940, p. 368) on the effect of the Dawes Plan and Olsen (1968, pp. 97–98) on domestic factors.

[83] He was the only member of the Foreign Exchange Conference who neither signed the joint statement nor wrote a separate statement as the representatives of the farmers' organizations did. *Valutakonferencens forhandlinger* (1923), p. 10.

[84] Archives National Bank of Denmark, *Direktionsprotokol*, 3 July 1925, p. 295.

[85] Lester (1939, p. 199) and Olsen (1968, pp. 102–103).

[86] Archives National Bank of Denmark, *Direktionsprotokol*, 25 August 1925, pp. 305 and 307.

the current level or to bring the krone completely back to prewar parity. In October, the *Wirtschaftsdienst* reported that the general opinion among the parties as well as in the population was decisively for a return to prewar parity regardless of the cost.[87] Only the Social Liberals (*Det Radicale Venstre*) asked for a stabilization of the krone at roughly 90 percent of prewar parity so that 20 kroner would be equivalent to £1 – a currency at such a rate was called the *shillingkrone*. But because they formed only the smallest of the four large parties and the party was divided on this issue, their opposition was rather weak.[88] Moreover, business and banking executives pointed out that a stabilization below the prewar parity might be seen as a sign of weakness and would only undermine the confidence of foreigners in the krone.[89] On 15 December, the parliament passed the amendment, which required the Danish National Bank to keep the krone above the level of 88 percent of prewar parity. Although it did not mention that the ultimate goal was the return to the prewar parity, it was clear to the speculators that they could drive the krone further upward. From December 1925 to March 1926, it appreciated by another 5 percent, thus reaching almost 98 percent of prewar parity. The process was completed and the gold standard was restored in January 1927.[90]

In conclusion, Denmark's return to the gold standard is yet more proof of how policymakers were unable to understand what new opportunities the suspension of the gold standard offered them. Instead of using exchange-rate management as a tool to improve macroeconomic performance, they burdened the economy with another deflationary shock, believing that the return to the old parity was in the best interest of the nation. In retrospect, it is particularly disturbing to see how even those in the business world who knew that the appreciation would be very costly did not form a powerful opposition. Apparently, the consensus that the old monetary order had to be restored was too widespread to be ignored.

Furthermore, the fact that Norway brought the krone back to prewar parity from an even lower level is strong proof that it was not specific economic structures and interests that guided the political process but deeply anchored convictions and fixed ideas. The process was nearly identical in Norway, with the only difference that the government and the parliament played only a minor role until the speculative attacks started in the spring

---

[87] *Wirtschaftsdienst*, 16 October 1925, p. 1592.
[88] *Wirtschaftsdienst*, 18 December 1925, pp. 1912–1913. Olsen (1968, p. 104). The Social Liberals suggested 91øre per schilling
[89] Haupt (1927, p. 299*).
[90] *Lov om Indløseligheden af Nationalbankens Sedler, "Lovtidende,"* Copenhagen, December 1926, No. 313.

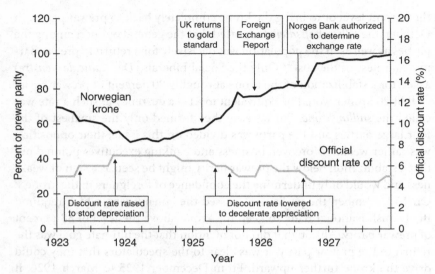

Figure 2.9. Danish krone and Norwegian krone (percentage of prewar parity) and Norwegian discount rate. (*Wirtschaftsdienst; Lester, 1939; Keilhau, 1952*).

of 1925. Not until September of that year did the government appoint a Foreign Exchange Committee that was to make proposals concerning the future parity of the krone. As noted, the Danish government appointed a committee as early as August 1923, and the prime minister and the parliament formed a Foreign Exchange Council in July 1924. This difference is not important enough, however, to change the chronology. We only have to add one more phase in order to take into account the period after the Danish krone reached prewar parity.[91]

The first phase, starting in May 1923, began with the increase in the discount rate from 5 to 6 percent, exactly as in Denmark. The step was motivated by the same rationale, namely, to stop depreciation of the krone. The outcome was identical as well: The currency continued to depreciate because the pessimistic mood in Europe following occupation of the Ruhr in January 1923 was too strong to be reversed by a discount-rate increase. But then, *Norges Bank* further tightened monetary conditions at an earlier date than the Danish National Bank. On 10 November 1923, it raised the discount rate from 6 to 7 percent, whereas Denmark didn't take this step until January 1924 (see Figure 2.9).

According to Lester (1939), this second rate increase, which was opposed by most private banks, was partially motivated by a speech given by Swedish

[91] See Jack (1927, pp. 77–78) for a brief description of the Norwegian case.

economist Gustav Cassel to the Norwegian Industrial Association in Oslo in which he criticized and even ridiculed Norwegian monetary policy. *Norges Bank* Governor Rygg rose after Cassel's speech and explained that Norway was legally and morally bound to bring the krone back to parity and that the Norwegian people had the "backbone" to sacrifice and conquer – almost the identical arguments that his Danish colleague Ussing had put forward in the *valutakonferencen*.[92] He concluded: "We must and we will go back and we will not give up." Prime Minister Berge endorsed Rygg in a press interview: "... [I]t may cost the nation much time, activity and labor to accomplish that goal. But the will is at hand and that this will show itself I do not doubt any minute. And I feel myself assured that we will reach that goal."[93]

The second phase began in the spring of 1924 as the Norwegian currency joined in the general upward movement initiated by the conclusion of the Dawes Plan in mid-August 1924. As noted, the government and the parliament still did not address the question of how to restore the gold standard. Only university professors of economics discussed the currency problem in public. For example, Wilhelm Keilhau gave a speech in November 1924 in which he proposed to stabilize the krone at the current level.[94] The only measure that was taken was lowering of the discount rate from 7 to 6.5 percent on 26 November 1924. Given that the exchange rate was appreciating and several banks fell victim to the deflationary course, *Norges Bank* saw a possibility to ease monetary conditions. Yet, at the same time, the bank talked the krone up by regularly issuing statements saying that the board foresaw a gradual return to prewar parity.[95]

One reason why the exchange-rate issue was hardly discussed was that Norwegian politicians were forced to devote their time to other issues. The first half of 1924 was marked by a long and violent labor conflict, and in the elections in mid-1924, the Communist Party received 6 of 150 seats in the Norwegian parliament for the first time. Since both the Conservatives and the Liberals lost seats, the ruling coalition was weakened, although the new government under Prime Minister Johan Ludwig Mowinckel of the

---

[92] For a good summary of the economic ideas of Rygg, see Sejersted (1973). The dispute with Cassel is mentioned on p. 29.

[93] Lester (1939, p. 205). His statements were printed in the daily newspapers *Aftenposten* (1923, no. 685, p. 6) and *Morgenbladet* (1923, no. 364, p. 4). See Keilhau (1952, p. 179).

[94] *Wirtschaftsdienst*, 22 May 1925, p. 802; Keilhau (1952, pp. 177–178); Lester (1939, p. 207). Keilhau, who was the head of a group of economics professors favoring devaluation, had already made this proposal in February 1924 in an article in *Dagbladet* (8 February 1924).

[95] Hodne (1983, p. 34).

Liberal Party (*Venstre*) still had 60 percent of total seats. Three years later they would lose their absolute majority.

The third phase, beginning in spring 1925, was marked by a steep appreciation of the krone leading to an intense public debate, just as in Denmark. As mentioned, the main reason for this strong upward pressure was that the United Kingdom, the Netherlands, and Switzerland had just restored the gold standard in late April and June, respectively, so international funds were looking for new investment opportunities in Europe, given that US interest rates were rather low at that point. Earlier than the Danish central bank, the *Norges Bank* tried to decelerate the appreciation by lowering the discount rates in three steps from 6.5 to 5 percent in May, August, and September 1925. These steps seem to have had some effect. The exchange rate dropped a few percentage points and remained stable until the end of the year. But then *Norges Bank* reversed its course once more by raising the discount rate from 5 to 6 percent in January 1926, and the krone resumed appreciating, again following the Danish currency. The third phase ended in June 1926 as the return of the Danish krone to prewar parity stopped the upward movement of the Norwegian krone.

In contrast to the first two phases, the government now actively addressed the currency question. Norwegian economist Wilhelm Keilhau, an outspoken advocate of a devaluation, observed: "It sometimes happens that all economic questions of a country are concentrated in a single one which is then in the center of economic life and on whose solution almost everything depends. This has been the case in Norway for months. There exists in fact only one economic question, namely, the currency problem."[96] In September 1925, the government appointed a Foreign Exchange Committee consisting of seven experts, chaired by Gunnar Jahn, director of the Central Bureau of Statistics. Yet, since the committee was divided on the issue, it could not clarify it.[97] In its report published on 23 January 1926, the committee advocated a de facto stabilization of the krone at the current level and proposed to postpone the final settlement of the question to gain more empirical knowledge.[98] Thus the conclusion was elusive, leaving much room for divergent interpretations.[99]

---

[96] *Wirtschaftsdienst*, 18 September 1925, p. 1436: "*Es kommt bisweilen vor, dass alle wirtschaftlichen Fragen eines Landes sich in einer einzigen konzentrieren, die dann im Mittelpunkt des Wirtschaftslebens steht und von deren Lösung beinahe alles abhängt. So ist es seit Monaten in Norwegen. Es existiert tatsächlich nur eine einzige wirschaftliche Frage, und zwar das Valutaproblem.*"

[97] Lester (1939, p. 206) assumes that the advocates of a deflation outnumbered the devaluationists. In any case, Chairman Jahn was in favor of returning to prewar parity.

[98] *Innstilling fra Valutakommisjonen*, Oslo, 1926, p. 15. The document also can be found in *Stortingets Forhandlinger 1926*, Appendix to St. prp. no. 62.

[99] Hodne (1983, p. 34).

The finance ministry sent the report to the *Norges Bank*, asking for a statement, but there was no answer until three months later, on 22 April. Not surprisingly, the central bank was even opposed to a temporary stabilization at the current level, arguing that this eventually would lead to a permanent devaluation. It also denied that the rise of the krone had resulted from speculation but ascribed it to rising profits of the productive sector and the increase in trade.[100] The position of the *Norges Bank* was backed by the public. When the report of the committee was released, a number of prominent businessmen and a former prime minister publicly criticized it and demanded a return to prewar parity. Lester (1939) reports that at a public meeting a businessman in the midst of a speech took out a 10-kroner note, saying that it should never be less valuable than a Swedish or a Danish krone.[101] Besides, the Norwegian currency, following the Danish krone, appreciated by another 5 percent during the first quarter of 1926, which further strengthened the case of the advocates of a return to prewar parity.

The final phase began in May of 1928, when the finance ministry and the central bank issued a joint press release stating that "the government as well as the *Norges Bank* were fully aware of the problems involved with a stabilization of the krone." Therefore, they would not engage in such an activity. Instead, the Norges Bank continued to regulate the exchange rate "in accordance with natural conditions."[102] This was nothing else but a clear signal to speculators that *Norges Bank* wished another appreciation of the krone because everybody understood that the central bank meant by "natural conditions" the return to prewar parity. On 11 June 1926, parliament adopted a bill in a secret session that legalized the sole responsibility of the central bank for the exchange-rate policy. At the conference of Nordic economists in Copenhagen at the beginning of September, there was a rumor that New York's big speculators had decided to drive the krone up further in the upcoming weeks.[103] The rumor proved to be correct: In October, the krone jumped from 88 percent of prewar parity to 94 percent. Since the *Norges Bank* continued to keep the exchange rate from depreciating and maintained the high level of interest rates – with another discount-rate increase in November 1927 – the krone eventually reached prewar parity at the end of 1927. On 1 May 1928, the gold standard was restored.

---

[100] Rygg (1950, p. 252).
[101] Lester (1939, pp. 207–208).
[102] Original version of press release printed in Keilhau (1952, p. 188).
[103] *Wirtschaftsdienst*, 31 December 1926, pp. 1825–1826.

THREE

Fear of Experiments

In the early 1920s, small neutral states were not willing to opt for a more flexible exchange-rate policy. They viewed the years after the end of World War I as a transitory period and were not interested in experimenting with new exchange-rate regimes. Eventually, they all restored the gold standard at prewar parity, with Denmark and Norway suffering from a particularly severe deflation. Only Belgium and Finland, two small states that had been involved in the war, stabilized their currencies at a lower level than prewar parity. A new window of opportunity opened in the early 1930s after the United Kingdom suspended the gold standard and allowed the pound to depreciate. The Scandinavian countries followed the British example and now were free to adopt whatever monetary regime they preferred. Did they seize the opportunity this time to make their exchange-rate regime more flexible?

Ever since that period, there has been a widely shared view that Sweden in fact broke with the past and implemented a new monetary policy. Two pieces of evidence are cited. First, the Swedish minister of finance announced in late September 1931 when Sweden abandoned the gold standard that monetary policy would be aimed at stabilizing the domestic price level. Second, Swedish prices were relatively stable after 1931, especially in comparison with countries that maintained the gold standard. Yet, the conventional view is not correct, and it remains a mystery why this overly positive view has been upheld so long because eminent economists have pointed out from the beginning that the policy change was modest. It it true that the discussions among economists and politicians were a historical novelty. But the words were not followed by deeds because the Swedish *Riksbank,* still longing for the old monetary order, continued to target the exchange rate. Although freed from the constraints of the gold standard, the *Riksbank* acted as if the gold standard still existed. In fact, as far as actual policies were concerned, Denmark and Norway had more success than Sweden. Norwegian prices were more stable than Swedish prices in 1932–1933, and Denmark at least used the new freedom to make competitive devaluations. This chapter will treat the Scandinavian experiences in the early 1930s in four steps. The first two sections discuss the causes leading to suspension of the gold standard in Scandinavia in September 1931. They also address the question of why the Benelux countries and Switzerland continued to adhere to the old monetary system until the mid-1930s. The third section deals with the gap between Sweden's official declarations and the monetary and exchange-rate policies pursued by the *Riksbank,* and the last section focuses on the experiences of Denmark and Norway.

TRADE AND CENTRAL BANK RESERVES

The end of the gold standard in September 1931 was a blessing for the Scandinavian countries. They recovered more rapidly from the depression than the Benelux countries and Switzerland, which did not devalue their currencies until the mid-1930s (Table 3.1). However, the early exit from gold was not the result of a sound strategy developed by Scandinavian central bankers and government officials. On the contrary, they were forced to devalue and felt shocked by the breakdown of the international monetary regime they had helped to rebuild only a few years earlier. Thus the crucial question is not whether Scandinavian policymakers were more foresighted than others, but rather what forces caused them to take a step they had tried to avoid.

The most obvious answer is that Denmark, Norway, and Sweden entertained particularly close trade relations with the United Kingdom. The *Economist,* for example, wrote shortly after the currency crisis of September 1931 that for this reason, "it was not unnatural that these three countries should be the first of our foreign neighbours to follow Great Britain's example in suspending the gold standard."[1] The argument is only partially correct, however, as Table 3.2 shows. It certainly holds for Denmark, a country that was selling 60 percent of its total exports to the United Kingdom corresponding to 17 percent of gross domestic product (GDP). Yet, as for Norway and Sweden, the trade argument is less convincing, especially if compared with Belgium and the Netherlands. The Benelux countries were much more open than Norway and Sweden, so trade with the United Kingdom

---

[1] *Economist,* October 3, 1931, p. 600. Similarly, Hodne (1983, p. 70) and Schön (2000, p. 342).

Table 3.1. *Regimes before and after Gold Standard*

Country	Stabilization 1920s: Percentage of Prewar Value	Regime Adopted after End of Gold Standard[a]
Austria	New currency	Capital controls
Germany	New currency	Capital controls
Belgium	14.3	New gold parity
France	20	New gold parity
Netherlands	Prewar parity	Sterling peg
Switzerland	Prewar parity	New gold parity
Denmark	Prewar parity	Exchange-rate targeting
Norway	Prewar parity	Exchange-rate targeting
Sweden	Prewar parity	Exchange-rate targeting
United Kingdom	Prewar parity	Exchange-rate targeting

[a] United Kingdom and Scandinavian countries: These classifications concern only the period from late 1931 to 1933 (Scandinavia) and to 1934 (United Kingdom).
Source: Aldcroft and Oliver (1998, p. 5).

Table 3.2. *Openness and Trade with Great Britain (1928)*

	Openness		Trade with Great Britain		
	Import and export/ GDP[a]	Import (Percentage of total)	Export (Percentage of total)	Import (Percentage GDP)[a]	Export (Percentage GDP)[a]
Denmark	60	15	60	3	17
Norway	41	19	26	6	4
Sweden	35	16	25	3	4
Belgium[b]	115	12	18	7	10
Netherlands	73	10	22	4	7
Switzerland	51	7	14	2	3

[a] Gross domestic product (GDP) used for Denmark, Norway, and Sweden; net national product (NNP) used for Belgium, the Netherlands, and Switzerland.
[b] Belgium: figures for 1927.
Source: Mitchell (2003), Ritzmann (1996) for Switzerland; author's calculations.

had roughly the same or even a higher importance for their GDP. As for Belgium, one also has to take account of the fact that some of its export industries, especially coal and iron, were competing directly with British exports.[2] And interestingly, the Netherlands linked its currency to sterling after the devaluation of 1936, a clear sign that the UK market was of vital importance for Dutch importers and exporters. Only if the Scandinavian countries are compared with Switzerland can one argue that the trade argument is valid. Yet, even for the Swiss economy, the fall of the pound proved to be a great problem.[3]

As for Norway, the major problem was the future of the shipping business. At the meeting of Nordic central bank officials a week after Britain's suspension of the gold standard, Governor Rygg of the *Norges Bank* declared: "The devaluation of sterling is a big blow for Norway, especially for shipping whose freights are calculated in sterling; in addition, many ships were chartered for a period of five to ten years, on the basis of freight contracts settled in sterling."[4] A second reason was that Norwegian officials were worried about the threat of another banking crisis.[5]

A closer look at the Swedish case reveals that the lack of sufficient gold and foreign-exchange reserves eventually forced the *Riksbank* to devalue in September 1931. As Figure 3.1 shows, reserves had been shrinking dramatically since June 1931. The central bank was already weakened when the fall of sterling triggered another run on the Swedish krona. Central banks in Belgium, the Netherlands, and Switzerland, by contrast, were able to maintain or even increase the levels of gold and foreign-exchange reserves during the months preceding the currency crises of September 1931 so that they were strong enough to avert the speculative attacks in September. What van Zanden (1998) observes in the case of the Netherlands is also true for Belgium and Switzerland: "In a way, it was just bad luck that the Netherlands was not thrust off gold in 1931 and that its gold reserves were so ample that a forced devaluation was out of the question."[6]

---

[2] Mommen (1994, pp. 34*ff.*).

[3] *Economist*, September 26, 1931, p. 563: "The principal strain will no doubt be felt in a decline of exports, both visible and invisible. Not less than 20 per cent. of Swiss exports of goods are taken by the UK, and the British contribution to the revenue from tourists is estimated to be as much as 35 per cent. of the total."

[4] Archives National Bank of Denmark, *Direktionsprotokol*, No. 2690g, 27 September 1931, p. 2: "*For Norges Vedkommende var Sterlings Nedgang et stort Slag, navnlig for Skibsfarten, hvis Fragt beregnedes i Sterling; dertil kom, at mange Skibe var udlegede paa 5 à 10 Aar med en Fragberegning i Sterling.*" See also Keilhau (1938, p. 1).

[5] Hanisch, Søilen, and Ecklund (1999, pp. 115–118).

[6] Van Zanden (1998, p. 106).

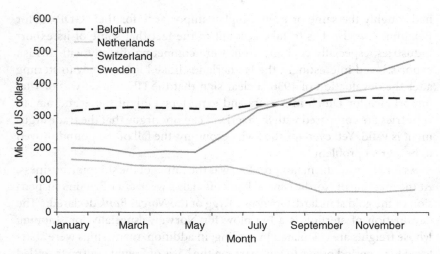

Figure 3.1. Gold and exchange reserves of Belgium, the Netherlands, Sweden, and Switzerland, 1931. (*Federal Reserve Bulletin.*)

The *Riksbank*'s final struggle for the gold standard began on Sunday, 20 September, after being informed of the British decision. The first measure was to keep the stock exchange closed. On Monday morning, the board met to discuss how to react to the new situation. Governor Rooth explained that it might be necessary to follow the Bank of England in increasing the discount rate from 4 to 6 percent. But he also believed that there was still enough time to wait and observe the situation. Accordingly, he proposed raising the discount rate by only 1 percent from 4 to 5 percent, and the board agreed.[7]

The measure did not have any effect, however. The *Riksbank* was losing gold and foreign-exchange reserves, mostly US dollars, at an alarming rate. On Thursday, 24 September, the board met again and decided to increase the discount rate from 5 to 6 percent to be effective from the next day.[8] One day later, in an attempt to disencourage speculators, the Swedish minister of finance declared that his country would never abandon the gold standard.[9] Yet both the discount-rate increase and the statement had only a temporary effect. On Saturday, the drain of reserves continued. Within one week, the *Riksbank*'s gold and foreign-exchange holdings had been reduced by 110 million kronor, corresponding to US$30 million. The gold

[7]   Archives *Sveriges Riksbank, Särskilt protokoll,* 21 September 1931, p. 63.
[8]   Archives *Sveriges Riksbank, Särskilt protokoll,* 24 September 1931, p. 65.
[9]   *Wirtschaftsdienst,* 20 November 1931, p. 1913.

stock had shrunk to 198.6 million kronor, and foreign-exchange reserves were virtually depleted, with only US$3.7 million and £1.1 million.[10] Only a minor part of this reduction, namely, a few million kronor, had been spent for foreign-exchange interventions in New York as well as in Amsterdam, Paris, and Zurich.

Owing to this shortage, the *Riksbank* tried to get a loan from France and the United States, but negotiations failed because the conditions imposed by the French and American interlocutors were too harsh. The German weekly *Wirtschaftsdienst* wrote that Paris and New York acted "as if Sweden was a Balkan state."[11] On Sunday morning, 27 September, one week after the fall of the British pound, central bank officials of the Nordic countries met in Stockholm. Governor Rooth mentioned the declaration by the French government to help all countries seeking to preserve the gold standard, but only under the condition that new loans would be covered by gold. Rooth was convinced that the *Riksbank* would not be able to maintain the current exchange rate for another month, and he agreed with Governor Rygg of the *Norges Bank* that one should not wait until all reserves were depleted. Finally, he pleaded for consultation in case a Nordic country decided to devalue.[12]

The definite decision to suspend the gold standard was taken a few hours later when the board of the *Riksbank* met on Sunday afternoon.[13] Governor Rooth explained that two reasons spoke in favor of a devaluation. First, the *Riksbank* had not received a loan in New York or Paris. It was only possible to obtain money if foreign demand for Swedish gold and foreign-exchange reserves started to weaken. Second, there was no sign that this was going to happen. On Friday, he continued, it had looked for a while as if the drain of reserves was about to end, but this hope had not been fulfilled. Even deposits that had not been due yet were now being withdrawn. The banks could have insisted on the observance of the terms, but this would have contradicted conventional banking practices and only intensified the fears of investors. Rooth concluded that the *Riksbank*

[10] Archives *Sveriges Riksbank, Särskilt protokoll,* 27 September 1931, pp. 69–70: The *Riksbank* lost gold worth 30.9 million kronor – 3.6 million kronor of gold at the main counter in Stockholm and 27.3 million kronor by shipping gold to France and the United States – which reduced the stock of gold from 229.5 to 198.6 million kronor. Additionally, it lost 76 million kronor of foreign-exchange reserves.

[11] *Wirtschaftsdienst,* 20 November 1931, pp. 1912–1913. Gäfvert (1979, pp. 83–108) describes the search for a loan in more detail. The *Riksbank* had tried to obtain it even before the fall of sterling. Archives *Sveriges Riksbank, Särskilt protokoll,* 5 September 1931, pp. 54–55.

[12] Archives National Bank of Denmark, *Direktionsprotokol,* No. 2690 g, 27 September 1931.

[13] Archives *Sveriges Riksbank, Särskilt protokoll,* 27 September 1931, pp. 69–72.

would not have enough means in the near future to fulfill the conditions of the law.

The board agreed with this assessment and decided to increase the discount rate by 2 percent in order to send a reassuring signal to those who feared a surge of inflation after the devaluation and in order to stop speculation counting on a further fall of the krona. This measure was thought to be temporary, however. The board wanted to lower the discount rate as soon as the situation would permit it. The *Norges Bank* took the same measures once it had been informed of Sweden's decision. The gold standard was suspended, and the discount rate was raised from 6 to 8 percent to be effective on Monday, 28 September.[14] Denmark abandoned the gold standard one day later.[15] The discount rate, however, was not raised but remained at 6 percent, as in the United Kingdom. In addition, the legal minimum gold cover was reduced from 50 to 33.33 percent.[16]

The Belgian, Dutch, and Swiss central banks fought the struggle for the gold standard more successfully, with the National Bank of Belgium and the Swiss National Bank having fewer problems than the *Nederlandsche Bank*.[17] In Belgium, the board of directors of the National Bank of Belgium decided on Sunday night, 20 September, to convert all foreign exchange except sterling into gold, and once the Council of Regency had confirmed this decision on Monday morning, the conversion was effected within the following 24 hours. Also on Monday, the National Bank of Belgium issued a press release stating that the gold cover ratio was at 67 percent, hiding the fact that the bank was still sitting on £12.6 million of sterling. The discount rate was left at the current level in order to avoid any sign of panic. Furthermore, the commercial banks formed a consortium to intervene in the market in case of a run on the Belgian currency. It was intended that the banks should spend as much as 1 billion belga (US$139 million), but since markets remained relatively calm, there was no need to intervene. On Wednesday, 23 September, the government and the central bank concluded an agreement that allowed the National Bank of Belgium to sell its sterling reserves at the old parity to the Belgian state. Thus, on Friday, 25 September, Louis Franck, governor of the National Bank of Belgium, could

---

[14] *Norges Bank*, Annual Report, 1931, p. 14. Cf. the report of the Danish representative: Archives National Bank of Denmark, *Direktionsprotokol*, No. 2690g, 27 September 1931, pp. 3–4.

[15] Archives National Bank of Denmark, *Direktionsprotokol*, No. 2690h, 28 September 1931.

[16] *Economist*, 3 October 1931, p. 601.

[17] The description of the Belgian case is based on van der Wee and Tavernier (1975, pp. 240–242) and Janssens (1976, pp. 222–227).

quietly explain on the radio that the Belgian monetary system was almost exclusively based on gold ("... *pratiquement, le billet de banque belge, c'est de l'or*"). His speech seems to have impressed Belgian listeners as well as foreign investors. In London, the quotation of the Belgian stabilization loan immediately experienced a strong rise. The nervousness following the devaluation of sterling was abating.

The Swiss National Bank chose roughly the same procedure as the Belgian central bank. On Wednesday, 23 September, the bank announced in a very short statement that it had sold all of its sterling reserves and was now holding only French francs and US dollars.[18] The bond market reacted positively; only shares were falling. What made Swiss officials nervous, however, was the outbreak of a banking crisis.[19] The weakest spot was Geneva. On 11 July 1931, two days before the crisis of the German *Danatbank* became public, the *Banque de Genève* closed its doors, triggering deposit withdrawals from other banks located in Geneva. On 20 September, one day before the United Kingdom suspended the gold standard, the *Comptoir d'Escompte*, one of the eight leading Swiss commercial banks, merged with the *Union Financière* to form the *Banque d'Escompte Suisse* and underwent a thorough restructuring. One week later, another large Swiss bank, the *Schweizerische Volksbank*, fell victim to the general nervousness. A run on the branch in Zurich lasted several days. The governing board of the Swiss National Bank was urged to issue a public statement but declined and preferred to act behind the scenes by lending one of its general members to the executive board of the *Volksbank*. The run on the bank ended when the *Volksbank* and the state government of Zurich reassured depositors by a press release.

In contrast to the Belgian central bank, however, the Swiss National Bank was in a much better position because it had withdrawn most of its sterling assets. On the eve of 20 September 1931, it had only £3.5 million in sterling[20] (Table 3.3). The table shows that this was not a mere accident but rather was a result of the fact that Swiss investors had begun to import gold from London earlier than other investors, which shows that uneasiness about the position of sterling was more pronounced in Switzerland than elsewhere. The table also shows that Amsterdam and Paris played a more important role in destabilizing the pound sterling especially in the crucial weeks in late July and early August.

---

[18] Müller (2001, pp. 81–82).
[19] On the Swiss banking crisis, see Ehrsam (1985), Halbeisen (1998), and Baumann (2004).
[20] Archives Swiss National Bank, *Protokoll des Direktoriums*, 17 September 1931, p. 823. Also see *Protokoll des Direktoriums*, 27 August 1931, p. 737.

Table 3.3. *United Kingdom Gold Exports (in Thousands of Pounds)*

Date	Holland	Switzerland	Belgium	France	Austria	Germany
April 27–May 4				13		
May 4–11				14	11	12
May 11–18				18		30
May 18–23		21		10	6	7
May 23–June 1				12	33	37
June 1–8		389		21	25	40
June 8–15	17	16		13	66	386
June 15–22	19	266		27	130	539
June 22–29	9	14		12		244
June 29–July 6	11			21		258
July 6–13	5	7		14		453
July 13–20	2,833	46	1,615	3,452	49	66
July 20–27	5,673	207	344	10,990	88	23
July 27–August 1	2,656	201	927	8,904	24	
August 1–10	1,957	81	1,052	1,186	31	
August 10–17	609	40		38	37	
August 17–24	507	1,391		1,163		
August 24–31	1,209	1,078	150	30	18	
August 31–September 7	22	1,310	4	42	7	
September 7–14	118	721		89	9	
September 14–21	1,884	46		20	51	17
September 21–28	2,183	10		17	26	

From The Weekly Bullion Letter of Samuel Montagu & Co., London.
Also exports to the United States of £ 309'500, July 20–27, and £ 211'000, September 21–28.
Source: William Hurst (1932, p. 639).

As noted earlier, the defense of the Dutch guilder was more protracted, which makes it a particularly interesting case in comparison with Sweden.[21] The *Economist* observed on 30 September, 10 days after the devaluation of sterling, that "in some circles the view was expressed that the only thing for the Netherlands to do in the circumstances was to abandon the gold

---

[21] For the following, see de Vries (1989, pp. 461–467).

standard too, and this was already being discounted by large offerings of bonds and demands for shares."[22] The *Nederlandsche Bank* had to issue a statement and to raise the discount rate in order to convince investors that the guilder would not be devalued. Thanks to abundant gold reserves, these measures had the desired effect, whereas in Sweden they failed to impress the markets.

One of the major factors undermining the confidence in the guilder was the rumor that the *Nederlandsche Bank* had failed to sell its sterling reserves before 20 September.[23] The exact amount, £11 million, was not known and also lower than the sterling holdings of the National Bank of Belgium (£12.6 million). However, whereas Belgian bank officials succeeded in keeping the secret and in reassuring investors by issuing a statement, Governor Vissering of the *Nederlandsche Bank* saw no necessity in making a public announcement, arguing that the figures did not indicate great uneasiness among investors. Only after journalists and bankers urged him to do so, pointing out that Belgium, Sweden, and South Africa had made such statements, did he begin considering it. Yet, since he remained convinced that the *Nederlandsche Bank* would not suffer any losses on its sterling holdings, believing that Britain's suspension of the gold standard was only temporary and that the Bank of England would continue to abide by the old rules, the statement that was published in the newspapers on Sunday morning 27 September sounded awkward and failed to convince markets.[24] It read:

In view of the questions which have been put to us, we desire to state that there is no reason for us to conceal the fact that our foreign bill portfolio does consist partly of sterling bills. In consideration of conversations held very recently with the Bank of England, and in view of the particular character of our sterling assets as the gold-bill portfolio of a bank of issue, we have every reason to believe that we need not fear any loss on these assets. The sterling bills held in our portfolio are yielding interest which in the meantime automatically offsets possible temporary losses in book value. For the Netherlands Bank, as a bank of issue, there can never be any reason for parting with its sterling bills at an inopportune moment. We declare most emphatically that our holdings of sterling bills will not impede the Netherlands Bank from fulfilling its function as bank of issue to the fullest extent. At the same time, we declare that we shall unconditionally maintain the gold standard. There is no inflation of Dutch currency, and no such inflation is to

---

[22] *Economist*, 3 October 1931, p. 614. The article was written on 30 September.
[23] On this point, see also *Wirtschaftsdienst*, 6 November 1931, p. 1850.
[24] On Vissering's exchange with the Bank of England, see de Vries (1989, pp. 441–460 and 467–478), Griffiths (1987, pp. 166–169), and Klemann (1990, pp. 38–44).

be expected. The gold position of the Netherlands Bank is stronger than it has ever been before."[25]

Ironically, only a few hours after the release of the statement, Vissering became aware of his misperception of the British situation when he was told by an Amsterdam banker that London's suspension of the gold standard was anything but temporary.

Because of Vissering's bad communication strategy, the situation remained unsolved. The bond market continued to be depressed, the US dollar and the French franc approached the gold export point. Some gold had already been shipped to France. The *Nederlandsche Bank* saw no other possibility than to raise the discount rate from 2 to 3 percent and the rate for advances on merchandise and securities from 2.5 to 4 percent on Monday, 28 September. This step proved to be more reassuring, and on Tuesday, the Dutch guilder began to recover.[26] However, there was one victim of those turbulent weeks: Governor Vissering resigned on 7 October 1931 for health reasons. He had been sick for some time – on 20 September, when the pound fell, he was in Lucerne (Switzerland) to recover. According to de Vries (1989), the big losses of the *Nederlandsche Bank* resulting from its sterling assets were not relevant for Vissering's decision.[27]

In sum, narrative evidence confirms the view that the *Riksbank*'s low level of gold and foreign-exchange reserves explains why Sweden suspended the gold standard in late September 1931. Belgium, the Netherlands, and Switzerland had ample reserves to defend their currencies. Thanks to the high gold cover ratio, the *Nederlandsche Bank* was not even punished for its bad communication policy. It was sufficient to raise the discount rate by 1 percent to reassure the markets. Sweden, by contrast, had seen its reserves diminished since July 1931 and therefore lacked the means to defend the krona after the fall of the British pound. This conclusion leaves us with the question of why Sweden's development in 1931 differed so strongly from that of Belgium, the Netherlands, and Switzerland.

IVAR KREUGER AND SWEDEN'S SHORT-TERM DEBTS

Theoretically, there are two possible explanations why the *Riksbank* experienced a dramatic reduction of its gold and foreign-exchange reserves after

---

[25] De Vries (1989, p. 465). The English translation is taken from the *Economist*, 3 October 1931, p. 614.

[26] *Economist*, 10 October 1931, p. 614.

[27] De Vries (1989, p. 467).

June 1931. Either investors were losing confidence in the commitment of the Swedish authorities to defend the gold standard, or Sweden was a short-term debtor and found itself in an untenable position when the Austrian and German crises led investors to convert short-term foreign assets into cash and gold regardless of the political situation of a country.

At a general level, the first explanation has been put forward by Simmons (1994) in her seminal work on the importance of political and institutional factors for the policy mix during the interwar period.[28] She observes that countries with a dependent central bank, high government instability, a strong Left, and a high number of strikes were more likely to devalue than countries with the opposite characteristics. There is some evidence supporting this view in the case of Sweden. First, in spring of 1931, a great strike broke out in a sawmill in Ådalen, a small town about 100 kilometers northwest of Stockholm. The strike was triggered by the announcement by management that wages would be cut drastically. When the conflict escalated, the provincial government sent troops, and several workers were shot during a clash.[29] Second, the *Riksbank* was more dependent than the central banks of Belgium, the Netherlands, and Switzerland. As we saw in Chapter Two, Sweden's early return to the gold standard in April 1924 essentially had resulted from its strong dependence on the Swedish political authorities. In fact, the Swedish parliament directly supervised the *Riksbank*.

However, despite this evidence, the explanation fails to convince in the case of Sweden. First of all, the chronology is not correct. The strikes were in spring, and the withdrawals of deposits began in mid-July. It is therefore hard to claim that investors were frightened mainly by the growing radicalism of the labor movement. Furthermore, there is no mention of this strike in the international financial press.[30] Second, Sweden's public finances were in good health, which should have reassured investors. Comparing the Swedish situation with the British one, the *Economist* wrote that "from the Treasury point of view, Sweden is better placed."[31] And finally, neither Denmark nor Norway experienced a drain of foreign-exchange reserves, although the political situation in those two countries was about as unstable as in Sweden. Especially the *Norges Bank* should have experienced a credibility problem. On 15 April, a major strike broke out endorsed by roughly

---

[28] Simmons (1994, pp. 11–19).
[29] Hadenius (1990, pp. 33–34).
[30] See, for example, *Economist,* 18 July 1931.
[31] *Economist,* 19 September 1931, p. 506. On the importance of public finances for the confidence of investors, see James (1992).

83,000 workers and lasting until mid-September.[32] In addition, the government resigned in May 1931 over a conflict between the government, the Dutch multinational Unilever, and both the Agrarian and Labor parties.[33] Nevertheless, the level of gold and foreign-exchange reserves of the *Norges Bank* remained relatively stable.

Thus Sweden's loss of reserves must have been due to the unfavorable balance of short-term foreign assets and liabilities.[34] The data in fact show a very clear picture. The Swedish commercial banks had allowed their short-term foreign balances to become negative in late 1930, and in May 1931, the deficit reached a record 141 million kronor (Table 3.4). This was particularly dangerous because a great number of the short-term liabilities were "hot money" pouring into Sweden. By borrowing short and lending long, the Swedish banks got into a situation similar to that of the London banks. The *Economist* observed on 19 September 1931, shortly before the fall of the British pound: "Such, briefly, appears to be the present situation in Sweden – a situation arising less from internal weakness than from causes abroad of which Swedish banking is the victim. It is a situation which closely parallels (*mutatis mutandis*) that of Great Britain."[35]

Accordingly, events in 1931 unfolded in a similar way as in the United Kingdom.[36] Until the summer of 1931, the situation remained stable because Sweden was still considered a "safe haven."[37] One reason was the relatively good condition of the Swedish economy. In 1930, the current account registered a surplus of 100 million kronor, and in the first semester of 1931, conditions did not deteriorate as dramatically as in most other European countries. Accordingly, the growing economic difficulties of Austria and Germany did not immediately exert a negative influence on Sweden. The Stockholm markets remained calm when on 26 May the rumor emerged that a German banking moratorium was to come soon that caused a stock market crash in Germany and pushed the German currency below the gold export point.[38] Likewise, when the German

---

[32] Keilhau (1936, p. 72).

[33] *Wirtschaftsdienst*, 21 August 1931, p. 1481; and *Economist*, 15 August 1931, p. 310. It was the so-called Lilleborg conflict.

[34] In general, *short term* meant a period of three months.

[35] *Economist*, 19 September 1931, p. 506. Cf. the abundant literature on Sweden in 1931: Kock (1931, pp. 141–154; 1933, pp. 343–346), Kjellström (1934, pp. 19–31), Lindahl (1936, pp. 82–87), Thomas (1936, pp. 178–186), and Fleetwood (1947, pp. 71–72).

[36] The BIS Annual Report, 1931–1932, also parallels the situation in Great Britain and Sweden. Cf. Einzig (1932, p. 156). Feinstein and Watson (1995) give a survey of private international capital flows in the interwar period.

[37] Fleetwood (1947, p. 75) and Jonung (1981, p. 299).

[38] Clarke (1967, pp. 189*ff*.).

Table 3.4. *Short-Term Balances of Riksbank and Commercial Banks*
(in Million Kronor)

		Swedish Riksbank	Commercial Banks	Total
1930	January	184	172	357
	February	182	145	326
	March	208	127	335
	April	293	106	399
	May	296	97	393
	June	324	10	333
	July	292	66	359
	August	282	60	342
	September	331	37	368
	October	332	39	371
	November	326	30	356
	December	326	−10	317
1931	January	304	−35	270
	February	286	−16	270
	March	232	−59	174
	April	223	−94	129
	May	218	−141	77
	June	240	−114	127
	July	189	−11	178
	August	93	23	117
	September	33	94	126
	October	25	142	147
	November	24	158	181
	December	49	178	227

Source: Sveriges Riks bank, Årsbok, 1930–1932.

central bank increased the discount rate from 5 to 7 percent on 13 June, a move that made foreign-exchange markets even more nervous, Sweden's position remained firm.

However, when the German banking crisis broke out in July, triggering a general rush for liquidity, the Swedish position deteriorated rapidly. The drain began on Monday, 13 July, when the management of the German Danat Bank announced that it had to close its counters, and the German government called a bank holiday. On the same day, the MacMillan Report was released, which revealed for the first time how great the amount of short-term liabilities of London's banks were.[39] On 15 July, sterling dropped below the gold export point. By the end of July, the Bank of England had lost US$200 million in gold and foreign-exchange reserves, corresponding roughly to one-quarter of its total reserves.

From June to August, the *Riksbank* lost 60 percent of its reserves as commercial banks brought their bills to the central bank to cover their short-term foreign deficits. In an attempt to stop the outflow, the *Riksbank* pursued the same policy as the Bank of England. On 31 July 1931, it increased the discount rate from 3 to 4 percent.[40] The Danish National Bank and the *Norges Bank* did not take this step and kept the discount rate unchanged until September[41] partly because their interest rates were higher (3.5 and 4 percent, respectively) than the Swedish rate. However, as noted, the main reason was that they did not suffer from the same drain of reserves. The tightening of monetary conditions by the Bank of England and the *Riksbank* had some success, but the British pound and the Swedish krona recovered only temporarily.[42] At the end of August, the Stockholm stock exchange experienced a "Black Friday," and in the beginning of September, Sweden tried to obtain a loan from France and the United States.[43] As described earlier, this mission failed, and since after the fall of sterling on 20 September the *Riksbank* was losing reserves at an alarming rate and still was not able to receive support from New York or Paris, the gold standard had to be abandoned on 27 September 1931.

Why was the Swedish banking sector borrowing short and lending long in 1930–1931? The reason was that one of the big commercial banks, *Skandinaviska Kredit AB*, was closely associated with the Swedish industrialist and financier Ivar Kreuger who was in need of liquidity after the

---

[39] There is, however, controversy over how great the influence of the MacMillan Report really was. The *Economist* wrote that publication of the report was overshadowed by the events in Germany. Moreover, the London magazine observed, the report was complex and its conclusions vague. On the devaluation of sterling, see Clarke (1967), Sayers (1976), Cairncross and Eichengreen (1983), Kunz (1987), Williamson (1992), Roberts and Kynaston (1995), Eichengreen and Jeanne (2000), and James (2001).

[40] Archives *Sveriges Riksbank, Särskilt protokoll*, 30 July 1931, p. 43: Governor Rooth explicitly hinted at the policy of the Bank of England when proposing the increase in the discount rate.

[41] Archives National Bank of Denmark, *Direktionsprotokol*, 3–4 September 1931, pp. 126–127; and *Norges Bank*, Annual Report, 1931, p. 6. The Danish discount rate was raised from 4 to 5 percent on 5 September 1931; the *Norges Bank* took the same step on 12 September 1931.

[42] Archives Swiss National Bank, *Protokoll des Direktoriums*, 20 August 1931, p. 715.

[43] *Economist*, 19 September 1931, p. 506.

stock market crash on Wall Street in 1929. Yet, since the *Riksbank*, urged by Prime Minister Carl Gustaf Ekman, who was associated to Kreuger, also gave loans, one could perhaps also interpret the unsound lending practices of *Skandinaviska Kredit AB* as a symptom of the lack of experience of leading figures of the Swedish financial elite in dealing with Stockholm's new role as a safe haven for hot money. Until World War I, Sweden had not played the role of a European financial center and therefore was ill prepared for the new financial geography after the war and particularly after 1929. Paul Einzig, the famous London financial journalist, observed in 1932 that "[the] international character of Stockholm after the war was largely the result of the expansion of Kreuger and Toll."[44] According to Fleetwood (1947), "[a] review of the years 1922 to 1932 shows Sweden gradually emerging as a capital exporting country, continuing direct investments abroad and even developing a market which attracted short-term funds from foreign capitalists seeking a safe haven. Moreover, in AB Kreuger & Toll a financial concern was built up which soon became responsible for transactions on a scale far beyond Sweden's own resources."[45] The whole nation was proud of Kreuger's rise in international finance, as Glete (1978) writes: "A reawakened pride in the achievements of capitalism mixed with nationalistic sentiments was present in the contemporary view of the Kreuger group. The term 'Sweden's second period of greatness' was coined, and it referred mainly to Kreuger's activities in disbursing government loans, activities that fascinated his countrymen."[46] Not surprisingly, this kind of admiration enhanced excessive risk taking and crony capitalism between Kreuger, the financial sector, and the government.

In the Netherlands and Switzerland, by contrast, two countries with a long tradition as international financial centers, commercial bankers seem to have been more experienced in dealing with capital inflows caused by international instability and never used "hot money" for long-term investments but parked these funds at the central bank.[47] The importance of Switzerland as a financial center also was documented by the fact that a Swiss city (Basle) became the seat of the Bank for International Settlements that was founded in 1930. Stockholm was never mentioned as a possible

---

[44] Einzig (1932, p. 180).
[45] Fleetwood (1947, p. 75).
[46] Glete (1978, p. 271). Cf. Lindgren (1982, p. 189).
[47] In the Netherlands, the sight deposits of commercial banks at the central bank continuously increased from Fl. 31 million at the end of December 1931 to Fl. 185 million at the end of August 1931 and in Switzerland from CHF 242 million to CHF 632 million. In Sweden, by contrast, they decreased from SKr. 301 million to SKr. 165 million.

location, and Amsterdam only failed to succeed because it was considered an ally of Germany.[48]

A closer look at Ivar Kreuger's life confirms the impression that his career was extraordinary by Swedish standards.[49] He was born in 1880 and trained as a civil engineer. In 1908, Kreuger founded a firm specializing in new building methods, together with Paul Toll, another young civil engineer. The new enterprise was a big success, AB Kreuger & Toll won several of the most prestigious assignments, among them the construction of the stadium for the 1912 Olympic Games in Stockholm. One of the foundations for this success was the division of labor between the two partners: Toll was in charge of the actual building work, whereas Kreuger took care of the financial aspects. Within a few years, Kreuger had developed contacts with the leading figures in the financial world, especially with Oscar Rydbeck, then managing director of one of the larger provincial banks and soon to be chief executive of one of the big commercial banks in Stockholm, *Skandinaviska Kredit AB*.

In 1913, Kreuger received the offer to become the managing director of the *AB Förenade Svenska Tändsticksfabriker* (United Swedish Match Factories), a new firm created from all the remaining independent match factories in Sweden. The offer was not accidental because Kreuger's father and uncle had been the owners of two match factories. He accepted the offer and began building a match empire. In a first phase, lasting until the mid-1920s, he managed to buy a majority of the shares of *Jönköpings & Vulcans Tändsticksfabriks AB*, the other giant of the Swedish match industry, to collaborate with one of its main competitors on the world market, Bryant & May, Ltd., in Britain and to issue a bond of the International Match Corporation, a newly founded subsidiary of Swedish Match, on the New York Stock Exchange.

Thanks to the international expansion, Kreuger now had access to the capital markets in London and New York, enabling him to finance his

---

[48] Baffi (2002, pp. 22 and 58), Toniolo (2005, pp. 43–44). Houwink ten Cate (1989, p. 177): Amsterdam was favored by the German *Reichsbank*, but the idea was rejected by the Belgians and the French on the grounds that Amsterdam had become a sort of German fiefdom after World War I. This claim was partly correct. In addition, the last German Kaiser, Wilhelm II, had chosen the Netherlands for his exile. Brussels was opposed by Germany. James (2001, p. 44) notes that Zurich was also rejected on the grounds that it was "too German." Geneva had already been chosen as the seat of the League of Nations. On the importance of Amsterdam for the financing of German business, see Broder (1991).

[49] The life of Ivar Kreuger and his businesses were thoroughly researched in the 1970s. Lindgren (1982) provides some research. Söderlund (1978, pp. 442–461) gives a detailed account of the growing dependence of the *Skandinaviska Kreditaktiebolaget* on Kreuger.

further expansion plans. In the second half of the 1920s, his main goal was to acquire leases of public match monopolies in exchange for long-term loans to capital-hungry governments, mainly in Eastern Europe and Latin America. The most important agreement (US$125 million) was made with Germany in 1929. The strategy worked: By the end of 1930, the Kreuger Group had made 18 loans to various governments totaling almost US$340 million and leased 15 national match monopolies and owned a majority of the shares of several other match monopolies. The Kreuger Group also was one of the underwriters of the Young Loan in 1930 (US$15 million corresponding to 5 percent of the total loan).

The second goal in the late 1920s was to invest risk capital in the Swedish stock market that had plunged to a low level during the postwar slump. By 1931, the investments in Swedish shares made by the Kreuger Group amounted to approximately US$125 million. Furthermore, he had put more than US$8 million into the huge Östrand pulp mill. Through these investments, the Kreuger Group bought a controlling interest of *Telefon AB L. M. Ericsson* and became a major shareholder of the *Grängesberg Company*, then the world's leading exporter of iron ore, and of various pulp and timber companies. It also acquired 80 percent of the stock of the Boliden Mining Company from *Skandinaviska Kredit AB*, the house bank of the Kreuger Group.

Yet, though impressive, Kreuger's business network was very vulnerable because it was financed largely by borrowed money, based on the expectation that his stocks kept rising. Thus, when the stock markets began to crash in autumn 1929, Kreuger needed other financial sources and turned to his long-time friend and business partner Oscar Rydbeck, managing director of *Skandinaviska Kredit AB*. Rydbeck was ready to help and almost ruined his bank. By September 1931, when the krona was devalued, almost a third of total lending (340 million kronor of 1,078 million kronor) was to Ivar Kreuger and his businesses.[50] The *Riksbank* played an important part in these transactions. In January and May 1931, when Kreuger needed US$8 million and US$27.5 million as a part of large payments to Poland and Germany, the *Riksbank* guaranteed a rediscount right of US$20 million (SKr. 75 million) to *Skandinaviska Kredit AB*.[51] In February 1932, it again supported Kreuger. Other big banks also gave loans, in particular

---

[50] See the history of *Skandinaviska Kredit AB* by Söderlund (1978). The figures are on pp. 482 and 493.

[51] The Banking Committee of the *Riksdag* documented the loans given to Kreuger by the *Riksbank*: *Bankoutskottet, Utlåtande* 40, 2 May 1932, pp. 20–33. For the figures, see also Gäfvert (1979, pp. 60–82 and 286–287).

Svenska Handelsbanken, the largest Swedish bank, which was closely tied
to Kreuger's pulp company.[52] Even the bank of the competing Wallenberg
family, the *Skandinaviska Enskilda Bank* (SEB), gave loans to Kreuger, especially in late 1930 and early 1931.[53] All together, Swedish commercial banks
increased their loans and advances to Kreuger from 357 million kronor at
the end of 1929 to 828 million kronor at the end of 1931.[54]

It is difficult to establish exactly what share of Sweden's short-term for-
eign debts was due to the financing of Kreuger's activities. According to
Söderlund (1978), though, there is no doubt that it was very substantial.[55]
It is therefore fair to conclude that it was the risky business of Ivar Kreuger
and the financing of his debt by the three big commercial banks and the
Riksbank that ultimately forced Sweden to suspend the gold standard in
September 1931. Obviously, Stockholm was not able to maintain an important role in European finance, whereas the Netherlands and Switzerland
were able to strengthen their positions as international financial centers.
Incidentally, it was a famous private banker in Zurich, Felix Somary, who
was one of the first to predict the end of the Kreuger concern.[56]

SWEDEN'S PRICE-LEVEL TARGETING: WORDS VERSUS DEEDS

When Denmark, Norway, and Sweden suspended the gold standard in
late September 1931, most policymakers were convinced that this was
only a temporary measure. However, as it became clear that the United
Kingdom did not intend to return to the old system in the near future, the
Scandinavian countries had the unique chance to pursue a more independent monetary policy, and according to official declarations, Sweden in fact
adopted an entirely new framework, so-called price-level targeting. When
Finance Minister Felix Hamrin announced on Sunday, 27 September 1931
that the gold standard was suspended, he added that "the monetary policy
was to aim at maintaining, by every possible means, the internal purchasing
power of the Swedish currency,"[57] and in the subsequent weeks and months,

---

[52] See the history of *Svenska Handelsbanken* by Hildebrand (1971).
[53] See the history of SEB from 1924 to 1945 by Lindgren (1988).
[54] Glete (1981, pp. 501–504).
[55] Söderlund (1978, p. 384).
[56] Somary (1986, p. 162). He made his prediction in the spring of 1931 in a conversation with
      high-level German government officials.
[57] This is the translation by Kock (1933, p. 346). The original wording was "*att med till buds
      stående medel bevara den svenska kronans inhemska köpkraft,*" as cited by Kock (1931,
      p. 154).

eminent Swedish economists developed a so-called monetary program for the *Riksbank*.

Yet, while there is no doubt that Sweden's official adoption of a new monetary target was a historical step and that the domestic price level remained quite stable, there is no consensus on whether or not the *Riksbank* truly adopted price-level targeting. Three different views can be distinguished. First, there is a group of economists, starting with Irving Fisher in the 1930s, claiming that there was in fact a major regime shift.[58] Swedish economist Lars Jonung, the main proponent of the second view, is more critical but supports the notion that a regime change occurred. While acknowledging that the *Riksbank* sometimes broke the principles of price-level targeting, he believes that the official goal of price stabilization, set up by the government and monitored by the parliament, served as a restriction on the *Riksbank*.[59] The third view was first developed by Princeton economist Richard Lester, who went to Sweden in the mid-1930s to study the monetary experiment. He was convinced that the Swedish *Riksbank* did not fully grasp the opportunity for conducting a better monetary policy and that it continued to follow the old rules of the gold standard.[60] In a similar vein, Swedish economists Erik Lindahl and Erik Lundberg concluded that the successful outcome of the Swedish monetary experiment was rather a consequence of fortunate circumstances than of a foresighted monetary policy.[61] Recent research, based on new narrative evidence and econometric tests, confirms Lester's skepticism.[62] In the remainder of the section I will argue that the last view is the most convincing one.

First of all, it took quite some time to develop the details of the new policy. What the minister of finance announced in September 1931 was only a vague statement that was not backed by a fully developed program. The sentence stating that monetary policy would be aimed at stabilizing the internal purchasing power of the krona was either Eli Heckscher's or Gustav Cassel's idea.[63] One day before the decision to abandon the gold standard

---

[58] Fisher (1934), Johnson and Keleher (1996, p. 280), Svensson (1995, p. 1), Bernanke et al. (1999, p. 180). In recent years, the *Riksbank* also expressed this view; see *Riksbank*, Annual Report, 1998, p. 4, and the speech given by Governor Bäckström (2000, p. 1).

[59] This position is most clearly spelled out in Jonung (1979a, pp. 477–479). See also Berg and Jonung (1999) and Fregert and Jonung (2004).

[60] Lester (1939, pp. 279–280).

[61] Lindahl (1936, p. 95) and Lundberg (1957, p. 107).

[62] Straumann and Woitek (2009).

[63] Lester (1939, p. 230) claims that Heckscher was the author; Berg and Jonung (1999, p. 529) think it was Cassel but also add that "the full account of the monetary program of 1931 remains to be written."

was formally taken by the *Riksbank*, the minister of finance had asked them how to draft the official statement. The main concern of economists as well as the government and the *Riksbank* was to reassure the public that they would not allow a surge of inflation. Consequently, it also was announced that the discount rate would be raised from 6 to 8 percent effective Monday, 28 September.

Even in the weeks and months after the initial statement, the so-called monetary program continued to be vague and confusing, although initially the *Riksbank* seemed to be interested in clarifying the issue. On 8 October, the board decided to ask three economists, Cassel, Davidson, and Heckscher, how to conduct monetary policy and sent them a detailed questionnaire.[64] The answers were returned after two weeks. All three economists recommended that the *Riksbank* opt for a so-called free standard based on price stabilization until circumstances allowed a return to the gold standard. As for the question of which indicators should be chosen, the *Riksbank* lacked the expertise to make reliable inflation forecasts. Heckscher suggested using wholesale prices as an indicator for future inflation and retail prices as an indicator for present inflation, arguing that wholesale prices changed far in advance of retail prices.

The opinions of the economists seem to have had little effect on actual monetary policy. In October 1931, the *Riksbank* lowered the discount rate in two steps back to 6 percent as the fears of inflation began to abate, but the level still was unusually high.[65] Politicians began to favor a more reflationary interpretation of the new policy, but the debate remained inconclusive.[66] In the Finance Bill introduced in the *Riksdag* in January 1932, the minister of finance repeated his original statement but also added that the new program did not preclude "certain modifications" in wholesale prices, meaning a moderate rise.[67] In February, the board of the *Riksbank* explained to the Banking Committee of the Parliament that it would allow prices to rise insofar as the rise was caused by higher exchange rates or higher prices abroad. The board also stated, however, that it would consider other indices besides its own weekly consumer price index that had been created shortly after suspension of the gold standard. In April, the board declared that the program was aimed at preventing price declines abroad from depressing the Swedish price level and added as another goal the maintenance of interest

---

[64]   The questionnaire is printed in Berg and Jonung (1999, p. 549).
[65]   For almost half a year, the discount rate remained at 6 percent. It was cut further in March, May, June, and September 1932 to 3.5 percent, each time by 0.5 percent.
[66]   Kock (1933, pp. 347–353), Lester (1939, pp. 232–234).
[67]   Kock (1933, p. 347).

rates for the benefit of industry. In May, the Banking Committee criticized the *Riksbank* for its failure to prevent prices from falling in the preceding months, but it also emphasized that monetary policy should not be bound up schematically to any particular index figure but was to be based on the internal price level and the needs of Swedish economic life.[68]

After wholesale prices had declined by about 5 percent from October 1932 to March 1933, the government appointed a Currency Committee (*Valutasakkunniga*). For the first time, the new framework was formulated in a clear way as the committee pronounced that the objective of Swedish monetary policy "should be to bring about a moderate rise in the internal wholesale price level."[69] In the parliamentary discussion of the report, the minister of finance, however, repeated the view of the Banking Committee of 1932 that monetary policy should not be schematically bound to any index and that the krona should continue to be regulated according to its internal purchasing power and the needs of Swedish industry.[70]

Yet, even if the monetary program had been developed more rapidly, it is still doubtful whether the *Riksbank* would have adopted it. Lester (1939) observes that "the *Riksbank* authorities operated during that period much as if Sweden were still on the gold standard and, therefore, they considered the Bank's foreign-exchange reserve as the limiting factor to an expansionary policy."[71] Two pieces of evidence strongly support this view. First of all, the *Riksbank* tied the krona to sterling in July 1933, that is, less than two years after suspension of the gold standard (Figure 3.2). If the *Riksbank* had been convinced that price-level targeting was a good substitute for the gold standard, it would not have taken this step. Of course, the monetary program continued to be the official guideline, and since the British price level was rising only gradually, the *Riksbank* could achieve both exchange-rate stability and price stability. Yet, when British prices began to rise more rapidly after June 1936 and the Swedish *Riksbank* ought to have either devalued or unpegged the krona in order to preserve price stability, it took neither of these two steps but preferred to have a stable exchange rate vis-à-vis the pound.[72]

The second piece of evidence is that the *Riksbank* tried twice to restore the old parity with sterling. The first attempt was made in November 1931, thus only a few weeks after suspension of the gold standard and the statement

---

[68] *Bankoutskottet, Utlåtande* 40, 2 May 1932, pp. 17–19.
[69] Cited in Lester (1939, p. 233).
[70] Proposition 260, pp. 24–25.
[71] Lester (1939, p. 279).
[72] *Ibid.*, pp. 258–261.

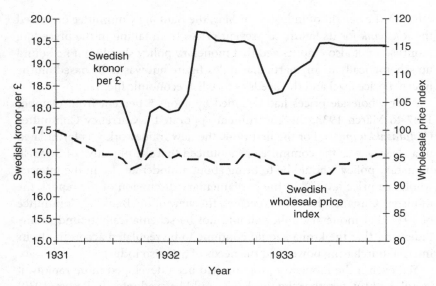

Figure 3.2. Sterling rate of Swedish krona and Swedish wholesale price index (January 1931=100), 1931–1933. (*Riksbankens Årsbok.*)

of the minister of finance that the price level was to be kept stable. Since late September, the krona had depreciated against the British pound and reached the old parity of 18.16 kronor on 17 November. On the same day, the board of the *Riksbank* declared that the krona rate should be fixed at the current level to be effective on the next day. The pegging lasted only three days because the *Riksbank* had too few reserves to prevent the krona from further depreciating and thus abandoned the plan. Ironically, however, the krona began to appreciate again in late November and was quoted at 17.94 kronor at the end of the year[73] (see Figure 3.2).

This intervention, aimed at stabilizing the exchange rate at the old level, clearly was against the spirit of the new monetary program. Wholesale prices had just started to recover after a long period of deflation, so the plan to prevent the krona from depreciating threatened to reverse this positive trend. Apparently, the board of the *Riksbank* was trying to save as much of the old monetary order as possible. After suspension of the gold standard, the main concern of Governor Ivar Rooth was to prevent inflation, and apparently, Economics Professor David Davison supported him in this view.[74] However, as the subsequent actions of the *Riksbank* would show,

[73] *Riksbank,* Annual Report, 1931, p. 16*.
[74] Lester (1939, p. 244).

even after this failure, Rooth did not give up on the idea that a peg to sterling, if possible at the old parity, was the best monetary arrangement for Sweden, for the most important lesson the *Riksbank* seems to have drawn from this episode was that first it had to replenish its reserves before trying to defend a fixed exchange rate.[75]

This conclusion leads directly to the second attempt that was made in late 1932. This time, the violation of the monetary program was even more striking because the forced appreciation of the krona deflated prices and depressed the economy even more than in the first attempt. To understand this episode, we have to go back to the first quarter of 1932 when the krona depreciated by 10 percent against sterling (see Figure 3.2). The main reason for this weakness was the final crash of Kreuger's business in March 1932, which frightened holders of krona assets and forced the *Riksbank* to purchase government securities amounting to roughly 200 million kronor. As for the business cycle, these reflationary measures proved to be a blessing because they isolated Sweden from the sharp fall of prices that was occurring abroad.[76] However, it appears that the board of the *Riksbank* was unhappy about the weakness of the krona and continued to be less concerned about the price level than about the exchange rate. It continued to purchase foreign-exchange reserves, with the consequence that the krona remained quite stable. Some Swedish economists, namely, Kock (1933), don't believe that the *Riksbank's* primary concern was to build up reserves. They think that the *Riksbank* finally accepted the new policy framework because the Banking Committee of the *Riksdag,* which was the body supervising the *Riksbank,* had criticized the board in May 1932 for its failure to prevent the fall of prices since suspension of the gold standard in September 1931.[77]

Yet this view is not convincing because it cannot explain why the *Riksbank* all of a sudden tried to bring the krona back to the old parity with the pound in late 1932 and early 1933. Kock (1933) argues that this was due to the rapid depreciation of the pound and that the main goal of the *Riksbank* was to steer a middle course between the pound and the US dollar.[78] Yet Lester (1939) is right in observing that in December the krona not only appreciated vis-à-vis the British pound but also vis-à-vis the US dollar owing to interventions by the *Riksbank*. It seems that the *Riksbank* had been accumulating foreign-exchange reserves over the preceding

---

[75] Lundberg (1957, p. 100) and Jonung (1979, p. 472).
[76] British wholesale prices decreased by 7 percent from March until June 1932.
[77] Kock (1933, pp. 350–351). Kjellström (1934, pp. 60*ff.*) also shares this opinion.
[78] Kock (1933, p. 352).

months in order to bring the krona back to the old parity. The attempt failed, just as in November 1931, because the British pound recovered in January 1933. The *Riksbank* tried once more to reverse exchange-rate movements in February and April, again to no avail. By June, the krona reached the same level as before the intervention. As a result of these interventions, Swedish wholesale prices fell by 5 percent, and recovery from the depression was delayed by a few months.[79]

Finally, there are several instances in which Governor Rooth himself openly admitted that the *Riksbank* continued to adhere to traditional principles.[80] In late September 1933, Rooth wrote to O. M. W. Sprague, Harvard professor of economics and temporary assistant to the U.S. secretary of the treasury. The U.S. government had suspended the gold standard in the spring of 1933 and was interested in Sweden's experience with managing its currency. Rooth answered that exchange-rate stability had been the priority, not price-level targeting on the basis of floating exchange rates: "My personal opinion is that it is of the utmost importance to the whole economic life of a nation which like Sweden for its standard of living is to such a great extent depending upon foreign trade, to have fairly stable quotations. I think that I dare say that also in order to get a rising price-level, stable foreign exchanges are better than the erratic movements of these rates which the world has suffered from ever since September 1931."[81] In February 1938, Rooth wrote to Randolph Burgess, vice president of the Federal Reserve Bank of New York: "Some American professors, e.g., Professor Irving Fisher, believe that it is an achievement by us in the *Riksbank* that prices have been fairly steady up to the middle of 1936. I have told Professor Fisher before and I am sorry to have to tell you now that what we have done is merely that we have carried out a fairly conservative central banking policy. In fact we have never tried to do anything directly with regard to prices."[82]

In sum, the claim that after suspension of the gold standard the *Riksbank* broke with exchange-rate targeting on the basis of the new monetary program is hard to maintain. The declaration that Swedish monetary policy would now be aimed at maintaining the internal price level, remarkable by itself, was not much more than a declaration of intent. The central bank continued to focus on the old parity with the British pound. Sweden's true

---

[79] Lester (1939, pp. 251–255).
[80] Ivar Rooth left his papers to the *Riksbank* archive, and they have not been fully exploited yet.
[81] Archives Bank of England, OV 29/26, 26 September 1933.
[82] Archives *Riksbank*, Rooth papers, Box 129, 10 February 1938.

break with the past did not come until the early 1990s when the *Riksbank* adopted inflation targeting.[83]

DENMARK'S AND NORWAY'S MONETARY POLICIES

What is true for Sweden also applies to Denmark and Norway: The opportunity to abandon exchange-rate targeting and to adopt an independent monetary policy was not seized. Danish economist Carl Iversen wrote: "From the beginning, the public debate on the goal of Danish exchange-rate policy was on the wrong track as many considered only the alternatives of pegging the krone to the British pound or the US dollar."[84] Iversen's Norwegian colleague Keilhau observed that as early as spring 1932 there was strong sympathy for a de facto stabilization with the British pound at roughly 20 kroner per pound (*shillingkrone*), and eventually, this was the rate at which the krone was stabilized in July 1933.[85]

Yet, besides this similarity, there also were two striking differences between the three Scandinavian countries. First, Norway, because it kept the krone stable vis-à-vis sterling at a discount of roughly 10 percent from early on, was most successful in stabilizing prices (Figure 3.3). The performance was far from optimal, but in comparison with Denmark, Norwegian wholesale prices did not register the same deflation in the first quarter of 1932, and in comparison with Sweden, they did not experience the same drop from late 1932 to early 1933. The reason for the latter difference was mentioned already in the preceding section. The *Riksbank*, still longing for the old monetary order, tried to bring the krona back to the old parity with sterling, although to no avail. The *Norges Bank*, by contrast, had no such ambitions and let the krone appreciate only slightly when sterling weakened (Figure 3.4). Similarly, the deep fall of the Danish price level was due to the ambition of the Danish government to maintain the old parity with sterling in the first half of 1932, although the Danish price level was considerably higher than the British level. On 30 January 1932, the *Rigsdag* had passed a law that tried to rebalance trade by import duties and capital controls instead of a devaluation.[86] The details of this law will be discussed below in more detail.

---

[83] See Chapter Eight.

[84] Iversen (1936b, p. 33): "*Die Diskussion über das Ziel der dänischen Währungspolitik in der grossen Öffentlichkeit kam von Anfang an auf ein unglückliches Geleise, indem viele nur die Alternative, entweder die Krone an das englische Pfund oder an das Gold (den Dollar) zu binden, vor Augen hatten.*"

[85] Keilhau (1936, p. 73).

[86] Iversen (1936b, p. 42).

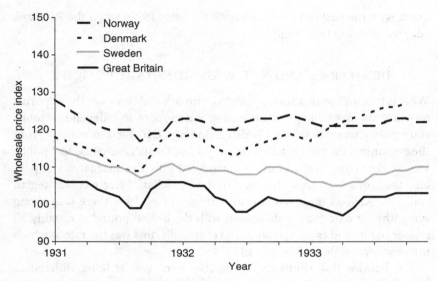

Figure 3.3. Wholesale prices of the United Kingdom, Denmark, Norway, and Sweden, 1931–1933 (1913 = 100). (*Federal Reserve Bulletin.*)

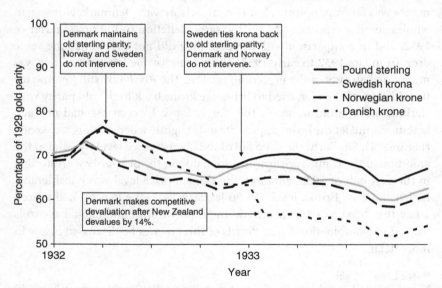

Figure 3.4. Exchange rates of sterling and Scandinavian currencies (percentage of gold parity), 1932–1933. (*Federal Reserve Bulletin.*)

The *Norges Bank* had abandoned the old parity with sterling as early as November 1931.[87] The krone initially continued to follow sterling more or less closely until March 1932, when Prime Minister Peder L. Kolstad unexpectedly died (5 March) and Kreuger committed suicide in Paris (12 March), and the ensuing nervousness spilled over into Norway.[88] Another contributing factor was that the ministry of finance appointed a Foreign Exchange Committee on 6 April to clarify the future status of the krone.[89] Since the krone fell by about 5 percent in March and continued to depreciate in April, the *Norges Bank* on 20 April urged the government to issue a statement to stop the downward movement of the krone. In late April, the markets began to ease, the depreciation rate decelerated, and the krone hit bottom in June.[90] It was now at the level of a *shillingkrone* (kr. 20 per pound), which was the rate the Foreign Exchange Committee preferred. One year later, in July 1933, this rate became the new guideline for Norway's exchange-rate policy.

The second difference between Scandinavian countries concerned the use of competitive devaluations. While Norway and Sweden abstained from using this instrument, Denmark devalued the krone by 17 percent in February 1933. It is true that this drastic measure was not taken voluntarily. New Zealand, its main competitor in the British butter market, had made a competitive devaluation of 15 percent in January 1933 (see Figure 3.4). Yet, in the European context, the Danish exchange-rate policy was quite remarkable. No other country used devaluations to improve the competitiveness of its exporting sector. The run-up to this devaluation will be discussed in more detail in the remainder of this section.

To simplify the narrative, four phases are distinguished. The first phase begins with devaluation of the Danish krone. As in Stockholm, policymakers in Copenhagen feared a strong rise of inflation, so credit rationing, which had been established a few days before the devaluation, was maintained. Soon, however, policymakers realized that this restrictive policy could not be pursued any longer because a major commercial bank in Copenhagen, *Handelsbanken*, had run into liquidity problems in the beginning of October. This serious threat to financial stability forced Danish authorities to reverse their policy completely, which marks the beginning of the second phase. The Danish National Bank gave a "standby declaration" to the management of

---

[87] *Norges Bank*, Annual Report, 1931, p. 15.
[88] Rygg (1950, p. 474).
[89] Keilhau (1952, p. 199): The chairman was again – as in 1925 – Gunnar Jahn, director of the statistical bureau. Keilhau was the only economist on the committee. See Chapter 2.
[90] Rygg (1954, p. 477).

the troubled bank, and the ministry of trade publicly announced that the Danish National Bank would soon relax credit conditions because abandonment of the gold standard offered more monetary freedom. With the liquidity problems solved, attention shifted from monetary policy to commercial policy. On 5 October, the board of the Danish National Bank met with ministry of trade officials and executives of big commercial banks to work out the so-called *Octoberplan*.[91] The plan was supposed to fulfill two goals, namely, to relax credit conditions for domestic producers and to protect foreign-exchange reserves by a further rationing of import credits.

Yet again, the policy was a failure. The relaxation of credit for domestic producers increased the demand for foreign goods, and because control of the import sector was not effective enough, the foreign-exchange reserves of the Danish National Bank dropped from 50 million kroner at the end of October to 20 million kroner in mid-November. The bank was forced to ship 20 million kroner abroad to replenish its stock of reserves.[92] Instead of allowing the krone to depreciate, thus abandoning the goal of maintaining the old parity with sterling, the ministry of trade and the Danish National Bank took more drastic measures to control capital exports and the import of certain goods that were not considered necessary, in particular luxury goods. The Parliament passed a first bill on 18 November, but the measures proved insufficient. A second bill was passed at the end of January 1932 covering all imports, not just luxury goods. The passing of the bill was accelerated by Germany's decision to drastically increase the duties on butter on 19 January.[93]

The new control system was thought to be temporary but was renewed constantly, which shows that the policy was not based on a clear plan.[94] The second bill led to establishment of an Exchange Control Office (*Valutakontor*), which supervised imports and decided on how to distribute the scarce foreign-exchange reserves.[95] Of course, the rationing of imports and foreign-exchange reserves was not popular, not least because of the laborious administration, but it was finally accepted because it worked reasonably well. In 1932, a reduction of the trade deficit to 6 million kroner was achieved, and since there was a considerable gain in invisible items,

[91] Hoffmeyer (1968, p. 165).
[92] National Bank of Denmark (*Nationalbankens Regnskab*), Annual Report, 1931–1932, pp. 4–5. Hoffmeyer (1968, p. 168).
[93] Menzel (1988, p. 260).
[94] Iversen (1932, p. 660).
[95] Iversen (1936b, pp. 41–42): *Lov om Foranstaltninger til Værn for den danske Valuta.* "*Lovtidende for Kongeriget Danmark,*" *Året* 1932, pp. 13*ff.*

the current account was in surplus. Foreign-exchange reserves of the central bank and the private banks were on the rise again.[96] As noted earlier, however, the strategy had a high cost: Danish wholesale prices decreased by almost 5 percent in the first two quarters of 1932 (see Figure 3.3).

Thus, not surprisingly, opposition to the control regime and the exchange rate grew as prices fell and the depression deepened. Farmers and business leaders, especially of the construction sector, started a campaign for a more expansionary monetary policy in February 1932, which marks the beginning of the third phase. The initiative came from the Currency Committee of the Parliament (*Valutaudvalg*), which sent two letters to the Danish National Bank demanding a change of course. Although the committee had no supervisory function, the bank reluctantly fell in line and sent two circular letters to all private banks advising them to redirect their credit policy to the needs of the industrial sector. Moreover, the bank gradually lowered the discount rate, starting in March 1932, against the opposition by the ministry of finance and the ministry of trade.[97]

After these measures had been taken, political attention turned to the Currency Bill, which had to be renewed at the end of March. Farmers were not only seeking a lower exchange rate but also demanded the end of the obligation to hand over their foreign-exchange holdings because the big commercial banks functioning as administrators of the system bought British pounds from exporters – mainly farmers – at a lower price than they sold them to importers. This difference made farmers believe that the exchange rate of the krone was artificially kept at a level below the market price. They could not accept the official claim that the Danish government wanted to prevent abuse of the system.[98]

The government realized that it would be hard to continue with this system and began negotiations with the Danish National Bank on how to abandon the obligation to deliver foreign-exchange holdings without destabilizing the exchange rate. The Currency Committee of the *Rigsdag* also demanded an answer to this question. The way the Danish National Bank replied is illustrative because it shows how afraid its management was of floating exchange rates: The bank claimed that abandonment of the obligation to deliver foreign exchange and the shift to free floating would entail the danger of depreciation and inflation. The executives of big commercial banks argued along the same lines. As a result, the Currency Bill was

---

[96] Iversen (1936a, pp. 75 and 82).
[97] Hoffmeyer (1968, pp. 170–171). The discount rate was cut further from 6 to 5 percent on 11 March 1932 and from 5 to 4 percent on 30 May 1932.
[98] Iversen (1936b, p. 45), Menzel (1988, p. 262), Hoffmeyer (1968, p. 171).

renewed until the end of May 1932. The opposition had demanded that they should examine how the transition to a flexible-exchange rate could be realized within the existing arrangement, but to no avail.[99]

In the following months, the Danish National Bank did not depart from this rigid position, but the government had to make a compromise with the oppositional Farmers' Party because general elections to be held in autumn were approaching. Everybody knew that the obligation to deliver the foreign-exchange holdings and the future of the exchange rate would be very successful campaign issues. Accordingly, when at the end of May the Currency Bill was again renewed until the end of October, the major parties agreed on eliminating the obligation to deliver foreign exchange by the end of August. Throughout the summer, the government and the Danish National Bank met several times to discuss the issue.

The Danish National Bank was reluctant to give in, but its arguments were too weak. Not only the upcoming elections but also new developments in British commercial policy led the Danish government to ignore the position of the Danish National Bank. In March 1932, the British government had introduced a general 10 percent *ad valorem* duty on all imports except those from the Dominions and the Crown Colonies of the Empire.[100] In the summer, from 21 July to 20 August, government officials of the United Kingdom, the Crown Colonies, and the Dominions met in Ottawa to deepen their trade relations and to further increase the import duties for other countries. The agreements foresaw that British duties on egg imports from Denmark would be increased from 10 to 15 percent and that the import quotas on bacon were further curtailed. At the same time, the direct competitors in Australia, Canada, New Zealand, and South Africa gained better access to the British market.[101] Since the Ottawa conference was held at the same time as the meetings between the Danish government and the Danish National Bank took place, the case for devaluation became stronger in Denmark. This trend was reinforced by the fact that the Norwegian and the Swedish kronor had depreciated by several percentage points since spring.[102] On 27 August, the obligation to deliver foreign exchange was finally eliminated, and the transition to a more realistic exchange rate succeeded.[103] The krone was allowed to depreciate by 6 percent and then kept within a narrow band until the end of the year (DKr. 19.20 to 19.30 per pound).

[99] Hoffmeyer (1968, p. 171).
[100] Menzel (1988, p. 252).
[101] For butter imports into Great Britain, see Kindleberger (1934).
[102] Hoffmeyer (1968, p. 172).
[103] *Ibid.*, p. 174.

The opposition was still not satisfied. Farmers and Conservatives representing business interests demanded a further relaxation of monetary conditions. This time the issue was not the rationing of credit, but the level of interest rates. The Danish National Bank had already lowered the discount rate to 3.5 percent on 12 October 1932, and since September, it had bought credit association bonds in the open market on a large scale: The stock of bonds increased by about 80 million kroner from September to December. The effect was modest because private banks, savings as well as commercial banks, lowered their interest rates only moderately. As a result, the idle money ended up as sight deposits at the Danish National Bank, and the purchase of bonds was halted in early 1933.[104]

Not least owing to these relatively high interest rates, the depression deepened further, and political tensions among parties and interest groups intensified. In late 1932, the fourth phase of Danish exchange-rate policy began with the demand of employers for a 20 percent wage reduction, which, in turn, triggered a political process that eventually led to a 17 percent devaluation of the krone. Employers played an important role at the beginning of the process because trade unions refused to even enter into discussion with them. The conciliator sent by the government tried to bring the parties together, but it proved impossible, so they gave up in January 1933. It was left to the government to come up with a solution. After long negotiations between the ruling coalition (Social Democrats, Liberals) and the Farmers' Party (*Venstre*), the so-called Kanslergade agreement was concluded on 30 January, named after the private home of the prime minister, where the negotiations had taken place.[105] The compromise allowed the government to implement its labor market policy, foresaw a competitive devaluation in order to boost the exports of farmers, and included some loose agreements about market arrangements for agricultural products.[106] That a devaluation was part of the compromise also was due to the fact that New Zealand had just devalued its currency by 15 percent. Denmark was forced to react in order to maintain its share on the British butter market. From then on, however, the rate of the Danish krone against sterling was not changed until World War II, although farmers demanded a further devaluation in 1935.[107]

[104] Johansen (1987, p. 65).
[105] Hoffmeyer (1968, p. 176).
[106] Johansen (1987, pp. 57–58).
[107] Iversen (1936b, p. 46).

FOUR

Dissolution of the Gold Bloc

Even more than the small Scandinavian states, Belgium, the Netherlands, and Switzerland failed to pursue a flexible-exchange-rate policy during the economic crisis of the 1930s. Although the devaluation of the British pound and a series of other currencies in September 1931 lowered the competitiveness of their exporting sectors, they were determined to defend the old monetary order. Not even devaluation of the US dollar in the spring of 1933 changed their minds. On the contrary, on 3 July 1933, Belgium, the Netherlands, and Switzerland joined France, Italy, and Poland in forming the "gold bloc" and signed a declaration stating that they would continue to maintain the gold standard at the current parities (Table 4.1). The statement was a reaction to Roosevelt's "bombshell message" to the London Economic Conference in which the U.S. president displayed no interest in international currency stabilization. Predictably, the plan of the gold bloc countries was unrealistic and highly damaging to their economies because maintenance of the gold standard required drastic deflationary measures.[1] In March 1935, Belgium threw in the towel, introduced exchange-rate controls, and then devalued. Eighteen months later, France announced that it would take the same step; the Netherlands and Switzerland followed one day later. The devaluation liberated the Belgian, Dutch, and Swiss policymakers from the straitjacket of the gold standard and had immediate positive effects.

This episode raises three major issues. First, why did Belgium, the Netherlands, and Switzerland fail to devalue earlier? Eichengreen and Temin (2000), as well as Mouré (2002), argue that a so-called gold standard

---

[1]   Bordo, Helbling, and James (2006) calculated the cost of the late devaluation in the case of Switzerland. If Switzerland had devalued with Britain in 1931, the output level in 1935 would have been some 18 percent higher than it actually was in that year. If Switzerland had waited until 1933 to devalue, the output level in 1935 would have been about 15 percent higher.

Table 4.1. *Chronology of the Gold Bloc*

1933	
March 6	United States introduces exchange controls
April 20	United States suspends gold standard
July 2	"Bombshell message" of president Roosevelt: No participation in international stabilization of exchange rates
July 3	France together with Belgium, Italy, the Netherlands, Poland, and Switzerland forms the gold bloc
1934	
May 26	Italy introduces exchange controls
1935	
March 18	Belgium introduces exchange controls
March 29	Belgian government devalues franc by 28%
1936	
September 25	France devalues franc by 30%; Tripartite Agreement between France, Great Britain, and United States
September 27	Netherlands suspends gold standard, guilder depreciates by roughly 20%; Switzerland devalues franc by 30%

Sources: Eichengreen (1992), Feinstein, Temin, and Toniolo (1997), Aldcroft and Oliver (1998).

mentality or gold standard belief determined the decisions of policymakers. Yet, since this explanation is based on the experience of the United States and the large European countries, it has not been clarified whether it holds for small states as well. In their recent paper on the Swiss exchange-rate policy, Bordo, Helbling, and James (2006) highlight the difficulty of making exchange-rate policy in a democratic setting and the problem of forming an effective alliance within a political arena that is characterized by a high degree of fractionalization of different interest groups. In turn, many Dutch and Swiss historians emphasize the advantages of a hard currency for commercial banks and multinational manufacturers. They believe that neither ideas nor institutional constraints but rather economic interests lead to the dismal policy outcome. I will strongly argue in favor of the first explanation. The comparison suggests that there was no fundamental difference between large and small European states. Regardless of the economic structure and the size of the country, policymakers were sincerely convinced that a devaluation would only worsen the situation, and therefore devaluation was to be avoided by all means. They also failed to understand the negative consequences of deflation. Instead of suspending the gold standard, business leaders and their political allies were demanding a series of state subsidies and protectionist measures despite their strongly held belief in a free-market economy.

The second important question is why Belgium left the gold standard earlier than the Netherlands and Switzerland. Economic historians have come up with three explanations. The most popular explanation highlights the combination of several factors: the importance of the British export market and of the British competitors on the world market, the growing power of the Belgian Left, and the deepening of the banking crisis. Second, Hogg (1987), the only economic historian arguing from a comparative perspective, has claimed that only the banking crisis truly distinguished Belgium from the Netherlands and Switzerland and that differences in trade and politics were of secondary importance. And finally, Chlepner (1943), who witnessed the devaluation as a professor and adviser of a major Belgian bank, argues that the banking crisis was not a cause but a consequence of the currency crisis and that this currency crisis was due to the increasingly apparent failure of the government to lower wages and prices.

Which of these three explanations is the most convincing? I will argue that they all highlight important aspects, but they fail to capture the dynamics of the Belgian "triplet crisis." Neither did the banking crisis lead directly to the currency crisis, as Hogg claims, nor was it purely a result of the currency crisis, as Chlepner argues. It is also imprecise to explain the devaluation by making a list of several independent factors. Rather, the drama followed a quite precise script that shows some similarities to the crises of emerging markets in recent years. It all began with a moderate banking crisis in the spring of 1934, but only when the government went through two crises in June and November did the stability of the currency begin to be threatened. The National Bank of Belgium suffered from gold losses and the Belgian banks ran into liquidity problems as their clients began to withdraw deposits. As this process developed, the banking crisis widened and also threatened the largest banks, so ultimately, the Belgian government was forced to devalue. In short, the road to devaluation began with a moderate banking crisis and ended with a severe banking crisis, but this deterioration could only happen because of two government crises in between.

The third and last issue concerns the exchange-rate regimes adopted after the devaluation. What lessons did policymakers learn from the failure of the gold bloc? The evidence shows that there was no fundamental break with the past but rather a cautious evolution toward a somewhat more flexible regime. There was still a strong consensus among policymakers that exchange rates needed to be fixed, and accordingly, policymakers were only debating whether the currency should be linked to gold or to the British pound and whether this step should be taken immediately or not, with the Netherlands deciding to wait and Belgium and Switzerland fixing a new gold parity, although the latter preferred to keep it provisional.

The chapter has five sections. The first section deals with the state of economic ideas during the 1930s and their implications for the decisions of policymakers in small states. The second, third, and fourth sections try to explain Belgium's early exit in March 1935. The fifth and final section takes a closer look at the exchange-rate regimes Belgium, the Netherlands, and Switzerland adopted after the devaluation in March 1935 and September 1936, respectively.

IDEAS AND INTERESTS

Why did Belgium, the Netherlands, and Switzerland fail to devalue earlier? They were open economies, entertained close trade relations with the United Kingdom and the sterling bloc, and could observe how the Scandinavian states were recovering from the depression after 1932. Especially at the London Economic Conference in the summer of 1933, they had the opportunity to learn about the advantages arising from suspension of the gold standard. Yet, instead, they formed the gold bloc together with France, Italy, and Poland and declared that maintenance of the existing parities was "essential for the economic and financial recovery of the world and of credit and for the safeguarding of social progress in their respective countries."[2] Consequently, the depression lasted longer than elsewhere.[3]

The question of why the gold bloc countries pursued such a counterproductive policy has been hotly debated ever since the 1930s. Today, most economic historians probably would subscribe to the view developed by Eichengreen and Temin (2000) and Mouré (2002). They argue that the economic ideas of policymakers were shaped by a so-called gold standard mentality or a gold standard belief. As the statements of the gold bloc countries suggest, its essence was the sincere convinction that the gold standard

[2] BIS, Annual Report, 1933–1934, p. 13. On 8 July 1933, the gold bloc members met in Paris and issued another statement. See Brown (1940, p. 1288). On the question of why the gold bloc failed, see Asselain (1993) and Bussière (1993).

[3] Eichengreen and Sachs (1985), Eichengreen (1992), Feinstein, Temin, and Toniolo (1997), Balderston (2003). On the Dutch economy during the 1930s, see van Zanden (1988, 1998) and van Zanden and Griffiths (1989); on the Swiss economy, see Kneschaurek (1952), Rutz (1970), and Zurlinden (2003).

was the precondition for stability and prosperity and that devaluation would have only a temporary effect or even worsen the situation. By the same token, they failed to recognize the harmful consequences of deflation and to understand that a drastic reduction in wages and prices was not possible under the new postwar conditions of regulated labor markets, mass politics, and organized labor. Eichengreen and Temin (2000) cite Tom Johnston, a former parliamentary secretary for Scotland and Lord Privy Seal, commenting on the devaluation of sterling in 1931 with the following words: "Nobody told us we could do that."[4] Mouré (2002) concludes: "Gold standard belief placed maintenance of the currency's gold value as the highest priority for monetary policy; gold standard rhetoric argued that doing so would provide a stable system adjusting naturally to economic changes in order to recover and maintain equilibrium."[5] In a recent study, Cesarano (2006) comes to the same conclusion, although he is not speaking of a gold standard belief. Policymakers were convinced that they were not allowed to use exchange-rate policy to cushion economic crises. In their view, the economy was flexible enough to adjust to the gold standard.[6]

Since this explanation was developed to describe the monetary policy of the United States and the large European countries, the question of whether or not it also holds for small countries such as Belgium, the Netherlands, and Switzerland has not been fully answered yet. There are, however, a number of studies suggesting that the gold standard mentality and other popular beliefs played a crucial role in the decision-making process. For example, a number of historians have highlighted the importance of Switzerland's stability culture. The most systematic test of the mentality thesis has been undertaken by Allgoewer in her study on Swiss monetary policy in the 1930s.[7] Her conclusion is that Swiss policymakers in fact shared the same views as their counterparts in Berlin, London, Paris, and Washington. They feared that devaluation would lead to inflation, the ruin of the middle class, and real wage losses, thereby making things worse than they already were. As for Belgium, Hogg (1987) comes to the conclusion that "general economic illiteracy" was the major reason for the opposition

---

[4]   Eichengreen and Temin (2000, p. 202).

[5]   Mouré (2002, p. 271). Mouré differs somewhat from Eichengreen and Temin in his characterization of the gold standard belief, but the essence of the explanation remains the same.

[6]   According to Cesarano (2006, p. 67) the neoclassical model of adjustment was "deeply ingrained in the policymakers' cultural baggage and influenced their behavior."

[7]   The importance of ideas are also highlighted by Bébié (1939, pp. 51–57), Rutz (1970, pp. 136–139 and 144–145), Baumann and Halbeisen (1999), Tanner (2000), and Zurlinden (2003).

to devaluation: "The same people who had been so slow to recognize the effects of inflation (or 'inflammation' as one leading Belgian advisor called it), were also unable to distinguish properly between inflation and devaluation. Even many exporters, who might have been expected to have had a practical grasp of the meaning of overvaluation, simply regarded the existing exchange rates as given."[8]

Yet not everybody agrees with this conclusion. Especially Dutch and Swiss economic historians have come up with other explanations.[9] They have argued that a combination or a selection of the following seven factors caused policymakers to defend the gold standard for as long as possible. First, it was hard to predict how a devaluation would affect the economy because of too many unknowns, including the possibility of further competitive devaluations or protectionist retaliations. Second, interest groups were too heterogeneous and therefore unable to formulate a convincing alternative to the maintenance of the status quo. The fractionalization of interest groups and the lack of a coherent alternative led various economic sectors to seek specific protection against the competitive disadvantage stemming from the overvaluation of the Swiss franc – such as export subsidies, trade quotas and tariffs, and privileged access to foreign exchange under clearing agreements. These measures, in turn, weakened the call for devaluation. Third, it was impossible to bring about a democratic consensus on the need for devaluation because the mere existence of a public discussion would have immediately triggered speculative attacks against the Swiss franc. Therefore, the decision-making process was enormously delayed. Fourth, as a rule, policymakers in general and central bankers in particular like consistency and do not revise their basic decisions unless forced to do so by external shocks. Fifth, the ideology of the conservative Calvinists and their alliance with the financial circles of Amsterdam had great influence on the then Prime Minister Colijn, also a conservative Calvinist. Sixth, there was a broad consensus among Swiss policymakers that a strong and stable currency was vital to maintain the eminent international position of the Swiss banking sector. Seventh, the Swiss ruling elites wanted to weaken the labor movement. And lastly, the Swiss exporting industries had some special features that made them less inclined to demand a devaluation: concentration on highly specialized niche goods, the relatively low share of wage costs and

---

[8] Hogg (1987, p. 207).

[9] Netherlands: Griffiths and Langveld (1987, pp. 10–12), Griffiths (1987, p. 165), and Bloemen (1993). Switzerland: Baumann and Halbeisen (1999), Guex (2003), Müller (2001), Müller (2002), Perrenoud et al. (2002), *Unabhängige Expertenkommission* (2002), Bordo, Helbling, and James (2006), and Bordo and James (2007).

a high degree of capital intensity, the great importance of clearing and cartel agreements, and finally, the long tradition of internationalization on the basis of a stable currency and a surplus in the current account.

Thus there are two different answers to the question of why Belgium, the Netherlands, and Switzerland did not devalue earlier. The first one argues that policymakers rejected devaluation mainly because of their conviction that it would not help. The second, broader explanation claims that not so much economic ideas but rather specific economic constraints and opportunities as well as political strategies and institutions played a crucial role. Contrary to what one might believe at first sight, these explanations exclude one another. Either policymakers failed to grasp the net macroeconomic benefits of devaluation and therefore tried to prevent it, or they understood them very well but delayed devaluation for a number of other reasons.

In the remainder of this section I will try to show that narrative evidence gives more support to the first explanation. An overwhelming majority of central bankers, national politicians, business executives, and union leaders, regardless of the economic structure of their countries, defended gold parity because of their sincere belief that a devaluation would not improve but would deteriorate the situation. Of course, there were dissenting voices, and the fact that it was politically sensitive to speak out publicly for a devaluation had a disciplinary effect on dissenters. Also, the situation was complicated by the existence of trade blocs, bilateral clearing agreements, and political tensions. Furthermore, national differences surely were relevant because, for example, the pro-devaluationists in Switzerland were somewhat weaker than in Belgium and the Netherlands. And finally, it is obvious that the increasing number of subsidies and protectionist measures mitigated the negative effects caused by overvaluation of the currency and the deflationary pressure and weakened the case for devaluation. The government stabilized or slightly raised agricultural prices, protected farmers against foreign competition, gave risk guarantees to exporters, and encouraged the formation of cartels. It is fair to assume that without these various protectionist measures, defense of the gold standard would have been much more difficult.[10] Yet the crucial point is that protectionism was a consequence of a monetary strategy that was endorsed by all major parties, business associations, and unions. Only because policymakers deeply felt that their strategy was the right one were they ready to resort to measures they would not have considered in normal times. Without this strong commitment to the gold

---

[10] The role of subsidies, price controls, and tariffs is highlighted by Helbling, James, and Bordo (2006).

standard, they would have given up much earlier – as in the late 1940s and after the collapse of the Bretton Woods agreement. Only in the latter stage of the depression, when it became obvious that it was impossible to lower wages and prices to the level required to restore the competitiveness of the trading sectors, did the problem of finding an exit strategy and the avoidance of a public debate become crucial.

A good starting point for a discussion of the two competing explanations is the statements of the central bank governors, finance ministers, and prime ministers because they were the most fervent advocates of the status quo and thus expressed conventional wisdom in its purest form. In Belgium, central bank Governor Louis Franck believed until the very last moment that a devaluation of the franc would not bring any advantages. In the annual meeting of the National Bank of Belgium on 25 February 1935, he declared that

those who believe that there is a safe and simple way to solve our severe problems are completely mistaken. The monetary manipulations in Belgium would not solve any of our problems, neither the unemployment problem, nor the budget problem, nor the debt problem that is largely a foreign debt, nor the export problem arising from quota and restrictions; the glorified alternative does not exist: it would only be a disaster in addition to all the difficulties of today. With reason, the government, the big parties, the public opinion reject it without any reservation.[11]

A few weeks earlier, on 19 January 1935, Prime Minister Georges Theunis, governing since November 1934 and appointed to defend the gold standard, had written a confidential letter to King Albert I. After speaking of the growing opposition to deflation, he concluded: "I will not lessen my struggle on the basis of our programme as long as Your Majesty gives me his confidence. I continue to believe that the monetary manipulations cannot help the economy in a durable manner. As long as the gold bloc does not collapse and neither the dollar nor the pound depreciate in a unforeseeable manner, we have no advantage as a nation from leaving the current parity for the time being."[12]

---

[11] Archives *Banque Nationale de Belgique*, A 006:3: *Procès-verbal de l'assemblée générale des actionnaires du 25 février 1935*, p. 5: "*J'ajoute que ceux qui croient qu'à la solution de nos graves problèmes il existerait une autre voie, sûre et facile, se trompent complètement. Les manipulations monétaires en Belgique ne résoudraient aucun de nos problèmes, ni celui du chômage, ni celui du budget, ni celui de notre dette, si largement étrangère, ni celui de notre exportation, vinculée par les contingents et les restrictions; l'alternative vantée n'existe pas: elle ne serait qu'un désastre ajouté à toutes les difficultés de l'heure. Avec raison, le gouvernement, les grands partis, l'opinion publique le rejettent sans réserves.*"

[12] Cited in Thielemans (1980, p. 58): "*Je n'en continuerai pas moins à lutter sur la base de notre programme tant que Votre Majesté me conservera sa confiance. Je persiste à croire que les*

In Switzerland, Gottlieb Bachmann, president of the Swiss National Bank, and Finance Minister Albert Meyer[13] defended the old gold parity until the very last minute. On Thursday evening, 24 September 1936, the French government informed the Swiss of its intention to devalue the franc the next day.[14] The next morning, the Swiss government (Federal Council) began to discuss the issue. Bachmann, who joined the discussion in the afternoon, tried to talk the ministers out of a devaluation and disclosed that the Dutch did not intend to follow the French. The discussion was continued on Saturday morning. Again, Bachmann was invited to the meeting. He had obtained another confirmation from Dutch central bank Governor Leonardus Trip that the Netherlands would not follow the French devaluation and therefore strongly recommended maintaining the existing parity. He argued that the Swiss National Bank had disposed of enough gold to avert all attacks. After this statement, he left, and the government continued with the discussion. Finance Minister Albert Meyer, endorsed by the minister of justice and police, also was opposed to a devaluation and explained, when the remaining five members of the government disagreed, as is reported in the minutes: "It should not be forgotten that it would be precisely the middle classes, the man in the street, the savers, the renters and the retired who would also suffer considerable damage. It would be impossible to prevent inflation, one would have to expect an early and strong rise of the prices of raw materials and of all imported goods, but also of wages etc. so that the advantages that a devaluation would bring to the competitiveness of our country in the international market would be eliminated again."[15] At this point, however, his words fell on deaf ears. The Swiss

---

manipulations monétaires ne peuvent aider l'économie d'une façon durable. A moins que le bloc-or ne s'effondre ou que le dollar ou la livre ne descende d'une façon imprévisible, actuellement nous n'avons pas avantage comme nation à quitter la parité actuelle."

[13] In 1936, Meyer also was president of the Confederation. But contrary to other nations, the Swiss President is elected for just one year and is regarded as *Primus inter pares* during that time. He chairs the sessions of the Swiss government (Federal Council) and undertakes special ceremonial duties.

[14] The devaluation of the French franc was announced on early Saturday morning, 26 September. See Mouré (1991, p. 262).

[15] *Protokoll des Bundesrats vom 26. September 1936* in *Diplomatische Dokumente der Schweiz 1848–1945*, Vol. 11 (1934–1936), Bern, 1989, p. 864: "*Es sei nicht zu vergessen, dass auch gerade der Mittelstand, die kleinen Leute, die Sparer, die Rentner und die Pensionierten ganz beträchtlich geschädigt würden. Eine Verhinderung der Teuerung werde nicht möglich sein, sondern man werde sogar recht bald mit einer starken Verteuerung der Rohprodukte und aller importierten Waren, aber auch der Löhne usw. rechnen müssen, wodurch die Vorteile der Abwertung mit Bezug auf die Erhöhung der Konkurrenzfähigkeit unseres Landes auf dem internationalen Markte wieder beseitigt würden.*" On the final debate, see also *Unabhängige Expertenkommission* (2002, pp. 89–90).

Federal Council decided to devalue the franc and informed central bank Governor Bachmann, who – according to his own words – was so surprised "that he could do nothing but utter a word of regret."[16] According to the minutes of the Federal Council, he even asked that another person implement the devaluation. Only when the government insisted did he agree to cooperate.[17] In any case, he was deeply disappointed. In a conversation with Felix Somary, a Vienna-born private banker in Zurich, he observed sarcastically: "Even 10 years ago, a devaluation in the case of a bank of issue with 100 percent gold coverage for its currency would have been termed a fraudulent declaration of bankruptcy. Nowadays they call it 'the theory of purchasing power.'"[18] Likewise, Minister of Finance Meyer also initially refused to do his duty. Eventually, however, he held the radio speech on the following day that announced the devaluation of the Swiss franc.

In the Netherlands, the gold standard was most fervently defended by Hendrikus Colijn, prime minister from May 1933 until August 1939. Against all odds, he remained convinced that a devaluation would be ruinous. Even devaluation of the Belgian franc in March 1935 failed to shatter his basic convictions. While Minister of Economic Affairs Max Steenberghe suggested that the cabinet follow the Belgian example, Colijn replied that "sacrificing the gold standard by the Netherlands means sacrificing every fixed point in the monetary confusion."[19] Even when his two closest allies, Finance Minister Oud and central bank Governor Trip, changed their minds after being informed of the Swiss decision to follow the French, the prime minister hesitated to accept the inevitable.[20] At last, Trip's argument that remaining on the gold standard as the only European country would lead to capital flight and to a steep increase in the discount rate managed to convince Colijn. On Saturday evening, 26 September 1936, the Dutch government decided to suspend the gold standard.

Thus the actions and statements of the leading policymakers were quite similar in Belgium, the Netherlands, and Switzerland. The crucial question now is whether other influential political groups shared this view or had different motives to support the strong currency, as some scholars have suggested. The two most important groups were the Left and the exporting

---

[16] Archives Swiss National Bank, *Bankausschuss*, No. 12, 28 September 1936, p. 370.

[17] *Protokoll des Bundesrats vom 26.* September 1936 in *Diplomatische Dokumente der Schweiz 1848–1945*, Vol. 11 (1934–1936), Bern, 1989, p. 865.

[18] Somary (1986, p. 178).

[19] Hirschfeld, Herinneringen, pp. 219–226, cited in Griffiths (1987, p. 180). See also Klemann (1990, p. 59).

[20] De Vries (1994, pp. 130–133) presents a detailed reconstruction of the discussions leading to the devaluation.

sector. As for the labor unions and the Socialists, the fear of inflation was clearly the greatest concern because it would reduce savings and real wages of workers. In Belgium, a sound majority of the Left was strongly opposed to devaluation.[21] In a parliamentary debate in late November 1934, four months before the devaluation, Socialist leader Émile Vandervelde endorsed the newly installed Theunis government in its defense of the gold standard.[22] In late January 1935, he renewed his support of Prime Minister Theunis: "... like you, we say: no printing of assignats, that goes without saying, and no monetary manipulations, which, as you have rightly said, can have only transitory results. It is a temporary euphoria, but a dangerous one, because the clearest final result of such an operation is speculation, are artificial manoeuvres which make the poor even poorer and enrich the others, the rich, precisely those who enrich themselves thanks to the devaluation."[23] It is true that in November 1934, Hendrik de Man, author of the *Plan du Travail*, together with Paul van Zeeland, deputy governor of the National Bank, had worked out a new economic policy plan that also included a devaluation.[24] But this plan was made in total secrecy because there was still a broad consensus across all parties and the public that a devaluation was to be avoided. The first public statements of politicians did not come until February 1935.[25]

The Dutch Social Democrats (SDAP) also remained conspicuously silent on the question of devaluation. Hess (1987) assumes that the most important factor was "the fact that the proponents of a devaluation had not succeeded in convincing the leadership that a reduction in the value of the guilder as an isolated measure would have a sufficient positive effect on the Dutch economy to be worth taking the risk."[26] In the course of 1934, party leader Johan Willem Albarda repeatedly pointed out that a devaluation would harm the middle class and workers. The Socialist Labor Union (NVV), however, seems to have had a more favorable

---

[21] Van der Wee and Tavernier (1975, pp. 254–255 and 271).
[22] Thielemans (1980, p. 32).
[23] Cited in Thielemans (1980, p. 53): "... *nous disons avec vous: Pas de planche aux assignats, cela va sans dire, et pas non plus de manipulations monétaires qui, comme vous l'avez dit justement, ne peuvent avoir que des résultats passagers. C'est une euphorie temporaire mais dangereuse, parce que le résultat final le plus clair d'une opération de ce genre, c'est la spéculation, ce sont les manœuvres artificielles qui appauvrissent les pauvres et qui enrichissent les autres, les riches, ceux précisément qui s'enrichissent à la faveur de la dévaluation.*"
[24] Van der Wee and Tavernier (1975, pp. 271–272).
[25] Gutt (1935, p. 58). Gutt was finance minister in the Theunis cabinet (November 1934 to March 1935). Janssens (1976, p. 279).
[26] Hess (1987, pp. 127–128).

attitude toward the devaluation. However, since the leadership remained strongly divided over this issue, the NVV remained silent like the SDAP.[27] Moreover, the Catholic and Protestant labor unions were staunch defenders of the old parity.[28]

In Switzerland, the Socialists and union leaders in favor of a devaluation were even weaker than in the Netherlands. Only Max Weber, chief economist of the Swiss Federation of Trade Unions (SGB), changed his mind in late 1935 after visiting a number of Scandinavian Social Democrats. In particular, he now understood the destructive forces of deflation leading to paralyzing "credit crisis."[29] He failed to convince his comrades, however. At an internal meeting in March 1936, Weber debated with Fritz Marbach, an economics professor and Social Democratic politician. Marbach rejected a devaluation, claiming that a devaluation was not the right measure to end the policy of deflation.[30] The party leadership followed Marbach and stated: "It [the Social Democratic Party of Switzerland] does not consider the demand for a devaluation of the Swiss franc to be a way out of the crisis, never mind a resolution thereof."[31] A few weeks later, Robert Grimm, the most prominent Swiss Social Democrat opposing a devaluation, wrote in a pamphlet stating that deflation and devaluation only differed with respect to the method of economic adaptation, not in substance: "The devaluation is another method of adjustment, nothing more." And he remained convinced that it was difficult to apply the experiences of countries that had devalued to Switzerland.[32] Since Weber nevertheless continued to advocate a devaluation, his colleagues accused him of weakening the labor movement.[33]

Thus a sound majority of Socialist and union leaders in Belgium, the Netherlands, and Switzerland was convinced that a devaluation would only worsen the situation. They could not imagine that the end of deflation would bring economic recovery and improve employment. The same holds for the exporting sectors. According to Hogg (1987), Belgium's main industrial peak organization, the *Comité Central Industriel*, rejected the devaluation option to the last, claiming that "any short-term advantage to be gained

---

[27] Langevelde (1987, pp. 66–73).

[28] *Ibid.*, pp. 73–80.

[29] Hohl (1983, pp. 112–116); Perrenoud (2000, pp. 83–121); Müller (2001, pp. 175–180).

[30] *Sozialdemokratische Partei der Schweiz* (1936, p. 62).

[31] *Sozialdemokratische Partei der Schweiz* (1936, p. 6): "*Sie [Sozialdemokratische Partei der Schweiz] vermag auch in der Forderung nach einer Devalvation des Schweizer Frankens keinen Ausweg aus der Krise oder gar ihre Überwindung zu erblicken.*"

[32] Grimm (1936, pp. 36–37): "*Die Abwertung ist eine andere Methode der Anpassung, nichts weiteres.*"

[33] Hohl (1983, p. 116).

from devaluation would soon be countered by rises in domestic prices."[34] The only body that favored devaluation was the Chamber of Commerce of Antwerp, probably because shipping was suffering tremendously from the overvaluation of the franc.[35]

In the Netherlands, there was more opposition from the exporting sectors, but as in the case of the labor unions, the pro-devaluationists failed to convince their skeptical colleagues, so most exporters continued to believe that a devaluation would have only temporary benefits because of the expected rise in inflation. The Union of Dutch Employers [*Verbond van Nederlandsch Werkgevers* (VNW)], by far the most important organization with the highest share of classic exporters, remained opposed to devaluation.[36] However, in June 1933, Sir Henry Deterding, chairman of Royal Dutch Petroleum Company, publicly advocated a devaluation of the guilder at a meeting of the Dutch Society for Industry and Trade [*Nederlandsche Maatschappij voor Nijverheid en Handel* (NMNH)].[37] His proposal met strong criticism, but it encouraged other exporters to take the option of devaluation seriously. In July, a group of economics professors, politicians, and managers sent a confidential message to Prime Minister Colijn in which they discussed three possibilities to end the crisis. The first one was a continuation of the existing policies, thus a combination of external protectionism and internal support. The second was an immediate managed devaluation, and the third an unmanageable depreciation in the future. The group was skeptical toward the first option because it required additional taxation and wage cuts to a degree unheard of in Dutch history. The second one was seen as a viable alternative, although it was added that not all the undersigned supported it unconditionally. The message pointed out, however, that all agreed "that given the able bank management and the healthy banking institutions enjoyed by the Netherlands, a devaluation managed and controlled by the powerful government is in no way such a disaster for Dutch society as the press repeatedly wants us to believe."[38] The third option was rejected. After a meeting with Colijn, which brought no results, a second message was sent in January 1934, this time openly demanding

[34] Hogg (1987, p. 201).
[35] Thielemans (1980, p. 62).
[36] Bloemen (1987, pp. 30–31, 33 and 37). Bloemen was the first to study the opinions of the Dutch employers, but not on the basis of archival material of the VNW, the most important employers' organizations. His study is based on the official VNW journal (*De Nederlandsche Werkgever*).
[37] Bloemen (1987, pp. 35–36).
[38] Cited in Griffiths and Schoorl (1987, p. 141).

a devaluation. Interestingly, however, fewer managers had signed it than in July 1933. Nevertheless, prominent names still were listed, for example, the chairman of Philips as well as two directors of Hoogoven, the largest steel maker in the Netherlands.[39] This message was not followed by another meeting with Prime Minister Colijn, however, so the group formed the Association for Stable Money [*Nederlandsche Vereeniging voor Waardevast Geld* (NVWG)] in October 1934.

This new pressure group could not change the course of events, however. The opposition to devaluation remained too strong, even among exporters. In November 1934, a few weeks after formation of the NVWG, the anti-devaluationists founded a group dominated by bankers but also including a considerable number of shipowners and industrialists.[40] Owing to its secret and informal character, the group was not a powerful political player either. However, its discussions reveal what the majority of the economic elite, including the exporters, thought about the devaluation issue. In a confidential message the group sent to the government in February 1935, it claimed that a devaluation would bring only temporary relief and would cause a series of new problems: "... [O]n past experience, nothing undermines confidence in the economic and financial field more than monetary experiments." In a manifesto written in July 1936 and signed by 78 bankers, shipowners, industrialists, politicians, and professors in the following weeks, the group repeated its critical view:

A deliberate reduction in the value of the Dutch guilder, as wanted by the advocates of devaluation, would not attack the causes of the malaise. The relief possibly afforded to some firms from such a measure would only be temporary and, certainly in a small country as ours, not long-lasting in view of the fact that such a reduction in the value of the guilder would undoubtedly result in price rises at home so that the devaluation strongly would push up the cost of living and, in all probability, unleash a violent wage struggle.[41]

With this view, the defenders of the gold standard were still in the majority, although the failure of the deflationary policies had become evident. In a secret poll taken in June 1936 in which 3,000 persons participated, no more than 37 percent were in favor of devaluation, with the transport sector having the highest share of devaluationists (62 percent), followed by shipping (59 percent) and agriculture (53 percent). Not

---

[39] De Vries (1994, p. 102).
[40] The members are listed in Griffiths and Schoorl (1987, pp. 154–155) and de Vries (1994, pp. 107 and 109).
[41] Citations in Griffiths and Schoorl (1987, p. 160).

surprisingly, the idea of a devaluation was least popular among lawyers (17 percent).[42]

As for the Swiss exporters, we can observe the same fear that a devaluation would lead to chaos and inflation. In July 1932, Ernst Wetter, managing director of the *Vorort*, the peak organization of Swiss business, considered a devaluation "a leap into the dark":

> Of course, one can initiate a devaluation, but no government is sure if it can stop the process at the point it wishes to. For, at that point, others who one has not thought of will have a word to say, for example, the owners of foreign capital. And we know that this capital in Switzerland is not small. If this capital starts moving because of a lack of confidence, if it is withdrawn, the situation then becomes critical for a relatively weak economy. In addition, there will be a loss in value of all property. And finally, do we want to compete with the economically weak and desperate in the area of inflation? Will we not always end up losing? All desire for inflation means playing with fire and is irresponsible.[43]

This view prevailed until a very late stage of the depression, and there were few dissenting voices. When at a meeting of the board of the *Vorort* in January 1934 Geneva banker Albert Pictet pointed out that Switzerland was "too expensive" and proposed to examine "the question of the franc," he met strong opposition. Robert Naville, a leading Swiss industrialist, declared that a devaluation of the franc would not bring a solution to the difficulties: "[I]t will result in the ruin of the middle classes, a genuine disaster."[44] The other members of the board of *Vorort* explained that the franc had to be maintained. Accordingly, Pictet changed his opinion, at least within the board. At a meeting in May 1934, he explained that "a decline of the franc would be a disaster."[45] After that meeting, the board never touched on

---

[42] Schwarz (1937, p. 377, footnote 1).

[43] Ernst Wetter, *Protokoll der am 2. Juli 1932 in Zürich abgehaltenen Ordentlichen Delegiertenversammlung des Schweizerischen Handels- und Industrievereins*, pp. 20–21: "*Man kann eine Währungsabwertung wohl einleiten, aber kein Staat ist sicher, ob er dann auch da Halt machen kann, wo es ihm beliebt. Denn dann sprechen andere mit, an die man nicht gedacht hat. Die Besitzer fremder Kapitalien im Lande. Und dass diese Kapitalien in der Schweiz nicht klein sind, wissen wir. Wenn diese Kapitalien aus Mangel an Vertrauen in Fluss kommen, wenn sie zurückgezogen werden, dann wird die Situation für eine verhältnismässig schwache Volkswirtschaft kritisch. Dazu kommt eine Entwertung allen Besitzes. Und schliesslich, wollen wir mit den wirtschaftlich Schwachen und Verzweifelten einen Wettlauf auf dem Gebiete der Inflation anstellen? Kommen wir da nicht immer zu kurz? Alle Inflationsgelüste sind ein Spielen mit dem Feuer und unverantwortlich.*"

[44] *Archiv für Zeitgeschichte, Vorortsprotokolle, Sitzung vom 12. Januar 1934:* "[I]l en résulterait la ruine des classes moyennes, véritable catastrophe."

[45] *Archiv für Zeitgeschichte, Vorortsprotokolle, Sitzung vom 4. Mai 1934:* "Une baisse du franc serait une catastrophe."

the question until early 1936. It was only in public that business executives continued to address the monetary issue; for example, Carl Koechlin, chairman of the chemical firm *Geigy AG*, in July 1934 said: "Any devaluation, even a so-called controlled or manipulated one, would immediately bring us a rise of prices of our foreign purchases of raw materials for the businesses and of our foodstuffs. This in turn would lead to a rise of the cost of living and production. That would result in bitter fights about wage conditions, and the internal conditions would suffer a strong shock."[46]

Only when it became clear that is was unrealistic to lower prices and wages to the level required to restore competitiveness did the industrialists begin to question their economic model. The impressive success of the Scandinavian states following suspension of the gold standard further destabilized the conventional wisdom. In particular, Denmark, Norway, and Sweden were not suffering from inflation but experienced a sustained recovery coupled with price stability. In the summer of 1935, a senior manager of a textile firm told his colleagues at a meeting of the *Vereinigung für gesunde Währung* that the option of a devaluation was becoming more and more popular.[47] However, Swiss exporters remained skeptical until the very last moment. They began to accept the inevitable but never embraced it enthusiastically. A typical example for this mixed view is the statement by Hans Sulzer at a meeting of the *Vorort* in February 1936. On the one hand, he regretted that Switzerland had not followed the devaluation of the British pound in 1931 as the Scandinavian small states had. On the other hand, he still did not recommend devaluation of the franc because of possible retaliatory measures by the countries that had already devalued. "I am against a devaluation as long as there are still any hopes that we may achieve the adjustment to the world market within a reasonable amount of time by directly lowering prices and wages. It is the ultima ratio of the fight against the crisis. It is good to wait until we can better assess the situation. However, I have lost any hope for an effective reduction [of costs and wages]."[48] Similarly, Carl Koechlin mentioned at the next meeting in late

---

[46] *Protokoll der am 7. Juli 1934 in Zürich abgehaltenen Delegiertenversammlung des Schweizerischen Handels- und Industrie-Vereins*, p. 28: "*Jede Abwertung, auch eine sogenannte kontrollierte oder manipulierte, würde uns sofort eine Verteuerung unserer ausländischen Einkäufe in Rohstoffen für die Wirtschaft und in Lebensmitteln bringen. Dies hätte wiederum eine Erhöhung der Lebens- und Produktionskosten zur Folge. Daraus würden sich heftige Kämpfe um die Lohnbedingungen ergeben, und die internen Verhältnisse würden eine starke Erschütterung erfahren.*"

[47] Tanner (2000, p. 65).

[48] *Archiv für Zeitgeschichte, Vorortsprotokolle, Sitzung vom 14. Februar 1936*, p. 10: "*Ich bin gegen die Abwertung, solange noch irgendwelche Hoffnungen bestehen, dass wir die*

March that "a large part of industry thinks that it will be impossible for our country to adapt to the current conditions without proceeding to a devaluation of the currency."[49]

When the Popular Front won the French elections in May 1936, some Swiss exporters began to prepare for a devaluation by investing their liquid funds in foreign exchange and by accumulating raw materials.[50] In June, a group of more than a 100 politicians, economists, industrialists, and traders of eastern Switzerland, which was dominated by the textile industry, organized a secret meeting in St. Gallen to discuss the question of devaluation. The organizers, afraid of leaving written traces, requested that those who did not follow the invitation send back their invitation card.[51] Within the *Vorort,* the question of the exit strategy came to the fore as insight into the inevitable grew stronger. In July 1936, the board of the *Vorort* discussed the idea of sending one or two economists on a secret mission to Belgium to study the effects of the devaluation.[52] The Swiss government took up the idea and sent a high administration official to Brussels. He returned with the conclusion that the devaluation had been very helpful to the recovery. Yet Swiss exporters still remained skeptical and were surprised when the devaluation of the Swiss franc in September 1936 had almost immediate positive effects. Notably, they did not expect such a rapid increase in demand.[53]

In summary, the claim that difficult circumstances rather than the poor state of macroeconomic understanding led the managers of exporting industries to favor maintenance of the gold standard is hard to reconcile with narrative evidence. Of course, the existence of clearing and cartel agreements and other regulations complicated the issue. At a more fundamental level, though, the problem was that they did not consider devaluation to be a viable option but a dangerous operation that could not be seriously considered. Had their knowledge of macroeconomics been more developed, they would have led a completely different discussion.

Anpassung an den Weltmarkt innert nützlicher Frist auf dem Wege des direkten Abbaues erreichen. Sie ist die ultima ratio der Krisenbekämpfung. Wir tun gut, zuzuwarten, bis sich die Lage noch etwas besser überblicken lässt. Ich habe allerdings jede Hoffnung auf einen wirksamen Abbau verloren."

49   *Archiv für Zeitgeschichte, Vorortsprotokolle, Sitzung vom 28. März 1936,* p. 2: "*Une grande partie de l'industrie considère qu'il sera impossible pour notre pays de s'adapter aux conditions actuellement en vigueur sans procéder à une dévalorisation de sa monnaie.*"

50   Müller (2001, p. 192), Halbeisen (2005, pp. 169–176).

51   Bosshardt (1970, p. 183).

52   *Archiv für Zeitgeschichte, Vorortsprotokolle, Sitzung vom 3. Juli 1936.*

53   Müller (2002, p. 249).

THE BELGIAN TRIPLET CRISIS

The reason why the gold bloc was doomed is obvious: It was impossible to implement the deflation necessary to compensate for overvaluation of the currency. By contrast, the question why Belgium left the gold bloc 18 months earlier than the Netherlands and Switzerland is harder to answer. The problem is not the lack of research but the fact that there has been neither a debate on which explanation performs best nor any reference to other banking and financial crises. This section therefore tries to take a step toward a more systematic understanding of the Belgian devaluation.

We can divide the existing explanations into three groups.[54] The first one claims that a combination of three developments was crucial: deepening of a banking crisis, deterioration of the trade balance, and increasing political unrest. For the American discussion, one of the most influential proponents of such an interpretation is Shepherd (1936): "As early as the autumn of 1934 Belgium was being regarded as the weakest member of the gold bloc. In the first place, its commercial banks were known to be in a precarious position. Secondly, the continued sharp contraction in foreign trade was an ominous development in a predominantly trading country such as Belgium, which has a limited home market. Thirdly, the strength of the Socialists – and particularly the widespread sympathy among the working population for the plan of the Socialist, Hendrik de Man – constituted a growing threat against continuing deflation."[55] For the Belgian discussion, the studies of Baudhuin (1936, 1946a) became conventional wisdom. Like Shepherd, Baudhuin highlights the importance of the banking crisis and the strength of the Socialists and views the renewed fall of the British pound as a "coup de grace."[56]

The second explanation is similar to the first one because it also highlights the importance of the banking crisis. The difference is that it rejects the two other factors. Hogg (1987) is the main proponent of this view.[57] He observes that "[i]t is beyond doubt that, in any case, the banking network was nearing the point of collapse by March 1935 ... The situation of the

---

[54] Baudhuin (1936, 1946a).

[55] Shepherd (1936, p. 199). Cf. p. 200: "Belgium was fighting a losing battle of deflation largely because of the steady depreciation of sterling." Cf. p. 222: "It is widely believed in Belgium that if devaluation had been delayed by two weeks a general banking moratorium would have been necessary to prevent wholesale bank failures."

[56] Baudhuin (1936, p. 77; 1946a, pp. 320–328). Van der Wee and Tavernier (1975, p. 274) also speak of a coup de grace and emphasize the importance of the Socialists and the banking crisis.

[57] Bernanke and James (1991, p. 53) and James (2001, p. 92) come to the same conclusion.

banks does not explain the long-term causes of the devaluation, but it does explain why it took place when it did."[58] He argues that the deeper reason for the banking crisis was the boom of the 1920s, leading Belgian banks to lend too generously and to participate more directly in the industrial sector. As the depression persisted, banks were increasingly confronted with frozen assets and liquidity problems that eventually resulted in a severe banking crisis, deposit withdrawals, and capital outflows.

The third explanation puts the same factors in yet another order. It argues that the banking crisis was a consequence of the currency crisis, which, in turn, had been caused by the persisting depression and the continued fall of sterling. The main proponent of this view is Chlepner (1943), a professor of banking and finance in Brussels and temporarily a chief economist of one of the leading Belgian banks. "As the conviction grew that the franc would be devalued, more and more people, individuals and corporations, wished to take precautions and to invest their funds in foreign currencies. This was the principal reason for deposit withdrawals in 1934 and 1935.... Contrary to what has been asserted by some people, the franc was not the victim of a banking crisis. Rather the banking organization, which had already suffered much from the depression, was the victim of the monetary crisis."[59]

In short, the three explanations differ in that they suggest various combinations of the same factors. Either the devaluation was caused by several factors including a banking crisis or only by a banking crisis, or it was the dwindling confidence in the government's ability to deflate the economy that caused a currency crisis and eventually a banking crisis. Which combination is the most convincing one? Owing to the lack of monthly statistics on individual Belgian banks, it is difficult to give a definite answer.[60] However, on the basis of the monthly balances of the National Bank of Belgium, it is at least possible to develop a plausible explanation. Also, the recent literature on the so-called twin crises in emerging markets can help to better understand the dynamics of banking and currency crises in the 1930s.

My main thesis is that from a strictly comparative perspective, the weakness of the banking sector is in fact the main factor that made Belgium special compared with the Netherlands and Switzerland. In this respect,

---

[58] Hogg (1987, p. 200).

[59] Chlepner (1943, pp. 73–74). By "monetary crisis," Chlepner means a currency crisis.

[60] Ferguson and Temin (2003) and Schnabel (2004a) have used monthly banking statistics to analyze the German twin crises of 1931. On the Belgian situation, see Hogg (1987, p. 199): "There are no detailed figures available on the extent of these withdrawals and indeed with the partial exception of the *Société Générale* there were no banking statistics released at all for the year 1934."

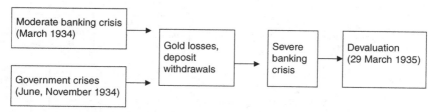

Figure 4.1. The course of the Belgian triplet crisis.

Hogg's explanation (1987) is the most convincing one. Yet, to understand the dynamic that led to the Belgian devaluation, it is not sufficient to focus on the banking sector alone. The government crises of June and November 1934 were just as important because they explain why investors began to withdraw their deposits and to sell Belgian francs and therefore why a moderate banking crisis could turn into a run on the currency and a large-scale banking crisis in early 1935 that eventually forced the authorities to devalue. Accordingly, it is more appropriate to speak of a "triplet crisis," a term coined by James (2001). To be sure, the Netherlands and Switzerland also experienced government crises that were due to the problems of deflation and fiscal policy. This is precisely the reason why, from a strictly comparative perspective, the weakness of the banking sector proved to be the crucial factor. However, if we concentrate only on the Belgian devaluation, it is necessary to include the government crises. In this respect, the explanation favored by Chlepner (1943) needs to be taken into account, at least partially (Figure 4.1).

As noted earlier, there are two ways to make this interpretation plausible. First, the chronology of events suggests that the banking crisis of March 1934 was not severe enough to cause a run on the franc. Only in combination with the two government crises in June and November that led first to a partial and then to a complete change of the cabinet did the National Bank of Belgium begin to lose gold (Figure 4.2). In particular, the second government crisis proved to be destabilizing. According to Baudhuin (1946a), the worst days in the whole year of 1934 were those following the resignation of the de Broqueville government on 13 November. Within four days, the National Bank of Belgium lost 500 millions francs, corresponding to 4 percent of its total reserves.[61]

Second, new research on twin crises in emerging markets has shown that the banking crisis usually predates the currency crisis and therefore is a

---

[61] Baudhuin (1946a, p. 326).

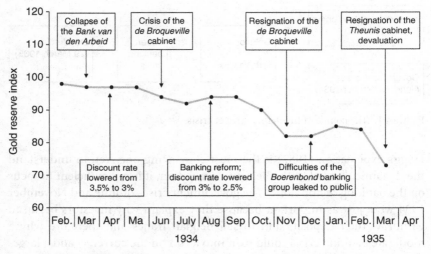

Figure 4.2. Belgium: crucial events and index of gold reserves (January 1934 = 100) [*For the data, see Commission d'enquête parlementaire (1936, pp. 141–142); for the events, see text.*]

rather reliable indicator for a coming currency crisis but that the peak of the banking crisis is after the currency crisis has broken out. Another relevant result is that a banking crisis is not necessarily the immediate cause of a currency crisis but only one of several factors.[62] As for the interwar years, recent research on the German crisis of 1931 has shown that the political shocks were of crucial importance. Schnabel (2004a) interprets the German currency crisis as a twin crisis based on two independent factors: political shocks and the liquidity problems of several German banks. Ferguson and Temin (2003) argue that the political shocks were even more important than the banking crisis.[63] James (2001) observes that not only the German but also the Austrian and Hungarian crises were in fact triplet crises: "The Austrian crisis started as a banking crisis, which then became

---

[62] Kaminsky and Reinhart (1999) have identified 26 cases for the period from the early 1970s to mid-1990s and have compared them with currency crises that were not coupled with a banking crisis. They define a twin crisis as "episodes in which the beginning of a banking crisis is followed by a balance-of-payment crisis within 48 months" (p. 478). Systematic research on twin crises did not really begin until the Asian crisis in 1997–1998, but the research on financial crises is abundant. A seminal paper on the interwar years is Eichengreen and Portes (1987), and a more recent paper on political and financial crises is Chang (2005).

[63] See the debate between Schnabel (2004b) and Ferguson and Temin (2004). For a longer version, see Temin (2008).

a foreign-exchange and fiscal crisis. In Hungary, a fiscal crisis set off a foreign-exchange panic and then a banking crisis. In Germany, a fiscal and banking crisis coincided and set off the foreign-exchange crisis. These were not 'twin' but 'triplet' crises."[64] Finally, Simmons (1994) has shown statistically that government instability enhanced the probability of a devaluation during the 1930s.

The course of the Swiss banking crisis is a good counterexample. As Baumann (2004) has argued, the political consensus was of vital importance for the successful prevention of a banking panic and currency crisis. Swiss bankers and policymakers agreed that both the *Banque d'Escompte Suisse* and the *Schweizerische Volksbank* were too big to fail and that political divisions should be secondary. Accordingly, both banks received financial help, and the banking crisis of 1931 was contained. The *Volksbank* was finally rescued in December 1933, and the *Banque d'Escompte* was allowed to close its doors in April 1934, when the danger of bank panic or currency crisis was not imminent anymore because the public perceived this failure as the end of an old story and not the beginning of a new crisis.[65] Thus, when the Swiss government was struck by a crisis triggered by the double resignation of Minister of Justice Heinrich Häberlin and Finance Minister Jean-Marie Musy in the spring of 1934, there was no run on commercial and savings banks.[66] It is true that the Swiss National Bank was suffering from gold losses, but this was only temporary: In May, the losses stopped, and in August, gold reserves were on the rise again. The confidence in the Swiss franc remained strong enough.

In summary, there is strong evidence that the outbreak of a banking crisis does not necessarily lead to a currency crisis and a devaluation. Only in combination with political shocks that can be due to various factors is a vicious circle set in motion. Of course, the political situation in central European countries in 1931 was much more explosive than in Belgium in 1934–1935. Obviously, though, the two government crises were severe enough to unsettle investors. The following two sections take a closer look at the course of events in Belgium, beginning with the first phase lasting from March to September 1934 when the situation still looked quite stable. The second phase started with the National Bank of Belgium suffering from new gold losses and ended with the devaluation in late March 1935.

---

[64] James (2001, p. 53).
[65] Baumann (2004, Chap. 3.3, pp. 145*ff.*).
[66] For a biography of Musy, see Kaiser (1999).

THE FIRST PHASE (MARCH TO SEPTEMBER 1934)

There is a strong consensus among economic historians, regardless of what overall explanation they favor, that a new phase began with the *Belgische Bank van den Arbeid* (BBA) closing its doors in late March 1934.[67] The bank had been founded in Ghent in 1913 with the purpose of serving the needs of the socialist cooperative societies and trade unions, but after the war, it also had begun to finance the Flemish textile industry. By 1930, it owned roughly 25 firms and had numerous participations in the industrial sector. According to Baudhuin (1946a), the problems of the BBA can be traced back to the late 1920s.[68] In 1929, the bank took over an artificial silk factory, which led to a marked deterioration of its asset-equity ratio, but management was convinced that it was a risk worth taking given that the Belgian economy was booming. This expectation proved wrong, however, because in 1930 and 1931 the export of textiles decreased dramatically. The BBA ran out of liquid funds and was forced to increase its share capital, but the operation failed completely. Only 1,351 of the 60,000 new shares were underwritten, the rest remained with the *Vooruit*, a socialist cooperative. As early as 1931, when confidence in the Belgian currency was still unshattered, the BBA was already doomed to fail because of its strong participation in the textile industry and its overexpansion. Thanks to advances from the government and new deposits by the cities of Ghent and Antwerpen, the bank managed to survive for a few more years. However, as the economic crisis dragged on, the bank's assets deteriorated further, the share of nonperforming loans increased, and the withdrawal of deposits continued. For some time, the problems were hidden from the public, but the bank became increasingly insolvent.

There is also a strong consensus among economic historians that the problems of the BBA were not unique but typical for a rather large segment of the Belgian banking sector.[69] The strong link with the industrial sector was partially a result of the system of mixed banking (universal banking) that had emerged in the nineteenth century, but the developments after

---

[67] Kurgan-van Hentenryk (1992, p. 320): In 1930, the assets of the BBA amounted to 316 million francs. The largest Belgian bank, the *Société Générale*, had 20 times more, namely, 6,515 million francs; the second-largest bank, the *Banque de Bruxelles*, had 10 times more, namely, 3,301 million francs.

[68] Baudhuin (1946b, pp. 174–183).

[69] For a comparative analysis of the banking crises in the 1930s, see Bernanke and James (1991) and Grossman (1994). Bernanke and James highlight the negative correlation between the degree of mixed banking and the likelihood of a banking crisis. Grossman does not test this variable.

World War I were more important. Because of the occupation and the expectation that war damages would be paid by Germany, Belgian authorities followed an expansionary course in the early 1920s – in contrast to the small neutral states, which registered a severe depression combined with a banking crisis.[70] As a result, the period of inflation and currency depreciation dragged on and even accelerated from 1923 to 1926, forcing Belgian banks to continue with the strategy they had pursued during the wartime inflation, namely, to transform nominal assets into "real" assets such as shares and to adopt a more aggressive credit strategy.[71] This trend toward a closer link with domestic industry was intensified by the fact that owing to the weakness of the Belgian franc, investments abroad became increasingly risky. Reconstruction, inflation, and depreciation created a climate of speculation leading to the founding of a series of new banks and brokers.

When the Belgian currency finally was stabilized in October 1926, the economy began to boom. Traditionally, economic historians explained this phenomenon with the fact that the franc was undervalued and that Belgian exporters therefore enjoyed a competitive advantage, especially vis-à-vis British competitors who suffered from an overvalued pound and labor unrest.[72] However, Cassiers (1989, 1995) has shown on the basis of sectoral studies that the domestic economy grew much faster than the export sector, which, despite an undervalued franc, became less competitive in the second half of the decade.[73] There were two other reasons for the exceptional boom of the domestic economy. First, labor unions were more successful in demanding higher wages after stabilization of the franc, whereas during the period of high inflation it was barely possible to preserve the purchasing power of workers. Real wages increased by 30 percent from 1927 to 1929 and fueled domestic demand.[74] Second, stabilization of the franc led to massive capital inflows, forcing commercial banks to seize any investment opportunities. The National Bank of Belgium tried to avert capital inflows by lowering the discount rate, but this relaxation of monetary conditions only fueled the boom.[75] In short, the reduction in inflation and the return to the gold standard did not normalize the Belgian economy and the business strategies of Belgian banks. On the contrary, the new boom led to a

---

[70] See Chapter Two.
[71] Jonker and van Zanden (1995, pp. 81–83).
[72] See Shepherd (1936, p. 192) for the older view.
[73] Cassiers (1995, p. 223).
[74] *Ibid.*, p. 222.
[75] Van der Wee and Tavernier (1975, p. 228): The discount rate was lowered from 7 to 4.5 percent in 1927 and to 4 percent in 1928.

Table 4.2. *Assets and Liabilities of Belgian Banks by Principal Items*
(in Millions of Francs)

	Number of banks	Cash Reserves	Discounts	Securities	Current Accounts	Advances	Other Assets	Total Assets
1913	67	172	777	717	1286	848		3802
1920	72	1,231	1,327	2,845	4482	827		10,713
1926	94	2,037	3,567	4,034	9992	1552		21,182
1927	101	3,030	5,281	4,198	12,910	2,080	338	27,828
1929	90	4,067	6,910	5,956	18,461	3,339	441	39,174
1930	92	4,346	8,385	7,201	19,571	2,692	572	42,767
1931	66	4,118	7,626	7,651	17,592		493	37,479
1932	66	5,642	5,881	7,568	13,223		518	32,832
1933	63	6,837	5,946	7,452	12,181		531	32,947
1913 (in %)		5	20	19	34	22	0	100
1920 (in %)		11	12	27	42	8	0	100
1930 (in %)		10	20	17	46	6	1.3	100

Source: Statistics of the Moniteur des Intérêts Matériels (Chlepner 1943, p. 58).

further strengthening of the links between banks and industrial enterprises. As stock prices at the Brussels stock exchange rose to new record levels, the banks profited directly from the high share of industrial securities in their portfolios.[76]

The transformation of the assets of Belgian banks during the 1920s is illustrated in Table 4.2. The most telling indicator is the share of current account credits. By 1930, these advances amounted to almost half of total assets. Theoretically, these advances were short-term loans, but in practice, they were the main channel through which commercial banks intensified their long-term link to industrial firms.[77] The second indicator is the composition of securities held by the leading 18 Belgian banks. From 1923 to 1929, the amount of obligations of public authorities decreased from 1,450 to 340 million Belgian francs, whereas the amount of industrial securities increased from 770 to 3,085 million Belgian francs, that is, from 35 to 90

[76] Kurgan-van Hentenryk (1992, S. 323).
[77] Chlepner (1943, p. 60) and James (2001, p. 51).

Table 4.3. *Assets of Banks in Belgium, Holland, France, and Switzerland in Percent of Total Assets, 1930*

	Cash, Banks, Bankers	Commercial Portfolio	Advances and Loans	Securities
All Belgian banks	10	20	53	27
Société Générale + *Banque de Bruxelles*[a]	28	13	31	28
Main five Dutch banks	18	22	54	6
Main eight Swiss banks (1926)	21	21	54	4

[a] Two largest Belgian banks.
Source: Hogg (1987, p. 197).

percent of total securities. A comparison with the composition of assets held by Dutch and Swiss banks shows the special position of the Belgian banks (Table 4.3). The latter had a much higher share of more liquid assets (i.e., cash and commercial portfolio) than the Belgian banks. In particular, the banks differed with regard to the share of securities.

In summary, there is a strong consensus that the commercial banks of Belgium were clearly more vulnerable to deflation and depression than the Dutch and Swiss banks and that the problems of the BBA were symptomatic. Yet, as far as the consequences of the failure of the BBA are concerned, there are two conflicting interpretations. On the one hand, a number of scholars argue that it marked the beginning of the end of the gold standard.[78] On the other hand, Chlepner (1943) claims that the currency crisis was not caused by the banking crisis but by the increasingly evident failure of the government to achieve a notable lowering of prices needed to avoid a devaluation.[79] As noted, since there are no monthly figures of deposit

[78] Roger (1936, p. 266): "*Als … Anfang 1934 die sozialistische Banque Belge du Travail, ein zweitklassiges Institut, dessen finanzielle Lage unhaltbar war, ihre Schalter schloss, setzte bei den Banken eine Spannung ein, die trotz verschiedener sogenannter Regierungsmassnahmen und trotz der durch das Gesetz vom 22. August 1934 angeordneten Bankreorganization nicht wieder verschwand.*" Van der Wee and Tavernier (1975, p. 263) write: "*La faillite de la Banque Belge du Travail et celle de quelques banques de moindre importance eurent un effet désastreux sur l'opinion publique et donnèrent lieu, dans tout le pays, à une nouvelle vague de retraits de dépôts bancaires.*" Hogg (1987, p. 199): "These measures provided too little, too late and were unable to prevent a major slump in public confidence together with heavy deposit withdrawals."
[79] Chlepner (1943, p. 73).

withdrawals available, this debate cannot be decided in a definite manner. However, there is enough circumstantial evidence to show that both views are only partially correct and that the truth lies somewhere in between.

What speaks for the first view is that the National Bank of Belgium lowered the discount rate because of banking problems, although these decreases undermined the overall goal of maintaining the gold standard. On 26 April, a month after failure of the BBA, the bank reduced the official discount rate from 3.5 to 3.0 percent; on 22 August, it reduced it to 2.5 percent in order to support the recovery of the industrial sector, as foreseen by the banking reform of 22 August. A second argument speaking for the first view is the mere fact that a banking reform became necessary in August 1934. Obviously, the situation had further worsened because of the failure of the BBA in late March. The banking reform foresaw two major measures. First, banks were forced to divide themselves into two juridically independent companies, namely, a bank and a holding company that would manage the industrial participations. And second, it enabled banks to transfer 2 billion Belgian francs of their outstanding loans to the National Industrial Credit Society (*Société Nationale de Crédit à l'Industrie*), a private bank patronized by the government. In return, the banks received bonds (3 percent) that were backed by the government and discounted by the National Bank.[80] Another problem of the banking reform was that more than 2 billion francs would have been needed to end the liquidity crisis and that it took several months until the reform was implemented.[81]

What speaks for the second view is that, first, the BBA was a bank of only minor importance (Table 4.4). Second, gold losses did not begin to become critical until June, but there were no notable bank failures during this time. The movement of the current account of the commercial banks held at the National Bank of Belgium confirms this impression: From April to July, it dropped from 2,245 million francs to 1,425 million francs, with the largest reduction in June. Third, according to outside observers, the August banking reform was a rather successful act of the government in that it succeeded in calming the public. The *Economist* even pointed out that "[t]he big Belgian banks have stood up to the crisis very well; they have no assets frozen in Germany or elsewhere. They have suffered losses through clients' insolvencies, and the market value of their industrial participations has fallen considerably. But they have been able to write down out of their reserves."[82] Similarly, the Swiss National Bank described the

[80] Baudhuin (1946a, pp. 305–306).
[81] Van der Wee and Tavernier (1975, p. 264).
[82] *Economist*, 25 August 1934, p. 357.

Table 4.4. *The Belgium Banking System in 1930*

Bank	Deposits (Million of Francs)
Société Générale group	
Société Générale	6,515
Banque d' Anvers	927
Subsidiaries of the Société Générale	6,212
Banque Italo-Belge	3,029
Total	20,731
Banque de Bruxelles group	
Banque de Bruxelles	3,301
Subsidiaries of the Banque de Bruxelles	2,712
Banque Belge d' Afrique	261
Total	6,274
Boerenbond group	
Algemeene Bankvereniging	1,463
Middenkredietkas	1,875
Crédit Général	495
Total	3,833
Solvay group	
Banque Générale Belge	1,470
Mutuelle Solvay	931
Other universal banks	
Banque Belge du Travail	316
Banque Industrielle Belge	242
Banque des Colonies	201
Total	759
Total deposits all Belgian banks	41,432

Source: Kurgan-van Hentenryk (1992, p. 320).

situation of Belgium in an internal report at the end of August without any sign of alarm, in contrast to later reports.[83]

In short, both views cover important aspects, but fail to be entirely convincing. The missing link that explains why the National Bank of Belgium lost gold in June and the commercial banks reduced their holding at the

---

[83] Archives Swiss National Bank, *Bankausschuss,* No. 28, 29 August 1934, p. 214.

central bank was a serious government crisis.[84] Young deputies of the Liberal Party had voted together with the Socialist camp to oppose two proposals of the government.[85] The first one concerned fiscal policy: The de Broqueville government wanted to shift the financing of family allowances to the communities and to special funds (*"caisses spéciales"*). The second proposal foresaw a reinforcement of the powers of the immigration authorities. The motives behind this attack of the "young turcs," as Thielemans (1980) describes them, are not entirely clear, but the effects were devastating.[86] Prime Minister Charles de Broqueville offered his resignation to King Alfred I but was charged to form a new government. Three ministers of the Liberal Party who had long served in senior positions and held key ministries, such as the ministry of foreign affairs and the finance ministry, were replaced. In addition, van Zeeland and Ingenbleek, two fiscal policy experts, entered the government as ministers without portfolio. Fiscal policy had become the main problem of Belgian politics, and Prime Minister de Broqueville hoped to solve it by seeking the collaboration of nonpartisan technocrats.

According to some observers, it was already clear by spring 1934 that the policy of deflation would not succeed and that the franc was doomed to fall. For example, Baudhuin (1936) wrote that toward the end of May, he had gotten the feeling that devaluation could no longer be avoided.[87] Simmons (1994) mentions a "source" that suggests that investors had begun to reduce their assets in Belgian francs.[88] However, the slight improvement of the gold reserves indicates that this assessment was still limited to a small group of professional investors and economists. In retrospect, it appears that there was still a chance for the Belgian government to solve the banking crisis in an orderly manner. The passage of the banking reform seems to have eased the situation so that the private discount rate fell slightly from 2.30 percent in August to 2.12 percent in October 1934. The yield of government bonds kept decreasing, for example, the 1925 bond from 6.36 percent in December 1933 to 5.36 percent in October 1934.

THE SECOND PHASE (OCTOBER 1934 TO MARCH 1935)

The second phase began in October when the National Bank of Belgium suffered new gold losses, and commercial banks reduced their current

---

[84]   Janssens (1976, p. 249).
[85]   Luykx and Platel (1985, p. 346).
[86]   Thielemans (1980, p. 9).
[87]   Baudhuin (1936, p. 50).
[88]   Simmons (1994, p. 253).

accounts at the National Bank by 40 percent. The private discount rate began to rise again while remaining stable in the other gold bloc countries. In November, the National Bank of Belgium continued to lose gold, and in early December, a bank panic spread through western Flanders and Louvain. After another banking bill was passed, the situation eased, but only temporarily. The private discount rate remained at the level of 2.37 percent. In mid-February, a deputy of the Belgian parliament openly asked for a devaluation, and from then on, the fall of the franc was only a matter of time. Gold reserves decreased at an alarming rate, and in mid-March 1935, a few days before he became prime minister of a government of national unity, Paul van Zeeland explained in a confidential conversation that Belgium had only two options: "save the franc or save the banks."[89] On 29 March, the franc was devalued by 28 percent.

Why did the situation deteriorate so rapidly? The timing of the gold losses suggests that the resignation of the de Broqueville government – which became foreseeable in late October – was the main trigger.[90] A representative example for the knowledge of observers was the report that the governing board of the Swiss National Bank gave to the Bank Council Committee on 7 November: "In the period under review [after 20 September], Belgium's currency was exposed to strong attacks. The causes are to be found in the strained economic situation and in political instability. Apparently there are differences of opinion within the government over the granting of credit to industry."[91] Similarly, the German weekly *Wirtschaftsdienst* observed in mid-November that the pressure on the franc was due to the change of cabinet.[92] Van Zeeland and Ingenbleek, who had joined the cabinet as ministers without portfolio in June, resigned on 9 November, the rest of the cabinet on 13 November.[93]

---

[89] Gutt (1935, p. 21). At that time, van Zeeland was still deputy governor of the National Bank of Belgium. See also *Documents parlementaires, Chambre*, 1935–1936, *rapport no.* 231 *du* 20 *avril* 1936, p. 10: "*Il fallait sauver ou le franc ou les banques.*"

[90] The government was doomed to fail from mid-August on, as de Broqueville later confessed: See his statement to the parliamentary committee that studied the causes of the devaluation: *Procès-verbaux, Enquête parlementaire chargée de rechercher les responsabilités de la dévaluation du franc*, 1935–1936, p. 72: "*Pendant près de deux ans, au sein du Gouvernement que je présidais les Ministres ont vécu dans l'union parfaite. Mais vers la mi-août 1934, il y eut de la zizanie dans le Gouvernement.*"

[91] Archives Swiss National Bank, *Bankausschuss*, 7 November 1934, p. 317: "*In der Berichtsperiode war die Währung Belgiens starken Angriffen ausgesetzt. Die Ursachen sind in der gespannten Wirtschaftslage und in der politischen Unstabilität zu suchen. Es scheinen sich in der Regierung Meinungsverschiedenheiten ergeben zu haben wegen der Krediterteilung an die Industrie.*"

[92] *Wirtschaftsdienst*, 16 November 1934, p. 1587.

[93] Janssens (1976, p. 249).

The de Broqueville government was divided over two issues: the future course of economic policy and the fate of the Boerenbond banking group.[94] Unlike the BBA, the Boerenbond was considered too big to fail because it was the third-largest bank after the *Société Générale* and the *Banque de Bruxelles* (see Table 4.4). The Boerenbond was a Flemish Catholic agricultural cooperative that had set up a banking network based on the model of Raiffeisen.[95] In 1934, the group consisted of 1,165 subsidiaries and counted 98,492 members, and its deposits amounted to more than 1.5 billion francs, which made it Belgium's third largest banking group. Its main purpose was to provide cheap credit to its members, but since there were considerable surpluses, the Boerenbond also was able to acquire a majority (85 percent) of the *Algemeene Bankvereeniging* and through it considerable industrial participation.[96] As noted earlier, such a strong involvement with the industrial sector proved deadly as the economic crisis persisted. The advances were immobilized, so the *Bankvereeniging* ran out of liquidity.

Actually, it wasn't so much the fact itself that the Boerenbond banking group was in difficulty but the way the Catholic ministers of the cabinet dealt with it. De Broqueville, Finance Minister Sap, and National Bank Governor Louis Franck had received warnings as early as August, but the Liberal ministers of the cabinet were not informed until the beginning of November. Even Cardinal Jozef-Ernest van Roey (Primate of Belgium), a highly respected and influential figure within the Catholic camp, was better informed than the Liberals. The plan of de Broqueville and Finance Minister Sap was to provide the Boerenbond with a big loan, but the Liberal ministers, annoyed by the fact that they had not been informed earlier, were not ready to go along. Moreover, they considered the current government, which had been divided by controversies over the budget, to be too weak to take such far-reaching measures and proposed that the government resign. De Broqueville took this step on 13 November.

From a comparative perspective, the question arises as to whether the government crisis was merely a result of a tactical struggle between Catholics and Liberals or whether there were more fundamental reasons why the government failed to overcome the internal divisions. As for the latter argument, two possibilities come to mind: Either Belgium's economic conditions were particularly severe or the Socialist opposition was stronger than in the

[94] Luykx and Platel (1985, p. 346).
[95] On the Boerenbond banking group, see Baudhuin (1936, pp. 184–199), Van der Wee and Tavernier (1975, pp. 265–267), Thielemans (1980, p. 13), and Kurgan-van Hentenryk (1992, p. 326).
[96] der Wee and Tavernier (1975, pp. 265–266), Thielemans (1980, p. 13).

Netherlands and Switzerland. In either case, the Belgian government would have been under more pressure and thus more vulnerable to conflicts about fiscal and economic policies than their Dutch and Swiss counterparts. As noted earlier, scholars highlighting the economic conditions have claimed that not only the banking crisis but also the extremely high degree of openness of the Belgian economy and the growing strength of the Belgian Left under the charismatic leader Hendrik de Man were important reasons for the early exit of the Belgian franc from the gold bloc.

A closer look at the data and some narrative evidence, however, suggest that the economic and political conditions were quite similar across the three small gold bloc countries. The persistence of the depression put the Dutch and Swiss authorities and politicians under a heavy strain and therefore caused deep conflicts and crises as well. It is true that Belgium was more open, that trade with Britain as a share of NNP was higher, and that owing to the similar industrial structure, Belgian manufacturers also were competing directly with British exporters in several segments of the world market.[97] In particular, the reduction of exports to the United Kingdom in terms of NNP was more dramatic for Belgium than for the Netherlands and Switzerland (Table 4.5). On the other hand, real GDP, GNP, and NNP figures suggest that Belgium's economic crisis was not deeper than the Dutch crisis (Table 4.6). On the contrary, from 1930 to 1934, Dutch real GDP as measured by Maddison (2001) had decreased by 9 percent and the Belgian economy by 5 percent. The difference between Belgium and the Netherlands is even bigger if we use the GNP and NNP figures provided by Mitchell (2003). Another indicator, the unemployment rate, also allows the conclusion that Belgium was not in a fundamentally worse position than the Netherlands. According to Mitchell (2003), the Belgian unemployment rate was 23 percent in 1934, and the Dutch rate was 28 percent; according to Grytten (1995), the corresponding figures were 11.8 and 9.8 percent. In short, there is no strong evidence for the claim that the renewed weakness of the British pound in early 1935 was an important contributing factor.

Furthermore, there is narrative evidence that the fall of the pound was not central to the debate. Camille Gutt, who served as minister of finance under Prime Minister Georges Theunis from November 1934 to March 1935, wrote that the renewed weakness of the British pound had been a shock, but one that could be dealt with: "In March, there was an abrupt fall. On 4 March, the pound sterling touched 100 francs. A decline of four percent. This was a hard blow. But, in reality, it was nothing to get

[97] Simmons (1994, pp. 241–243).

Table 4.5. *Trade Statistics of Belgium, the Netherlands,
and Switzerland (1928, 1934)*

	Belgium	Netherlands	Switzerland
Trade openness (imports + exports/NNP)			
1928a	115	73	51
1934	56	38	28
Main export markets (percentage of total exports)			
1928	United Kingdom (17)	Germany (24)	Germany (18)
	Germany (14)	United Kingdom (22)	United Kingdom (14)
	Netherlands (13)	Belgium (9)	United States (9)
	France (13)	Indonesia (9)	France (7)
1934	France (15)	Germany (25)	Germany (22)
	United Kingdom (12)	United Kingdom (20)	France (14)
	Germany (10)	Belgium (12)	United Kingdom (10)
	Netherlands (10)	Indonesia (4)	Italy (9)
Exports to GB (percentage of NNP)			
1928[a]	10	7	3
1934	4	3	1
Main export products (percentage of total exports)[b]			
Food	6	34	7.5
Raw materials	39	23	10.5
Manufactured articles	55	43	82

[a] Belgium 1927 because NNP available only for 1927; Switzerland 1929 for the same reason.
[b] Belgium and Luxembourg are taken together.
Sources: Mitchell (2003) and League of Nations, Statistical Year Book 1935/36; author's calculations.

hysterical about. Our industries had seen other things happen in the past; in particular since the dissociation and the following depreciations of the [British] pound."[98]

[98] Gutt (1935, pp. 73–74): "*En mars, ce fut la chute brusque. Le 4 mars, la livre sterling touchait 100 francs. Quatre pour cent de baisse. C'était un coup dur. Mais, réellement, il n'y avait pas*

Table 4.6. *Real GDP, GNP, and NNP of Belgium, the Netherlands, and Switzerland (1927–1936)*

	Belgium		Netherlands		Switzerland	
	GDP	GNP	GDP	NNP	GDP	NNP
1927	97	80	94	93	92	
1928	102		99	96	97	
1929	101		100	98	101	99
1930	100	100	100	100	100	100
1931	98		94	94	96	98
1932	94		93	91	93	95
1933	96		92	88	97	99
1934	95	97	91	88	97	100
1935	101	102	94	90	97	100
1936	102	114	100	92	97	100

Sources: Maddison (1995), Mitchell (2003).

Conversely, there is narrative evidence showing that the renewed fall of sterling was a blow to the Dutch economy as well. In November 1934, the *Economist* observed "a serious decline in Dutch trade with Great Britain, due to the protectionist policy of that country and the extremely low prices prevailing there."[99] In December, it reported that "the Netherlands Association of Employers has addressed a letter to the Prime Minister, Dr. Colijn, containing the following words: 'Our anxiety about the future of Holland and her inhabitants is such that we felt compelled to give expression to our misgivings, especially as our alarm has been accentuated by the recently presented Budget figures. Wherever we look, there is no escape from the impression that Holland's sources of prosperity are definitely drying up.'"[100] And in mid-March 1935, the *Economist* added: "A further blow has been struck at Dutch trade and industry by the rather unexpected and steep decline in sterling.... For not only on these trades, but on the entire commerce and industry of the country every new depreciation of sterling imposes the necessity of additional measures of deflation, with all their disagreeable results. Owing to the new fall in sterling, Holland is now a good

---

de quoi s'affoler. Nos industries en avaient vu d'autres, dans le passé; particulièrement, depuis le décrochage et les chutes successives de la livre."

[99] *Economist,* 10 November 1934, p. 876.

[100] *Economist,* 22 December 1934, p. 1204.

Table 4.7. *Political and Economic Indicators of Belgium, the Netherlands, and Switzerland*

	Belgium	Netherlands	Switzerland
Seats of socialists in parliament (in %)			
1925–36	38	23	30
Industrial disputes (number)			
1934	79	152	20
Industrial disputes (workers involved in 1000s)			
1934	34	6	3
Population (in million)			
1930	8.1	7.9	4.1
Wholesale prices (1929 = 100)			
1934	56	63	64
Consumer prices (1929 = 100)			
1934	76	83	80
Nominal wages (1929 = 100)			
1934	84	89	94
Real wages (1929 = 100)			
1934	111	107	118

Sources: Caramani (2000), Mitchell (2003).

deal farther than it was from the achievement of the necessary readjustment of costs with prices."[101]

The political argument fails to be convincing as well. It is true that Belgium's opposition to deflation was stronger because the Left and the labor unions had more power than in the Netherlands and Switzerland. Table 4.7 shows that the Socialists held more seats in the Belgian Parliament and that more workers were involved in industrial disputes in 1934 (even if the figures are corrected for population levels). Moreover, the threat of a miners' strike in early 1935 frightened employers and government officials and led them to withdraw their plan to cut the miners' pensions. Outside observers even got the impression that the conflict "almost caused

[101] *Economist,* 16 March 1935, p. 591.

revolutionary excitement" in Belgium, as the governing board of the Swiss National Bank put it.[102]

Yet, again, there are serious doubts whether these differences were important enough to give evidence to the claim that the Belgian government was particularly vulnerable. First, if it is true that opposition to deflation was fiercer in Belgium than in the Netherlands and Switzerland, it is hard to explain why Belgian workers accepted a larger reduction of their nominal wages than Dutch and Swiss workers[103] (see Table 4.7). Likewise, if the Belgian Socialist Party had been particularly militant, the *Economist*, a magazine with little sympathy for socialism, hardly would have praised it for its "exceptionally realistic" appreciation of workers' interests:

when the sterling countries went off gold and the British iron and steel tariff aimed what might have proved a mortal blow at one of Belgium's principal export industries, it was relatively easy for the Government to make drastic cuts in money wages at the same time as they preserved the continuity of Belgium's "free imports" policy. Belgium did not run amok with import restrictions and quotas; in the interests of the workers' real purchasing power she kept such restrictions at a level which, even to-day, makes her one of the lowest-tariff countries.[104]

Third, there were political tensions in the Netherlands and Switzerland as well. In early 1935, the situation in the Dutch coal-mining area became "threatening," as the *Economist* wrote.[105] The private mine owners terminated the labor agreements, and the miners' unions petitioned the prime minister to order a thorough inquiry. In the weeks and months after the devaluation of the Belgian franc, the Colijn cabinet stumbled from one crisis to another.[106] In the April elections, all but one of the five parties represented in the government lost votes, with the fascist NSA being one of the major winners. In May, Minister of Education Hendrik Marchant was dropped. In June, the cabinet clashed over the future course of exchange-rate policy with the result that Minister of Economic Affairs Max Steenberghe, who advocated a devaluation, resigned when he saw himself isolated. In

---

[102] Archives Swiss National Bank, 20 February 1935, p. 59: "*Ein Abbau der Bergarbeiter-Pensionen verursachte beinahe eine revolutionäre Erregung.*" Gutt (1935, pp. 44–49) also highlights the importance of this conflict.

[103] *Economist*, 23 March 1935, p. 666: "The cost of living has been reduced more than in other countries of the gold bloc; but it is still far from being in proportion to the low level of Belgian wholesale prices."

[104] *Economist*, 23 March 1935, p. 666. Cf. the discussion of the Belgian policy mix depending on the openness of the economy in Simmons (1994, pp. 241–256).

[105] *Economist*, 23 February 1935, p. 418.

[106] Griffiths (1987, pp. 179–184).

July, the Dutch parliament rejected the budget, which almost led to the resignation of Colijn and triggered a run on the guilder. On 24 July, one day after the parliamentary debate, the *Netherlandsche Bank* lost gold and foreign-exchange reserves worth 62 million guilder, and the discount rate was increased from 3 to 5 percent. Together with two top officials, central bank Governor Trip drafted a statement saying that the Netherlands was forced to suspend the gold standard: "The political development, which is generally known, has led to such a large and continuous capital flight, that the Directors have come to the conviction that it can no longer bind itself to its declaration of 1925."[107] The statement was not released, however.

In Switzerland, as noted earlier, two out of seven members of the Swiss government, Minister of Justice Heinrich Häberlin and Finance Minister Jean-Marie Musy, resigned in spring 1934 when the Swiss electorate rejected a new law on state security. It was especially the resignation of Musy, a fierce advocate of a balanced budget, that shattered the confidence in the franc and led to a reduction of the gold reserves of the central bank.[108] Tensions grew further when, together with employee organizations and progressive farmers, the Swiss trade unions launched the so-called crisis initiative in late April 1934. It foresaw an expansionary fiscal policy and a works program that was strongly opposed by the center-right government, the majority of the parliament, and the Swiss National Bank. The idea was very popular, however, and more than 300,000 Swiss voters signed the proposal, which by far exceeded the number of signatures required to bring about a referendum. The crisis also was followed closely by foreign observers, as was noted within the Swiss National Bank.[109] On 2 June 1935, the crisis initiative was almost adopted: 43 percent endorsed it.[110]

To summarize, the view that the government crisis of November 1934 was a logical consequence of Belgium's difficult economic and political conditions is not sustainable. The differences between Belgium, the Netherlands, and Switzerland were differences in degree, not fundamental ones. Accordingly, the de Broqueville government had the means to overcome the internal divisions and may have succeeded in managing the banking crisis and avoiding a devaluation in March 1935. Of course, sooner or later Belgium would have abandoned the gold standard anyway, and it was certainly fortunate that this step was taken 18 months before France, the Netherlands, and Switzerland. But contrary to a widely held

---

[107] Cited in Griffiths (1987, p. 183).
[108] Müller (2001, p. 122).
[109] Archives Swiss National Bank, *Bankausschuss*, 5 April 1935, pp. 119–120.
[110] The exact result was 567,425 (57 percent) no versus 425,242 (43 percent) yes.

belief, Belgium's early exit from the gold bloc does not seem to have been so clearly predetermined.

In any case, whatever the causes of the government crisis of November 1934, there is no doubt that from then on, devaluation of the Belgian franc was only a matter of time. The combination of a banking crisis and a political crisis proved deadly. The trend was stopped temporarily because only one week after de Broqueville's resignation Prime Minister Georges Theunis was sworn in. Yet the main problem remained unsolved: The government had to find a solution if it wanted to prevent the banking system from collapsing. According to Finance Minister Camille Gutt, the fate of the Boerenbond was the most urging issue they had to deal with.[111] On 20 November, when the new cabinet met for the first time, Prime Minister Theunis received a message that deposit withdrawals from the *Caisse générale d'Epargne et de Retraite*, the public savings bank, had doubled for several days.[112] In the course of 1934, the Caisse had lent 700 million francs to the Trésorerie, but now it was forced to borrow from the National Bank. In addition, the Socialists, young Catholics, and Liberals and parts of the press denounced the Theunis cabinet as a "government of bankers" because several ministers had strong ties to the world of finance.[113] On 27 November, when the Theunis government was confirmed by the parliament, a liberal deputy made public mention of the difficult situation of the Boerenbond banking group for the first time, which only served to accelerate deposit withdrawals: 35 to 40 million francs within two days.[114] Thanks to a series of new laws that were passed almost unanimously in the course of December, a bank panic was avoided.[115] But the situation remained unstable.

When the Belgian parliament returned from recess on 21 January 1935, the final run on the Belgian franc began.[116] Initially, the losses were moderate: From 21 January to 5 March, the bank lost gold worth less than

---

[111] See the statement of Gutt to the parliamentary committee that studied the causes of the devaluation: *Procès-verbaux, Enquête parlementaire chargée de rechercher les responsabilités de la dévaluation du franc*, 1935–1936, p. 37: "*Nous avons eu la crainte d'une catastrophe bancaire dès le jour de notre entrée au Gouvernement.*"

[112] Thielemans (1980, p. 29). See also the statement of Theunis to the parliamentary committee that studied the causes of the devaluation: *Procès-verbaux, Enquête parlementaire chargée de rechercher les responsabilités de la dévaluation du franc*, 1935–1936, p. 42: "*Au cours du débat sur la déclaration gouvernementale on a parlé du Boerenbond dont le crédit a été par cela même gravement touché. Ses liquidités étaient épuisées et les retraits commençaient à prendre un ampleur inquiétante.*"

[113] Gutt (1935, pp. 20–21), Thielemans (1980, pp. 30–31).

[114] Thielemans (1980, pp. 33 and 34).

[115] Van der Wee and Tavernier (1975, pp. 267–268).

[116] Gutt (1935, p. 64).

500 million francs. But then confidence collapsed. During the week from 11 to 16 March, the bank lost almost 2 billion francs in gold. The main events leading to the devaluation are well known.[117] On 12 February, several deputies openly advocated devaluation during a parliamentary debate. On 18 March, exchange controls were introduced, and a Belgian delegation tried to obtain a new loan and trade concessions from the French government, but the negotiations failed. One day later, the Theunis government resigned and was replaced by a government of national unity led by Paul van Zeeland. On 29 March, the franc was devalued by 28 percent. By that time, not only the small commercial and savings banks were threatened by the deposit withdrawals but also the second-largest Belgian bank, the *Banque de Bruxelles*. On 25 March, it received an emergency loan from the government.[118] Even the largest bank, the *Banque de la Société Générale de Belgique*, was faced with serious problems and was forced to implement a restructuring plan.[119]

THE NEW REGIME AND THE LIMITS OF CHANGE

By any standards, the strategy for maintaining the gold standard at the old parity had failed completely. Accordingly, policymakers were forced to revise their basic assumptions about the exchange-rate regime and in fact adjusted the exchange-rate regime to the new international environment. However, the regime change did not go as far as might be expected by scholars who regard the 1930s as a decade of fundamental policy innovation. Policymakers continued to be convinced that fixed exchange rates served the economy best and that deviations from this principle should be only temporary. The Bretton Woods system certainly was more flexible than the gold exchange standard of the interwar years, but it inherited two important principles from its predecessor: pegged exchange rates and gold convertibility.[120]

Owing to this strong consensus, policymakers disagreed only on what kind of peg should be adopted in the aftermath of the devaluation and on how rapidly the exchange rate should be fixed again (Table 4.8). The Belgian

---

[117] Van der Wee and Tavernier (1975, pp. 274–278).

[118] Vanthemsche (1980, p. 392), Hogg (1987, p. 200).

[119] Vanthemsche (1997, pp. 296–303). The bank was created in reaction to the new banking legislation passed in August 1934 that foresaw a separation of the *Société Générale*'s banking business and its industrial participations.

[120] On the lessons drawn from the interwar experience and their impact on the Bretton Woods system, see Bordo (1993), Eichengreen (1996b, pp. 93–96), and Bordo and James (2001).

Table 4.8. *The New Regimes of the Gold Bloc Countries*

	Introduction of Exchange Controls	Suspension of Gold Standard	Devaluation or Depreciation	New Regime
Belgium	March 1935	March 1935	March 1935	New gold parity (March 1936)
France	–	–	September 1936	New gold parity (October 1936)
Netherlands	–	September 1936	September 1936	De facto sterling peg (January 1937)
Switzerland	–	–	September 1936	Provisional new gold parity (September 1936)

Source : Renou (1939), p. 133.

government chose the most rigid regime: First, it introduced capital controls, devalued the franc by 28 percent, and fixed a new provisional gold parity; then, one year later, it removed capital controls and fixed a definite gold parity. Similarly, the Swiss suspended convertibility, devalued the franc, and fixed a new gold parity, but unlike in the Belgian case, the new parity remained provisional and was less rigid because the exchange rate was allowed to fluctuate between 26.9 and 34.5 percent of the old parity. De facto, however, the franc was stabilized at the level of 30 percent. The Dutch, by contrast, were more cautious: They introduced a gold embargo, let the guilder depreciate, and stabilized the exchange rate at the level of 20 to 25 percent below the old parity without fixing a new parity. Thus, in the strict sense of the word, the guilder was not devalued. But de facto, it was a sterling peg.

When the van Zeeland government in Belgium decided to devalue the franc, it was not clear that a new gold parity would be fixed.[121] There were notable advocates of a sterling peg, in particular, influential professors of economics at the University of Louvain, Fernand Baudhuin and Léon Dupriez, and van Zeeland himself, who had studied in Louvain and had spent a year at the Economics Department at Princeton University, attending, among others, the seminars of Edwin Kemmerer, who helped establish

---

[121] On the implementation of the Belgian devaluation, see Baudhuin (1946a, pp. 332–347), van der Wee and Tavernier (1975, pp. 278–285), and Janssens (1976, pp. 256–259).

the International Finance Section in 1929 and became its first director. The main argument of the Louvain economists was that the British pound might depreciate again, forcing Belgium to return to a deflationary policy as before 1935. They also reckoned that there was only a small risk of imported inflation because the British had shown since the devaluation of the pound that they were able to maintain price stability without a hard peg.[122] This proposal met strong opposition, however. Central bank Governor Louis Franck succeeded in convincing the *Conseil de Régence* of the National Bank of Belgium that such a regime change was too dangerous. Van Zeeland eventually backed down from his position, acknowledging that a new gold parity was perhaps more suited to reassure the public and to facilitate the return of capital.[123] Perhaps the timing was important as well. In March 1935, the gold bloc was still functioning and showed no sign of an early collapse despite all its economic and political difficulties. Belgian policymakers therefore wanted to minimize the break with the past.

In Switzerland, there was a similar debate as in Belgium.[124] But it was the Swiss National Bank that came up with the idea to peg the franc to the pound, as President Bachmann explained to the *Bankausschuss:* "At an earlier stage, the Governing Board had a different solution in mind, namely, following the English pound. We did not want to tie the franc to gold anymore because, under certain conditions, this might have entailed difficulties again. We were thinking to keep the currency at a certain distance from the pound and the dollar, but also to follow the fluctuations of the pound and the dollar."[125]

Eventually, the idea was rejected for two reasons. First, the pound had only been attractive as an alternative anchor currency as long the French franc remained on gold. But now, since the French franc had left the gold standard as well, the need to find an alternative was less urgent. Second, the gold price of the dollar and the pound had been quite stable for some time. It thus made little difference whether the Swiss franc was pegged to the pound or whether a new gold parity was established. Yet, at least, policymakers

---

[122] Baudhuin (1936, p. 46).
[123] Baudhuin (1946a, pp. 332–333) and van der Wee and Tavernier (1975, p. 281).
[124] On the Swiss devaluation, see Bébié (1939, pp. 209–218), Renou (1939, pp. 130–148), and Rutz (1970, pp. 140–144).
[125] Archives Swiss National Bank, *Bankausschuss*, 28 September 1936, pp. 370–371: "*In einem frühern Stadium hatte dem Direktorium eher eine andere Lösung vorgeschwebt, nämlich die Anlehnung an das englische Pfund. Man wollte keine Bindung mehr an das Gold, welche unter Umständen wiederum Schwierigkeiten hätte bereiten können. Man dachte daran, die Währung einfach in einem gewissen Abstand von Pfund und Dollar zu halten, aber auch die Schwankungen von Pfund und Dollar mitzumachen.*"

understood that they needed to introduce some flexibility into their new regime and therefore decided to adopt a broad exchange-rate target: The franc was allowed to fluctuate between 25.9 and 34.5 percent of the old gold parity (between 215 and 190 milligrams).[126] However, it was always understood that the Swiss National Bank was expected to keep the exchange rate within a narrow band of 28.5 and 31.5 percent.[127] Thus Switzerland pursued a similar strategy as Belgium, namely, maintaining as much continuity with the former exchange-rate regime as possible. The signal was understood by the markets, as Tanner (2000) points out. The fact that Switzerland was among the last countries to devalue and maintained a gold parity reassured foreign investors.[128]

The Netherlands was the only former gold bloc country that waited before fixing a new parity.[129] It had only decreed a gold embargo on 27 September and created an Exchange Equalization Fund, but as noted, this approach did not mean that the Dutch authorities had embraced managed floating as a new exchange-rate regime. On the contrary, the reluctance to fix a new parity was due to the fear of new turbulences, as central bank Governor Trip explained in the Annual Report: "No decision has as yet been taken as to the new gold parity of the guilder. The authorities have reserved themselves full freedom of action on this point. This does not mean, however, that the guilder has been abandoned to its fate. The Equalization Fund was created in order to prevent or at least to restrict, in the interest of industry and trade, undesirable influences of capital movements or speculative operations."[130] Hans Cohrssen, an assistant of Irving Fisher, who traveled through Europe in order to learn more about the monetary experiences during the depression, wrote: "The truth seems to be that the same cautious mentality which caused the Dutch to hold onto the deflationary gold standard for such a long time, now makes them proceed slowly and tentatively. The Dutch are a conservative people...."[131] Schwarz (1937), who compared the devaluations of the guilder and the franc, made a similar observation: "From a legal point of view the guilder has been left to the interplay of demand and supply of the foreign-exchange market. In reality, this is not true. Even if it is only out of consideration for the basis on which calculations are made in commercial

---

[126] *Bundesratsbeschluss vom 27. September 1936 betreffend Währungsmassnahmen.*
[127] *Schweizerische Nationalbank* (1957, pp. 118–119).
[128] Tanner (2000, pp. 2 and 58–60).
[129] On the Dutch devaluation, see Schwarz (1937, pp. 376–380) and de Vries (1994, pp. 135–150).
[130] *Nederlandsche Bank*, Annual Report, 1936, p. 28.
[131] I thank Claude Million for providing me with the reports of Cohrssen.

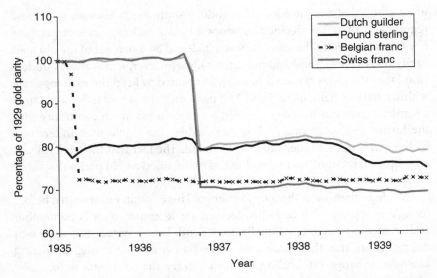

Figure 4.3. Exchange rates of sterling and the currencies of Belgium, the Netherlands, and Switzerland (percentage of 1929 gold parity). (*League of Nations.*)

life, it is impossible for a country that is closely linked to the world market to refrain from influencing the exchange rates in the desired manner by buying and selling gold and foreign exchange."[132] Finally, in an internal memo, the Statistical Bureau of the Swiss National Bank came to the same conclusion that the exchange rate was only theoretically determined by the market but in reality by the intervention of the central bank.[133]

Accordingly, although the Dutch regime officially differed from the Belgian and the Swiss regimes, the basic approach was very similar, as Figure 4.3 shows. Instead of being fixed to gold, the Dutch guilder was tied to the British pound from January 1937 to October 1938. It is thus fair to conclude that the small gold bloc states, despite introducing some flexibility into their new exchange-rate regimes, continued to be cautious and conservative. As after World War I, they considered the instability of the international monetary environment to be temporary and were waiting

---

[132] Schwarz (1937, p. 378): "*Der Gulden wurde, … juridisch betrachtet, in seiner Kursgestaltung dem Spiel von Nachfrage und Angebot auf dem Wechselmarkt überlassen. Praktisch trifft dies allerdings nicht zu. Schon mit Rücksicht auf die Kalkulationsbasis des kaufmännischen Lebens kann es sich kein weltwirtschaftlich verbundenes Land erlauben, die Wechselkurse durch An- und Verkäufe von Gold und Devisen nicht im gewünschten Sinne zu beeinflussen.*"

[133] Archives Swiss National Bank, 5135 (501.1). *Währung und Wirtschaft in Holland im Vergleich mit der Schweiz*, p. 1.

for better times. The idea that some day they might have a system of permanently flexible exchange rates was completely unrealistic at the time. They all shared the view of Nurkse (1944), who in his report on interwar monetary history wrote: "If there is anything that the inter-war experience has clearly demonstrated, it is that paper currency exchanges cannot be left free to fluctuate from day to day under the influence of market supply and demand.... If currencies are left free to fluctuate 'speculation' in the widest sense is likely to play havoc with the exchange rates."[134]

[134] Nurkse (1944, pp. 137–138).

PART TWO

AFTER BRETTON WOODS

After almost three decades of relative exchange-rate stability, the collapse of the Bretton Woods system in the early 1970s created a situation that resembled in many ways the monetary chaos after World War I. Exchange rates were fluctuating wildly, currency crises and devaluations were frequent events, and the fight against inflation became a top priority for governments and central banks. However, despite all resemblances, the differences between the period after the end of Bretton Woods and the interwar years were more fundamental. First, some countries, notably the United States and Japan, made a permanent shift to flexible-exchange-rate regimes during the 1970s. Exchange-rate policies were not determined by the expectation that the old system would be restored. Second, the fixed-exchange-rate arrangements created by the members of the European Community (EC), namely, the Snake and the European Monetary System (EMS), were much less rigid than the interwar gold standard. The pegs were fixed but adjustable, capital mobility was limited until the late 1980s, and it was possible to leave the arrangement temporarily or to change the conditions of membership. It wasn't until introduction of the euro at the end of the century that many European countries again gave up their monetary policy independence. From 1973 to 1999, the options were much more numerous than during the interwar years.

What regime choices have small European countries made during this period? Since the general conditions have been quite different from those of the interwar years and the macroeconomic knowledge has evolved since the 1930s, we would expect that they have been much more inclined to monetary experiments than ever. Surprisingly, however, this expectation is only partly confirmed. Of course, there was not a single small European state that sought to restore or to defend an old parity at any cost. But the idea that exchange rates should be fixed proved to be remarkably persistent in the 1970s and 1980s. Only Switzerland permanently abandoned the fixed exchange rate in 1973, but even in this case, the regime shift was entirely against the will of policymakers and became permanent only when France rejected the Swiss plan to join the Snake in 1975. All other small European states maintained a fixed exchange rate. The small EC members, the Benelux countries and Denmark, participated in the Snake and the EMS. Norway and Sweden first joined the Snake in 1972–1973 and then shifted to a currency basket peg in 1977–1978, respectively. And Austria linked the peg to a currency basket and then adopted a hard deutsche mark (DM) peg.

Not until the 1992 EMS crisis, when Norway and Sweden were forced to abandon their unilateral European currency unit (ECU) peg they had adopted in 1990–1991 did the idea that small European states needed a fixed exchange rate lose its power in the minds of policymakers. Sweden immediately adopted inflation targeting and a flexible exchange rate and showed by successfully managing the krona that conventional wisdom was flawed. Norway was more hesitant in adopting inflation targeting but eventually took the same step de facto in 1999 and *de jure* in 2001, thus further increasing the number of small European states with a flexible exchange rate. In other words, until the last decade of the twentieth century, small states were continuously seeking more flexibility within the framework of a fixed exchange rate. The Benelux countries and Denmark revalued or devalued their currencies but never considered leaving the Snake or the EMS. Norway and Sweden left the Snake but adopted a currency basket peg, not a flexible exchange rate. And Austria always kept the schilling as stable as possible vis-à-vis the DM.

By contrast, the large European states – France, Germany, Italy, and the United Kingdom – abandoned the fixed exchange rate in order to pursue an independent monetary policy. Germany let the DM float in March 1973 and could allow itself to introduce monetary targeting because the DM was the de facto anchor currency of the Snake. The United Kingdom, Italy, and France left the Snake in the period from 1972 to 1974 because it became obvious that they were not able to maintain a fixed exchange rate against the strong DM. Thus, while all currencies of the small states – with the exception of the Swiss franc – remained tied to the DM or were pegged to a currency basket, the currencies of the large states were floating during the greater part of the 1970s. Only with the start of the EMS did the period of divergence come to an end. France and Italy joined from the beginning and eventually adopted the euro, together with Germany, Spain, and most small EC member states. From then on, there is no divide between small and large European states anymore. We find that both large and small states outside and inside the European area and even very small European states have adopted different regimes: Luxembourg introduced the euro in 1999, and Iceland shifted to inflation targeting in 2001.

The following four chapters will discuss the changing choices of small and large states since the end of Bretton Woods system in more detail, like the four chapters of Part One. However, the basic structure is not chronological but analytical. Chapters Five and Six deal with two processes of divergence. Chapter Five tries to explain why small and large European states made different choices during the 1970s and why in 1973 Switzerland and in 1992 Norway and Sweden abandoned their fixed-exchange-rate regime. Chapter Six is focused on the divergence among small European states that maintained a fixed exchange rate. Austria and the Netherlands defended a hard peg against the DM, Belgium and Denmark were forced to effect a series of devaluations within the Snake and the EMS, and Norway and Sweden left the Snake in 1977–1978 and readjusted their currency baskets several times.

Chapters Seven and Eight deal with the regime shifts and experiences of Switzerland, Norway, and Sweden. As noted, the Swiss franc was the only currency of a small European state to begin to float in 1973, and this regime shift became permanent only after the failed attempt to enter the Snake in 1975. Chapter Seven explains in more detail why the decision to float was taken and why France rejected the Swiss request. Furthermore, it takes a look at how the Swiss National Bank has managed the floating Swiss franc since 1973. Chapter Eight poses and tries to answer one question, namely, why Norway and Sweden were forced to abandon their exchange-rate pegs and how the central banks have managed their floating currencies.

Again, as in Part One, the approach is, highly selective. Only the fall of the Finnish markka during the 1992 EMS crisis will be treated in some detail because it enables us to better understand the regime shift in Norway and Sweden. However, the selection is not random. As during the interwar years, Finland, Ireland, and Portugal were still at the periphery of the European economy during the 1970s. Only in the last 10 to 20 years have they been catching up. And, of course, the small Eastern and Central European countries were planned economies until 1989, which makes them special cases. Even the choices of Finland were strongly influenced by the Socialist camp headed by the Soviet Union. The major reason why the Finnish markka was not linked to the Snake in 1973, as was the currency of neighboring Sweden, was the concern over the neutral status of the country.[1] Thus Part Two will focus on the same group of small developed states as Part One. Only Austria has been added to the group because its economic and political history after the end of Bretton Woods has not been marked by the catastrophic consequences of the world war, as was the case in the interwar years.

[1]   Moses (1995, pp. 214–223).

FIVE

Fixed versus Floating

During the 1970s, small and large states reacted differently to the dis-integration of the Bretton Woods system and the first attempt by the European Community (EC) to deepen monetary cooperation.[2] From 1972 to 1976, the United Kingdom, Italy, and France left the Snake, the monetary arrangement of the EC, and switched to a floating regime.[3] And Germany, whose strong currency was the anchor of the Snake, abandoned exchange-rate targeting and focused on control of the central bank money stock. By contrast, the overwhelming majority of small states maintained a peg, either by staying in the Snake, by adopting a currency basket, or by maintaining a deutsche mark (DM) peg (Table 5.1). Only one small state, Switzerland, abandoned the fixed-exchange-rate regime in the early 1970s, and it remained the only exception until the European Monetary System (EMS) crisis in 1992, when Norway and Sweden made the same regime shift. Thus not until the end of the twentieth century did a floating exchange rate become a normal option for small European states.

Why did most small states maintain a peg during the 1970s, whereas large countries chose to float? And why did Switzerland in 1973 and Norway and Sweden in 1992 make a regime shift toward floating? As to the first question, country size obviously played a role, but not exclusively, as the Swiss exception shows. The crucial question, then, is by what chan-nel did country size exert its influence?[4] A survey on the criteria by which countries choose their exchange-rate regime suggests that there are two

---

[2] The name *European Community* (EC) was used from 1967 to 1993. The Maastricht Treaty changed the name to *European Union* (EU).

[3] France reentered in July 1975 and left again in March 1976.

[4] So far there have been only two studies dealing with exchange-rate policies of small European states during the 1970s: Thygesen (1979) and Argy and De Grauwe (1990). Thygesen does not cover Austria and Switzerland, however.

Table 5.1. *Exchange-Rate Regimes of Large and Small European States (1972–1979, 1990–1993, 1999)*

Monetary Regime		Large EEC Countries			Small EEC Countries			Small EFTA Countries			
		France	Italy	UK	BG	DK	NL	NOR	SWE	AUT	SWITZ
Snake	1972	Snake	Snake	Snake/Float	Snake	Snake	Snake	Snake			
	1973		Float						Snake	DM peg	Float
	1974	Float									
	1975	Snake									
	1976	Float									
	1977								Basket		
	1978							Basket			
EMS	1979	EMS	EMS	EMS	EMS	EMS	EMS				
EMS crisis	1990			EMS				Ecu-peg			
	1991								Ecu-peg		
	1992			Float				Float	Float		
	1993							Ecu-peg			
Euro	1999	Euro	Euro	Float	Euro	Euro-peg	Euro	Float	Float	Euro	Float

Germany is not on the list because the DM was the anchor currency of the Snake and the EMS.

possibilities. Either small states disposed of more flexible wage bargaining systems than large states and therefore were better capable of making the price adjustments required to maintain a pegged exchange rate, or the economies of small states were so much more open that it was almost natural to keep the exchange rate pegged to the currencies of the main trading partners.

As this chapter will show, the first possibility is clearly at odds with the evidence. It is true that small states had more flexible institutions than large states, but they were not flexible enough to prevent the real exchange rate from sharply appreciating during the crucial phase from 1972 to 1976 when large states left the Snake. It must have been the second channel that made a difference. The problem with this factor, however, is that not all small states were significantly more open than large states. It thus would be wrong to make an automatic connection between trade openness and the choice of an exchange-rate regime. I will argue that the solution to this problem can be found in how policymakers *perceived* their economies and the risks of foreign-exchange markets. Small states maintained a peg during the 1970s because policymakers *thought* that a small, open economy needed a stable currency. They feared that an erratically moving exchange rate would harm trade and complicate the conduct of monetary policy and the wage bargaining process. As a result, a floating regime was never seriously taken into consideration. Only after the regime change of Norway and Sweden in 1992 did the fixed idea that a small, open economy needed a fixed exchange rate begin to lose its power.

This finding has implications for the second question. The regime shift of Switzerland in 1973 and of Norway and Sweden in 1992 did not result from careful considerations but from the lack of alternatives. A combination of two factors caused this impasse: financial openness and nonmembership of the EC – a combination that we find only in the case of small states. The first factor made the currencies of Switzerland, Norway, and Sweden possible victims of speculative attacks. The second one explains why the fixed regime could not be maintained and why the authorities were reluctant to return to the fixed regime. During the 1970s and 1980s, Switzerland was the only small European state meeting both conditions and therefore was forced to abandon the fixed regime. As Norway and Sweden liberalized their financial markets and unilaterally pegged their currencies to the European currency unit (ECU), they found themselves in the same situation: Their currencies were vulnerable, and they lacked the credibility, the domestic mandate, and the support by other central banks needed to defend a currency.

The remainder of this chapter has four parts. The first two sections discuss and reject the institutional argument stating that small states had more flexible wage bargaining systems and thus were better able to maintain a pegged exchange rate. The third section highlights the importance of economic ideas. And the last section explains the regime changes of Switzerland in 1973 and of Sweden and Norway in the 1990s and compares them with those of large states from 1972 to 1976.

COUNTRY SIZE, INSTITUTIONS, AND DOMESTIC ADJUSTMENT

The literature on what factors countries should consider when choosing their exchange-rate regime is abundant. Inspired by the theory of optimum currency areas (OCA), Eichengreen et al. (1999) have made a comprehensive list of the most important criteria[5] (Table 5.2). It shows that only two criteria are relevant for the choice of a floating regime: trade openness and the type of shocks. In contrast, a pegged exchange-rate regime that includes a crawling peg and a fixed rate requires a much more specific country profile:

- A high level of reserves
- Capital controls
- Labor mobility
- Nominal flexibility
- A diversified production and export structure
- Fiscal flexibility and sustainability
- Close economic relations with partner countries (high degree of trade openness, symmetric shocks, nominal shocks)

Which of these criteria explain the choices of small and large states?[6] To make the discussion easier, we can divide them into two groups. The first group consists of all the factors highlighting domestic flexibility, whereas the second group emphasizes the importance of economic integration. Were small states more capable of making the adjustments required to maintain a pegged exchange rate? This question is crucial because if the answer is positive, the preference of small states for a peg loses all its mystery, and the only problem to be solved is Swiss exceptionalism. If not,

---

[5] Eichengreen et al. (1999, p. 4). The seminal papers on OCA theory are Mundell (1961), McKinnon (1963), and Kenen (1969).

[6] Note that this chapter deals only with the choice fixed versus floating. Chapter Six will treat the reasons why Sweden and Norway shifted to a basket in 1977 and 1978, respectively.

Table 5.2. *Criteria for Choice of Exchange-Rate Regime*

	Float		Target Band		Peg		Currency Board	Currency Union
	Pure	Managed	Wide	Narrow	Crawling	Fixed		
Inflation								
High	X	X	X		X			
Low	X	X	X	X		X	X	X
Level of reserves								
High	X	X	X	X	X	X	X	X
Low	X	X	X					X
Capital mobility								
High	X	X	X				X	X
Low	X	X	X	X	X	X	X	X
Labor mobility and nominal flexibility								
High	X	X	X	X	X	X	X	X
Low	X	X	X	X				
Production and export diversification								
High	X	X	X	X	X	X	X	X
Low	X	X						
Fiscal flexibility and sustainability								
High	X	X	X	X	X	X	X	X
Low	X	X	X					
Relative to partner countries								
Trade integration								
High			X	X	X	X	X	X
Low	X	X						
Political integration (similarity of policy preferences)								
High			X	X	X	X	X	X
Low	X	X	X	X	X	X	X	
Preponderance of shocks								
Symmetric	X	X	X	X	X	X	X	X
Asymmetric	X	X	X					
Type of shocks								
Real	X	X						
Nominal			X	X	X	X	X	X

Source: Eichengreen et al. (1999, p. 21).

the mystery remains because we would have to explain why small states preferred a peg despite their failure to prevent the real exchange rate from appreciating sharply. Because of its central role for the argument, we start with the discussion of domestic institutions. This section tries to assemble evidence supporting the view that small states in fact had more institutional flexibility than large states. The subsequent section then will argue against this view and draw a conclusion.

The most important proponent of the view that during the 1970s small states infact had more flexible institutions than large states is Katzenstein (1985). He showed that because of their high degree of economic openness and their great vulnerability to shifts in the world economy, small states had developed a distinct "democratic corporatism" in order to cushion the negative effects of external shocks.[7] He identified three characteristics of this type of corporatism: "an ideology of social partnership, a centralized and concentrated system of economic interest groups, and an uninterrupted process of bargaining among all of the major political actors across different sectors of policy."[8] Thanks to these cooperative features, small states were able to combine political stability with economic flexibility. Among large states, by contrast, these corporatist arrangements were less common, Katzenstein argues.[9]

Recent research on the causes of inflation and unemployment during the postwar era can be read as a confirmation of Katzenstein's view, although this research has never been undertaken with the purpose of linking institutional structures to country size. Following the seminal paper of Calmfors and Driffill (1988), economists and political scientists have focused on the interaction between central banks and wage bargaining systems.[10] Two of their findings are relevant for our topic. First, all small states had either an independent central bank or a highly centralized wage bargaining system[11] (Figure 5.1). By contrast, most large states

---

[7] Precursors of Katzenstein are Wright (1939) and Kindleberger (1951). Huberman and Lewchuk (2003) provide econometric evidence for the first globalization period before World War I. For a skeptical view, see, for example, Iversen (1999).

[8] Katzenstein (1985, p. 80).

[9] *Ibid.*, p. 9.

[10] Important papers are Cukierman and Lippi (1999), Iversen (1999), and Franzese and Hall (2000). See also Franzese's book (2002).

[11] There is some disagreement on the precise extent of central bank independence. However, in all indices, the central banks of France, Italy, and the United Kingdom are considered to be very dependent. See Freitag (1999, p. 105) for a comparison of the indices of Alesina (1989), Grilli, Masciandaro, and Tabellini (1991), Eijffinger and De Haan (1996), and Cukierman (1992). A new review of CBI is provided by Crowe and Meade (2007).

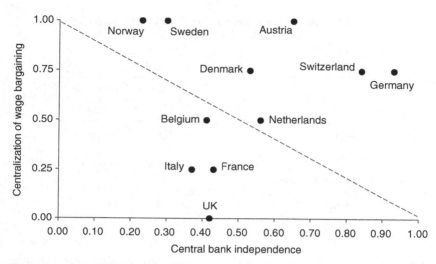

Figure 5.1. Central bank independence and centralization of wage bargaining. (*Franzese and Hall, 2000, p. 198.*)

lacked both these institutions. Only Germany does not fit the picture, and this may be the reason why most scholars have overlooked the fact that country size mattered. But the German case does not violate the rule. The small-country argument claims only that small states *always* have either an independent central bank or a highly centralized wage bargaining system or even both. It does not preclude that large states also *sometimes* have one or both institutional specialities.

The second finding is that owing to their institutional features, small states had lower inflation rates than the three large countries that left the Snake[12] (Table 5.3). The data clearly show that countries having a weak central bank and a highly centralized wage bargaining system (e.g., Norway and Sweden) perform better than countries with a weak central bank and a decentralized system (e.g., France, Italy, and the United Kingdom).

Since maintaining a stable exchange-rate regime was mainly about controlling inflation, it is fair to conclude that small states pegged their exchange rate throughout the 1970s because their institutions were particularly flexible. These institutions also allowed successful devaluations: The

---

[12] Lane (1995) also comes to the conclusion that openness and inflation are negatively correlated for OECD countries. Romer (1993), by contrast, does not find any correlation between openness and inflation for OECD countries but only for countries outside the OECD.

Table 5.3. *Average Inflation Rates in OECD Countries under
Alternative Institutional Arrangements (1955–1990)*

		Inflation Rates	
		Central Bank Independence	
		Low	High
Coordinated	Low	7.5	4.8
Wage bargaining	High	6.2	4.8

Note: Cases were coded as follows:
CWB: low = 0 and 0.25, high = 0.75 and 1; CBI: low = below 0.50,
high = above 0.50. Cases where CWB = medium (0.5) are omitted here.
Source: Franzese and Hall (2000, p. 187).

government was able to pursue a restrictive monetary policy or to demand wage restraint from labor unions that was needed to reap the competitive advantages resulting from a weaker currency. The United Kingdom, Italy, and France, by contrast, let their currencies float because they lacked these institutional capabilities.

There is also some narrative evidence suggesting that large states had more problems in containing inflation than small states and therefore left the Snake. In the United Kingdom, Italy, and France, the decision to float the currency always was preceded by a shift to more expansionary monetary and fiscal policies that could be pursued only because the central bank lacked the power to prevent such policies. These decisions were motivated by the fear of losing the next election or of violent clashes with labor unions that were weakly organized but, depending on the sector, highly politicized and militant. The German weekly magazine *Die Zeit* observed after the second defection of the French franc from the Snake in March 1976: "This is the European reality. Discipline is not in demand anymore. The class conflicts are greater in countries such as France, Italy, and England than in the Federal Republic, Holland, or Denmark."[13]

The most evident example is the defection of sterling in June 1972. Under the Labor government of Harold Wilson (1964–1970), it had already become clear that the lack of a strong central bank and the decentralized structure of the British labor movement made it hard to manage

[13] *Die Zeit*, No. 14, 26 March 1976, p. 25: "*Das ist die europäische Realität. Disziplin ist nicht
gefragt. Die Klassengegensätze sind in Ländern wie Frankreich, Italien und England noch
immer grösser als etwa in der Bundesrepublik, in Holland oder Dänemark.*"

the economy and control inflation. As a result of the lack of confidence in Wilson's economic policy and the mounting level of wage costs, sterling was devalued by no less than 14.3 percent in the autumn of 1967.[14] And since the underlying problems persisted, the situation only eased temporarily. Wages continued to grow faster than productivity, and the government appeared helpless in the face of increasing labor militancy.

The advent of the Conservative government in 1970 did not change much. Only at the beginning did Prime Minister Edward Heath try a new approach. Instead of using income policies, he tightened fiscal and monetary policies in order to reduce inflation. Yet the government did not have the courage or the power to stay its course as unemployment grew because of its restrictive policies. This led to a complete reorientation of economic policy. At the beginning of the year 1972, the government decided to stimulate both consumption and investment, which lead to the so-called Barber boom, named after Chancellor of the Exchequer Anthony Barber.[15] At the same time, Heath reached out to the unions to strike a deal to get moderate wage increases for his expansionary policies that were supposed to create jobs. Yet, again, the strategy failed mainly because of the militancy of labor unions. As a result, the foreign-exchange markets grew uneasy about the future of sterling. According to the bank for international settlements (BIS), "[T]he crisis was sparked off by the imminent prospect of a national dock strike."[16] The run on sterling began on June 14, 1972. The Bank of England and the EC central banks tried to turn the tide, but after 10 days, on June 23, they stopped their interventions in the foreign-exchange market. Sterling began to float, and despite several official statements that it would soon be fixed again, it continued to remain outside any monetary arrangement of the EC until 1990.

The Italian government was trapped in the same dilemma. On the one hand, it knew that the stop-and-go-policy was doomed. Wage increases were too high, confidence in the economic policy had evaporated, and with increasing creativity, Italians brought their money to Switzerland.[17] On the

[14] Cairncross and Eichengreen (1983, pp. 156–217).
[15] Hellmann (1976, pp. 43–47), Solomon (1982, p. 221), de Vries (1985, pp. 47–49), Hatton and Chrystal (1991, p. 70), Bean and Crafts (1996, pp. 146–147), James (1996, pp. 239–240), Dyson and Featherstone (1999, pp. 537–538), Howson (2004, p. 155).
[16] BIS, Annual Report, 1972–1973, p. 138. Tsoukalis (1977, p. 122) also highlights "the growing fear of an industrial strife in Britain." In his memoirs, Heath (1998, p. 409) confirms that the ongoing docker dispute was an important factor. He also mentions that "the vulnerability of sterling was greatly enhanced by nervousness about the rate of inflation in Britain as compared with that in other countries..."
[17] Hellmann (1976, pp. 50–51), Tsoukalis (1977, p. 126).

other hand, the authorities were too weak to confront the unions, and the Bank of Italy, though highly respected, was not independent enough to pursue its own monetary policy.[18] In the late 1960s, the growing discontent of workers had resulted in a series of strikes, with the most powerful one being the general strike in September 1969. In Torino alone, there had been 600,000 metal workers demonstrating in the streets.[19]

Accordingly, the new center-right government under Christian Democrat Giulio Andreotti, formed in June 1972, gave in when the left wing of the party opposed deflationary measures suggested by the finance minister.[20] The *Banca d'Italia* was told to lower interest rates, leading to another wave of capital flight. And despite this expansionary policy, strikes and social unrest continued, which further unsettled foreign-exchange markets. In January 1973, a two-tier system was introduced, but renewed capital flight in February caused the Italian authorities to let the lira float.[21] The strategy of combining expansionary policies with capital controls had failed completely.

France experienced the same kind of militant labor unionism in the late 1960s as Italy. In May 1968, the economic life of France came to a halt as unions successfully organized several stay-in strikes across the country, and large student demonstrations took place in Paris. In April 1969, President Charles de Gaulle resigned after losing a referendum on regional reform and on the de facto abolition of the senate which he had declared to be a personal confidence vote. As the political crisis continued and markets became increasingly nervous, France was losing foreign-exchange reserves at a high rate. Finally, de Gaulle's successor, Georges Pompidou, devalued the franc by 12 percent in August 1969.[22]

The events of 1968 had a strong impact on French economic policy during the 1970s.[23] Pompidou, afraid of another outburst of popular discontent, wanted the economy to grow at almost any cost. With the poor performance of the Gaullist Party in the national elections of 1973, the pressure to pursue expansionary policies increased further. When a few months later the oil crisis led to a further inflationary wave and a sharp reduction in foreign-exchange reserves, Pompidou was not willing to

---

[18] Goodman (1992, pp. 143, 146–147).
[19] Rossi and Toniolo (1996, pp. 442–445), Ferrera and Gualmini (2000, p. 356).
[20] Goodman (1992, pp. 146–147).
[21] Hellmann (1976, p. 52).
[22] Solomon (1982, pp. 151–165).
[23] Loriaux (1991, p. 190), Goodman (1992, p. 110), Levy (2000, pp. 320–321).

switch to a restrictive monetary policy. In January 1974, France announced the independent floating of its currency.[24]

As for the second French exit two years later – the franc had reentered the Snake in May 1975 – we can observe the same mechanism.[25] The weakening of the franc was preceded by a shift to expansionary policies initiated by Prime Minister Jacques Chirac in the second half of 1975 (*"relance Chirac"*). By creating a boom and increasing employment, Chirac was hoping to win the cantonal elections taking place in March 1976, a policy that was not consistent with a fixed exchange rate against the deutsche mark (DM). The strategy failed to bring the desired results. The Left won the cantonal elections, and President Valérie Giscard d'Estaing decided to let the franc float in order to keep the economy growing.

In summary, there is statistical and narrative evidence supporting the claim that the United Kingdom, Italy, and France left the Snake from 1972 to 1976 because they lacked the institutional prerequisites to contain inflation in accordance with Germany. Already in 1967 and 1969, respectively, the United Kingdom and France had experienced severe currency crises with subsequent devaluations. And the Italian economy had suffered from violent strikes and inconsistent economic policies since the late 1960s. In small states, by contrast, we don't find situations that were as conflicting as in these three large states. Apparently, the institutions of small states were more flexible and thus more capable of adjusting to the pegged regime than those of large states.

THE LIMITS OF THE INSTITUTIONAL APPROACH

Yet, although small states had fewer domestic problems than large states, it would be wrong to conclude that they easily managed to adjust to the restrictive course of Germany. Quite the reverse is true: Small states avoided floating from 1972 to 1976 *even though* they had problems with their deutsche mark (DM) peg. Inflation rates may have been lower than in France, Italy, and the United Kingdom, but they still were too high in comparison with the German rate (Table 5.4). Accordingly, real exchange rates continued rising sharply until 1976.

---

[24] Hellmann (1976, pp. 63–65), Tsoukalis (1977, pp. 129–130), Goodman (1992, pp. 112–113), McNamara (1998, pp. 119–120), Dyson and Featherstone (1999, p. 111), Walsh (2000, pp. 27–28).

[25] Hellmann (1976, pp. 79–85), Goodman (1992, pp. 117–118), Gros and Thygesen (1998, p. 18); Giscard d'Estaing (1988, pp. 136–142), with a different, but obviously incomplete account. See the criticism by Szász (1999, p. 42).

Table 5.4. *Average Inflation Rates of Germany
and Small European States (1973–1979)*

Switzerland	4.7
Germany	5.0
Austria	6.5
Netherlands	7.3
Belgium	8.2
Norway	8.5
Sweden	9.3
Denmark	10.6

Source: Iversen, Pontusson, and Soskice (2000, p. 12)

Why did the small states fail to adjust? The most obvious explanation
is that for historical and institutional reasons, the forces seeking a disinflationary policy were weaker than in Germany. In particular, small
states lacked a central bank enjoying the same independence as the
Bundesbank, and all measurements of central bank independence in fact
rank Germany at the top.[26] Yet this factor should not be overrated.[27] In
the 1970s, central banks underwent dramatic changes despite the fact
that the legal framework remained the same. And as Johnson (1998) correctly argues, the *Bundesbank* was only truly independent *after* the shift to
floating: "Monetarism fostered the central bank's independence, not vice
versa."[28] Also, Germany's fear of inflation was not the only historical experience inherited from the interwar years. The fear of mass unemployment,
caused by the deflationary policies that brought Hitler to power, was just as
vivid in the nation's memory. In the 1970s, public polls indicated that the
German public was more concerned about unemployment than inflation.
Even the *Bundesbank*'s own confidential polling led to such results.[29]

---

[26] See the references of footnote 11, Neumann (1999) and Manow and Seils (2000, p. 268).

[27] For example, Campillo and Miron (1997, p. 336) come to the conclusion that "institutional arrangements play almost no role in determining inflation outcomes, once other
factors are held constant." On potential theoretical weaknesses of the concept of central
bank independence, see, for example, Posen (1995, 1998), Forder (1996, 1998a, 1998b),
and Siklos (2002). Berger and Woitek (2005) come up with a new solution ("time-series
approach") to the problem of whether conservatism matters or not.

[28] Johnson (1998, p. 24). von Hagen (1999, pp. 411*ff.*) speaks of an "emancipation of monetary policy."

[29] Johnson (1998, p. 101).

Two other reasons seem to have been at least as important. First, the change from the late Bretton Woods system with a weak dollar at its center to the Snake based on a strong DM was too abrupt to be immediately understood by Snake members. Even in Germany itself, most observers were not able to react adequately to the restrictive course pursued by both the *Bundesbank* and the Brandt government.[30] Consequently, it must have been particularly difficult for policymakers outside Germany to foresee the consequences of this policy turn. Scharpf (2000) observes that "in countries practicing forms of 'imported monetarism' as a consequence of their membership in the Snake, governments and unions were less directly exposed to the ex-cathedra teachings of the *Bundesbank* and thus had greater difficulty in learning the same lesson."[31] Germany had the advantage of being the first mover, whereas the small states were confronted with all the problems of lagging behind.

Even in Austria, where the postwar consensus had remained relatively unshaken and the orientation toward Germany was particularly important, the adjustment to the new economic and monetary environment almost failed. The schilling was pegged against the DM not because economic and income policies were in tune with those of Germany but precisely because they were too expansionary during the 1970s.[32] At least the social partners reacted promptly when it became clear that the recession would be severe and that Germany had embarked on a restrictive course: In 1975, real wages increased by only 1 percent after almost 10 percent in 1974. But fiscal and monetary policies aimed at maintaining full employment clearly were too expansionary to justify the peg. As a result, the current-account deficit became unsustainable in 1977, and the DM peg had to be replaced temporarily by a basket peg. Chapter Six will show in more detail how Austria had great difficulty adjusting to German policies.

The second, more important reason why small states failed to adjust was that their corporatist institutions had begun to fall apart in the late 1960s owing to erosion of the postwar consensus.[33] There has been debate about whether institutional, structural, or ideational reasons were the most important driving forces behind this process.[34] For my argument, this debate is

---

[30] Scharpf (1991, pp. 127–143), Johnson (1998, pp. 84–95).

[31] Scharpf (2000, p. 46).

[32] On Austria, see Handler (1989), Scharpf (1991), Kurzer (1993), Hochreiter and Winckler (1995), Hemerijck, Unger, and Visser (2000), and Bachinger et al. (2001).

[33] On wage explosion and wage conflict, see Eichengreen (1996a, 2007) and Notermans (2000, pp. 160*ff.*).

[34] See, for example, the discussion in Blyth (2001) and Lindvall (2004), who explain the Swedish case by ideational changes.

not central. The crucial point is that even before the end of Bretton Woods system and Germany's shift to a restrictive course, the ability of small states to adjust was seriously hampered just as in the large states. Formally, wage bargaining systems were still centralized, but in reality, there was great competition between various fractions of the labor movement leading to uncontrolled wage increases from 1972 to 1976. And since the process of wage bargaining was impeded, the monetary authorities found themselves in a hopeless situation. If they pursued the same restrictive course as the *Bundesbank,* they would cause a steep increase in unemployment. On the other hand, accommodating real wage increases would contribute to a further rise of inflation. Fiscal policy faced a similar dilemma: On the one hand, the government tried to maintain demand during the recession years in order to contain the rise in unemployment; on the other hand, by financing this expansionary policy with new corporate or payroll taxes, the government only contributed to the general profit squeeze and the rise in labor costs.

Of course, the situation was not identical across all small states. Aside from Switzerland, though, with its very specific labor market and its exceptional regime shift in January 1973 (see Chapter 7), the similarities among small states were more relevant than the differences. The breakdown of the postwar consensus was most visible in Belgium and the Netherlands. Once admired for their strong cooperative spirit across ethnical and religious divides, both societies became increasingly unable to cope with centrifugal forces. At the beginning of the 1970s, corporatist institutions were almost completely hollowed out.[35]

Although the general trend was the same in Belgium and the Netherlands, the chronology differed considerably. Corporatism in the Netherlands had been at its height in the 1950s.[36] Wage increases were moderate, gross domestic product (GDP) growth rates were high, and the balance of payments was mostly in surplus. Yet toward the end of the decade, the consensus began to falter. First cracks appeared during the wage round of 1957, when the Nederlands Verbond van Vakverenigingen (NVV), the Socialist trade union leadership, agreed to moderate wage increases, whereas many union members demanded substantial increases and turned their backs on the unions.[37] Equally, many employers felt that the postwar system of

[35] Jones (2008) coined the formula "corporatism without consociationalism"; Visser and Hemerijck (1997) speak of "corporatism without consensus."
[36] On the Netherlands, see Windmuller (1969), van Zanden and Griffiths (1989), van Ark, de Haan, and de Jong (1996), Visser and Hemerijck (1997), van Zanden (1998), and Hemerijck, Unger, and Visser (2000), and Jones (2008).
[37] Jones (2008, p. 101).

wage determination was malfunctioning. In order to attract well-trained workers, they began to offer higher "black wages."

The break with the postwar growth model came in the autumn of 1963 when real wages increased by 12 percent.[38] In contrast to the late 1950s, when the sign of an imminent recession disciplined politicians as well as social partners, the early 1960s were a time of full employment, and with the exception of a short recession in 1966–1967, labor markets remained tight until the crisis of the mid-1970s. Marius Holtrop, governor of the *Nederlandsche Bank* from 1946 to 1967, observed in 1970 that "the golden rules of sound economic behavior seem to have lost their compulsion without any new ones being offered in their stead."[39] Wages increased at a higher rate than productivity, thus hampering the competitiveness of the Dutch economy and squeezing profit margins. As the situation became unsustainable in the early 1970s, firms began to reduce their investment.[40]

Not only the economy but also society underwent a dramatic change during the 1960s and the 1970s, perhaps more than in any other small European country.[41] The confessional parties – the Catholic People's Party (KVP), the Anti-Revolutionary Party (ARP), and the Christian Historical Union (CHU) – shrank from almost 50 percent of votes in 1963 to little more than 30 percent in 1972. New parties such as Democrats '66 (D66), Democratic Socialists '70 (DS'70), and the Farmers' Party (BP) were the main winners of this shift. The most visible symbol of this deep cultural change was that Amsterdam became an international center of the hippie movement. The forces of traditional authority and hierarchy, marked by Calvinism, ceased to be relevant. Thus, when the Bretton Woods system broke down in the early 1970s, the Netherlands had definitively lost the institutional capacity to engineer a flexible policy best suited to the difficult challenges of the new age of stagflation. The institutions were still in place, but they had stopped functioning properly.

In Belgium, the 1950s had not been a particularly good decade, neither economically nor politically.[42] In return for this, the 1960s became a sort of golden period, with high rates of economic growth and smooth

---

[38] BIS, Annual Report, 1963–1964, p. 14; BIS, Annual Report, 1964–1965, p. 61. In retrospect, the country report of the OECD (1979, p. 7) identified this increase as a turning point. On the forces behind this wage explosion, see van Zanden (1998, pp. 82–84).

[39] Holtrop (1970, p. 371).

[40] OECD (1979), The Netherlands, p. 9.

[41] Kennedy (1995) gives an excellent description of the cultural changes taking place during the 1960s.

[42] On Belgium, see Mommen (1994), Cassiers, de Villé and Solar (1996), and Hemerijck, Unger, and Visser (2000), and Jones (2008).

cooperation between employers and union leaders. Yet the Belgian honey moon was only of short duration. As in the Netherlands, the atmosphere of full employment led to higher wage claims, higher wage drift, and ultimately, higher rates of inflation. In addition, Belgium began to suffer from a regional divide because the Flemish economy had grown faster in the postwar years than the Wallonian economy, formerly the economic center of Belgium. In the parliamentary elections of 1968, the regionalist parties won more than 16 percent of total votes, and in 1971, even 23 percent. In the same year, the Belgian parliament passed a first revision of the constitution giving regional councils some, though only limited power.[43]

Also in the early 1970s, strike activity picked up again. From 1969 to 1975, the number of strikes tripled from 88 to 243; in 1970 and 1971, the number of days lost was 10 times higher than in 1969.[44] Real wages increased by almost 10 percent in 1973, and the inflation rate reached a record high of 12.7 percent in 1974.[45] Clearly, the union peak organizations were not able to moderate the wage claims of their members anymore. Torn apart by regional divides and class conflicts, the Belgian cabinets of the 1970s were incapable of governing the country, and a swift adjustment to Germany's restrictive course was out of the question.

Of the three Scandinavian countries treated in this study, Denmark had the weakest collective wage bargaining system, and the dominance of the Social Democrats was less pronounced than in Norway and Sweden.[46] Often, they had to lead a minority government, thus depending on the cooperation of smaller parties. This instability made Danish corporatism particularly vulnerable to the erosion of the postwar consensus in the 1960s. As elsewhere, the position of the labor unions had become stronger during the 1960s. From 1965 to 1971, nominal wages rose by 150 percent, whereas prices increased by 60 to 70 percent.[47] Labor unions began to pursue a solidaristic wage policy aimed at improving the wages of unskilled workers with the result that the general wage level increased considerably because skilled workers secured an additional share by negotiating directly with their employers. In the early 1970s, labor unions grew more militant and often resorted to strikes. 1973 was the record year: 205 strikes

---

[43] On the regional divide, see Fitzmaurice (1996).
[44] Mitchell (2003, p. 177).
[45] Scharpf and Schmidt (2000a), Statistical Appendix.
[46] On Denmark, see Johansen (1987), Andersen and Risager (1990), Pedersen (1996a), Benner and Vad (2000), and Iversen, Pontusson, and Soskice (2000).
[47] Johansen (1987, p. 150).

with 4 million days lost.[48] Also in 1973, real wages increased by a record 10 percent, contributing to an outburst of inflation that peaked at 15 percent in 1975.[49] Johansen (1987) characterizes the situation of Denmark in the 1970s as "a house divided against itself."[50]

In Norway, the system of centralized wage bargaining was more elaborate and built on a more solid base. However, it could not escape the erosion of the postwar consensus either.[51] First cracks in the facade became visible in 1961 when wage increases went far beyond the level that was compatible with maintaining the competitiveness of Norway's exporting industries.[52] Partly the reason for this failure was bad timing: Wage negotiations coincided with parliamentary elections, which complicated the process of finding a compromise. However, as in other small states, the main reason was that tight labor markets gave labor unions a strong position in the bargaining process. Owing to these difficult circumstances, negotiations at the peak failed and disintegrated to the federation level, leading to a price and wage explosion.[53]

After this failure, the government tried to change the rules of the game by making it more transparent. Yet the measures proved insufficient. The government, sometimes with the support of parliament, had to resort to forced arbitration, especially in 1964 and 1966. In the early 1970s, the government tried to convince unions to restrain wages by granting subsidies. At the same time, it introduced a price freeze and prohibited wage drift.[54] The success was only temporary, however. The inflation rate was lowered from 10.6 percent in 1970 to 6.2 percent in the following year but then accelerated again and reached 11.7 percent in 1975. Clearly, the wage bargaining process produced results that were not compatible with a fixed exchange rate anymore. The system did not collapse yet, but even in Norway it became much more difficult to link fiscal and monetary policies with income policies.

In Sweden, the system of centralized bargaining began to be transformed from the mid-1960s onward.[55] In the late 1960s and early 1970s,

---

[48] Mitchell (2003, p. 177).

[49] Scharpf and Schmidt (2000a), Statistical Appendix.

[50] Johansen (1987, pp. 164–205).

[51] On Norway, see Rødseth and Holden (1990), Hanisch, Søilen, and Ecklund (1999), Iversen, Pontusson, and Soskice (2000), Moses (2000), and Notermans (2000).

[52] Moses (2000, pp. 103*ff.*).

[53] *Ibid.*, p. 105.

[54] *Ibid.*, p. 108.

[55] The transformation of the "Swedish model" is among the most researched topics in comparative political economy. Here is a short selection: Calmfors and Forslund (1990),

a wave of labor unrest hit the country, with the strikes at some iron ore mines in 1969 being the most important event. These wildcat strikes showed that the hegemony of the Svenska Arbetsgivareföreningen-Landsorganisationen i Sverige (SAF-LO) agreements had come to an end. There was also increasing competition among unions, especially between the LO and the union of the public sector, which resulted in higher wage drift.[56] Toward the end of the 1960s, the growing tensions between capital and labor were reflected in the political arena. Not least because of the constitutional reform of 1968, the Social Democrats lost their absolute majority in the elections of 1970. Only with the help of the Communists could they pass their legislation. In 1973, the Social Democrats again lost some seats so that the new parliament was evenly divided between the Left and the center-right parties.

In addition, the late 1960s marked the end of an era in the history of the Swedish Social Democratic Party (SAP). Tage Erlander, party leader and prime minister since 1946, stepped down in 1969.[57] He was followed by Olof Palme, who had been minister for education and a leading figure of the younger generation and had positioned himself more to the left than the old generation of Social Democrats. Furthermore, Palme was less interested in economic affairs than his finance minister, Gunnar Sträng, an exponent of the old generation who thought that price stability was just as important as solidaristic income policies. A clear sign that collective wage bargaining did not work properly anymore was the agreement of 1972 that led to real wages increasing by 12.7 percent. It is true that the unions eventually could be convinced to restrain their wages in the following two years, but in 1975–1976, the government completely failed to moderate the bargaining process even though it had offered new subsidies. Clearly, the postwar system did not produce the desired results anymore.[58] It would be wrong to claim that the system had collapsed by the mid-1970s. However, as in Norway, there were clear signs that the government could not count on the automatic cooperation of the social partners anymore. Accordingly, the real exchange rate appreciated steeply from 1974 to 1976.

In summary, the claim that small states maintained a pegged regime because their domestic institutions were flexible enough to adjust to Germany's monetary policy is not correct. On the contrary, small states

Fregert (1994), Henrekson, Jonung, and Stymne (1996), Lindbeck (1997), Benner and Vad (2000), Iversen, Pontusson, and Soskice (2000), Blyth (2001), and Lindvall (2004). See also Schön (2000, pp. 468*ff*.) for the economic history of the 1970s and beyond.

[56] Lindbeck (1997, p. 73).

[57] See the biography of Erlander by Ruin (1990).

[58] Calmfors and Forslund (1990, pp. 79–82).

maintained their DM peg *even though* real exchange rates appreciated dramatically from 1972 to 1976. Even in Austria, where the postwar consensus was still quite intact, the adjustment failed because of the difficulty in correctly interpreting the German monetarist turn in 1973–1974. Consequently, small states had about the same incentives to leave the Snake and to let the currency float as large states. Therefore the reasons why small states preferred a pegged regime must have been related to the kind and degree of their international integration.

TRADE OPENNESS AND EXCHANGE-RATE REGIME

As noted earlier (see Table 5.2), several aspects of international integration are relevant for the choice of a pegged exchange-rate regime. Eichengreen et al. (1999) list five of them:

- A high level of reserves
- Capital controls
- Labor mobility
- A high degree of production and export diversification
- Close economic relations with partner countries (high degree of trade openness, symmetric shocks, nominal shocks)

This survey also comes to the conclusion that *political integration* is secondary for a country with a pegged rate. Only the reverse is true: If a country wants to float its currency, it is better not to belong to a political union. The crucial question is: How are these criteria related to country size, and what decisions did policymakers take when these criteria were in conflict with each other? Theory does not provide any guideline to the latter question, as Eichengreen et al. (1999) explain: "… [T]here is no agreement on how precisely to quantify the various criteria, nor, to the extent that they conflict, on which should take priority."[59]

A closer look reveals that three criteria can easily be excluded: a high level of reserves, labor mobility, and a high degree of production and export diversification. As for the level of reserves, it is true that the defense of large state currencies required more reserves on the part of the *Bundesbank* than those of small states.[60] The pound was the world's second reserve currency until the late 1970s. The British authorities had

[59] Eichengreen et al. (1999, p. 4). See also, for example, Sutherland (1994, pp. 56–58) on choices by Nordic countries.

[60] Thygesen (1979, p. 27): "Absolute amounts matter; the European Community and its main creditor country, Germany, have been able to take a fairly relaxed attitude to the absence of formal policy coordination with the smaller member countries."

guaranteed free access to the London capital market to sterling area countries in exchange for holding sterling balances. This agreement with former British colonies made the British currency particularly vulnerable despite capital controls restricting the use of sterling outside the sterling area.[61] France also was more vulnerable than most small states. In January 1974, German Finance Minister Helmut Schmidt had to offer 9 billion DM in order to dissuade the French from leaving the Snake.[62] In March 1976, the *Banque de France* was forced to buy 8 billion French francs (roughly 4 billion DM) within two weeks. By contrast, the defense of the Belgian franc and the Danish krone immediately after the exit of France in that same month cost only 2 billion and 1.5 billion DM, respectively.[63]

Yet, differences in the level of reserves do not explain the choices of small and large states. The currencies of large states may have been more vulnerable than those of small states, but that does not explain why they let their currencies float instead of devaluing them. Furthermore, the level of reserves not only differed between small and large states but also among small states: Belgium, the Netherlands and Switzerland disposed of ample reserves owing to their traditionally strong current-account surplus and their position as international financial centers, whereas Austria, Denmark, and Norway were never able to accumulate many reserves (Table 5.5). Nevertheless, all small states, with the exception of Switzerland, preferred to have a stable exchange rate.

With the same argument, we also can exclude two further criteria from the list of relevant factors: the extent of labor mobility and the degree of production and export diversification. While, for example, many Austrian workers near the border preferred to have a job in Germany or Switzerland that paid higher wages, the mobility of Norway's or Sweden's workforce toward Germany was very limited. And whereas, for example, Sweden had a diversified production and export structure, Austria's trade was focused on the German market. Nevertheless, all these small states had a pegged regime.

This leaves us with the following three factors: political integration, capital mobility, and economic relations with partner countries. We can further simplify the discussion by assuming that the degree of trade openness was correlated with the type and preponderance of shocks. In other

---

[61] James (1996, pp. 185–186), Dyson and Featherstone (1999, p. 538), Battilossi (2002, pp. 11–12).
[62] Tsoukalis (1977, p. 129).
[63] Hellmann (1976, pp. 81 and 83).

Table 5.5. *Total International Reserves, 1973*

	In Billions of US Dollar	As Percentage of GDP
Austria	4.3	15.52
Belgium	8.1	19.93
Denmark	1.5	3.23
France	15.6	7.17
Germany	41.5	13.50
Italy	12.2	7.36
Netherlands	10.4	17.30
Norway	1.6	8.21
Sweden	2.9	6.06
Switzerland	14.3	41.48
United Kingdom	7.9	5.13
Total	182	

Source: Maddison (1991, p. 178).

words, countries entertaining strong trade relations with Germany were most likely to suffer from symmetric and nominal shocks, and vice versa. On theoretical grounds, this simplification may not be entirely legitimate, but as the remainder of this chapter will show, it is useful and leads to plausible results. I therefore will argue with the three following factors: EC (non)membership, financial openness, and trade openness.

Of these three layers, the most important one clearly was trade openness – or rather how policymakers *perceived* the problems of country size and trade openness – because the differences between small and large states were not as considerable as the statements of policymakers suggest[64] (Table 5.6). There was a strong consensus that small European countries were too open to have a flexible exhange-rate regime. They argued that, owing to destabilizing speculation, a floating exchange rate would hamper trade and complicate monetary policy.[65] It was the old argument made by Nurkse in his book entitled, *International Currency Experience*, commissioned by the League of Nations and published in 1944.[66] Policymakers

[64] See Hey (2003, p. 3), citing Rothstein (1968) and Keohane (1969) on the importance of how small states perceive themselves.
[65] Krugman (1989, p. 63), Frankel (1999, p. 10), Tobin (1978, p. 519). See Cohen (1996) and McNamara (1998) on the power of ideas in monetary history.
[66] Bordo and James (2001).

Table 5.6. *Trade Openness (1974–1979)*

	Import and Exports as Percentage of GDP (1974–1979)
France	39
Italy	41
United Kingdom	55
Belgium	101
Netherlands	96
Denmark	61
Norway	89
Sweden	58
Austria	66
Switzerland	66

Source: McKeown (1999, p. 13).

also believed that a pegged exchange rate was best for a centralized wage bargaining system because employers and unions needed reliable projections of the inflation rate.

This said, it is imprecise what Giavazzi and Giovannini (1989) have written in their influential book on the EMS, namely, that all Europeans, whether inhabiting a small or a large state, dislike exchange-rate fluctuations for three reasons: "First, they all live in relatively open countries. Second, many of them hold the floating rates of the 1920s and 1930s responsible for the ensuing collapse of national economies and of the international trading and monetary systems. Third, postwar European institutions – particularly the common agricultural market – depend in their survival on exchange-rate stability."[67] During the 1970s, not all Europeans disliked exchange-rate fluctuations to the same extent. In small countries, they believed that the openness of their economies made them particularly vulnerable, whereas in large states, policymakers were ready to take the risk at least temporarily.

According to this fear of floating, small states abandoned their pegged regimes only when they were forced to – as did Switzerland in 1973 as well as Sweden and Norway in the wake of the EMS crisis in 1992, which will be treated in the next section. The regime shift of Switzerland did not change

[67] Giavazzi and Giovannini (1989, p. 1).

the general perception, however, because it was considered an exception resulting from its extraordinary position as an international financial center and the conservative stance of its authorities. Only when Sweden successfully adopted inflation targeting with a flexible exchange rate from 1993 on was the conviction that exchange rates of small open economies needed to be fixed challenged. Now everyone could see how a country that formerly had clung to a pegged rate came to grips with the volatility of the foreign-exchange market. From then on, Switzerland ceased to be considered as an exception, and a new era in the history of European exchange-rate regimes began.

It is true that the fear of market volatility was widespread among policymakers in large European countries as well. But we can observe a slow change of mind during the Bretton Woods era.[68] In Germany, Minister of Economic Affairs Ludwig Erhard was in favor of floating exchange rates in the early 1950s, and in 1957, Otmar Emminger, who was in 1970 to become vice president of the *Bundesbank*, published an article in which he explained that floating was compatible with the International Monetary Fund (IMF) agreement.[69] In 1971, Karl Schiller, another German minister of economic affairs, publicly supported a floating exchange rate.[70] In the United Kingdom, as early as 1952, a number of officials proposed the so-called robot plan, which would have allowed sterling to float within a wide band. The plan was without any chance of success at the time, but the mere fact that it was brought up is remarkable.[71] Guido Carli, governor of the Italian central bank from 1960 to 1975, was in favor of a more flexible system.[72] It is true that these opinions were shared only by a minority, but they had been circulating for some time and were seriously discussed.

The conviction that small states needed a fixed exchange rate was not shattered by the fact that many academic economists considered this mistrust of flexible rates ill founded. Following Milton Friedman's "Case for Floating Exchange Rates" in the 1950s, economists were convinced that long-run macroeconomic performance was not affected by

---

[68] Helleiner (1994, pp. 115–118), James (1996, pp. 215–216, 224, 226, 234–235, 240), Toniolo (2005, p. 431).

[69] Emminger (1986, pp. 290–292), Johnson (1998, pp. 74 and 81–83).

[70] Von Hagen (1999, p. 411). On Schiller's strong impact on German economic policy, see Nützenadel (2005).

[71] James (1996, p. 99). Robot was named after the three authors Leslie Rowan, George Bolton, and Otto Clarke and was intended to convey a sense of automaticity. See the study by Burnham (2003) on the history of robot.

[72] Hellmann (1976, p. 53).

the exchange-rate regime.[73] Their main microeconomic argument was that importers and exporters could hedge their exchange-rate risks.[74] Policymakers, by contrast, were concerned primarily about short-run stability and believed that economists underestimated the negative effects of speculation. Their preference was to keep their exchange rate as stable as possible, be it as a DM peg or as a basket peg.

The weight of the conviction that small states could not float was most visible in the cases of Sweden and Norway because, theoretically, Sweden and Norway could have let their currencies float after leaving the Snake in 1977 and 1978. But they decided to adopt a currency basket peg instead. True, the new regime allowed for more flexibility, yet the crucial point was that the authorities controlled the degree of flexibility.[75] Some Swedish politicians may have seen many parallels to a free float, such as Kjell-Olof Feldt, who later became the finance minister of the newly formed Social Democratic government in 1982. He accused the Swedish government of having thrown Sweden into "a new and unfamiliar experiment": "Little Sweden shall be the sole industrial country in Europe that floats freely."[76] But that was an allegation motivated by politics, not by economics.

Figure 5.2, which shows effective exchange rates, illustrates the continuity of the approaches of Norway and Sweden. The rates of the Norwegian krone and the Swedish krona followed a linear path – in contrast to sterling, for example. Sweden and Norway thus softened their peg in order to save the most important element of their traditional exchange-rate policy,

---

[73] Important advocates of floating were Friedman (1953), Meade (1955), Sohmen (1961), and Johnson (1969). On the discussion among economists, see Zis (2004).

[74] Recently, this finding has been questioned. See Begg et al. (2003) and De Grauwe (2003) on the new literature. According to Rose (2000) and others, lower exchange-rate variability is correlated with more trade. Their argument is that forward and futures markets do not exist for most trading partners and for most longer-term horizons. Thus a floating exchange-rate regime involves transaction costs and risk premia between the forward rate and the expected future spot rate. The opponents also argue that the econometric evidence has largely been based on the experience of large states and obtained by time-series analysis that is not good at sorting out other influences on trade.

[75] Hörngren and Lindberg (1994, p. 138): "By shifting to the basket, Sweden made it easier to maintain an unchanged peg, at the same time making room for somewhat higher domestic inflation." Moses (1998, p. 204): "Swedish monetary history can easily be read from two different perspectives. Generally, supporters of fixed exchange rates can find comfort in Sweden's long-standing commitment to such regimes... Proponents of flexible exchange rates, however, can also draw on much of Swedish history."

[76] *Riksdagens protokoll*, No. 10, 1977–1978, p. 115. Cited in Moses (1995, p. 279); translation by Moses.

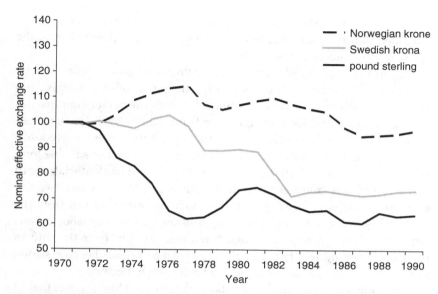

Figure 5.2. Nominal effective exchange rates of Norwegian krone, Swedish krona, and British pound sterling (1972 = 100). (*Scharpf and Schmidt, 2000a*).

not to abandon it altogether.[77] In its annual report of 1977, the Swedish *Riksbank* highlighted the fact that "the new system gives the krona a stable effective exchange rate."[78] The same rationale was relevant for the majority of the board of directors of *Norges Bank* when it decided to switch to a basket regime. The crucial argument was that the krone would be more stable than before: "The majority expected an appreciation of the EMS currencies, and such a development could create problems for Norwegian economic policy. Especially at a time of prices and incomes freeze, it was imperative to keep exchange rates as stable as possible, since an appreciation would thwart the aspirations and a depreciation could jeopardize the prices and incomes freeze."[79] Accordingly, devaluations were not an integral part of the strategy but rather a temporary measure to regain the old equilibrium. And the stabilization of the peg in the 1980s, as the figure shows, should not be seen as another regime break but as the end point of

---

[77] *Per Kleppe, S.tid.* (1978–1979), p. 1788, 14 December 1978: "Therefore, such a basket solution will give us the greatest stability in an effective, or average krone exchange rate." Cited in Moses (1995, p. 311); translation by Moses.

[78] *Sveriges Riksbank,* Annual Report, 1977, p. 14.

[79] *Norges Bank,* Report and Accounts, 1978, p. 61.

the transition from the Snake to the basket.[80] A stable exchange rate had remained the goal ever since Sweden and Norway had defected from the Snake in 1977 and 1978, respectively.

Why didn't Sweden and Norway adopt a floating regime? As for Sweden, perhaps the best statement demonstrating the power of ideas comes from Urban Bäckström, who was economic adviser to the center-right parties during the 1980s and *Riksbank* governor from 1994 to 2002. He explained in retrospect: "It is interesting to note that before the 1990s the predominant view was that a floating exchange rate regime was not suitable for a small open economy."[81] High government and central bank officials recall that floating was considered "almost immoral."[82] When a few Swedish economists proposed to adopt a flexible exchange rate after exit from the Snake, they met almost unanimous opposition.[83] Especially labor unions were against such a regime change.[84] Yet, interestingly, once the shift to inflation targeting was taken in the 1990s, labor unions became strong supporters of inflation targeting with a flexible exchange rate.

In Norway we find a similar situation. Notermans (2000) writes that in 1973 "the move to a more flexible exchange rate was interpreted as a threat to international trade and growth."[85] The reluctance to let the currency float remained even stronger than in Sweden, as we will see in Chapter Eight.[86] Whereas Sweden did not hesitate to abandon exchange-rate targeting in late 1992, Norway continued to stabilize the exchange rate against

---

[80] In this point, I disagree with Moses (1995, p. 319), who regards the 1982 devaluation as a regime shift.

[81] Bäckström (2000, p. 1). See the debate between former *Riksbank* Governor Lars Wohlin (1979–1982) and former *Riksbank* Senior Adviser Lars Hörngren (1989–1996) in *Ekonomisk Debatt* (1998, pp. 21–30 and 295–298). Wohlin writes that the *Riksbank* should have shifted to a floating exchange rate in 1985; Hörngren replies (p. 297): "It is my opinion that Wohlin's reasoning lacks historical context... Right or wrong, there was a nearly total agreement that Sweden, like other small European countries, should have a fixed exchange rate" (my translation; in Swedish: "*Här tacker jag att Wohlins resonemang saknar historisk förankring... Rätt eller fel, rådde närmast total enighet om att Sverige, i likhet med andra små europeiska länder, skulle ha fast växelkurs.*")

[82] Lindvall (2004, p. 125). Cf. Gylfason (1990, p. 163): "The Nordic EFTA members have decided against free floating mainly out of fear of the potentially destabilizing effects of excessive volatility of exchange rates on trade, investment, employment, and inflation." Åkerholm (1990), in his comment on the paper of Gylfason, confirms this view (p. 193): "The preference for a fixed exchange rate has reflected the belief that such a regime best serves the development of foreign trade in a small, open economy."

[83] Werin et al. (1993, p. 224). Jonung (1978) and Myhrman (1978) were two rare examples.

[84] Moses (1995, p. 247).

[85] Notermans (2000, p. 203).

[86] See Chapter Eight.

the ECU until the late 1990s. A typical statement was given by the governor of *Norges Bank* in 1997:

In large countries where foreign trade accounts for a relatively small share of total GDP, changes in the exchange rate will have little effect on the general economy. Less emphasis can therefore be placed on exchange-rate stability in large countries, whereas domestic stability must be assigned greater importance. In small countries with substantial foreign trade, changes in the exchange rate will be of greater importance, particularly in countries where export sectors also account for a high share of employment. It is, therefore, not possible to apply directly the experience of large countries with a relatively small share of foreign trade to small countries, like Norway, with an open economy.[87]

Despite these caveats, however, Norway eventually adopted inflation targeting with a floating exchange rate.

In the case of the small EC members Belgium, the Netherlands, and Denmark, it is more difficult to demonstrate how their choices were determined by the idea that a flexible exchange rate would hamper trade and monetary policy. It seems more obvious to argue with political integration because small states are in general more loyal to the rules of international institutions than large states.[88] Yet narrative evidence suggests that political considerations were secondary. In those rare instances when the monetary authorities expressed their opinion about the pros and cons of fixed and flexible regimes, they always highlighted the negative economic consequences, not the political risks they would encounter, if they left the Snake.

As for the Netherlands, Jelle Zijlstra, president of the Dutch central bank from 1967 to 1981, explained in 1977, looking back at the regime shifts of the United Kingdom, Italy, and France: "It has been claimed as a further advantage of floating rates that they give a country more room for manoeuvre, a greater measure of freedom in the conduct of monetary policy. But experience in this respect has not been encouraging... The situation in a number of countries then resembles the freedom of the slipway, the freedom which results in a steadily accelerating (downward) motion. A fixed rate of exchange, on the other hand, can serve as both a signal and a support to domestic policy."[89]

---

[87] Annual address by Governor Kjell Storvik at the meeting of the Supervisory Council of *Norges Bank* on Thursday, 6 February 1997.

[88] On the foreign policy of small states, see von Dosenrode (1993) and Hey (2003).

[89] *De Nederlandsche Bank n.v.*, Report for the Year 1976, presented to the General Meeting of Shareholders, 26 April 1977, p. 14.

André Szász, a top central bank official, wrote that the *Nederlandsche Bank* preferred exchange-rate stability because "it ensures maximum certainty about the prices of goods sold or bought abroad in terms of the domestic currency. More importantly, in an open economy such as the Netherlands the goal of internal price stability is inextricably linked to exchange rate stability."[90] And like Zijlstra, he did not believe in the theory that floating exchange rates would bring more autonomy: "Many countries sought refuge in flexible exchange rates, believing that flexible exchange rates provided protection against inflationary influences from abroad. The Dutch monetary authorities never fully shared this optimism. Instead, they continued to attach great importance to stable exchange rates."[91]

As for Belgium, one also can hardly find any hints of a discussion about the option of a flexible-exchange-rate regime. In an annual address held in early 1977, Governor Cecil de Strycker explained, alluding to the exit of France in March 1976: "Consequently, the Bank, with the Government's agreement, made it the foremost aim of monetary policy to oppose any developments which could have brought about a fall in the pivot rate for the Belgian franc within the Snake, or even Belgium's abandonment of its participation in this fixed exchange rate area."[92] Like Zijlstra, he observed that flexible exchange rates did not bring the advantages promised by their adherents. At the general meeting in early 1979, de Strycker devoted a great part of his speech to the experiences with flexible exchange rates since 1973. His verdict was negative: "But the abandonment of the old rules was accepted all the more easily in many cases because the new system was presented as being capable of bringing about a more painless adjustment of the external imbalance – an illusion which was partly fostered by the criticisms levelled against fixed parities in the economic literature." And he added

---

[90] Greef, Hilbers, and Hoogduin (1998, p. 7). Cf. Szász (1988, p. 255): "*Op het eerste gezicht lijkt het belang dat wird gehecht aan wisselkoersdoelstellingen in strijd met de grote betekenis die wird gehecht aan de noodzaak, de geldhoeveelheid te beheersen. Daarbij kann het volgende worden aangetekend. Ten eerste beseften de Nederlandse autoriteiten dat zeker voor een kleine open economie de mogelijkheid om ter wille van een binnenlandse monetaire doelstelling wisselkoersbewegingen te aanvaarden beperkt was. Voorts vreesden zij de internationale gevolgen van ongereguleerde wisselkoersen.*" Den Dunnen (1985, p. 10): "Small open economies usually give priority to maintaining a stable exchange rate, which may be accompanied by a preference to lay this down in a formal arrangement. The Netherlands are a case in point."

[91] Cited in Greef, Hilbers, and Hoogduin (1998, p. 12).

[92] National Bank of Belgium, Report on the Activities of the Year 1976, presented to the General Meeting, 28 February 1977 p. XII.

that exchange rate fluctuations, rather than solving the existing problems, have created new ones, and that they have been particularly subject to amplification through speculation when the markets have been left to themselves. It is moreover clear that, in all the industrialised countries, the authorities have retained or ultimately reassumed control over the rates for their currencies. The hope that the authorities' autonomy of choice would be increased by floating has therefore not been fulfilled. The opinion is even gaining ground that this autonomy might perhaps, when all is said and done, be more limited under a system of fluctuating exchange rates.[93]

In Denmark, the consensus in favor of exchange-rate stability was just as strong as in the Benelux countries. In October 1976, the government and *Danmarks Nationalbank* published a report on the Frankfurt realignment in which they highlighted the "very great advantage that the rates of exchange have remained stable in relation to countries which account for almost one half of Denmark's foreign trade." The logical conclusion was: "From the Danish point of view, therefore, it has been a matter of crucial importance that the Snake co-operation should be maintained."[94] There seemed to have been a strong consensus, as a Danish economist observed in the early 1990s: "... [T]he official Danish attitude has always been that the Kingdom was best served by participating in a fixed exchange rate system – and given the size and the openness of the economy that is hardly worthwhile debating."[95]

In Austria, not a member of the EC, the preference for a fixed exchange-rate regime was just as self-evident as in the Benelux countries and Denmark. In May 1971, shortly after the DM had begun to float, Hans Kloss, general director of the Austrian National Bank, told the board that "a floating exchange rate would hamper trade because the schilling would not be suited as a currency for international payment anymore."[96]

---

[93] National Bank of Belgium, Report on the Activities of the Year 1978, presented to the General Meeting, 26 February, 1979, pp. XX and XXIV.

[94] Memorandum: Report by the Government and *Danmarks Nationalbank* on the Ministerial Meeting of the "Snake" Countries Held in Frankfurt on 17 October 1976, printed in Annual Report of the National Bank of Denmark for the Year 1976, Annex, p. 81. The argument that the CAP depended on exchange-rate stability also was relevant for France. Nevertheless, the French government decided to let the franc float.

[95] Nielsen (1994, p. 64).

[96] *OeNB-Archiv, Protokoll der ausserordentlichen Sitzung des Generalrates der OeNB vom 10. Mai 1971*, p. 3: Generaldirektor Hans Kloss: "*Entscheidend war auch der Umstand, dass eine feste Kursrelation bestehen soll, so dass der Exporteur mit festen Kursen rechnen kann. Wir dürfen dabei nicht übersehen, dass, würde der Schilling auch [wie die DM] noch zu einer floatierenden Währung werden, sich der Handel dadurch erschweren würde, weil ja der Schilling sich auch nicht mehr als Fakturierungswährung eignen würde. Es würde also*

Finance Minister Hannes Androsch explained in the parliament two days later: "For a small country like Austria, there is only a slight possibility to solve the question of parity by letting the currency float."[97] And when the Austrian parliament discussed the collapse of the Bretton Woods system in March 1973, not a single deputy challenged the finance minister when he declared that Austria needed stable exchange rates in relation to the currencies of the most important trading partners.[98]

Finally, the monetary authorities of Switzerland shared the same aversion to flexible exchange rates as their counterparts in other small states until the decision of the Swiss National Bank to let the franc float changed everything.[99] True, in the 1950s, Friedrich A. Lutz, a liberal economist and widely respected professor at the University of Zurich, advocated flexible exchange rates, but his theory resonated only with Swiss economists, not with policymakers.[100] Max Iklé, a member of the governing board of the Swiss National Bank until 1970, expressed the standard small-country argument in a conversation with Milton Friedman in the late 1960s: "The exchange rate of a small country can be influenced much more easily by capital movements than the rate of a big or medium-sized country." And with respect to Switzerland, he explained: "Scientists assume that within a system of flexible exchange rates the 'correct' rate is automatically formed. When the trade balance is negative, the rate depreciates so that the exporting industry becomes more competitive and the deficit is reduced. In the case of Switzerland this scientific scheme is simply not correct, because the stream of goods is superseded by streams of capital which obey other laws."[101]

bedeuten, dass eine grosse Anzahl von Geschäften, die heute doch schon in Schilling abgewickelt werden, wieder in anderen Wärungen abgewickelt würden."

[97] *Stenographisches Protokoll, No. 43. Sitzung des Nationalrates der Republik Österreich, XII. Gesetzgebungsperiode, 12. Mai 1971, pp. 3164–3165: "Die Möglichkeit, die Frage der Parität durch gleitende Kurse befriedigend zu lösen, ist für ein kleines Land wie Österreich nur sehr gering."*

[98] *Nationalrat XIII. GP, 66. Sitzung, 20. März 1973, pp. 6191ff.*

[99] Birchler (1979, p. 89): *"Es ist nicht auf einen grundlegenden theoretischen Gesinnungswandel – wenigstens nicht in jenem Zeitpunkt – zurückzuführen, dass 1972/73 die Tiefzinspolitik sowie das System der festen Wechselkurse aufgegeben wurden, sondern Ursache dafür war der Zwang der Umstände, der ohne Alternative zum Sachzwang führte, von Tiefzins- und Fixkurspolitik abzurücken."*

[100] For example, Lutz (1954). Prader (1981, pp. 505ff.) shows how some Swiss economists embraced the idea of flexible exchange rates.

[101] Iklé (1984, pp. 318–319): *"Prof. Milton Friedman, der später den Nobelpreis erhielt, bat mich einmal, mit ihm zusammen das Mittagessen einzunehmen, um die Gründe meines hartnäckigen Widerstands kennenzulernen. Ich legte ihm die Gründe dar, weshalb ein Land wie die Schweiz kein Interesse an flexiblen Wechselkursen haben könne. Der Wechselkurs*

Fritz Leutwiler, member of the governing board of the National Bank, explained in 1971 that floating was "utopian."[102] Accordingly, the bank tried to protect the Swiss financial market with capital controls. In this it was supported by the big commercial banks. On behalf of them, a senior economic adviser explained in 1970 that the banks "unconditionally reject the idea of expanding the possibilities of monetary policy by adopting floating exchange rates." The main reason for this negative attitude was that such a regime change "would destroy essential foundations of Swiss foreign economic relations and of Swiss prosperity."[103] This opinion was shared by the *Schweizerische Kreditanstalt* (SKA), one of the big three Swiss commercial banks. In an article published in 1971, a senior manager pointed out that the experiences with floating exchange rates had been "particularly bad," and he warned of the loss of monetary discipline and the rise of international conflict owing to manipulated exchange rates.[104]

When the shift to floating finally occurred, Swiss banks reacted with little enthusiasm to the decision of the Swiss National Bank to float the franc. The *Neue Zürcher Zeitung*, the leading Swiss business newspaper, wrote on the following day that in banking circles one could hear the opinion that the Swiss National Bank had perhaps stopped its interventions prematurely.[105] The governing board took notice of this criticism uttered

---

eines kleinen Landes könne viel leichter durch Geldströme beeinflusst werden als derjenige eines grossen oder mittelgrossen Landes. Ein kleines Land wie die Schweiz, mit einem starken Finanzzentrum, sei stärker von Geldströmen abhängig als ein Land, dessen Bankensystem weniger stark ausgebildet sei. In der Schweiz fielen die Geldströme weit stärker ins Gewicht als die Warenströme, da kurzfristige Gelder zeitweise ins Land strömten, zeitweise dieses wieder verliessen. Dazu komme das Vertrauen in den Schweizerfranken, welches dazu führe, dass die Schweiz bei gestörten Währungsverhältnissen als Zufluchtshafen diene. Die Wissenschaftler gingen davon aus, dass sich in einem System flexibler Wechselkurse der 'richtige' Wechselkurs automatisch herausbilde. Bei negativer Handelsbilanz falle der Kurs, wodurch die Exportwirtschaft leistungsfähiger werde und das Defizit bilde sich zurück. Dieses Denkschema der Wissenschaft stimme im Falle der Schweiz ganz einfach nicht, weil die Warenströme von den Geldströmen überlagert werden, welch letztere ganz andern Gesetzen gehorchten."

[102] Ferrari (1990, p. 284).

[103] Mast (1971, p. 294): *"Mit diesen Feststellungen gehen die Banken ebenso einig wie in der unbedingten Ablehnung des Gedankens, die strukturbedingten Grenzen der Geldpolitik durch flexible Wechselkurse erweitern zu wollen, müsste doch ein solcher Eingriff wesentliche Grundlagen zerstören, auf denen die schweizerische Aussenwirtschaft und damit der schweizerische Volkswohlstand ruht."* Hans Mast was director and economic adviser of the executive board of the *Schweizerische Kreditanstalt (SKA)*.

[104] Cited in Ferrari (1990, pp. 287–288).

[105] *Neue Zürcher Zeitung,* No. 37, January 24, 1973: *"In schweizerischen Bankenkreisen war denn auch die Ansicht zu hören, das Noteninstitut habe mit dem Rückzug vom Devisenmarkt vielleicht etwas voreilig gehandelt..."* Cf . Bundesrat Celio, *Stenographisches Bulletin des*

by Swiss banks in its first meeting after the decision to float.[106] The London foreign-exchange market had not expected such a move either: "In any case, the floating of the Swiss franc has surprised professional circles, and foreign exchange traders are looking for reasons."[107]

In summary, the options of small states were constrained by the idea that a floating regime would impede trade and complicate monetary policy and wage bargaining. Many academic economists have never really understood this mistrust of markets, and developments in the last 15 years have shown that this fear was in fact exaggerated. Nevertheless, there was a strong consensus among policymakers that a flexible exchange rate would be subject to destabilizing speculation with negative consequences for the real economy. Large states, by contrast, were not constrained by this idea. They adopted floating rates even though their central banks lacked the credibility to maintain price stability.

WHY SWITZERLAND, SWEDEN, AND NORWAY?

Given that policymakers wanted to avoid floating, why did Switzerland in 1973 and Sweden and Norway in 1992 abandon their fixed-exchange-rate regime? To understand this decision, we have to include the two other dimensions of international integration mentioned earlier, namely, financial openness and political integration. Switzerland, Sweden, and Norway were forced to make a regime shift because of open financial markets and nonmembership in the EC[108] (Tables 5.7 and 5.8). The first factor explains why their currencies became victims of speculative attack. And the second factor, nonmembership in the EC, was the main reason why the currency

---

Ständerats, 20. März 1973: "*Man hat uns zwar schwer kritisiert, weil wir das Feld so rasch verlassen haben.*"

[106] Archives Swiss National Bank, *Protokoll des Direktoriums*, No. 90, 25 January 1973, p. 124: "*Natürlich ist unser Entscheid nicht ohne Kritik geblieben. Die Vorwürfe scheinen aber bis jetzt lediglich von den Banken zu kommen, nicht von der Industrie. Die Banken machen geltend, wir seien ängstlich gewesen und hätten die Nerven verloren; wenn wir im Markt geblieben wären, hätten wir 'nicht sehr viel' bekommen.*" Fritz Leutwiler (III. Department) is speaking.

[107] *Neue Zürcher Zeitung*, No. 37, 24 January 1973: "*Auf jeden Fall hat das Floating des Schweizerfrankens in hiesigen Fachkreisen* [in London] *etwelches Erstaunen hervorgerufen, und die Devisenhändler suchen nach Begründungen. Die Überraschung war um so grösser, als vor allem der amerikanische Dollar an den internationalen Devisenmärkten seit längerer Zeit eine relative feste Haltung aufgewiesen hat. Die erfolgreiche Inflationsbekämpfung in den Vereinigten Staaten hat das Vertrauen in den Dollar gestärkt.*"

[108] The regime shift of Switzerland, Norway, and Sweden will be discussed in more detail in Chapters Seven and Eight.

Table 5.7. *External Constraints and Opportunities (1970s)*

	EC Member	Non-EC Member
Capital controls		Austria (DM peg)
		Norway (Basket)
		Sweden (Basket)
Capital mobility	Belgium (Snake)	Switzerland
	Denmark (Snake)	(*Floating*)
	Netherlands (Snake)	

Table 5.8. *External Constraints and Opportunities (1990s)*

	EC Member	Non-EC Member
Capital controls		
Capital mobility	Austria (Euro)	
	Belgium (Euro)	
	Denmark (Euro-peg)	
	Netherlands (Euro)	
	Sweden (*Floating*)	Norway (*Floating*)
		Switzerland (*Floating*)

peg was not maintained or adjusted and why the authorities hesitated to return to a pegged regime after the crisis. If Switzerland, Norway, and Sweden had been EC members, markets would have perceived the currency peg as more credible, and policymakers would have felt more obliged to seek a new peg within the existing exchange-rate regime.[109] At first sight, a third factor should be included: the vulnerability of a peg. The Swiss franc was attacked not only because Swiss financial markets were open but also because investors considered it to be undervalued owing to the notorious anti-inflationary stance of the Swiss authorities. On the other hand, the Norwegian and Swedish currencies were considered overvalued and enjoyed little credibility because of the traditionally high inflation rates. But this factor only explains why the attack was launched, not why the authorities made a regime shift. Again, if Switzerland, Norway, and

---

[109] For a comparative view of the relationship between small states and the EC, see the contributions in Miles (1996) and Grädel (2007).

Sweden had been EC members, they would have readjusted their exchange rates within the existing regime.

There was, however, one exception: the Austrian schilling. At the time of the EMS crisis, Austria had open financial markets and was not a member of the EC, and yet, the DM peg of the schilling was maintained without major problems.[110] The reason for this stability was, as Chapter Six will show, the close link between the Austrian and German economies. In 1970, one-quarter of total exports went to Germany, and imports from Germany accounted for 41 percent of total imports. Austria also entertained close trade relations with Switzerland, another hard-currency country – the corresponding figures were 10 percent of total exports and 7 percent of total imports. Owing to these exceptionally close trade relations with two hard-currency countries, Austria had developed a hard-currency policy in the course of the 1970s and 1980s. By the late 1980s and early 1990s, when financial markets were being liberalized, the DM peg of the schilling had become highly credible. Thus the Austrian case may have been an exception, but it was one that confirmed the rule.

As for the Swiss case in 1973, the comparison with the Netherlands, another small state with open financial markets and a strong currency, is illustrative. The Dutch guilder was equally under upward pressure during that time, but thanks to the cooperation of Snake members, especially Germany, the central bank could defend the fixed exchange rate. As for the Norwegian and Swedish cases, the comparison with Denmark is interesting. The Danish krone came under enormous pressure, not least because of the negative outcome of the referendum on the Maastricht Treaty in June 1992, yet thanks to interventions of the EC central banks and the domestic backing of the hard-currency policy, the krone could be defended.[111]

Once their currencies were thrown out of a fixed-exchange-rate system, the authorities saw no easy way back because they feared that the same attacks could happen again. And owing to nonmembership in the EC, they were not forced to return. So they waited until the markets had eased, yet because this period of transition lasted so long, they began to develop a strategy outside a fixed-exchange-rate system. Since this strategy proved to be viable, the rationale changed: Instead of returning to the old system, they began to accept and appreciate the flexible exchange rate. In Sweden, inflation targeting became such a success that a sound majority of voters declined to adopt the euro in 2003. In Norway, the government did not

---

[110] On the high credibility of the Austrian DM peg, see Kleinewefers (1997, pp. 163–209).
[111] Gros and Thygesen (1998, pp. 97–98).

even dare proposing such a step in combination with a referendum on EC membership.

The Swiss case is somewhat more complicated. Initially, the Swiss authorities declined to join the Snake, but in 1975, after another sharp appreciation of the Swiss franc as a result of a sudden weakening of the dollar, the Swiss National Bank sought membership. But again, nonmembership in the EC was the crucial factor prohibiting a return to a fixed exchange rate: The French government was strongly opposed to letting the Swiss in because they feared a strengthening of the DM bloc. And since Switzerland continued to have open financial markets, making an unilateral peg against the DM or the Snake, as Austria chose to do, was not a solution.[112] As a result, the floating of the Swiss franc became a permanent solution.

This type of regime transition was very typical for small states. As seen, they were forced to abandon their fixed-exchange-rate regime mainly because they were not EC members. Large states, by contrast, were all EC members at the time they changed their regime – or, as in the case of the United Kingdom, they had already signed the accession treaty and had joined the Snake as a full member before the *de jure* entry.[113] Accordingly, their regime shifts were voluntary, not forced by market forces. The United Kingdom, Italy, and France could have devalued instead of letting the currency float, and they always had the possibility of rejoining the Snake or the EMS. Houben (2000) correctly summarizes the choices of large states with respect to the French exit: "During the Snake period, France had generally prioritised domestic objectives and when the franc came under untenable downward pressure, it had opted to leave the system rather than accept a devaluation – an approach common to all the large countries at the time."[114]

The reason for the regime shifts of large states thus largely was political.[115] During the 1970s, in the initial phase of European monetary cooperation,

---

[112] Cf. Hellmann (1976, p. 73): "*Die österreichische Formel eines Mitziehens mit der Schlange aus eigenem autonomen, sonst niemand bindenden Entschluss, erschien für die Schweiz wenig geeignet. Der Schweizer Franken benötigte, um den Gleichschritt mit der Schlange glaubhaft und beständig erscheinen zu lassen, des gegenseitigen Interventionsversprechens. Allein konnte die Nationalbank keinen Schweizer Riegel gegen die stetige Selbstaufwertung des Frankens aufbauen.*"

[113] Sterling left the Snake in June 1972. On 22 January 1972, the EC had signed the treaties of accession with the United Kingdom, Denmark, Ireland, and Norway. Denmark and the United Kingdom participated in the Snake. The United Kingdom, Denmark, and Ireland joined the EC on January 1973, but not Norway, owing to the negative outcome of the referendum. The United Kingdom did not hold a referendum.

[114] Houben (2000, pp. 206–207).

[115] On the relationship between politics and exchange-rate policy, see Andrews (2006).

France, Italy, and the United Kingdom were powerful enough to play an important role outside the Snake in order to influence the institutional process. Therefore, they were facing a tradeoff between national autonomy and European cooperation that was different from that of small states. On the one hand, large states were interested in having a stable monetary environment in Europe and in shaping the institutional framework, just as small states were. On the other hand, however, they were able to set a price for their participation. Eventually, they all opted for more auton- omy because they felt that the Snake was dominated by German monetary policy.[116] Staying in the Snake would have meant begging for German revaluation or opting for devaluation of their own currencies and thereby losing face vis-à-vis Germany. This strong dependence was not acceptable to large EC states. Therefore, they tried to change the rules by boycotting the whole process.

The dilemma between staying in the game and keeping enough national autonomy was perhaps most evident in the case of the United Kingdom.[117] As described earlier, at the time when the United Kingdom was about to join the Snake, the Heath government initiated a boom that was not consis- tent with adhering to a fixed exchange-rate system. Anthony Barber, chan- cellor of the exchequer after whom the boom was named, explained in his annual budget speech in April 1972: "It is neither necessary nor desirable to distort domestic economies to an unacceptable extent in order to retain unrealistic exchange rates, whether they are too high or too low."[118] On 26 June 1972, when Barber was asked by the press why his government had joined the Snake eight months before the official entry into the EC, he gave the frank answer that the United Kingdom wanted to shape the institu- tional process from the beginning.[119]

Italy had been a founding member of the EC, but the weakness of its domestic institutions and the strength of its labor movement in the wake of the revolts in the late sixties had made it difficult to pursue the restrictive monetary course required to maintain the stability of the lira. Accordingly, the Italian governments (Colombo and Andreotti) opposed an early intro- duction of the Snake.[120] However, as the formation of the Snake gained momentum, Italy had no choice but to participate in order to stay in the

---

[116] Walsh (2000, p. 27). In fact, this European monetary arrangement was more rigid than the Bretton Woods system or the subsequent EMS.

[117] Moravcsik (1999, pp. 274–285).

[118] Cited in James (1996, p. 239).

[119] Hellmann (1976, p. 43).

[120] Dyson and Featherstone (1999, p. 473).

game. At the same time, it was clear to Italian politicians that they would not participate at any price. After the United Kingdom had left the Snake, the Italians threatened to follow the pound if the other EC members would not make any concessions, and they obtained what they demanded: The Bank of Italy was allowed to use dollars (and not only EC currencies) in its interventions in the foreign-exchange market, and it was freed of the obligation to exchange gold for the lira the other EC members bought during exchange crises.[121] This concession, as well as the introduction of a two-tier system, proved insufficient because the Andreotti government was not interested in taking restrictive measures to stop capital flight. In February 1973, the lira began to float. The Italians offered to reenter the Snake if all EC countries pooled their reserves, but Germany and other EC members were not interested in financing the expansionary policy of Italy.[122]

France as the main architect of the EC besides Germany had even less interest in giving in to German hegemony than Italy.[123] Leaving the Snake twice was a clear expression of the will not to sacrifice domestic goals to European monetary cooperation at any price. The French position became especially clear in the Fourcade Plan that was submitted to the council of ministers consisting of the ministers of economics and finance (Ecofin) in September 1974. The plan was an attempt to reconcile national interests with the desire for European monetary stability. It made four proposals: larger short- and medium-term credit facilities to support the Snake, more use of intramarginal interventions, a joint dollar policy, and use of the European unit of account (EUA), which was to be renamed the ECU in 1978.[124] Germany and the Netherlands declined because they feared an even distribution of the burden of adjustment. Consequently, France stayed outside and waited for a better opportunity. In the medium term, the French approach was successful. The EMS was less rigid than its predecessor, the Snake.[125]

As for the second French exit in March 1976, the same dilemma can be observed. On Sunday evening, 14 March 1976, Snake members held a meeting because of relentless speculation against the French franc since March 5, resulting from another fall of the pound. The French franc was

---

[121] Hellmann (1976, pp. 50–55), Tsoukalis (1977, pp. 123–124).

[122] Tsoukalis (1977, p. 144), Goodman (1992, p. 147).

[123] Goodman (1992, pp. 111–118), Loriaux (1991, pp. 248–252), Moravcsik (1999, pp. 259–274).

[124] Tsoukalis (1977, p. 156), Dyson and Featherstone (1999, pp. 112–114).

[125] For a detailed account of the EMS, see Ludlow (1982). For the making of the EMS from the French point of view, see Loriaux (1991, pp. 260–261).

not the only victim. The Belgian franc also came under strong pressure and reached the limit of the lower band of the Snake and violated the narrow band of the "worm"– the monetary arrangement of the Benelux countries – because the guilder was among the strong currencies.[126] The international press expected that the finance ministers and central bankers would agree to a realignment at their regular meeting on Monday, 15 March. An exit of the French franc was considered "absolutely unthinkable."[127]

Yet, when the finance ministers held a press conference on Monday just before the regular meeting was about to begin, it was exactly this decision that had been taken the night before. The main culprit was France and, to a minor extent, the Benelux countries. Initially, a consensus had appeared to be possible. French Finance Minister Jean-Pierre Fourcade could offer a devaluation of 3 to 4 percent and his German counterpart, Hans Apel, a revaluation of 2 percent, if necessary even 3 percent. Yet, for Fourcade, this offer was not sufficient. He wanted a more comprehensive realignment and asked the officials of the Benelux countries and Denmark to devalue their currencies as well.[128] Obviously, the most important goal of the French was to keep face. Had France devalued as the only country, it would have been clear to outsiders that it was the weakest link of the Snake. France wanted to be perceived as an equal partner of Germany.

The officials of the small countries were reluctant. Nevertheless, a consensus still seemed possible, and in order to readjust their positions with their governments, the finance ministers decided to split and to meet later in the evening. Yet, when they gathered again shortly before midnight, Fourcade was not interested in a realignment anymore apparently because in the meantime Paris had informed him of the negative results in the cantonal elections that had been held that weekend. The French government now felt too weak to devalue the franc and to secure the resulting competitive advantage by implementing restrictive policies. The defeat at the election polls forced them to continue their expansionary course. Thus Fourcade let his colleagues know that France had decided to leave the Snake, blaming the small members for their reluctance to devalue, an accusation that he repeated to the press after the meeting. He also blamed

---

[126] BIS, Annual Report, 1975–1976, p. 101.
[127] *Frankfurter Allgemeine Zeitung,* No. 63, 15 March 1976, p. 9.
[128] There are divergent versions. Hellmann (1976, pp. 81–85), a German journalist and long-time observer of the European monetary scene, reports that France wanted to see the Dutch guilder revalued and the Belgian franc devalued. Yet Szász (1999, pp. 41–43), a high Dutch central bank official participating in the meeting, writes that France wanted to see the guilder devalued as well. I follow the version of Szász.

the British and the Italians for having allowed a "wild depreciation" of their currencies that caused speculative attacks against the French franc.[129] The French government was highly interested in avoiding the impression that it had left the Snake because it had lost the election. Only a month before, on February 11, Fourcade had explained that he did not know the word *devaluation*.[130]

Small EC member states were in a very different position. In the process of European monetary unification, they had no power as single nations.[131] The only way to reach their goals was to make coalitions with large EC members within the Snake.[132] Accordingly, we can never observe that they left the Snake in order to promote their interests. More than large states, they were interested in institutional continuity and monetary stability. Only two small states that were not members of the EC during the 1970s, namely, Norway and Sweden, dared to abandon their participation in the Snake. The reasons for this decision will be discussed in Chapter Six.

---

[129] *Frankfurter Allgemeine Zeitung*, No. 64, 16 March 1976, p. 1.
[130] *Ibid.*, p. 9.
[131] Von Dosenrode (1993), Alesina and Spolaore (2003), and Hey (2003).
[132] See Maes and Verdun (2005) on the role of Belgium and the Netherlands as pace setters and gatekeepers in the creation of the EMU.

SIX

Hard and Soft Pegs

It was shown in Chapter FIVE that the small European states preferred to have pegged exchange rates during the 1970s and 1980s and that Switzerland's shift to a floating regime in 1973 was viewed as an exception confirming the rule, not as a new model. Yet, although small states shared this common approach, the strength of their currencies and the type of exchange-rate pegs they used diverged, starting with the Frankfurt realignment in October 1976.[1] Three groups can be distinguished (Figures 6.1 and 6.2):

1. Austria and the Netherlands maintained a hard peg to the deutsche mark (DM) with only minor changes – Austria independently and the Netherlands as a member of the Snake and the European Monetary System (EMS).
2. Belgium and Denmark participated in the Snake and the EMS, but made several devaluations until 1982. From then on, both currencies maintained a hard peg against the DM.
3. Sweden and Norway devalued their currencies several times within the Snake and then left the Snake and adopted a currency basket peg in 1977–1978. After changing the peg, Sweden undertook three devaluations, among them a "big bang" devaluation in 1982 (by 16 percent). The Norwegian krone, by contrast, remained a stable currency from 1979 on, with the exception of a one-time devaluation in 1986.

How can we explain these different trajectories? As in Chapter FIVE, I propose to divide the numerous explanations into two groups, one based on domestic institutions and policy preferences and one based on external factors. The starting point of the first explanation is that during the 1970s, policymakers had to choose between price stability and full employment,

---

[1] Thygesen (1979, p. 14) and Thygesen and Gros (1998, p. 16).

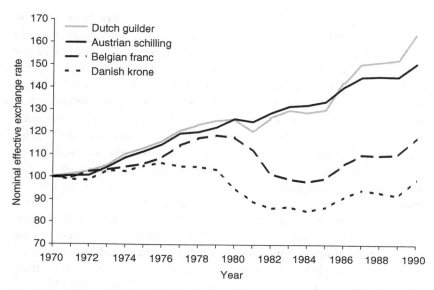

Figure 6.1. Small states with DM peg: Austria, Belgium, Denmark, and the Netherlands (effective nominal exchange rates, 1970–1990). (*Scharpf and Schmidt, 2000a.*)

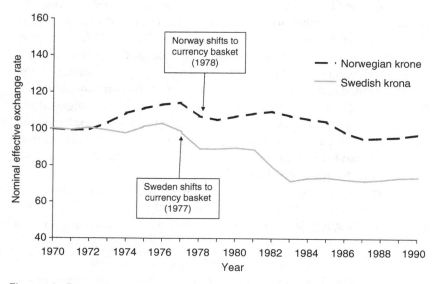

Figure 6.2. From DM peg to currency basket peg: Norway and Sweden (effective nominal exchange rates, 1970–1990). (*Scharpf and Schmidt, 2000a.*)

and their decisions depended on the position of the central bank, the system of wage bargaining, and the power of labor unions. Accordingly, Norway and Sweden, two countries with a strong Social Democratic tradition, highly centralized labor unions, and weak central banks, preferred to maintain full employment, accepted high inflation, and left the Snake in 1977–1978 to pursue an independent exchange-rate policy. By contrast, the Netherlands, a country with a weak commitment to full employment, a strong central bank, and a more fragmented labor movement, considered price stability the most important policy goal, maintained a strong currency and accepted a steep increase in unemployment. Finally, Austria, Belgium, and Denmark can be regarded as mixed cases. Austria had the capability of maintaining full employment and exchange-rate stability owing to a nearly perfect policy mix, whereas in the two latter cases the institutional capability apparently was particularly weak: The Belgian franc and the Danish krone were weak currencies, but at the same time, unemployment rates climbed to record-high levels.

The second explanation highlights external factors. They range from trade structures and political integration European Community (EC) and European [Free Trade Association (EFTA) membership] to financial openness and the degree of oil dependence. The Benelux countries were EC members, were financially open, and entertained close trade relations with Germany and each other, so maintaining a peg to the DM was the obvious choice. Conversely, Norway and Sweden belonged to the EFTA, were financially less open, and had equally close trade relations with Germany and the United Kingdom, so the exit from the Snake was only a matter of time once the United Kingdom left. Finally, Austria and Denmark combined features of both groups. Austria, an EFTA member, was closely integrated into the German market and therefore was interested in a stable exchange rate against the DM. And Denmark, despite entertaining close trade relations with the United Kingdom and Sweden, remained in the Snake and the EMS because of its EC membership.

The crucial question is how to combine these two explanations. Not many scholars have addressed this question. Only Moses (1995) can claim to have used a systematic comparative framework.[2] His conclusion is that

---

[2]　Very helpful are Argy and De Grauwe (1990), Åkerholm and Giovannini (1994), Gerlach (1997), and Jones, Frieden, and Torres (1998), but none of the three studies includes a systematic comparative discussion. Important contributions also have been made by Kurzer (1993), Notermans (2000), and Jones (2008), yet their studies are confined to a selected group of (small) European countries. See also the country studies in Scharpf and Schmidt (2000b) and Scharpf (2000), who gives a short overview on macroeconomic policies from 1970 to 2000.

external factors, which he labels as "geo-economico-political positioning," largely determined the choice of the exchange-rate regime, whereas domestic institutions, economic fundamentals, party politics, and interest-group pressures were almost irrelevant.

Yet, since the study of Moses is confined to the Nordic countries, the mystery of why some currencies of small states were stronger than others has not been fully solved yet. This chapter tries to fill the gap. Enlarging the number of countries, however, does not make it easier to find an answer. On the contrary, it entails a new difficulty that I call "the problem of double difference." As noted earlier, small European states differed not only with respect to domestic institutions and policy preferences but also regarding external structures. Accordingly, there was no continuum among them that would allow us to isolate the decisive factors. For example, Sweden had institutions and political traditions that were very different from those of the Netherlands, but in addition, Sweden also was outside the EC, had capital controls and a more diversified trade structure than the Netherlands. It is therefore hard to find out what mattered more during the 1970s: domestic institutions and policy preferences or the varying international integration. Of course, the two dimensions were linked to each other, but this observation is of little help if we want to identify the individual driving forces behind the divergence of exchange rates.

My suggestion for coping with this problem of double difference is to start with the discussion of external constraints and then to focus on domestic differences. This procedure seems all too obvious, but a look at the literature shows that it is not. Many political scientists have proceeded in the other direction: They focus on domestic factors and resort to ad hoc explanations when it comes to the importance of external structures. And economists studying the importance of central bank independence sometimes ignore external constraints altogether. The comparative discussion will lead to the following result: External constraints and opportunities largely explain the differences in the exchange-rate policies of the small states. Differences in domestic institutions and policy preferences also were relevant but clearly less important.

The remainder of this chapter is structured as follows: Because of the general bias toward domestic factors, I will first treat this type of explanation in more detail and develop the problem of double difference. Then I discuss the influence of external constraints and domestic factors on exchange-rate policies. I will, however, separate the discussion of the Benelux and Scandinavian countries from the analysis of the Austrian case because the latter has been considered an exception by scholars arguing

with institutional differences. The chapter thus ends with a closer look
at Austria.

THE DOUBLE DIFFERENCE

Until recently, political science research on European macroeconomic policies during the 1970s was dominated by models explaining how countries
reacted to the tradeoff between unemployment and inflation. Roughly
speaking, countries with a weak central bank, a strong Left, and highly centralized labor unions preferred to minimize unemployment at the price of
a higher inflation rate. By contrast, countries with a strong central bank,
a weaker Left, and less centralized labor unions focused on price stability
and accepted an increase in unemployment in the short run. Norway and
Sweden fulfilled the conditions of the first scenario, the Netherlands those
of the second, and the remaining small states with a pegged exchange rate
can be regarded as mixed cases (Figure 6.3).

As we will see below, this explanation has lost its dominant position
in political science because of the rise of the globalization thesis in the
1990s. Yet it is still useful to start the conceptual discussion with this
model, given that institutional models are still widely popular among
economists. The best starting point for a discussion is the seminal work of
Scharpf (1987, 1991) because he is a major proponent of the institutional

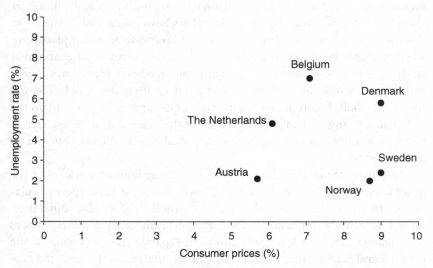

Figure 6.3. Inflation and unemployment, 1970–1985. (*Franzese and Hall, 2000.*)

approach and has influenced most scholars working in this field.[3] He compared Austria, Germany, Sweden, and the United Kingdom, focusing on the question why countries with Social Democratic parties had varying success in coping with the crisis of the 1970s. He developed a game theoretical framework that is very similar to the formal models developed recently by economists and political scientists who have studied central bank independence and labor market institutions.[4] Three players are involved in Scharpf's game: the government, the central bank, and the labor unions. And there are two types of games to be played. The first game is a monetarist one in which either the government or the central bank is expected to fight inflation regardless of what labor unions do. In a Keynesian game, by contrast, the government and the central bank abstain from restrictive measures and thus leave the responsibility to the labor unions to maintain price stability by wage moderation. Scharpf concludes: "The social democratic–Keynesian coordination can thus succeed only if the unions orient themselves not only toward common as opposed to individual interests but also toward future as opposed to present interests."[5]

According to Scharpf, Germany is a typical example for how the monetarist game works. In 1973, the *Bundesbank* and the German government tightened monetary policy to bring down inflation, while the role of labor unions was secondary in this process. In Austria, Sweden, and the United Kingdom, by contrast, the authorities tried to cushion the recession by playing the game of Keynesian coordination. Yet only Austria managed to find the ideal mix to reduce inflation and preserve full employment because the Austrian labor unions were able to moderate their wage claims during the crucial years, whereas the British and Swedish labor unions failed to do so. According to Scharpf, the main reason for this difference is institutional: "Austria had the optimal set of institutional arrangements for cooperative coordination in its relationship between the unions and the employers as well as in its relationship between the unions and government policy."[6]

---

[3] English version: Scharpf (1991). Bruno and Sachs (1985) also highlight the importance of wage bargaining systems. Other milestones in comparative political economy were Goldthorpe (1984), Katzenstein (1985), Gourevitch (1986), and Therborn (1986).

[4] See Chapter FIVE for a discussion of these models.

[5] Scharpf (1991, p. 176).

[6] Scharpf (1991, p. 193). Froats (1995), Guger (1998), and Hemerijck, Unger, and Visser (2000) also mainly argue with institutional factors in the Austrian case.

Since the mid-1980s when Scharpf's study was published, comparative political economy has made two extensions to the conventional model. First, the employment success of the Social Democratic governments lost some of its glory during the 1990s.[7] Accordingly, political scientists have started to see the different trajectories as a matter of timing, not as completely distinct paths. Kurzer (1993) was one of the first to make this argument. She compared four small European states: Austria, Belgium, the Netherlands, and Sweden. She claims that there were two reasons why Austria and Sweden were able to maintain their postwar model of social partnership until the late 1980s in comparison with Belgium and the Netherlands, which had dismantled it by the early 1980s. First, their business and banking sectors had a greater orientation toward the domestic market, and second, their central banks were controlled by the government or the social partners.[8] Accordingly, interest rates could be kept at a low level during the recession. In the Netherlands and Belgium, by contrast, "the concerns of financial agents (and their fear of inflation) induced, despite high unemployment and foreign trade dependence, monetary restrictiveness and appreciated exchange rates."[9]

Notermans (2000) also argues that the different experiences of European states were a matter of timing. He compares five countries with strong Social Democratic parties: Germany, the Netherlands, Norway, Sweden, and the United Kingdom. His starting point is the observation that in all five countries Social Democrats failed to combine full employment with price stability after 1973 because income policies did not work appropriately. Eventually, this failure led them to reduce inflation by shifting to a restrictive monetary policy, causing a rise in unemployment. Germany and the Netherlands were the first countries to shift to a regime of disinflation, then came the United Kingdom in the early 1980s, and eventually, Norway and Sweden arrived there in the late 1980s. The reason for the different timing was that the goal of full employment was more deeply anchored in Norwegian and Swedish society than elsewhere owing to the exceptionally strong position of the Social Democrats.[10] Germany and the Netherlands, by contrast, switched to a regime of macroeconomic disinflation that included stable exchange rates as a main ingredient "not because they were confronted with the most serious inflationary pressures, but because the political commitment to a growth regime was most precarious there."[11]

---

[7] See the Introduction of Kitschelt et al. (1999).
[8] Kurzer (1993, p. viii).
[9] *Ibid.*, p. 189.
[10] Notermans (2000, p. 170).
[11] *Ibid.*, p. 167.

The second extension that has become necessary since the mid-1980s is the inclusion of open-economy and open-state models. Moses (2000) rightly observes that "the external account enters ad hoc, and rather problematically, into his [Scharpf's] analysis. Solutions to unemployment are interpreted in a closed-economy framework and the effects of aggregate policies are interpreted without systematically considering their effects on the external balance."[12] Again, one of the first to apply this dimension to small European states was Kurzer (1993). Her claim that the international orientation of business and banking was the crucial factor behind the dismantlement of the postwar institutions is obviously based on an open-economy argument. The importance of external constraints is also emphasized by Jones (2008), who compares Belgium and the Netherlands. He argues that these countries pursued a hard-currency policy for the following three reasons: the deep liberal, free-market tradition, the extreme openness to international trade, and the breakdown of the wage bargaining systems before the end of Bretton Woods.[13] Since the mid-1990s, as the globalization thesis became popular among political scientists, the number of authors who have included the world economy has increased greatly.[14]

As for the exchange-rate policies of the small European states, the most relevant and systematic contributions have been made by Moses (1995, 2000).[15] His work on exchange-rate regimes of the Nordic countries clearly shows how relevant external constraints and opportunities are. His finding is that the "geo-economico-political positioning," that is, the degree and structure of economic, financial, and political integration, largely determined the choices of policymakers. The detailed case study on Norway further demonstrates how intertwined international and internal policies are. For example, the discovery of oil in the North Sea not only led to a persistent current-account surplus since the 1980s but also enabled Norway to borrow foreign capital at low interest rates before the current-account balance had become positive. The mere expectation of an oil bonanza made it possible to run high budget deficits and to finance social programs during the 1970s.

---

[12] Moses (2000, p. 5). Another example of an ad hoc explanation can be found in Therborn (1986, p. 29).

[13] Jones (2008, pp. 140–145). Hemerijck, Unger, and Visser (2000, p. 231) put forward the same explanation.

[14] For example, Garrett (1998), Iversen (1999), Kitschelt et al. (1999), and Iversen, Pontusson, and Soskice (2000). For a theoretical foundation, see Soskice (2000). Scharpf (2000) also has reacted to the challenge raised by the globalization thesis.

[15] A short and lucid comparative analysis of Nordic exchange-rate policies also can be found in Mjøset (1987).

Finally, there also has been new statistical research combining institutional and political structures with external constraints. Freitag (1999) is the first to have studied the influence of these factors on market expectations and exchange rates – in a similar way as Simmons (1994) has done for the interwar years. Altogether, he tested more than a dozen factors for 18 OECD countries during the period from 1973 to 1995. His results suggest that international constraints mattered.[16] In particular, EMS membership made it more likely that a currency was weak – and vice versa. However, Freitag also points out that domestic institutions were the most important factors, namely, the degree of fiscal policy leeway and the degree of central bank independence.

In sum, the evidence that the exclusive focus on domestic policy preferences and institutions is too narrow is overwhelming. Yet it is also clear that there is still a lack of comparative analysis. Scholars have either focused on individual small states or selected small-state groups, but the monetary history of the seven countries covered by Katzenstein (1985) has not been studied systematically yet. The following sections will try to fill this gap with respect to their exchange-rate policies. The starting point of my argument is that small states were subject to a "double difference"; that is, they differed not only with respect to domestic structures but also regarding external constraints. Accordingly, there is no perfect continuum between these countries, so it is impossible to identify every relevant factor individually.

Table 6.1 illustrates this point: The Benelux countries and Denmark were EC members and had open financial markets, whereas Austria, Norway, and Sweden were EFTA members and maintained tight capital controls. At the same time, these two country groups differed with respect to domestic structures. Only with respect to trade integration was there some sort of continuum: Denmark traded less with Snake participants than Belgium and the Netherlands; Austria, more than Norway and Sweden. Moreover, Scandinavian countries traded intensely with each other. Therefore when Sweden shifted to a currency basket in 1977, the Snake became even less optimal for Denmark and Norway. Because of EC membership, Denmark did not leave the Snake, whereas Norway followed Sweden in 1978.

The second point of my argument is that given this "double difference," it is better to start with the discussion of external constraints and then to ask for the role played by domestic policy preferences and institutions – not vice versa, as some political scientists have suggested. This method will allow us

---

[16] Freitag (1999, p. 199) interprets the fact that central bank independence is not the most important factor as a sign that institutional conditions of credibility are not confined to the legal and political status of the central bank.

Table 6.1. *The "Double Difference" among Small European States (1973–1982)*

	Independent Central Banks Centralized Wage Bargaining (0.50–0.75) Weaker Left	Dependent Central Banks Highly Centralized Wage Bargaining (1.00) Strong Left
EC member	Belgium	
Capital mobility	Netherlands	
Trade with EC	Denmark*	
EFTA member		Austria*
Capital controls		Norway
Less trade with EC		Sweden

Note: * With respect to trade integration, Austria and Denmark are special within their group: Austria traded more with the Snake area than Norway and Sweden, Denmark traded less with the Snake area than the Benelux countries.

to find out whether we can directly compare exchange-rate policies at all, and if yes, which elements of these policies. My conclusion will be that the scope for a direct comparison is very limited. Thanks to their trade relations, their capital controls, and their nonmembership in the EC, Norway and Sweden had options that were not available to the Benelux countries and Denmark. It is true that the weak position of the Norwegian and Swedish central banks had an impact on monetary policy and thus on exchange-rate policy. But the reverse is not true: The Benelux countries and Denmark had no choice but to adjust to the restrictive monetary policy of Germany regardless of whether their central banks were independent or not. Similarly, Austria had options that were not available to either of these two country groups.

The third and final point of my argument is that not only trade integration, the degree of financial openness, and EC (non)membership were important external factors but also the extent to which small countries depended on natural gas and oil (Table 6.2). The Netherlands and Norway were net exporters of these raw materials and therefore enjoyed current-account surpluses despite inconsistent domestic policies – the Netherlands almost throughout the whole period (with the exception of 1978 and 1980) and Norway from 1980 onwards. Accordingly, the Dutch guilder was stronger than the Belgian franc and the Danish krone, and the Norwegian krone was stronger than the Swedish krona. It is true that domestic policies also influenced the current account and the strength of a currency. The above-average growth of Belgian wages as well as Belgium's and Sweden's

Table 6.2. *External Constraints of Small European States*

	EEC	Trade Integration		Financial Openness	Natural Gas/Oil
		Trade Openness (X+I/GDP) (1974–1979)	Three Most Important Trading Partners (1973)		
Belgium	EEC	101%	Germany France Netherlands	Open	–
Netherlands	EEC	96%	Germany Belgium UK	Open	Natural gas
Denmark	EEC	61%	Germany UK Sweden	Open	–
Norway	–	89%	Sweden UK Germany	Closed	Oil (expected)
Sweden	–	58%	Germany United Kingdom Denmark	Closed	–
Austria	–	66%	Germany Switzerland Italy	Closed	–

Source: McKeown (1999), Mitchell (2003).

expansionary fiscal policy from 1978 to 1980 certainly contributed to the deterioration of the current account. However, from a comparative perspective, the dependence on oil and natural gas had a greater impact on the strength of a currency than the differences in domestic policies. In all small states with a pegged exchange-rate regime (including Austria), the government pursued rather expansionary fiscal policies, and income policies adjusted only slowly to the new economic realities after 1973.

In the remainder of this chapter I will try to develop this argument in four steps. The next three sections will discuss the experiences of the Benelux and Scandinavian countries, and the last section is devoted to the Austrian case.

A separate treatment has been chosen because Scharpf (1991) and others have claimed that the smooth functioning of Austria's institutions was the main reason why the government managed to maintain full employment and reduce inflation during the 1970s. My conclusion will be that this view not only exaggerates the success of Austrian policies but also underestimates the favorable external constraints that made the Austrian policy mix possible in the first place.

FINANCIAL OPENNESS, MONETARY POLICY, AND REAL WAGES

The first external factor that made a crucial difference was the degree of financial openness.[17] The conventional view claims that the degree of central bank independence determined whether monetary policy was restrictive in 1973–1974 or not. This may have been true for a large European country such as Germany but not for those small states that participated in the Snake and had relatively open financial markets, namely, the Benelux countries and Denmark. Regardless of whether their central banks were independent or not, these small states had no choice but to raise interest rates following Germany's policy turn in 1973, whereas Norway and Sweden were able to keep interest rates low (Figures 6.4 and 6.5).

This restrictive monetary policy put the Benelux countries and Denmark on a completely different trajectory as the rise of interest rates slowed down gross domestic product (GDP) growth, increased unemployment, and decelerated wage increases. Figure 6.6 demonstrates this mechanism for the Netherlands: After 1974, unemployment doubled, and real wages stagnated. Of course, one can argue that the Benelux countries and Denmark would have tightened monetary policy anyway in 1973 because their central banks were quite independent. Yet, since there is no comparable case, namely, a small European state with tight capital controls and an independent central bank, this conclusion is hard to prove.

It is true that some scholars have classified Austria as a country with tight capital controls and an independent central bank. Yet only the first half of this claim is true: Austria did indeed have capital controls during the 1970s, but the assumption that the Austrian National Bank was independent is incorrect. On the contrary, the essence of Austrian corporatism was that there was no such thing as strong institutional independence. Unions,

---

[17] For a comprehensive treatment of financial market integration, see Simmons (1999) and Obstfeld and Taylor (2004).

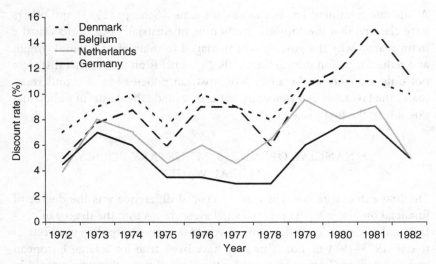

Figure 6.4. Central bank discount rates: Germany, Belgium, Denmark, and the Netherlands (end of year). (*Federal Reserve Bulletin.*)

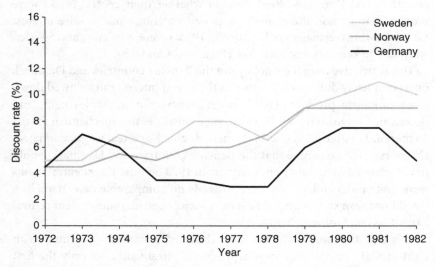

Figure 6.5. Central bank discount rates: Germany, Norway, and Sweden (end of year). (*Federal Reserve Bulletin.*)

associations, political parties, manufacturing firms, banks, and state institutions pervaded each other to a larger degree than anywhere else. The state owned 50 percent of the shares of the *Österreichische Nationalbank,* and the remaining shares were held by interest groups. Accordingly, the central

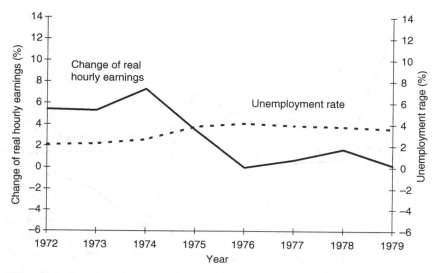

Figure 6.6. The Netherlands: unemployment rate (in percent) and real hourly earnings in manufacturing (percentage change from previous year). (*Scharpf and Schmidt, 2000a.*)

bank could not react without the consent of the government and the social partners.[18]

Only with respect to Norway and Sweden, which maintained tight capital controls, can one argue that central bank independence mattered. These two countries not only had the possibility to pursue an expansionary monetary policy but also used it to maintain full employment during the recession. This successful policy had far-reaching consequences because the persistence of full employment encouraged labor unions to make high wage claims. Figure 6.7 demonstrates this mechanism for Sweden: Unemployment remained low, and real wages literally exploded in 1975–1976 while stagnating in the Netherlands. If the *Norges Bank* and the Swedish *Riksbank* had been more independent and powerful vis-à-vis the government, the countercyclic policies surely would have been less pronounced. Yet this assumption is unrealistic because if central banks had been more independent, financial markets also would have been more open, and central bank independence would not have mattered anymore so long as Norway and Sweden maintained a DM peg. There is no easy solution to the problem of the double difference.

---

[18] See Katzenstein (1984), Kurzer (1993), and Scharpf (2000).

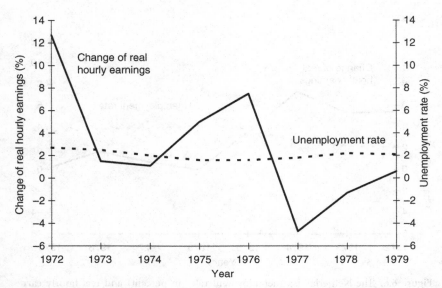

Figure 6.7. Sweden: unemployment rate (in percent) and real hourly earnings in manufacturing (percentage change from previous year). (*Scharpf and Schmidt, 2000a.*)

One could argue further that the degree of financial openness was not truly an external factor but rather the result of domestic political decisions. This observation is certainly correct in the medium or long term. For example, countries with a strong Social Democratic tradition such as Norway and Sweden were reluctant to dismantle capital controls during the postwar era.[19] Yet, in the short term, the degree of financial openness was exogenous because the liberalization required extensive political bargaining, and history has shown that the introduction of capital controls is only possible during a war or a severe economic crisis such as the Great Depression during the 1930s. Thus, when the Bretton Woods system fell apart and the German authorities tightened monetary policy, policymakers had to accept the instruments they inherited from their predecessors and tried to muddle through. The following short sketches of the individual country experiences attempt to illustrate this point in more detail.

The case of the Netherlands is a particularly good example to show the constraints stemming from capital mobility because Dutch financial

---

[19] For the link between political factors and capital mobility, see, for example, Frieden (1991), Helleiner (1994), and the review article by Cohen (1996), which develops a useful typology.

markets were among the most open during the 1970s.[20] After the final collapse of the Bretton Woods system in March 1973, Dutch policymakers immediately felt the pressure stemming from Germany's policy change. Since *De Nederlandsche Bank* (DNB) can be regarded as an independent central bank, and since the financial sector has a particularly strong position in economic and political life, it seems plausible to assume that the Dutch authorities would have raised interest rates anyway. Surprisingly, though, narrative evidence shows that at least in the first half of 1973 the tightening of monetary policy was not voluntary but forced on Dutch policymakers. When German short-term interest rates began to rise in the second quarter, the DNB actually was trying to keep interest rates low because it wanted to stimulate domestic demand, particularly private investment, which had been weak since 1971. It also wanted to encourage capital outflows because in the final weeks of the Bretton Woods era, the Netherlands had been one of the safe havens for foreign capital, which led to excess liquidity. Accordingly, the Bank for International Settlements (BIS) observed in its Annual Report that "in view of the domestic economic situation, the DNB refrained from adjusting its discount rate fully in line with the sharp rise in money-market rates at home and abroad."[21]

Yet this policy of low interest rates became unsustainable when German short-term interest rates reached double-digit numbers and Dutch money-market rates followed the international trend.[22] The guilder came under pressure and became the weakest currency of the Snake during the first four months of its operation.[23] Eventually, the DNB decided to defend the

[20] For an overview of Dutch monetary policy, see Bosman (1984), Szász (1988, 1999), De Grauwe and Vanhaverbeke (1990), Kurzer (1993), Wellink (1994), Jones (1995, 1998b), Greef, Hilbers, and Hoogduin (1998), van Zanden (1998), Hemerijck, Unger, and Visser (2000), and Notermans (2000). The official history of the period from 1948 to 1973 is covered by Fase (2000), a former top official of *De Nederlandsche Bank*. The memoirs of central bank Governor Zijlstra (1992) give some insight into his difficult relationship with Prime Minister Joop den Uyl from 1973 to 1977 but contain little about the discussions within *De Nederlandsche Bank*.

[21] *De Nederlandsche Bank*, Annual Report, 1973, pp. 74 and 121. Cf. BIS, Annual Report, 1973–1974, p. 66.

[22] *De Nederlandsche Bank*, Annual Report, 1973, p. 74. An interest-rate distortion emerged in the second quarter of 1973. The interest rates of advances of the commercial banks that were tied to the discount rate were lower than the rate for time deposits. This had two consequences: First, the public borrowed money from the banks to deposit them, and second, there was a shift from sight deposits (which lowered M1) and savings to small time deposits. Consequently, credit to the economy and M2 skyrocketed, while M1 was strongly negative.

[23] BIS, Annual report (1973/74), p. 144: "During the first four months of the joint float, however, while sharing in the general appreciation against the dollar, the guilder was, mainly for interest rate reasons, one of the weakest participating currencies."

exchange rate by increasing the liquidity requirements for the banking sector and by raising the discount rate from 4 to 6.5 percent in the period from
June until August.[24] Thanks to these measures, the guilder became strong
again by the end of August.[25] However, the tightening of monetary policy
was only sufficient to reassure foreign-exchange markets but not to curb
inflation. Short-term real interest rates remained negative, so the claim
that the Dutch pursued the same approach as Germany is incorrect.[26] The
OECD even wrote in its country report on the year 1973 that Dutch monetary policy was not restrictive at all in 1973.[27]

Confronted with rising inflation but still hesitant to weaken domestic demand with higher interest rates, the center-left government under
Prime Minister Joop den Uyl decided to revalue the guilder by 5 percent in
September 1973.[28] The revaluation was fully backed by the DNB but was not
well received by the exporting sectors.[29] Then, shortly after the revaluation
in September 1973, the Dutch economy was hit by the oil crisis in October
1973 – more than most other European countries because the Netherlands
was among the few countries that fell under a complete oil embargo imposed
by the Organisation of the Petroleum Exporting Countries (OPEC). Again,
because the Netherlands was financially open, the guilder immediately came
under pressure. Snake members had to intervene in the foreign-exchange
market, and the DNB was forced to tighten monetary policy once more by
taking several measures, among them an increase in the discount rate to 8
percent in December – which was 1 percent higher than in Germany.[30] Thus
only then had Dutch monetary policy become relatively restrictive. And
since Germany did not lower interest rates until the last quarter of 1974

[24] BIS Annual Report, 1973–1974, p. 66.
[25] *Ibid.*, p. 144: "Toward the end of August, however, following a progressive tightening of
the domestic monetary situation, it reached the top of the Snake and stayed there almost
uninterruptedly until its revaluation."
[26] This is the thesis of Notermans (2000, p. 167).
[27] OECD, *Pay-Bas*, June 1974, p. 16.
[28] Press archives De Nederlandsche Bank: Zitting 1972–1973 – 12505: *Revaluatie van de
Nederlandse gulden: Brief van de Minister van financieën aan de Heer Voorzitter van de
Tweede Kamer der Staten-Generaal,* No. 1: s'Gravenhage, 14 September 1973.
[29] For the support of De Nederlandsche Bank, see Press archives De Nederlandsche
Bank: Persbericht financiën, No. N240, 1 October 1973. For the reactions of the industries,
see Press archives De Nederlandsche Bank, Handelsblad NRC, 17 September 1973.
[30] BIS, Annual Report, 1973–1974, p. 144: "From late October onward, however, the oil crisis,
aggravated in the Dutch case by the Arab embargo on oil supplies, produced a rather drastic decline against the dollar of almost 19 percent to a low point of Fl. 3.01 on 23 January.
In addition, the guilder needed support in the Snake during November and December.
Since late January the situation of the guilder has reversed again, both vis-à-vis the dollar
and in the joint float."

when the recession began to make itself felt throughout Western Europe, it remained restrictive during most of the year.[31] Yet the degree of restrictiveness was still moderate in comparison with Germany. In 1974, real short-term interest rates were at 0.9 percent in the Netherlands (−1.4 percent in 1973), whereas they amounted to 2.9 percent in Germany.[32] If the Dutch authorities had wished to clamp down on inflation, they would have taken more drastic measures. The truly interesting question, therefore, is not why DNB raised interest rates in 1973 but why it was not more restrictive in the face of the ongoing expansion of the money supply.[33]

The tightening of monetary policy had strong effects on the Dutch economy. It slowed down GDP growth, reduced inflation, and increased unemployment – from 2.2 percent in 1973 to 4.1 percent in 1976. Rising unemployment, in turn, decelerated real wage growth, which contributed to a further reduction in inflation. In 1975, real wages rose by 3.5 percent; in 1976, they stagnated, and inflation decelerated after its peak in December 1974.[34] In the short term, the dismal performance of the economy and the rise in unemployment were unfortunate. At the same time, however, the restrictive measures decelerated the real appreciation of the exchange rate. Most important, the current account remained in surplus, which helped the DNB to maintain a strong guilder.

Since German interest rates were low from 1975 to 1978, it became easier to reconcile external constraints with domestic priorities. Yet when the United States changed course and tightened monetary policy in the late 1970s, the negative consequences of capital mobility became fully evident again because the Dutch authorities were forced to allow interest rates to rise to a record high. When in the early 1980s a recession set in, the DNB had little power to counteract it with an expansionary monetary policy. As a result, the Netherlands experienced the worst economic crisis in the post-war period, with real GDP growth being negative in two consecutive years and the official unemployment figure jumping from 4 percent in 1980 to 11 percent in 1983. The fiscal deficit more than doubled from 3 percent of GDP in 1979 to 6.6 percent in 1982. By the early 1980s, the costs of inconsistent policies had become visible to everyone, and employers and

---

[31] BIS, Annual Report, 1975, p. 55.

[32] OECD, Historical statistics. Cf. van Zanden (1998, p. 169): "Real interest rates were negative between 1972 and 1976 and remained low until the end of the decade, ... Looking back, it is surprising that the Central Bank, focused as it was on the battle against inflation, allowed the ongoing expansion of the money supply that went along with these processes."

[33] Van Zanden (1998, p. 149).

[34] BIS, Annual Report, 1975–1976, p. 26. Cf. Den Dunnen (1985, p. 10).

labor unions were ready to strike a deal to restore the competitiveness of the Dutch economy.

Like the Netherlands, Belgium belonged to the group of countries with a financially open economy.[35] Accordingly, we can observe the same trajectory. Just as the Netherlands, Belgium failed to check the rise of inflation in due time and had to accept a real appreciation of the exchange rate vis-à-vis the DM.[36] Like the Dutch authorities, the Belgian government and the National Bank of Belgium should have fought inflation at an earlier stage and with more rigorous steps if they had been willing to give priority to price stability, as had their German colleagues. Thus the claim that Belgium was making the same policy turn as Germany in 1973 is incorrect, just as in the case of the Netherlands.

But there also were some interesting differences between the two neighboring countries. First, Belgium had a dual exchange-rate system from 1955 to 1990. Current-account transactions were controlled and settled at a fixed exchange rate, whereas capital-account transactions were subject to exchange-rate fluctuations depending on the supply and demand of the currency.[37] However, at first sight, the difference from the Dutch system looks bigger than it really was. According to Tsoukalis (1977), Belgian officials were well aware of the fact that the effectiveness of this system was limited. The main reason why they continued to uphold it was that it gave the impression to the public that there was a mechanism protecting the Belgian economy against speculation.[38] More important, the Belgian system is not comparable with the Norwegian or Swedish systems, in which capital movements were strictly controlled.[39]

The second difference is that in the first quarter of 1973, the Belgian authorities were facing other challenges than their Dutch colleagues. The main problem was the stagnation of exports, not of domestic demand, as in the Netherlands. Exports rose from 1972 to 1973 from 711 to 870 billion francs, but imports jumped from 682 to 856 billion francs. Accordingly, the Belgian authorities were less reluctant to raise interest rates to fight inflation

[35] On Belgian monetary policy, see Vandeputte (1985), De Grauwe and Vanhaverbeke (1990), Kurzer (1993), Mommen (1994), Jones (1995, 1998a), and Hemerijck, Unger, and Visser (2000).

[36] OECD, *Union Economique Belgo-Luxembourgeoise, Juin* 1974, p. 30.

[37] Bakker (1996, pp. 12 and 134–136).

[38] Tsoukalis (1977, p. 134): "The officials of the Belgian central bank have not had many illusions about the effectiveness of the two-tier market system. They argued that the main reason that the system was kept was to create the impression to the public opinion that there existed a mechanism which served to protect the Belgian franc from speculation."

[39] OECD (1988, p. 116).

but also less interested in revaluing the currency in September 1973.[40] The National Bank of Belgium started to raise the discount rate in May, whereas the DNB began in June, and until August, the Belgian rate rose from 5 to 6.5 percent, whereas the Dutch rate stopped at 6 percent.[41] Owing to this more restrictive policy, the Belgian franc never came under pressure during this period.[42]

In the late 1970s, the Belgian dilemma was very similar to the Dutch one. The steep increase in interest rates in the United States from 1979 onward constrained Belgium's possibility to cope with the recession of the early 1980s. The crisis of the Belgian economy was even more severe. Real GDP decreased by 1.3 percent in 1981, and the official unemployment figure almost doubled from 7.6 percent in 1979 to 13.3 percent in 1983. The fiscal deficit, which had already been exceptionally high during the 1970s, reached the record level of 12.7 percent of GDP in 1981. The Belgian economy was at the brink of collapse. The government had no other choice but to make a big devaluation, urge labor unions to moderate their wage claims, and tackle the fiscal problems.

The third country being subject to the tightening of German monetary policy was Denmark.[43] According to the general International Monetary Fund (IMF) index, the Danish financial market has been considered as rather closed.[44] But the index is too rough. Only the purchase of Danish securities by nonresidents and of foreign securities by residents was prohibited, but with EC membership, many of these regulations were abolished.[45] And, as early as 1971, central bank Governor Erik Hoffmeyer declared that international financial markets largely determined short-term interest rates and therefore domestic monetary policy.[46] The increase in the discount rate

---

[40] They were asked by the Dutch but declined. See next section for details.

[41] BIS, Annual Report, 1973–1974, p. 63.

[42] *Ibid.*, pp. 144–145.

[43] On Denmark's monetary policy, see Thygesen (1979), Johansen (1987), Mjøset (1987), De Grauwe and Vanhaverbeke (1990), Nannestad (1991), Mikkelsen (1993), Andersen (1994), Nielsen (1994), Iversen and Thygesen (1998), Iversen (1999), and Abildgren (2004a, 2004b, 2005).

[44] Scharpf and Schmidt (2000a, p. 369).

[45] The first regulation was upheld until 1 January 1975, the second until 1 January 1978. This transitional period was part of the accession treaty signed by the EC and Denmark. See Bakker (1996, p. 145, footnote 38) and Abildgren (2004a, p. 29).

[46] Mikkelsen (1993, p. 121): "*I sin tale på Danske Bankers Fællesrepræsentations årsmøde den 9. november 1971 udtrykte nationalbankdirektør Erik Hoffmeyer det således: 'Vi er kommet så langt du i vor kortfristede gældsætning til udlandet, at dette dominerer den generelle pengepolitik. En stram pengepolitik er nødvendig alene for at kunne fastholde den låntagning, som vi har foretaget for at dække de forløbne års store underskud. Det er så at sige fortiden,*

from 7 to 8 percent in July 1973 was explained by the increase in foreign interest rates – besides the growing demand pressure of the domestic economy.[47] Also, the further tightening in January 1974 had its cause in the international arena: The French exit from the Snake nurtured speculation against weaker currencies such as the krone.[48]

Rising interest rates made it impossible to maintain growth and full employment. In fact, Denmark was the only European economy that registered negative growth in 1974 (–0.9 percent) after it had grown by 3.6 percent in 1973, and the increase in the official unemployment figure therefore was particularly steep (+4.2 percent from 1973 to 1975). The link to German monetary policy was not the only cause for the dismal performance, however. Owing to the low credibility of the DM peg, Denmark was forced to pay a high risk premium to maintain the exchange rate.[49] Nevertheless, despite this Danish specialty, the basic story was the same as in the Benelux countries: Financial openness forced the Danish authorities to follow the German policy change.

There seems to be a second specialty, however, stemming from domestic factors. While in Belgium and the Netherlands real wage increases decelerated gradually in 1974–1975 as a result of recession and rising unemployment, the process took longer in Denmark. Real wage increases decelerated only in 1974 (+6.2 percent) but then accelerated again in 1975 (+9.3 percent). Some scholars have concluded that Danish labor unions must have been particularly short sighted with respect to the role of wages in a nonaccommodating monetary environment.[50] This may be true in general, but a closer look at the concrete circumstances suggests otherwise. The main problem for wage setters in the negotiations for the year 1975 was to foresee the sharp drop in consumer prices from 15.3 to 9.6 percent.[51] Nominal wage

---

der begrænser vor handlefrihed.'" Cf. Mjøset (1987, p. 431) and Iversen (2000, p. 222):"The problem of combining flexible monetary policies with integrated capital markets was particularly acute in Denmark, where credit markets had always been comparatively open and left to the oversight of the central bank. These monetary-policy constraints – which were acerbated by EC membership and participation in the European currency arrangements (first the 'Snake' and then the EMS) – created a double problem for the government."

[47] Mikkelsen (1993, p. 124). Cf. BIS, Annual Report, 1973–1974, p. 71: "The official discount rate, which had been raised from 7 to 8 per cent. in July mainly for external reasons, was increased to 10 per cent. in two steps around the turn of the year, largely to help counteract inflation."

[48] Mikkelsen (1993, pp. 126–127).

[49] Iversen and Thygesen (1998, pp. 64–65).

[50] For example, Scharpf (2000, pp. 48–49) emphasizes "cognitive misperceptions."

[51] Nannestad (1991, p. 161). Wrong inflation projections were frequent during the mid-1970s. See, for example, Fregert (1994, p. 207) for Sweden and the section on Austria below.

increases were not extraordinary compared with those in other European countries.[52] Once the unions had realized this wrong prediction, they swiftly adjusted their claims, which shows that they were less short sighted than usually assumed: In 1976, real wages increased by only 3.9 percent.

Like the Benelux countries, Denmark suffered from the steep increase in interest rates in the United States from 1979 on. Real GDP growth became negative in 1980 and 1981, the official unemployment figure reached 10.3 percent in 1983, and the fiscal deficit rose from 1.7 percent in 1979 to almost 10 percent in 1982. In reaction to this crisis, the government as well as employers and labor unions became ready to strike a deal, just as in the Benelux countries. The following reforms were so successful that Denmark turned into a model for orthodox economic reforms.[53]

Sweden's path was fundamentally different from the one followed by the Benelux countries and Denmark.[54] Sweden had tight capital controls and therefore was able to keep interest rates low when Germany changed course in 1973.[55] As a result, the Social Democratic government succeeded in maintaining full employment during the recession of 1974–1975. Initially, it was particularly lucky in pursuing this goal.[56] As a result of the resolute fight against inflation and the current-account deficit in the early 1970s, the Swedish economy was less overheated in 1973, which left room for expansionary measures in 1974. Domestic demand increased by about 6 percent in 1974, while slowing down elsewhere.[57] And given that the unemployment rate was unusually high by Swedish standards (2.5 percent in 1973), labor unions moderated their wage claims for 1974, which proved to be the ideal response to the inflationary pressure in the wake of the oil crisis. Finally, Swedish exports profited from the rise in raw material prices, so corporate profits increased steeply.[58] The external balance was so favorable in 1974 that some economists proposed a revaluation in order to dampen

---

[52] For the international comparison of nominal wage increases in 1975, see Mitchell (2003, p. 187): Austria +13.6, Belgium +17.6, Denmark +19, Finland +12.2, France +17.6, Italy +12.6, Netherlands +11.1, Norway +16.3, and United Kingdom +12.2. Only Germany, Sweden, and Switzerland registered significantly lower nominal wage increases.

[53] Wyplosz (1994) calls it "the Danish fairy-tale."

[54] On Swedish monetary policy, see Gourevitch et al. (1984), Mjøset (1987), Calmfors and Forslund (1990), Eklöf (1990), Gylfason (1990), Feldt (1991), Scharpf (1991), Kurzer (1993), Werin et al. (1993), Hörngren and Lindberg (1994), Bergström (1995), Moses (1995, 1998), Lundberg (1996), Lindbeck (1997), Jonung (1999), Magnusson (2000), and Notermans (2000).

[55] Iversen (2000, p. 223).

[56] Scharpf (1991, p. 97).

[57] OECD, Sweden, April 1976, p. 32.

[58] Scharpf (1991, S. 97), Fregert (1994, S. 204).

the expected rise in demand and inflation.[59] However, Finance Minister Gunnar Sträng, an old-school Social Democrat, was strongly opposed to it. For his conservative position, the *Economist* called Sträng "moderate, respected and long-serving."[60] And in retrospect, Erik Lundberg, who had been member of the Studieförbundet Näringsliv och Samhälle (SNS), called the revaluation idea "a clear instance of political naïveté."[61]

Yet, in the course of 1974, the favorable situation deteriorated unexpectedly. Because of his restrictive fiscal policy in the early 1970s, Sträng came under pressure from his party colleagues and the opposition. They expected that he would make up for the "lost years."[62] And since the Social Democrats had suffered losses in the elections in September 1973 and now held only 50 percent of the seats in the new *Riksdag* ("*lotteririksdagen*"), it proved completely impossible to insulate economic policy from power politics. As a result of all these developments, the parliament agreed on expansionary fiscal measures – against the will of Sträng – and the *Riksbank* lowered long-term interest rates. At the same time, high corporate profits in 1974 and expansionary polices encouraged Swedish labor unions to demand large concessions from employers. In April 1975, after a long struggle, the social partners concluded a two-year agreement that was very favorable for workers. Real wages increased by 5 and 7.5 percent in 1975 and 1976.[63]

The government had tried to prevent the labor unions from making excessive wage claims by offering an income tax cut for 1975 in combination with an increase in employers' social charges. The so-called Haga agreement, concluded in May 1974 and named after the location where Palme, the union leaders, and Gunnar Helén, chairman of the *Volkspartei*, met to strike a deal, was initially hailed as "the great political sensation of the season."[64] However, the agreement failed to convince labor unions, and the rise in payroll taxes only further worsened the situation of Swedish businesses. The second Haga agreement, concluded in March 1975, failed as well.[65] As a result of the steep wage increases in 1975–1976, the competitiveness of the Swedish sectors exposed to trade deteriorated, and a big

---

[59] Thygesen (1979, p. 12). Dahlfors (1991) reviews the opinions of economists on the Swedish exchange-rate policy. See also Gourevitch et al. (1984, p. 293).

[60] *Economist*, November 17, 1973, p. 82.

[61] Lundberg (1996, p. 69).

[62] Eklöf (1990, Secs. 28–29).

[63] See Landsorganizationen (1986), Fregert (1994, pp. 204 and 207).

[64] *Svenska Dagbladets Årsbok*, 1974, p. 137.

[65] Gourevitch et al. (1984, p. 292).

current-account deficit emerged.[66] Sweden had no option but to devalue the krona.

However, the center-right government under Prime Minister Thorbjörn Fälldin that came to power in the fall of 1976 initially hesitated to take this unusual step, just as its Social Democratic predecessor did.[67] The employers warned during the wage negotiations for 1977 that "a cost development which leads to a devaluation and that the exchange-rate cooperation is abandoned leads to uncontrollable consequences."[68] Yet soon the government realized that wage earners were not able to moderate their wage claims because "they did not trust one another," as Fälldin recalls.[69] The Swedish *Riksbank* wrote in its Annual Report of 1977: "The decisive adjustment of costs was assumed to occur through internal measures. In the event this proved not to be possible. The results of the wage-agreement in Sweden did not involve any noticeable improvement of Sweden's competitive position."[70] As a result, the current-account deficit deepened further, and confidence in the krona began to dwindle. By now, the government accepted that a large devaluation had become the only realistic option. A first devaluation by 3 percent was made at the meeting of Snake members in Frankfurt in October 1976. It proved to be too small, however, so the Swedish government requested a devaluation of between 10 and 12 percent in April 1977 but got only 6 percent. As capital outflows continued, Sweden made the same request in August 1977, but again it met strong opposition. After this second defeat at the negotiating table, Sweden left the Snake and adopted a currency basket like Finland had done four years earlier.[71]

As noted in Chapter FIVE, capital controls also enabled Sweden to adopt a currency basket and to avoid floating, in contrast to Switzerland in 1973, which had open financial markets. These controls contributed to the relative good performance during the early 1980s because Sweden could at least partially escape from the consequences of tight US monetary policy. With the liberalization and deregulation of financial markets from 1983 on, it became more challenging to manage the basket. The *Riksbank* increasingly had to use interest rates to stabilize the exchange rate and lost the

---

[66] Thygesen (1979, p. 19).

[67] Lindvall (2004, pp. 47–48).

[68] Cited in Fregert (1994, p. 207).

[69] Lindvall (2004, p. 48). A major problem was the competition between blue- and white-collar workers. See, for example, Calmfors and Forslund (1990) and Iversen, Pontusson, and Soskice (2000).

[70] *Sveriges Riksbank*, Annual Report, 1977, p. 13.

[71] Eklöf (1990, pp. 46–47), Moses (1995, pp. 274–275), Notermans (2000, p. 203). On Finland, see Moses (1995, pp. 253–258).

instrument of monetary policy for demand management.[72] And since fiscal policy failed to be restrictive enough to contain domestic demand pressure in the aftermath of the 1982 devaluation, maintaining a stable currency became increasingly costly. In May 1991, following Sweden's decision to apply for EC membership in the autumn of 1990, the *Riksbank* unilaterally tied the krona to the European currency unit (ECU) in order to strengthen the commitment to the fixed exchange rate. Norway had made this shift in October 1990, shortly after Britain's decision to enter the EMS. With this step, Sweden definitely lost its special status as a country with an independent exchange-rate policy backed up by closed financial markets.

Like Sweden, Norway had a comprehensive system of capital controls.[73] Accordingly, the Norwegian policies and its consequences were almost identical to the Swedish ones. Thanks to capital controls, the Norwegian authorities were able to ignore the rise in German interest rates and allow long-term interest-rate differentials to increase – in 1974, the differential amounted to 5.9 percent and in 1975, 7.2 percent. The expansionary policy succeeded in fueling growth and maintaining full employment but also encouraged labor unions to make excessive wage claims, threatening the competitiveness of the exporting and import-competing sectors. The Social Democratic government tried to prevent labor unions from realizing these wage claims by offering subsidy and support measures. Yet the strategy failed to convince workers. Real wages increased steeply by 7.7 and 7.3 percent in 1975–1976, so the relative unit labor costs rose more than in Germany, the Benelux countries, and Denmark.[74] Norway thus had no choice but to devalue. From October 1976 to February 1978, the rate of the krone was changed four times and lost more than a quarter of its value vis-à-vis the DM. In December 1978, Norway left the Snake.

Also as in Sweden, capital mobility made it easy to replace the DM peg with a currency basket and to combine a stable exchange rate with a policy of low interest rates. Monetary policy was expansionary during the recession of the early 1980s, and unemployment remained low. Finally, when the Norwegian authorities decided to deregulate and liberalize financial markets at about the same time as their Swedish counterparts, the *Norges Bank* ran into similar problems as the Swedish *Riksbank*.[75] In order to strengthen the credibility of the fixed exchange rate, Norway followed the United

[72] Hörngren and Lindberg (1994, pp. 146–148).
[73] On Norwegian monetary policy, see Mjøset (1987), Gylfason (1990), Moses (1995), Moses (2000), and Notermans (2000).
[74] Moses (2000, pp. 128–130), Notermans (2000, pp. 197*ff.*).
[75] Moses (2000, pp. 145–151).

Kingdom in pegging the currency to the ECU in October 1990, although only unilaterally.

In sum, the different degrees of financial openness mattered enormously. The Benelux countries and Denmark had relatively open financial markets and therefore no choice but to follow Germany's policy change in 1973. As a result, GDP growth slowed down, unemployment increased, and real wage claims were reduced. The positive effect was that the real appreciation of their currencies was reversed with a certain time lag. Norway and Sweden, by contrast, were free to pursue an independent monetary policy, to fuel growth, and to maintain full employment during the recession of 1974–1975. The negative effect was that real wages increased steeply at a time when they began to stagnate in Germany, which led to a dramatic deterioration of the competitiveness of the exporting and import-competing sectors.

These results suggest that the conventional thesis that Sweden and Norway devalued and left the Snake mainly because of different institutions and policy preferences misses the crucial point. These two Scandinavian countries had options that the Benelux countries and Denmark lacked, so a direct comparison cannot be made. It is true, however, that Norway and Sweden probably would have pursued another course from 1974 to 1976 if their central banks had been more independent. In this case, however, they also would have had more open financial markets, which would have confronted them with the same dilemma as the Benelux countries and Denmark.

EC MEMBERSHIP, TRADE INTEGRATION, AND THE OPTIMAL PEG

The second and third factors that shaped the exchange-rate policies of the small European states were the structures of political and economic integration.[76] They determined whether a small state could opt for an independent exchange-rate regime or not. States that were members of the EC and entertained strong trade relations with Germany had no choice but to participate in the Snake and the EMS and to follow the rules of these European monetary regimes. By contrast, small states that were only associate members of the Snake and were not particularly integrated with the German economy had the freedom to replace the DM peg with a currency basket, and

---

[76] Frieden (2002) also highlights the importance of manufacturing exports to the DM zone as a percentage of GDP.

after leaving the Snake, they were free to make many and large competitive devaluations.[77] The small EC members, by contrast, had to comply with the rules of the regime. The decision to adjust the peg was made jointly, and the size of adjustment was limited because countries asking for an exchange-rate change were not allowed to fully offset inflation differentials.[78]

The reason why the small EC members were reluctant to leave the Snake was that they had nothing to gain from violating the rules of monetary cooperation.[79] They only opened themselves to be marginalized and to lose their ability to make coalitions or engage in "horse trading" that could bring advantages in other policy areas of the EC. They did not have the power to ignore the EC bodies when it contradicted their interests. Accordingly, there is not the slightest narrative evidence suggesting that small EC members even considered changing the monetary regime.[80]

The constraints stemming from trade integration and EC member-ship were most evident in the cases of Belgium and the Netherlands. The Netherlands were one of the six founding signatory states of the Treaty of Rome in 1957. The Dutch government was particularly interested in the success of the Common Agricultural Policy (CAP) because of the great importance of its agricultural exports. And since the Dutch economy was very open and closely linked to the German and Belgian economies, fixing the guilder to the DM and the Belgian franc was the obvious choice, regardless of central bank independence, the strength of the Left, and the structure of the labor movement.[81]

Of course, in theory, the Netherlands could have adopted a currency basket, as had Sweden and Norway, given that the British pound lost about a third of its value from 1972 to 1977. But the difference to the existing regime would have been much smaller than in the case of the Scandinavian countries. In addition, the costs in terms of lost credibility and higher interest rates would have been more considerable for the Netherlands than for Norway and Sweden because the high degree of financial openness would have made it impossible to control the level of domestic interest rates.[82] For example, in

---

[77] Note that the constraint stemming from EC membership is only relevant for what kind of peg small states chose but not for the question of fixed versus floating. See Chapter FIVE.

[78] Argy (1990, p. 7). On the rules of realignment in the Snake and the EMS, see Gros and Thygesen (1998, pp. 15–20 and 77–79).

[79] See the last section of Chapter FIVE.

[80] Von Dosenrode (1993, pp. 62–65) and Hey (2003, p. 188). See Chapter FIVE.

[81] Van Zanden (1998, p. 164): "In view of the increased importance of Germany for the Dutch economy and the growing role of the eastern neighbour in the EC, it was only natural to try and maintain a close link with the deutsche mark."

[82] OECD (1988, p. 98).

1983, the Dutch government decided not to follow the appreciation of the DM by 2 percent – against the advice of the DNB.[83] Consequently, a risk premium emerged again after it had disappeared in the preceding years.[84] Moreover, the devaluation was too small to improve the competitiveness of the Dutch economy.[85] After this failed devaluation, the Dutch authorities decided to link the guilder explicitly to the DM.

Belgium was in a similar situation as the Netherlands. EC membership and close trade relations with Germany and the Netherlands, combined with a high degree of trade openness, made a peg to the DM and the guilder the most obvious option. What was different in comparison with the Netherlands, however, was that Belgium suffered from a weak French franc from 1976 to 1983, and France was the second most important trading partner of Belgium. Consequently, the markets speculated that Belgium would follow France in leaving the Snake in early 1976.[86] The weak franc also aggravated the problems of the Belgian currency during the initial phase of the EMS. Another difference between Belgium and the Netherlands was that Belgium, a net exporter of coal and steel, was mainly interested in promoting trade of raw materials and had no stakes in the CAP.[87] Yet, despite these differences, Belgium had the same incentive to stay in the Snake and the EMS as the Netherlands. The Swedish scenario – leaving the Snake and shifting to a currency basket – was not an option either for Belgium or for the Netherlands. It is therefore problematic to blame Belgian or Dutch labor unions for their failure to advocate a Swedish policy.[88]

Accordingly, the Benelux countries had to accept the rules of the Snake and the EMS. For the Netherlands, these rules were not relevant because the guilder remained a strong currency, mainly owing to the strong current account, as we will see below. In the case of Belgium, though, they represented a serious constraint when in 1982 the Martens government sought a competitive devaluation by 12 percent, whereas Germany and most other EMS members only conceded a devaluation by 8.5 percent.[89]

---

[83] Devaluations and exchange-rate regime changes were the responsibility of the government. The central bank, however, was entitled to give a public comment on the decisions of the government. The *Dutch central bank* had already opposed the devaluation of the guilder in 1979 by 2 percent against the DM.

[84] Wellink (1994, p. 69), Hemerijk, Unger, and Visser (2000, pp. 216–217).

[85] Szász (1999, pp. 198–201).

[86] BIS, Annual Report, 1975–1976, pp. 100–101.

[87] Hemerijck, Unger, and Visser (2000, p. 176).

[88] For example, Notermans (2000, pp. 186–187) is critical toward the policy of Dutch labor unions.

[89] Jones (2008, p. 197).

For the Dutch, it was another kind of political constraint that proved to be a problem, namely, that Belgium insisted on a common exchange-rate policy during the 1970s. Until the spring of 1976, they had formed a special exchange-rate regime, the so-called worm in the Snake, but following the weakness of the French franc that put the Belgian franc under pressure, the formal agreement was withdrawn.[90] The special relationship was still visible in the first year of the EMS, however. In September 1979, when France devalued the franc by 2 percent and Germany revalued the DM by the same amount, the Benelux countries had to decide whether or not to follow Germany. The Netherlands were willing to go along, but France and Germany would not allow the weak Belgian franc to be revalued. In this situation, the Dutch gave in.[91]

The case of Denmark is more complicated. On the one hand, the Snake was not an optimal exchange-rate regime because the share of trade with Germany was relatively small in comparison with the Benelux countries. The fact that Denmark had made a temporary exit from the Snake following the British shift to floating in June 1972 showed that the United Kingdom was an important market for Danish exporters.[92] Accordingly, Denmark's exports suffered more strongly from the appreciation of the DM and the fall of the British pound than the Benelux countries.[93] And once Sweden, the second most important trading partner, had shifted to a currency basket in 1977 – to the great annoyance of the Danish authorities[94] – participation in the Snake became even less optimal. Only at the end of the 1970s had trade with Germany become important enough to justify the DM peg, but not from 1972 to 1976, when the large EC members adopted floating. Thus,

[90] BIS, Annual Report, 1975–1976, p. 101; Bosman (1984, p. 11), Jones (1998b).

[91] Wellink (1994, pp. 71–72), Szász (1999, p. 199). An additional reason was that the Dutch guilder had been in a weak position as well but still not as weak as the Belgian franc.

[92] Tsoukalis (1977, pp. 122–123). Denmark's temporary exit was motivated by the British decision to adopt floating and the fact that the referendum on entering the EC was still to be held. Moreover, the Danish government declared after the exit that it would continue to keep the fluctuation of the krone within the band of 4.5 percent as agreed in the Smithsonian agreement. In other words, the krone stayed de facto in the Snake. And once it became clear that the United Kingdom was not willing to reenter, the Danish authorities joined the Snake again *de jure*. For an overview of Denmark's changing views toward the EC, see Pedersen (1996b).

[93] Thygesen (1979, pp. 18–19).

[94] *International Herald Tribune*, 30 August 1977: "The Governor of the National Bank of Denmark, Mr. Erik Hoffmeyer, said on 29/8 in Copenhagen that Denmark would not have devalued the krone but for the Swedish exit from the European joint float. He called the Swedish move extremely unfortunate. Combined with the Norwegian decision to devalue the krone by 5 percent, it had obliged Denmark to follow suit."

from an economic point of view, leaving the Snake would have been an option for Denmark.[95]

On the other hand, Denmark had had a pending application for EC membership for many years and had finally joined in January 1973, after a referendum held on October 2, 1972. Almost two-thirds of Danish voters favored this step, mainly because the United Kingdom had become a member of the EC and Denmark needed the EC market for its agricultural exports.[96] Leaving the Snake thus would have complicated the cooperation within the CAP and overshadowed the good relationship with other small EC members, so the vast majority of politicians readily accepted the restrictions of the EC exchange-rate regimes without further discussion.[97] Obviously, trade integration was seen as a function of political integration.[98]

The loyalty to the Snake had a high price, however. Denmark was never allowed to make devaluations large enough to decisively improve the competitiveness of its exporting sectors because the rules of the Snake were rather rigid. The devaluations only prevented the effective exchange rate from further appreciating but did not bring about any improvement in real terms. Figure 6.8 shows how Sweden and Norway succeeded in making real depreciations once they had left the Snake, while Denmark's competitiveness remained at the same level.[99] Under the EMS, the room for maneuvering increased, but Denmark still was constrained by the rules of the monetary system. In February 1982, Denmark wanted to make a large devaluation, following the Belgian devaluation, but the EMS members rejected this demand.[100]

Sweden had almost the same trading partners as Denmark, so the DM peg was clearly not an optimal regime for Sweden. The main reason why the *Riksbank* had decided to join in March 1973 had been the lack of alternatives. Most politicians, government officials, and labor union leaders wanted a stable exchange rate with the most important trading partners, and since Germany and Denmark had been participating in the Snake, Sweden followed.[101] This step was taken despite strong anti-EC sentiments. Swedish citizens, proud of the neutral status of their country, believed that joining

---

[95] Thygesen (1979, p. 22).
[96] The precise result was 63 to 37 percent; the turnout amounted to 90 percent of the electorate.
[97] Moses (1995, pp. 230–231 and 315).
[98] Mjøset (1987, p. 432).
[99] Thygesen (1979, p. 14).
[100] Ludlow (1982, p. 288).
[101] Moses (1995, pp. 244–253).

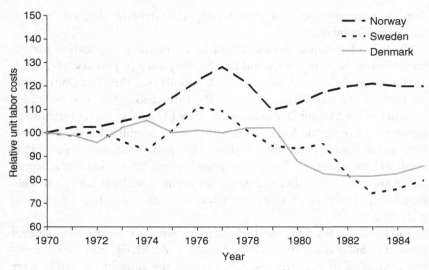

Figure 6.8. Scandinavia: relative unit labor costs, 1970–1985. (*Scharpf and Schmidt, 2000a.*)

the EC would limit their sovereignty.[102] Besides Switzerland, Sweden had been the only small neighbor of Germany that had not been invaded during World War II. A further reason for Sweden's cool feelings toward the EC was that agricultural exports were of little importance. For these two reasons, the Swedish government did not even consider EC membership in 1972, whereas Denmark and Norway held a referendum, and Sweden joined the Snake only when the Bretton Woods system collapsed in March 1973, whereas Denmark and Norway had readily entered the Snake in 1972, even before the referendum on EC membership was held.[103] Sweden, however, was not as reluctant to consider EC membership as Finland, which strongly depended on the Soviet Union and therefore adopted a currency basket in June 1973.

It is against this historical background that Sweden's exit from the Snake in August 1977 must be studied. Sweden showed no interest in the institution building of the EC, and it always had the option to change the exchange-

---

[102] Miles (1997, pp. 89–113).

[103] Moses (1995, pp. 212–214). Interestingly, the governing board of the *Riksbank* decided in March 1972 to join the Snake along with Norway, but Governor Erik Åsbrink did not follow up on this decision. Moses supposes that Åsbrink declined to act because Social Democrats were split on the question of EC membership and didn't want to deepen this conflict.

rate regime. Accordingly, Swedish officials could allow themselves to act on their own after they had realized that the Snake was a straitjacket. Officially, the Swedish government argued that it wanted to maintain full employment, which was not compatible with staying in an international monetary regime dominated by Germany's monetarist policy.[104] This official statement and later comments by Swedish officials often have served as clear evidence that Sweden had a deeper commitment to the social welfare of its citizens than other European states.[105] Such a view is too narrow, however. From a comparative perspective, the crucial point is that Sweden's policy options were not the same as those of the Benelux countries and Denmark owing to differences in economic and political integration. Regardless of whether their commitment to full employment was strong or weak, the small EC members could not leave the Snake. Conversely, if Sweden had been a member of the EC during the 1970s, it probably would have stayed in the Snake.[106]

It is evident that Sweden had more freedom to pursue its own exchange-rate policy once it left the Snake. There were three large devaluations: one by 10 percent in August 1977, another one by 10 percent in September 1981, and the "big bang" devaluation by 16 percent in October 1982. In 1983, after all these devaluations had taken place, the krona was clearly the weakest of all small-state currencies: The effective nominal exchange rate was 30 percent lower than in the basis year of 1970. The next weakest currency was the Danish krone, which had lost 13 percent of its value.

Norway was even less linked to the German market than Denmark and Sweden. The most important trading partner was the United Kingdom, followed by Sweden and Germany. On the other hand, the relationship to the EC was less cool than Sweden's – Norway had joined NATO in 1949, whereas Sweden had remained neutral. In September 1972, a referendum on EC membership was held, and membership was rejected by a rather small majority of 53.6 percent.[107] Expecting that the voters would say yes, the *Norges Bank* had decided to join the Snake as early as May 1972, only a few weeks after the Snake started to operate. The negative outcome of the referendum did not change the choice of the exchange-rate regime, however, because Snake membership was seen as a technical, not a political issue.[108]

---

[104] *Frankfurter Allgemeine Zeitung,* No. 199, 29 August 1977, p. 9, and *Frankfurter Allgemeine Zeitung,* No. 200, 30 August 1977, p. 9. Cf. Eklöf (1990, p. 47).
[105] Gylfason (1990, p. 167) and Notermans (2000 p. 203).
[106] Thygesen (1979, p. 23).
[107] Sœter (1996, p. 135) calls the referendum "the 1972 trauma."
[108] Moses (1995, p. 207).

Norway withdrew from the Snake in December 1978, three months before the start of the EMS, and introduced a basket peg. The official statement was similar to the one made by Swedish officials in August 1977. During the parliamentary debate of 18 December 1978, when the new basket regime was dealt with, several deputies pointed out that Norway needed to have a weaker currency in order to maintain full employment. For example, Einar Førde of the Labor Party said: "Binding our exchange rate to the German mark shouldn't be evaluated only in light of considerations for stability, but equally in terms of that which has been our constant theme while defending our economic policies in recent years. We have rejected the economic policies pursued by most of the other West European countries. We have done this first and foremost because these countries have tolerated a level of unemployment that we could not."[109]

Yet, like in the Swedish case, the statement is misleading from a comparative perspective. First and foremost, Norway had the option to leave the Snake, whereas the small EC members did not. It is therefore impossible to prove that a deeper commitment to full employment was the crucial reason for Norway's regime change. Second, there is strong narrative evidence that Norway declined to join the EMS and adopted the currency basket in December 1978 mainly because the United Kingdom and Sweden did not join and because Norway's voters were opposed to EC membership.[110] The *Norges Bank* wrote in its Annual Report that a majority of the board stressed "that the participants in the EMS would only account for some 32 per cent of Norway's foreign trade. If the United Kingdom at a later date should become a full member, and if Sweden should apply for association, there would, however, be reason for a reconsideration of the question of Norway's attitude to the EMS."[111] Thus the question of full employment was dependent on issues of trade integration and EC membership.

In sum, the structures of political and economic integration made a crucial difference. The small EC members – the Benelux countries and Denmark – had no choice but to participate in the Snake and the EMS. The political costs of leaving would have been too high, and in the case of the Benelux countries, the difference between the EC monetary system and a currency basket would not have been considerable anyway. Norway and

---

[109] Einar Førde, Labor Party representative before Parliament on 18 December 1978, cited in Moses (2000, p. 123). See also Notermans (2000, p. 203).

[110] Moses (1995, pp. 291–309, especially p. 292).

[111] *Norges Bank*, Report and Accounts 1978, Oslo, 1979, p. 61. This is what happened in 1990: The United Kingdom entered the EMS on 8 October 1990, and Norway linked the krone to the ECU on 22 October 1990. See Chapter EIGHT.

Sweden, by contrast, had the option to leave the Snake, and since their trade with Germany was less important than in the case of the Benelux countries, it was rational to opt for a currency basket. For economic reasons, Denmark should have followed Sweden in leaving the Snake, but EC membership proved to be primordial.

If we combine these results with those of the preceding section, the following picture emerges: Thanks to capital controls and the weak position of their central banks, the Norwegian and Swedish governments were able to pursue a countercyclic policy during the recession of the mid-1970s, resulting in high wage increases and a dramatic deterioration of competitiveness. Since the correction of these imbalances required a large devaluation that was not granted by Snake members, and since trade with the Snake countries was modest, Sweden and Norway replaced the DM peg with a softer peg. By contrast, the Benelux countries and Denmark had the option neither to pursue a countercyclical policy during the recession nor to carry out large devaluations or to leave the Snake. Their actions were determined primarily by financial openness and EC membership, not by domestic institutions or specific policy preferences.

NATURAL RESOURCES, DOMESTIC POLICIES, AND THE CURRENT ACCOUNT

The list of external factors is not complete yet, however, because capital mobility, trade integration, and (non)membership in the EC only explain why Norway and Sweden left the Snake in 1977–1978 but not why exchange-rate movements also varied within the two country groups. The Dutch guilder was stronger than the Belgian franc and the Danish krone and the Norwegian krone was stronger than the Swedish krona after the exit from the Snake. The missing additional factor is the extent to which small European states depended on oil and natural gas. Countries exporting natural gas or oil registered a current-account surplus and were able to keep their currency stable or even to revalue despite structural problems. Countries with a net import of oil and natural gas, by contrast, were forced to devalue during the second oil-price shock – regardless of the strength of the Left, the status of the central bank, or the structure of wage bargaining.

Of course, the current account also was influenced by wage movements as well as fiscal and monetary policies, and in two instances, the domestic policies in fact made a difference. First, Belgian real wages rose above average from 1973 to 1979 and continued to increase in 1980 and 1981, whereas they decreased in Denmark and the Netherlands. Second, the expansionary fiscal policies of Sweden in 1979 and 1980 contributed to the weakening of the krona. However, in both cases, domestic policies were only a contributing factor, not the main reason for the divergence of exchange rates within the two country groups. Or put differently, if Belgium and Sweden had been net exporters of oil or natural gas, their currencies would have been stronger despite overly expansionary domestic policies.

Among the Benelux and Scandinavian countries, the Netherlands was the country with the highest current-account surplus during the 1970s, and accordingly, the guilder was the strongest currency (Figures 6.9 and 6.10). In part, the surplus was due to the traditional structure of the Dutch economy. Owing to the long tradition of capital exports, the country enjoyed high yearly interest earnings from abroad, and thanks to the importance of the port of Rotterdam for the European economy, the service sector always had been particularly strong. Yet, during the 1970s, the most important cause of the current-account surplus was the high revenue from natural gas exports in the wake of the first oil crisis. Natural gas reserves had been discovered in the 1950s and 1960s in the northern Groningen Province. Production rose rapidly from 1.7 billion cubic meters in 1965 to almost 100 billion cubic meters in the mid-1970s.[112] And when oil prices quadrupled as a result of the first oil crisis in October 1973 and the Dutch government decided to raise the price of natural gas, domestically as well as for exports, the revenues increased further.[113] In a country report, the OECD calculated that Dutch natural gas improved the current account by more than 10 percent in 1975 and 1976 (10.4 and 12.8 percent).[114]

1976 also was the year in which the current-account surplus peaked. Accordingly, when the Snake members met in Frankfurt in October of that year to discuss a realignment, the Netherlands was in a strong position. Finance Minister Wim Duisenberg explicitly highlighted the strong surplus of the Dutch current account during the proceedings, and on this ground, Dutch officials – together with their Belgian colleagues, who also argued on the basis of their current-account surplus – rejected a devaluation.[115] The arguments seem to have been convincing: The Dutch guilder

---

[112] OECD, *Pays-Bas,* March 1978, p. 34.

[113] *Ibid.,* p. 35.

[114] *Ibid.,* p. 34: "*Calcul de l'incidence sur la balance des paiements, y compris les économies d'importations.*" In 1965, the figure was 0.1, and in 1973, it was 4.6.

[115] *Archief De Nederlandsche Bank,* HA 01234: 2.312.22/73/1: *geldmarkt Bijeenkomst van Ministers en Centrale Bank Presidenten van deelnemers aan de "Slang" op zondag 17 oktober 1976 te Frankfurt: "Minister Duisenberg wijst op de sterke betalingsbalanspositie van nederland, die geen enkele grond geeft tot wijziging van de koersverhouding tot the D-mark.*" Cf. Thygesen (1979, p. 18).

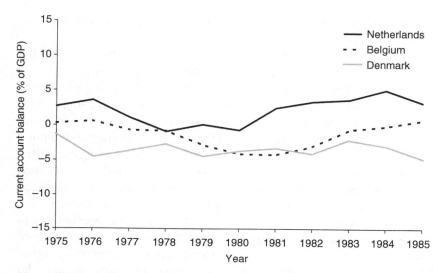

Figure 6.9. EC members Belgium, Denmark, and the Netherlands: current-account balance (in percent of GDP). (*Mitchell, 2003.*)

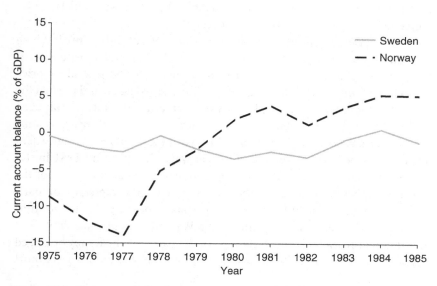

Figure 6.10. Norway and Sweden: current-account balance (in percent of GDP). (*Mitchell, 2003.*)

and Belgian franc remained untouched, while the DM was revalued and the Scandinavian currencies devalued.

Yet, if there had not been a second oil-price shock in the late 1970s, the Netherlands would have been forced to devalue the guilder despite the high revenues from natural gas. For, as is well known from the literature on the "Dutch disease," the strong guilder in combination with rising relative unit labor costs resulting from wage indexation and a strong labor movement weakened the competitiveness of the non-gas-exporting and import-competing sectors. In 1977, the year after the Frankfurt realignment, the current-account surplus therefore diminished by two-thirds, and it turned into a deficit in 1978. The guilder came under attack, the DNB was forced to raise short-term interest rates, and some Social Democratic deputies in the Second Chamber, since 1977 seated on the opposition benches, began to speak out against a strong guilder. Until that moment, there had been only one prominent voice criticizing the hard-currency policy of the central bank, namely, Harry Langman, a former minister of economic affairs, who demanded a devaluation coupled with an austerity package to improve the competitiveness of the exporting industry. In his public speech, Langman made the link between Colijn and Zijlstra: The latter was said to be an adherent of Colijn in his early student years.[116]

However, the current-account deficit remained small and did not last long enough to generate a consensus in favor of devaluation and a suspension of wage indexing, as Langman had proposed. Thanks to the second oil-price shock, the income from natural gas exports increased again and pushed the current account back into surplus. In nominal terms, the surplus was even slightly bigger in 1981 than in the record year of 1976. Pressure against the guilder subsided, and the voices in favor of a devaluation went silent again. It is true that the reduction of real wages in 1980 and 1981 by 1.9 and 3.4 percent contributed to an improvement in competitiveness of the non-gas-exporting sectors. The real wages of Belgian workers, by comparison, continued to rise in those two years mainly because Wallonian miners were particularly well organized and Wallonian politicians could not afford to ignore their claims, regardless of the party to which they belonged (Table 6.3). But export statistics also show that the rise in natural gas export

---

[116] Szász (1981, pp. 306–311). See *Bank- en effectenbedrijf, Oktober* 76/194, p. 366, on the debate. It refers to Langman as soloist: "… *heeft oud-minister Langman nu een solisten-rol op zich genomen.*" Zijlstra (1992, p. 225) shows a cartoon of Zijlstra as new Colijn which appeared in the Social Democratic *Volkskrant* in January 1981. Colijn was the most important defender of the gold standard during the 1930s (see Chapter FOUR). For a comparison of the 1930s and the 1970s see Siebrand and Van der Windt (1983).

Table 6.3. *Real Wages in Belgium, Denmark, and the Netherlands (1972 = 100)*

	1973	1980	1981	1982
Belgium	101.4	115.6	118.0	115.1
Denmark	100.6	100.1	98.1	98.7
Netherlands	99.8	103.9	101.2	100.1

Source: OECD, Economic Surveys, Belgium-Luxembourg, May 1983, p. 11.

prices contributed to the improvement in the Dutch current account by almost half.[117] If we also take into account the fact that in the early 1980s natural gas accounted for about 7.5 percent of national income and 8 percent of merchandise export values, it becomes even more evident that the Dutch exchange-rate policy would have been quite different without this natural resource.[118]

Belgium also enjoyed much room to maneuver during the greater part of the 1970s because the current account registered a surplus until 1976 and only a minor deficit in 1977–1978. The reason was that from 1974 to 1979, incomes from the invisible balance increased mainly because of rising expenditures by international organizations based in Belgium.[119] Accordingly, in the initial phase lasting from 1973 to the Frankfurt realignment in 1976, Belgium was in a similarly strong position as the Netherlands, and the Belgian franc was considered a strong currency. Thus, when the Belgian government decided not to follow the revaluation of the Dutch guilder by 5 percent in September 1973, markets were surprised.[120]

---

[117] OECD, The Netherlands, January 1993, p. 53: "The swing on current account to the tune of 5.5 percent of GNP (1980–1982) was composed as follows: +2.5 percent due to natural gas exports prices, –0.5 percent due to natural gas exports volumes, +3.25 percent due to the nonenergy merchandise balance, +0.25 percent due to the services balance."

[118] OECD, The Netherlands, January 1993, pp. 13–14.

[119] Mommen (1994, p. 156).

[120] BIS, Annual Report, 1973–1974, p. 150: "Following the guilder revaluation in mid-September market attention was immediately focused on the franc, partly because of its link to the guilder in the worm and partly because, like the Netherlands and Germany, Belgium's current balance of payments was strong." *Economist*, 22 September 1973: "The Belgians were quick to deny that they would follow Holland's example, but dealers were more impressed by statistics suggesting that they should. Belgium's rate of inflation has been catching up with the unhappy 8 per cent a year now standard throughout most Europe. Its current balance of payments surplus is now equivalent to nearly 4 per cent of its grip, and does not look like disappearing of its own accord. Despite their denials, the Belgians will probably have to upvalue...."

However, the Belgians had a good reason to make this decision: They feared that a revaluation would hurt the export business. Finance Minister Willy de Clercq explained that the primary goal was to maintain the employment level in the exporting sector, and he did not believe that a revaluation would have a great anti-inflationary impact.[121]

Furthermore, as in the Netherlands, the willingness of labor unions to change course and to suspend wage indexation was small as long as the current account registered a surplus or only a minor deficit. And as long as wage indexation was never questioned, all political groups knew that a devaluation would not work, especially in a very open economy such as the Belgian one.[122] However, from 1979 to 1981, when the current-account deficit became excessive in the wake of the second oil crisis and markets lost confidence in the franc, the Belgian situation became completely different from the Dutch one.[123] Slowly but steadily, policymakers began to question the conventional wisdom, and a consensus emerged that a devaluation was the only option to restore competitiveness, provided that labor unions were ready to accept real wage reductions.[124] In February 1982, the Belgian government carried out a devaluation by 8.5 percent that proved to be very successful, thanks to the concomitant tightening of fiscal and monetary policy and the temporary abolition of wage indexation. The current-account deficit disappeared in 1983.[125]

The situation of Denmark was completely different. The current-account balance had been mostly negative in the postwar years and continued to be a major constraint after 1973. The most important disadvantage was that the low level of foreign-exchange reserves made the krone vulnerable to speculative attacks.[126] Besides, as a result of the low credibility of the DM peg and the need to borrow abroad to replenish reserves, Denmark was forced to keep interest rates well above the international level. Mjøset (1987) concludes that "balance-of-payments problems made full employment policies

---

[121] *Trouw,* 17 September 1973; *Handelsblad NRC,* September 17, 1993. Dutch Finance Minister Duisenberg contacted Belgian Finance Minister W. de Clercq as early as July.

[122] Hellmann (1976, p. 83), Jones (1998a, pp. 44–47).

[123] ECD (1988), p. 117: "In 1981, outflows of private capital amounted to almost 5 per cent of GDP."

[124] In a best-selling book, the Belgian journalist Hugo de Ridder described the change of opinion (de Ridder, 1991). Prime Minister Martens also tells important details in his memoirs (Martens, 1985).

[125] De Grauwe (2003, p. 38). See also De Grauwe and Vanhaverbeke (1990).

[126] Johansen (1987, p. 194): "During the 1970s the main concern of Danish monetary policy was the external situation with an emphasis on creating foreign-exchange holdings sufficiently large to avoid sudden speculative capital movements undermining domestic economic policy." See also Nielsen (1994, p. 63).

impossible in Denmark."[127] Furthermore, Denmark was very dependent on oil imports, which, in combination with wage indexation, led to the highest inflation rate in Western Europe in 1974 (15.3 percent).[128] Thus, not surprisingly, the Danish krone lost more of its value from 1973 to 1982 than the Belgian franc.

Since the Danish authorities had almost no room to maneuver, the political deadlock resulted in a stop-and-go policy.[129] To reduce the current-account deficit and inflation, monetary policy was tightened in 1974, and fiscal policy was restrictive in the first half of 1974.[130] Yet the measures were too drastic, making Denmark the only country in Western Europe to register a negative growth rate in 1974 (–0.9 percent), and its unemployment also was rising faster than elsewhere. Accordingly, the authorities changed course. In 1975, real M1 and M2 increased at a record pace, and fiscal policy was much more expansionary than in all small countries with the exception of Austria (Table 6.4): Adjusted for the business cycle and inflation, the structural budget deficit increased by 1.1 percent (from 0.4 to –0.7 percent). Consequently, the steep fall in the inflation rate that had started in 1974 came to a halt again. At the end of 1975, the newly elected Social Democratic government that had taken power from Venstre continued with an expansionary fiscal policy in order to reduce unemployment.[131] By contrast, all other small states and Germany changed course because they realized that the recession had ended. As a result of this ill-timed measure, the Danish current-account deficit quadrupled in 1976 despite a tightening of monetary policy.[132]

Not surprisingly, Snake members considered the Danish currency the weakest link in the system when they discussed realignment at the conference in Frankfurt in October 1976. The krone was devalued by 6 percent against the DM, but since this realignment proved insufficient, the krone was devalued further in April and August 1977 by 3 and 5 percent against the DM. As explained in the preceding section, these steps were too small to improve the competitiveness of the trading sectors of the Danish economy. Only temporarily did they take some pressure from the krone, but since wage indexation was still widespread, devaluations translated themselves

---

[127] Mjøset (1987, p. 428), Iversen and Thygesen (1998, pp. 64–65).

[128] Johansen (1987, p. 169). BIS, Annual Report, 1975–1976, p. 30. Denmark, France, Italy, and Spain were particularly dependent on oil imports.

[129] For example, Scharpf (2000) ignores the current account and thus explains the stop-and-go policy only by domestic factors, notably central bank independence.

[130] BIS, Annual Report, 1975–1976, p. 58.

[131] Thygesen (1979, p. 17).

[132] Johansen (1987, p. 167).

Table 6.4. *Inflation-Adjusted Trend (Mid-cycle) Structural Budget Balances
(Percent of GDP/GNP)*

	Austria	Belgium	Denmark	Netherlands	Norway	Sweden
1971	2.7	−1.3	3.1	0.7	4.0	2.8
1972	1.8	−2.3	1.5	0.7	4.3	2.3
1973	2.0	−2.2	1.6	0.7	5.7	0.8
1974	2.2	1.1	0.4	0.1	4.4	−3.5
1975	0.5	1.4	−0.7	0.4	3.8	−2.5
1976	−1.7	−2.5	−2.0	−1.2	2.5	−0.3
1977	−1.3	−1.7	−2.6	−0.6	1.9	−1.0
1978	−1.0	−3.3	−1.5	−1.9	1.3	−1.9
1979	−1.9	−4.0	−3.8	−2.3	2.0	−4.8
1980	−0.2	−4.8	−3.4	−1.4	4.1	−6.9
1981	1.3	−5.6	−3.8	−1.3	5.3	−5.4
1982	−0.1	−2.9	−7.0	−1.7	5.4	−4.8
1983	−1.6	−2.5	−5.7	−2.5	5.3	−3.3
1984	−0.2	−2.3	−4.4	−1.6	2.3	−2.4

Source: Muller and Price (1984, p. 58), table 8.

into higher inflation, so the current account hardly improved. In 1977, consumer prices still increased by 10.1 percent, whereas the Benelux countries had succeeded in bringing them down to 6 to 7 percent. Denmark ended up in the worst of all worlds: Both inflation and unemployment rates were high in comparison with other small countries.

In 1979, when the second oil crisis started, the situation became even worse. The current-account deficit reached another record high, and further devaluations were needed. From September 1979 to March 1983, the krone was devalued six times, resulting in a total devaluation of almost 30 percent (28.7 percent) against the ECU. Most of these adjustments were carried out within a general realignment of the EMS, with the exception of the one made in November 1979 by 5 percent.[133] However, these devaluations proved successful, as in the case of Belgium, because they were combined with suspension of wage indexing and the launch of fiscal reform.[134]

---

[133] Moses (1995, p. 289).
[134] According to Bergman and Hutchison (1999, p. 254), the Danish experience "was the largest fiscal adjustment among the OECD countries reviewed."

Nominal interest rates decreased rapidly, and the interest-rate spread against Germany almost disappeared until the end of the 1980s.[135]

Sweden also was among the countries those were confronted with the problem of a persistent current-account deficit. However, initially, this international constraint was not as strong as in the case of Denmark. The main reason was that commodities and commodity-related products made up a large share of exports, whereas agricultural exports were much less important.[136] In 1973, the current-account surplus peaked; in 1974, the deficit was small. On the other hand, Sweden, just like Denmark, greatly differed from the Netherlands, for, in contrast to the prices of natural gas and oil, commodity prices soon fell back to the pre-1973 level, so the exceptional increase in relative unit labor costs in 1975 and 1976 translated directly into a deepening of the current-account deficit. In 1977, the deficit amounted to 2.6 percent of GDP. With hindsight, this deterioration of the external balance proved to be a blessing because it forced the authorities and social partners to act, whereas in the Netherlands it took more time for authorities to realize the extent of the external imbalance. And since Sweden had more policy options than the small EC members, the government and the *Riksbank* could make a real difference by changing the exchange-rate peg and by devaluing the krona.

Thanks to a competitive devaluation, a softening of the peg, and a reduction in wage costs, Sweden almost succeeded in annihilating the current-account deficit by 1978.[137] But the steep increase of oil prices beginning in the spring of 1979 reversed the trend, so the current account reached a record deficit in 1980 (−3.5 percent). The worsening of the external balance was not fully caused by the oil crisis, however. A domestic factor, fiscal policy, contributed to it: The inflation-adjusted trend (midcycle) structural budget balances show a fiscal deficit rising from 1.9 percent of GDP in 1978 to 6.9 in 1980 – not even Belgium registered such a steep increase of the fiscal deficit. Thus domestic policies continued to play a role. Yet it would be wrong to assume that fiscal policy was the crucial factor. All small states depending on oil experienced a rapid deterioration of the current account in 1979. An explanation based exclusively on domestic policies is flawed.

With this dramatic deterioration of the current account, a further devaluation was needed to push the current account back into surplus. In 1981, the

---

[135] Andersen, Jensen, and Risager (1999, pp. 14–17).
[136] OECD (1988, p. 100).
[137] Gourevitch et al. (1984, p. 303).

center-right government devalued the krona by 10 percent, and in October 1982, the newly elected Social Democrats engineered a "big bang" devaluation of 16 percent – against the opposition of the IMF – combined with a decrease in real wages.[138] Interestingly, the Social Democrats first planned to peg the krona to the DM, but the *Bundesbank* didn't seem to be thrilled by this outlook.[139] It is interesting to compare the Swedish devaluation of 1982 with the approach pursued by the Danish authorities mentioned earlier. While Sweden linked a large competitive devaluation to a policy package, Denmark simply declared in late 1982 that from now on it would never devalue again. Andersen (1994) observes that both policies, the "no-more" strategy of Denmark and the "once-and-for-all" strategy of Sweden, have their pros and cons. The main advantage of the Swedish approach was that it didn't involve heavy strain in the short term, but the backside was the persistence of the credibility problem. Conversely, the Danish policy had negative short-term effects but was very effective in curbing inflationary expectations. He concludes that "in retrospect the 'no-more' strategy has worked surprisingly well."[140]

In any case, the two devaluations of the Swedish krona gave the exporting industry a large competitive advantage, and thanks to the upswing in the world economy, profits rose rapidly. Ultimately, however, the strategy failed. Policymakers had hoped that a devaluation would increase the share of the exporting sector, but this hope was not fulfilled because the nominal devaluation did not result in a real devaluation.[141] There were two important reasons for this failure. First, in order to contain the inflationary effects of the devaluations, to shift resources to the tradables sectors, and to help keeping real wages in check, fiscal policy should have been more restrictive. Second, the deregulation of the credit market that started in the fall of 1985 ("November revolution") was poorly executed. Most important, the authorities failed to adapt the tax system to the new situation.[142] The current account fell back into deficit, the krona continued to be a vulnerable currency and was attacked during the EMS crisis of 1992.

That oil revenues mattered greatly for exchange-rate movements is particularly evident in the case of Norway. Oil was discovered in the late 1960s and early 1970s, but the rising revenues didn't generate a current-account

---

[138] OECD (1988, p. 102).
[139] Kjell-Olof Feldt (1991, pp. 74–77), Hörngren and Lindberg (1994, p. 139).
[140] Andersen (1994, p. 123).
[141] Henrekson (1991). For a shorter English version, see Henrekson (1990). A discussion of the effects of the devaluations also can be found in Hörngren and Lindberg (1994).
[142] Henrekson (1991, pp. 74–76). Hörngren and Lindberg (1994, pp. 147–148) agree.

surplus until 1980. Nevertheless, the pure expectation that the Norwegian oil business would be very profitable in the near future completely changed economic conditions and macroeconomic policies after the oil shock of October 1973. Most important, the expected revenues allowed the government to run a high current-account deficit during the 1970s and to borrow cheaply abroad to finance the high investment needed in the oil sector.[143] Until that point, Norway had been in the same situation as Denmark: The almost permanent current-account deficit required the authorities to avoid high fiscal deficits. From the 1970s on, by contrast, they were able to mitigate an economic crisis by increased spending.[144] The investment rate was by far the highest in Western Europe during the 1970s.

The expectation of an oil bonanza also explains why Norway, despite a widening current-account deficit, could afford to revalue the krone by 5 percent in November 1973 as a measure to contain inflation.[145] The Netherlands, which had been the first small state to use this instrument in September 1973, took this step in the presence of a rising current-account surplus. Yet, despite the expected oil revenues, Norway could not maintain a hard peg against the DM in the medium term. One reason was, as noted earlier, that labor costs got out of control because expansionary fiscal and monetary policies maintained full employment. Another reason was the drop in revenues from shipping.[146] As a result of these factors, the Norwegian krone lost roughly a quarter of its value vis-à-vis the DM in the period from the Frankfurt alignment in October 1976 to the exit from the Snake in December 1978.

Yet, once the krone left the Snake and the second oil crisis brought the expected revenues, the current account registered a strong surplus, and the krone became a stable currency in comparison with the Swedish krona. From then on, Norwegian exchange-rate policy was completely determined by the oil price and followed its own course (Figure 6.11). When the oil price was high, as in the period from 1979 to 1985, the nominal effective exchange rate remained stable, with the exception of two minor

---

[143] Moses (2000, pp. 125–127 and 144–145).

[144] BIS, *Annual Report*, 1974–1975, p. 60; OECD, *Norvège*, 1977, p. 6; Hodne (1983, p. 265), Moses (2000, p. 125). Notermans (2000, pp. 197–200) disagrees: "Oil revenues certainly influenced the extent to which the government was willing to spend, but the policy strategy started in 1975 was by no means predicated on the oil wealth. In the opinion of Labor's Finance Minister Per Kleppe, 'Even without prospects of oil incomes, Norway, like Sweden, should have pursued the same general policy, namely, to maintain activity and employment despite recession abroad.'"

[145] BIS, *Annual Report*, 1973–1974, p. 72.

[146] OECD, *Norvège*, 1976, pp. 15*ff.*, on shipping.

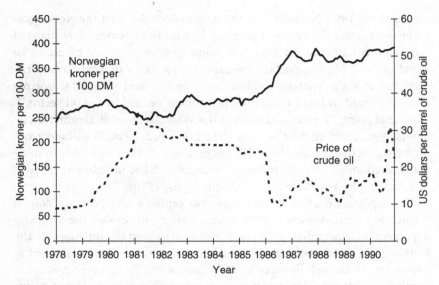

Figure 6.11. Norwegian krone and oil price, 1978–1991. (*Norges Bank and US Depart-ment of Energy.*)

devaluations in 1982 and 1984.[147] And when the oil price became weak, as in the first quarter of 1986, the current-account surplus turned into a high deficit, and the krone was devalued by 10.2 percent in May 1986. Clearly, without the existence of oil reserves, the exchange-rate policy of Norway would have been completely different regardless of domestic policy goals and institutions.

In sum, not only did capital mobility, trade integration, and (non)mem-bership in the EC determine the exchange-rate policies of small European states but also the dependence on oil and natural gas. The Dutch guilder remained a strong currency mainly because of high revenues from natural gas exports; the Norwegian krone, because of oil exports. By contrast, Belgium, Denmark, and Sweden were forced to devalue because they depended on the import of these natural resources and suffered from rising prices, especially during the second oil crisis. Of course, differences in domestic policies con-tributed to the weakening of the currency. By the early 1980s, Belgium's real wage gap was considerably larger than elsewhere. Belgium also pursued a more expansionary fiscal policy in 1980 than Denmark and the Netherlands. Similarly, Sweden's fiscal policy was more expansionary than Norway's in

---

[147] August 1982: devaluation by 3.5 percent; September 1982: devaluation by 3 percent; July 1984: devaluation by 2 percent; September 1984: devaluation by 2 percent.

1979 and 1980. But these domestic policy differences were not large enough to explain the divergence of exchange rates after 1976.

All external factors taken together, the discussion leads to the following conclusion: External constraints largely explain why the Benelux currencies and the Danish krone continued to participate in the Snake and the EMS despite the failure to adjust to the German policy turn in 1973–1974. They also largely explain why the Dutch guilder was the strongest of these three currencies, the Danish krone the weakest, and the Belgian franc in between the two. It is possible to argue that owing to their domestic institutions and policy preferences, the Benelux countries would have pursued roughly the same policy even if these external constraints had been different. But this argument cannot be proved, and in the case of Denmark, it is not very plausible. If Denmark had not joined the EC in 1973, the exchange-rate policy would have been different.

Norway and Sweden, by contrast, had more room to maneuver, thanks to capital controls, their nonmembership in the EC, and their strong trade relations with each other and with the United Kingdom which stopped its participation in the Snake as early as June 1972. In this case, it is more convincing to include domestic factors in the argument: The weak position of the central bank and the strength of the Left and labor unions were prerequisites for the boom that was generated in 1974–1975 and lead to a steep increase of real wages and a rapid deterioration of competitiveness. However, it is important to note that the weak position of the central bank and the existence of capital controls were strongly related to each other, which makes it impossible to isolate central bank independence as a single factor. There was no small European state that combined capital controls with an independent central bank, and vice versa. The "double difference" between small European states excluded such a combination of factors.

AUSTRIA

The explanation just presented seems to be flawed in one case: Austria. As with the Netherlands, Austrian authorities managed to maintain a hard DM peg, but unlike the Dutch economy, the Austrian economy did not suffer from high unemployment in the early 1980s. Accordingly, scholars arguing with domestic factors have taken Austria as a sort of "poster boy" proving that institutional differences and policy preferences mattered. Scharpf (1991) has claimed that "Austria had the optimal set of institutional arrangements for cooperative coordination in its relationship between the unions and the employers as well as in its relationship between the unions and government policy."[148] This view also has been shared by policymakers themselves. In 1979, one government official in the Austrian ministry of finance coined the term "Austro-Keynesianism."[149] The policy mix included the following elements: A hard currency and wage moderation reduced inflation, labor hoarding and expansionary fiscal and monetary policies maintained full employment.

As most scholars argue, the reason why Austrian institutions worked better than elsewhere was their traumatic experience during the interwar years.[150] As in Germany, the republic that emerged from the ashes of World War I remained weak because of the strong opposition of traditional elites and the radicalization of the labor movement. Economic crises further undermined the confidence in the new political system. The hyperinflation of the early 1920s led to the impoverishment and radicalization of the middle classes, and the depression of the early 1930s further convinced many citizens that Austria needed an authoritarian regime. In March 1933, Chancellor Engelbert Dollfuss, a Christian Democrat (Christlichsoziale Partei), eliminated the parliament, based on a war amendment dating back to 1917. A year later, the political struggle between the government and the Social Democrats resulted into a civil war between the police, the army, and armed right-wing militias on the one hand and workers on the other. The Social Democrats and Communists were completely defeated, and in May 1934, a new authoritarian and corporatist constitution became effective. The country was so deeply divided that after World War II, a strong consensus emerged that such a civil war was never to happen again in the Second Republic.[151]

Was Austria really an institutional exception? The good results achieved during the 1970s cannot be disputed. Austria succeeded in maintaining a stable currency and reducing inflation. Consumer prices declined from 9.5 percent in 1974 to 3.6 percent in 1978, the effective exchange rate of the schilling appreciated by a quarter from 1970 to 1980, and the exchange rate against the DM was stable. The unemployment rate remained below 2 percent until 1980 and below 4 percent in 1983, whereas, for example, the Dutch employment rate rose from 4 percent in 1980 to 11 percent in 1983.

---

[148] Scharpf (1991, p. 193). Cf. Other proponents of the institutional view: Froats (1995), Guger (1998), and Hemerijck, Unger, and Visser (2000).

[149] The term was coined in 1979 by Hans Seidel, then head of the Austrian Institute of Economic Research (WIFO). On the origin of the term, see Seidel (1982).

[150] Scharpf (1991, pp. 193–194), Guger (1998, p. 41).

[151] Bachinger (2001, pp. 114–134).

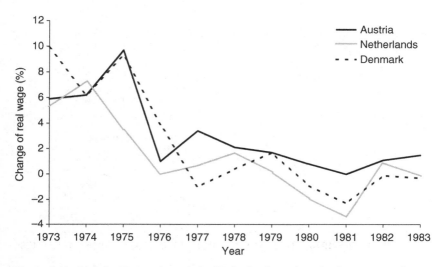

Figure 6.12. Austria, Denmark, and the Netherlands: real wages (percentage change from previous year). (*Scharpf and Schmidt, 2000a.*)

Yet, despite these impressive results, it appears that even in the Austrian case the conventional explanation arguing with domestic institutions and policy preferences seems to be too narrow.[152] It has three weaknesses. First, the adjustment process did not work smoothly at all. The Austrian institutions may have worked better than the British, German, or Swedish ones but not well enough to compensate for the negative consequences of the hard-currency policy, as a comparison with Denmark and the Netherlands shows.[153] Austrian real wages rose even more than Danish and Dutch wages from 1973 to 1983 (Figure 6.12) – nevertheless, Denmark and the Netherlands performed much worse in terms of unemployment. Second, the time period under study is too short to make a firm conclusion. It is true that Austrian unemployment was lower than elsewhere from 1973 to 1983, but as soon as we extend the period to the late 1980s, we see that Austrian unemployment kept increasing during almost every year after 1980, whereas it decreased in most other European states after 1983 (Figure 6.13). Obviously, the performance until 1983 was better because

[152] For a critical view, see Butschek (1985, 2001).
[153] OECD, Austria, January 1981, p. 38: "This exchange rate policy ... was successful in achieving a marked slowdown in inflation. However, as the rise in incomes was adjusted only slowly to the hard currency approach, the currency appreciated in real terms, imply- ing a loss of competitiveness which manifested itself in rising import penetration. Export industries were also affected, particularly by lower profits."

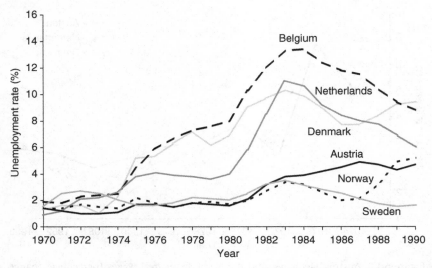

Figure 6.13. Austria: unemployment rate in comparison with other small states. (*Scharpf and Schmidt, 2000a.*)

the Austrian authorities were successful in delaying the full impact of the post-1973 problems, not in solving them.

Third, and most important, the institutional explanation completely ignores that Austria was in a very special situation as far as external constraints and opportunities were concerned.[154] It is true that it shared three features with Sweden: capital controls, a rather weak current account, and EFTA membership. But these common features were secondary to the economic and political relations that Austria entertained with Germany and Switzerland, two countries with particularly strong currencies. Trade relations with Germany were unusually strong. In 1970, 23 percent of Austrian exports went to and 41 percent of imports came from the big neighbor. Austria's trade with Switzerland accounted for 10 percent of total exports and 7 percent of total imports. Thus Austria imported about 50 percent of total imports from Germany and Switzerland – a clear contrast to the Scandinavian countries. In 1970, their imports from and exports to Germany were below 20 percent of total imports and exports, respectively.

Furthermore, Austria had always entertained close cultural and political ties with its big neighbor. It is true that the government and the central bank

---

[154] Butschek (1985), Hochreiter and Winckler (1995).

often had been eager to signal to the public that Austria was not a satellite of Germany. However, such a problem of identification emerges only if these ties in fact exist. There is narrative evidence suggesting that the Austrian National Bank was always in close contact with the *Bundesbank* and the Swiss National Bank in times of crisis. A telling example is the revaluation of the schilling in May 1971 – the first one since 1945 and thus a defining moment in the monetary history of Austria.[155] In a meeting on 5 May 1971, when the markets were shut down following speculative attacks against the dollar, the governing board of the Austrian National Bank came to the conclusion that it was important "to avoid the impression of depending to a large extent on the economic and exchange-rate policy of Germany."[156] In a special meeting held on 10 May 1971, when the board explained to the general at why it had decided to revalue the schilling by 5.05 percent, the managing director Hans Kloss summarized:

For Austria, the question emerged whether to take the same measures as Switzerland or Germany. Apart from the political question that we did not want to act on the coat-tails of the measures of Germany, … The National Bank was in permanent contact with the other central banks, in particular the President of the National Bank maintained personal contact with President Edwin Stopper of the Swiss National Bank and President Zijlstra in his capacity as President of the BIS. Switzerland then declared that she would revalue the Swiss franc by 7 percent.[157] … The question was: how high was the exchange rate supposed to be? … And thus, 5 percent appeared to be the minimum, whereupon we also got the confirmation by the de facto revaluation of the Swiss franc by 5 percent. We also hear from Germany that it is planned to seek a revaluation of 5 percent – but please, this is strictly confidential.[158]

---

[155] Androsch (1985, p. 77): "*Die im Mai 1971 vorgenommene Schillingaufwertung war die erste seit 1945 und muss zweifellos als Markstein in der österreichischen Währungspolitik angesehen werden.*"

[156] OeNB-Archiv 25 B/II/1971: *Besprechung der Mitglieder des Unterausschusses für Währungspolitik mit dem Präsidium und den Mitgliedern des Direktoriums am 5. Mai 1971, um 16'30 Uhr, p. 4 (Punkt b): "den Eindruck vermeiden, von der Wirtschafts- und Währungspolitik Deutschlands in hohem Masse abhängig zu sein.*"

[157] The formal revaluation by 7 percent corresponded to a de facto revaluation by 5 percent.

[158] OeNB-Archiv, *Protokoll der ausserordentlichen Sitzung des Generalrates der OeNB vom 10. Mai 1971, pp. 2–4: "Für Österreich ergab sich nun die Frage, Massnahmen zu treffen wie die Schweiz oder wie Deutschland. Abgesehen von der politischen Frage, dass wir nicht im Schlepptau der Massnahmen der Bundesrepublik agieren, … Die OeNB stand dabei in ständigem Kontakt mit den übrigen Notenbanken, insbesondere hat der Herr Präsident den persönlichen Kontakt aufrecht erhalten mit Präsident Stopper von der Schweizerischen Nationalbank und Präsident Zijlstra in seiner Eigenschaft als Präsident der BIZ. Es wurde also dann von der Schweiz mitgeteilt, dass sie die Parität des Schweizer Franken um 7 percent erhöhen wird. … Die Frage war: wie hoch soll der Kurs sein? … Und so erschien uns 5 percent als das Minimum, wobei mir die Bestätigungen ja noch bekommen haben durch*

Furthermore, the importance of Germany for the Austrian exchange-rate policy was not only discussed in secret meetings but debated in parliament. In December 1971, when the Smithsonian Agreement was concluded, Austrian Minister of Finance Hannes Androsch confirmed that the exchange rate of the DM and the Swiss franc were crucial for the decision to revalue the schilling: "When we took our decision, we accounted for the past and future exchange-rate movements of the DM and the Swiss franc. Adhering to the old parity would have triggered additional inflationary impulses caused by higher import prices."[159] When in March 1973 the schilling had been revalued against Special Drawing Rights (SDR) by 2.25 percent, Androsch again explained in parliament that Austria followed Germany and Switzerland.[160]

The close ties with Germany did not concern only trade relations, but also labor mobility – an important criterion in the literature on optimum currency areas (OCAs). Many Austrians living at the border worked in Germany and Switzerland because of higher wages. A devaluation would have led to an increased outflow of skilled workers. Austrian central bank officials explained at the occasion of the double revaluation of the schilling in 1971 that the lack of a revaluation would have accelerated the exodus of Austrian workers.[161] Minister of Finance Androsch told the parliament in July 1973, after another revaluation, that keeping the schilling at the old parity with Germany would have led to emigration to Germany and thus to a considerable aggravation on the Austrian labor market.[162] In July 1971,

die faktische Erhöhung von 5 percent in der Schweiz. Wir hören auch von Deutschland, dass die Absicht besteht – aber bitte, das ist streng vertraulich –, dass sie einen Satz von 5 percent anstreben."

[159] *Nationalrat XIII. GP, 17. Sitzung, 20. Dezember 1971, p. 1359: "Bei der damaligen Entscheidung wurde die mit 1969 eingetretene und die voraussichtliche künftige Entwicklung des DM-Kurses sowie des Kurses des Schweizer Franken berücksichtigt. Ein Festhalten an der vorherigen Parität hätte durch die Importe zusätzliche inflationäre Impulse in Österreich ausgelöst."*

[160] Androsch (1985, pp. 88–89): *"Als die Mitgliedstaaten der EG eine gemeinsame Freigabe ihrer Wechselkurse gegenüber dem Dollar vereinbarten und die D-Mark gegenüber dem Sonderziehungsrecht um 3 percent aufgewertet wurde und überdies auch die Schweiz im Wege der Kursfreigabe eine weit über 3 percent hinausgehende Aufwertung des Schweizer Franken zuliess, wurde in Österreich am 13. März 1973 der Beschluss gefasst, den Schilling gegenüber dem Sonderziehungsrecht um 2,25 percent aufzuwerten."*

[161] For December 1971, see Androsch (1985, p. 81). Cf. OeNB-Archiv, *Protokoll der ausserordentlichen Sitzung des Generalrates der OeNB vom 10. Mai 1971, p. 2:* Generaldirektor Hans Kloss speaks of *"dem Abengagieren von Arbeitskräften aus Westösterreich bis herein nach Linz, bis nach Wien und in die Steiermark."*

[162] *Nationalrat, 76. Sitzung, XIII. Gesetzgebungsperiode, 4. Juli 1973, p. 7278: "... für den österreichischen Arbeitsmarkt eine wesentliche Verschärfung durch Abwanderungen in die Bundesrepublik...."*

the *Vereinigung Österreichischer Industrieller* (VÖI) publicly complained about the drain of Austrian workers.[163]

There was a final specialty in Austria's relations with its neighboring countries. As in Switzerland, migrant workers from the Balkans or Southern Europe did not have permanent work permits but had to renew them at the end of each year. If the economic outlook allowed it to extend their work permits, employers welcomed foreign workers; if not, they simply let the permits expire. This legal specialty proved to be an effective buffer during the recession of 1975, as we will see below. Less important, however, was Austria's dependence on foreign borrowing. Sweden had the same problem that the devaluations of the krona increased the debt burden, but it did not prevent it from doing it even so.[164]

Of course, there also were arguments in favor of a devaluation. Most important, exports to Italy, amounting to 7 percent of total exports, were hurt by the real appreciation of the schilling vis-à-vis the Italian lira, one of the weakest European currencies during the 1970s. Furthermore, Austrian tourism suffered from the strong schilling because of the high demand elasticity of this service sector. Yet these arguments were relatively weak in the political debate. Even the leader of the Christian Democratic opposition (ÖVP), Stephan Koren, a former professor of economics, who was to represent the interests of the exporting industry, supported the hard-currency policy. He had been finance minister until 1970 when the Social Democrats came to power, and in this function he had favored a revaluation of the schilling in 1969, following revaluation of the DM by 9 percent. The government eventually abstained from such a step, fearing losses in the upcoming elections – a decision that proved to be irrelevant because the ruling Christian Democrats suffered an electoral defeat anyway.[165] In the parliamentary debate following revaluation of the schilling in May 1971, Koren endorsed the decision of the government. The same stance was taken by Rudolf Sallinger, president of the *Bundeswirtschaftskammer* (1964–1990) and deputy of the ÖVP (1966–1990).[166]

Summarizing these three weaknesses of the institutional explanation, we can conclude that Austria did not pursue a hard-currency policy mainly because labor unions managed to moderate their wage claims particularly well. Rather, owing to close relations with Germany and Switzerland, Austria

---

[163] *Pressedienst der Industrie*, 6. *Juli* 1971, *Folge* 4.783.

[164] Butschek (1985, p. 171).

[165] Androsch (1985, p. 74).

[166] *Nationalrat, XII. GP*, 43. *Sitzung*, 12. *Mai* 1971, pp. 3170–3175 (Koren) and pp. 3188–3192 (Sallinger).

was condemned to maintain a hard DM peg *even though* the increase in real wages was too big during the 1970s. Consequently, the government had to find other ways to compensate exporters for the loss of competitiveness resulting from a rising real exchange rate. It came up with three measures enabling them to postpone the hard choices for Austrians.

The first one has already been mentioned: the reduction of "migrant workers." According to official statistics, the number was reduced from 227,000 to 172,000 from 1973 to 1976. This covered the whole reduction in the manufacturing sector, which decreased from 676,000 to 629,000 during the same time period.[167] If migrant workers had gone to the employment agencies, the unemployment rate would have been almost 2 percent higher in 1976, that is, 4 percent instead of 2 percent – as in the Netherlands. Other countries also used the instrument of reducing the foreign workforce to keep unemployment low, but Austria and Switzerland used it far more extensively than other small European states (Table 6.5).

The second measure was excessive labor hoarding in industry. According to Butschek (2001), Austria had the highest share of state-owned companies during the 1970s, comprising almost 20 percent of total employment in the industrial sector.[168] These companies also were the most export-intensive.[169] Private employers reduced their workforce from 1973 to 1976 by almost 9 percent, whereas public enterprises were prohibited to lay off workers. The German weekly magazine *Der Spiegel* observed that, for example, the public steel company *VOEST* told its employees without work to clean up the courtyard or to walk around the factory. Other firms recommended that their workers report sick so that social insurance would pay for them.[170] In the medium term, this policy had negative consequences because it squeezed profits and prevented the state sectors from modernizing.[171] Yet, in keeping official unemployment at a low level, labor hoarding was highly successful: From 1975 to 1982, the employment rate in the industrial sector (including construction) was stabilized at a relatively high level, whereas it decreased in the other small European states (Table 6.6).

The third measure was subsidies, in particular, for investment and exports. In the mid-1970s, an OECD report concluded: "As compared with other member countries, the financial inducements offered to the

---

[167] Butschek (1985, tables on pp. 160 and 188). This aspect is also mentioned by Hemerijck, Unger, and Visser (2000, p. 197) but downplayed.

[168] Butschek (2001, p. 304).

[169] Kurzer (1993, p. 173).

[170] *Der Spiegel*, No. 37, 5 September 1977, pp. 117–118.

[171] Butschek (1985, p. 173).

Table 6.5. *Net Migration as Percentage of Total Population*

	Switzerland	Austria	Denmark	Belgium	Norway	Sweden	Netherlands
1974	0.03	−0.09	−0.14	0.24	0.1	0.11	0.24
1975	−0.91	−0.18	−0.18	0.25	0.12	0.21	0.53
1976	−0.85	0.03	0.06	0.07	0.12	0.24	0.15
1977	−0.36	0.05	0.12	0.05	0.12	0.28	0.17
1978	−0.11	0.01	0.1	−0.03	0.1	0.17	0.2
1979	0.06	−0.01	0.1	0.02	0.07	0.17	0.32
1980	0.27	0.12	0.02	−0.02	0.1	0.12	0.37
1981	0.37	0.38	−0.04	−0.2	0.12	0.12	0.12
1982	0.32	−0.46	−0.02	−0.04	0.15	−0.08	−0.01
1974–1982	−1.18	−0.15	0.02	0.34	1	1.34	2.09

Source: Scharpf and Schmidt (2000a, p. 352).

Table 6.6. *Employment Rate in Industrial Sector as Percentage of Population 15–64 Years*

	Austria	Belgium	Denmark	Norway	Netherlands	Sweden	Switzerland
1970	27.5	25.2	27.6	23.0	22.3	28.1	35.4
1971	28.2	25.2	27.2	23.3	21.8	27.4	35.4
1972	28.4	24.5	25.1	22.9	20.6	26.9	35.1
1973	28.9	24.4	25.0	22.6	20.1	27.1	34.8
1974	28.7	24.5	23.5	22.8	19.5	27.9	34.3
1975	25.7	23.2	22.7	23.4	18.5	28.2	31.5
1976	25.1	22.3	23.8	23.5	17.6	27.5	29.9
1977	25.6	21.5	23.2	23.3	17.3	26.7	29.6
1978	25.7	20.6	22.7	23.0	17.3	25.7	29.5
1979	25.7	20.1	24.1	22.0	17.0	25.6	29.2
1980	25.5	19.6	22.6	21.6	16.7	25.6	28.3
1981	25.2	18.5	20.8	21.5	16.0	24.7	28.4
1982	25.5	17.4	20.0	20.9	15.0	23.8	27.4
1983	24.4	16.7	20.1	19.9	14.3	23.5	26.6
1984	24.3	16.2	19.5	20.2	14.3	23.5	26.4
1985	24.2	16.0	20.9	20.2	14.4	23.8	26.6

Note: Employment in industrial sector includes ISIC 2–5: ISIC 2: mining and quarrying; ISIC 3: manufacturing; ISIC 4: electricity, gas, and water; ISIC 5: construction.
Source: Scharpf and Schmidt (2000a, p. 346).

Table 6.7. *Gross Fixed Capital Formation as Percentage of GDP*

	Austria	Belgium	Denmark	Norway	Netherlands	Sweden	Switzerland
1970	24.0	22.7	28.3	26.0	26.5	22.3	28.5
1971	25.8	22.0	27.8	29.1	26.0	21.8	30.3
1972	28.0	21.3	28.1	27.2	24.2	22.0	30.8
1973	26.5	21.3	28.4	28.7	23.6	21.7	30.5
1974	26.4	22.6	27.5	29.9	22.5	21.3	28.6
1975	24.7	22.4	24.2	33.5	21.6	20.8	24.9
1976	24.2	21.9	26.3	35.6	19.9	21.0	21.4
1977	25.2	21.5	25.3	36.4	21.6	20.9	21.5
1978	23.3	21.5	24.8	31.2	21.8	19.3	22.2
1979	23.3	20.5	23.9	29.9	21.4	19.7	22.6
1980	24.1	21.0	21.6	26.9	21.4	20.0	24.7
1981	23.9	18.1	17.9	27.1	19.6	18.8	25.0
1982	21.8	17.1	18.4	27.3	18.6	18.6	23.9
1983	21.2	15.8	18.3	27.9	18.6	18.6	24.5
1984	20.8	15.6	19.7	26.4	19.1	18.7	24.3
1985	21.5	15.7	21.5	24.8	19.7	19.3	24.4

Source: Scharpf and Schmidt (2000a).

individual industrialists in Austria are among the highest available."[172] In the late 1970s, about 40 percent of the volume of domestic credit was subsidized. In this system, Austria's nationalized banks played an important role by granting cheap credit. Accordingly, Austria registered one of the highest investment rates in the 1970s and early 1980s (Table 6.7). The strategy was risky, however. As economic conditions worsened in the late 1970s and early 1980s, the rate of nonperforming loans increased and almost caused the collapse of the second-largest commercial bank in 1981.[173]

The government not only encouraged investment on a large scale but also subsidized exports with unusually high contributions. From 1973 until 1982, utilization of these export subsidies (*"Ausnützungsstände"*) increased by more than seven times in real terms (from 11 billion to 80 billion schillings in 1973 prices).[174] The bulk of these subsidies (*"Zusagen- und*

[172] Cited in Katzenstein (1985, pp. 75–76).
[173] Katzenstein (1985, pp. 76–77).
[174] Breuss (1983, p. 56, table 12).

Ausnützungsstände") went to firms exporting to Eastern Europe.[175] From 1974 on, this system began to aggravate the budget deficit, particularly in 1976 and 1979. As a result of this rising demand for export subsidies, capital imports by the *Österreichische Kontrollbank* (OeKB) increased enormously from 1977 on.[176] Helmut Kienzl, a leading Social Democrat and top official of the central bank, observed in retrospect that the export promotion had led to an enormous demand for public subsidies.[177] From a comparative perspective, it is difficult to measure how important these contributions were for the better performance of the Austrian economy.[178] Most other small states also subsidized exports. Yet one figure suggests that it must have been considerable: The share of insured exports jumped from 21.7 percent in 1974 to 44.8 percent of total exports in 1981.[179] The transactions were made by the OeKB, but later, as this institution ran into problems, the state had to cover the losses and the increasing interest-rate payments, which were reflected in the official budget.[180]

Thus the secret of Austria's success was "horse trading" between the government and the exporting industry: price and exchange-rate stability in exchange for massive subsidies.[181] The managers of the exporting sectors were in fact talented lobbyists. Already during the debate following the moderate revaluation in May 1971, Koren and especially Sallinger insisted on compensations for the exporting sectors.[182] When the government hesitated to give such guarantees, the *Vereinigung Österreichischer Industrieller* (VÖI) complained in public.[183] And from then on, this claim was repeated whenever the schilling appreciated or was revalued – and, as the figures reveal, the exporters received what they wanted.[184]

---

[175] *Ibid.*, p. 59, Table 14. In 1978, it amounted to 39 billion schillings, corresponding to 50.6 percent of all exports that were subsidized. It then declined to roughly 40 percent.

[176] Breuss (1983, p. 69).

[177] Kienzl (1993, p. 71): "*Eine enorme Forderungsposition kam zustande, als man in Österreich vor allem in den 70er Jahren die Vollbeschäftigung durch Exporte in die Oststaaten aufrechterhielt, die Finanzierung dieser Exporte durch österreichische Kreditgewährungen ermöglichte und dafür auf den westlichen Finanzmärkten entsprechende Kredite aufnahm.*"

[178] OECD, Austria, February 1984, p. 47: "The high level of subsidies ... covers a large number of promotion schemes which are complex and difficult to assess."

[179] Breuss (1983, p. 52).

[180] Breuss (1983, pp. 64–71).

[181] Androsch (1985, p. 105).

[182] *Nationalrat, XII. Gesetzgebungsperiode*, 43. *Sitzung*, 12 *Mai* 1971, p. 3174 (Koren) and pp. 3190–3191 (Sallinger).

[183] *Pressedienst der Industrie*, Wien, 8 June 1971 (*Folge* 4.759).

[184] *Pressedienst der Industrie*, Wien, 8 March 1973 (*Folge* 5.252), 3 July 1973 (*Folge* 5.344), 5 July 1973 (*Folge* 5.346), 13 July 1973 (*Folge* 5.353), 3 September 1973 (*Folge* 5.391), 19 September 1973 (*Folge* 5.403), 11 April 1974 (*Folge* 5.552).

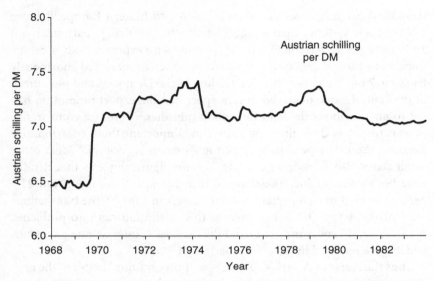

Figure 6.14. DM rate of Austrian schilling, 1968–1983 (1968 = 100). (*Deutsche Bundesbank.*)

From 1971 to 1973, the amount of subsidies remained moderate because Austrian authorities revalued the schilling only when the *Bundesbank* revalued the DM, and in each case, they chose to revalue by a smaller amount than the *Bundesbank* (Figure 6.14; see also Table 6.8). Moreover, since the closing of the gold window in August 1971, the schilling was pegged to a basket of currencies that was dubbed the "indicator."[185] In fact, Austria was the first country to design such an exchange-rate regime; Finland followed in early 1973.[186] Thus, the government did not pursue a truly hard-currency policy yet. Finally, the schilling had been kept at the old parity in October 1969 after revaluation of the DM by 9 percent, resulting in a 2.5 percent devaluation of the nominal effective exchange rate of the Austrian schilling.[187] This weakening gave Austrian exporters a certain competitive advantage for a few years.

Yet, with the strong appreciation of the real exchange rate, the size of subsidies began to grow. In May 1974, the government revalued the

---

[185] Handler (1989, pp. 32–33). The following currencies were included in the indicator basket: the DM, the Swiss franc, the Dutch guilder (representing also the Belgian franc), Swedish krona (representing also the Danish krone), Italian lira, and pound sterling.
[186] Hochreiter and Knöbl (1991, pp. 33–61).
[187] Handler (1989, p. 30).

Table 6.8. *Chronology of Austrian Exchange-Rate Policy*

1969	
October	Germany revalues DM by 8.5% against US dollar; Austria keeps schilling unchanged.
1971	
May	Germany, Belgium, and the Netherlands let their currencies float (until December), and Switzerland revalues the franc by 7% against dollar; Austria revalues schilling by 5.05% against dollar and widens band width.
August	Austria suspends dollar peg and introduces basket peg ("Indikator").
December	New central rate against dollar is fixed (6.22% revaluation of schilling against new dollar rate fixed in May).
1973	
March	Germany revalues DM by 3% within the Snake, Austria revalues schilling by 2.25% against currency basket. Austria unilaterally ties schilling to Snake currencies.
July	Germany revalues DM by 5.5% within the Snake; Austria revalues schilling by 4.8% against SDR.
1974	
May	The schilling comes under upward pressure so that Austria extends band width vis-à-vis Snake from 2.25% to 4.5%. The schilling appreciates against the DM.
1976	
July	Austria ties schilling to DM with a band width of 2% (7.049 to 7.189 schilling per DM).
1977	
December	Austria abandons DM peg and ties schilling again to the Snake, yet without any official band width.
1979	
September	The new goal of Austrian exchange rate policy is to stabilize the real exchange rate of the schilling. From 1981 on, the schilling is de facto fixed to the DM.

Source: Breuss (1983), Handler (1989).

Austrian schilling for the first time on its own, which can be regarded as the beginning of the hard-currency policy.[188] Technically, it was only a widening of the fluctuation margin from 2.25 to 4.5 percent against the Snake

---

[188] For the chronology of Austria's exchange-rate policy, see Breuss (1983), Handler (1989), Hochreiter and Winckler (1995), and Hemerijck, Unger, and Visser (2000, pp. 196–197).

currencies, but de facto it meant a considerable revaluation.[189] The exporters were particularly upset because the step was taken without any previous consultation.[190] The competitive position further deteriorated when the social partners agreed to high wage increases for 1975 mainly because of a forecasting error. Real wages rose by almost 10 percent. It is true, as conventional wisdom points out, that the *Österreichische Gewerkschaftsbund* (ÖGB) soon agreed to a minor real wage increase in the following year to correct the error. However, the correction was not sufficient to compensate for the previous increase in relative unit labor costs. In July 1976, the authorities decided on a further hardening of the exchange-rate policy by abandoning the "indicator" and pegging the schilling to the DM. Yet again, income policies were not consistent with the exchange-rate regime: Real wages increased by 3.4 percent, which was less than in Germany (5 percent) but still too much to improve competitiveness. As a result, the current-account deficit widened. In 1976, it amounted to 2.6 percent; in 1977, it moved to a record 4.4 percent. Austria was on a downward path, as the international press observed.[191]

By now, the government was in a delicate situation. On the one hand, the finance ministry as well as National Bank officials and union leaders wanted to maintain a strong currency. They were convinced that a devaluation would not remove the basic imbalances but only fuel inflation.[192] Accordingly, they were forced to take restrictive measures to reduce the current account. On the other hand, the change of course had to be

---

[189] Hochreiter and Knöbl (1991, p. 35, footnote 6): "Between May and July of that year the Schilling appreciated by 4.4 percent in nominal effective terms and 4.0 percent in real effective terms."

[190] Cf. *Pressedienst der Industrie*, 16 May 1974 (*Folge 5,586*): "*Energischer Protest der Industrie gegen Manipulation des Schilling-Kurses.*" See the Austrian daily *Die Presse*, Friday, 17 May 1974, p. 1: On Monday, the finance minister had excluded a revaluation at the occasion of the "*Gipfelgespräch*" between SPÖ and ÖVP. (*The Presse* is dominated by the ÖVP and champions the employers' views.) For 1976, see *Jahrbuch der österreichischen Wirtschaft* 1976, Band 1, Wien 1977, pp. 19–21. *Pressedienst der Industrie*, 21 May 1974 (*Folge 5.590*), 22 May 1974 (*Folge 5.591*), 26 June 1974 (*Folge 5.622*). See Koren and Sallinger in *Nationalrat XIII. GP,* 108. *Sitzung,* 22 May 1974, pp. 10532–10538 (Koren) and pp. 10578–10582 (Sallinger).

[191] *Der Spiegel*, No. 37, 5 September 1977, pp. 116*ff.*

[192] Androsch (1985, p. 121): "*Einer Verschlechterung der Wettbewerbsposition durch Abwertung zu entgehen, ist abzulehnen, da inflationäre Prozesse dadurch gefördert werden.*" Androsch (1993, p. 201): "*Bayer hingegen hat immer mit dem Verlust des italienischen Marktes argumentiert. Was auch gestimmt hat. Auf die Frage: 'Herr Generaldirektor, wieviel Abwertung des Schillings würden Sie denn brauchen, damit das kompensiert wird?' antwortete er: '30 percent.' Dann sagte ich: 'Wie lange würde das halten?' 'Eineinhalb Jahre.' Damit war das Thema sozusagen via facti zwischen uns vom Tisch.*" See also Butschek (2001, pp. 293–294).

realized without causing unemployment because otherwise the days of the Social Democrats as the ruling party would have been numbered. The situation was further complicated by the fact that not only the exporters openly demanded "the return to a more flexible exchange-rate regime," which meant more than a devaluation.[193] The IMF, the OECD, and even Chancellor Bruno Kreisky, a long-time friend of the Swedish model, demanded a devaluation as well. Kreisky had spent his exile years in Sweden and had been deeply impressed by the economic policy of the Swedish Social Democrats during the 1930s. During the 1970s, he also was a major figure in the Socialist International, together with German Chancellor Willy Brandt, who also had been in Norway and Sweden during the Nazi era, and Swedish Prime Minister Olof Palme. Possibly, another reason for Kreisky's demand for a devaluation was that Hans Igler, president of the VÖI, was Kreisky's neighbor in Vienna.[194]

The finance minister, the ÖGB, and the National Bank officials who wanted to maintain a strong schilling decided to combine restrictive policies with more of the same, that is, more subsidies to the exporting sector outside the formal budget, leading to a further aggravation of the future budget deficit.[195] At the same time, interest rates were raised, the fiscal deficit was narrowed, and import taxes on luxury goods were raised. Moreover, the DM peg was replaced by a currency basket in December 1977, and the schilling did not completely follow the revaluation of the DM in October 1978. The DM was revalued by 2 percent against the Benelux currencies and 4 percent against the Danish krone and the Norwegian krone; the schilling was revalued by only 1 percent. The contribution of labor unions was to agree to moderate real wage increases in 1978 and 1979, but again, this wage restraint was not exceptional: The real wage increases were even higher than in Belgium, Denmark, and the Netherlands. Thanks to this package, it was possible to continue the hard-currency policy. The current-account deficit narrowed in 1978, and unemployment remained low despite a marked slowdown in economic growth (from 4.4 percent in 1977 to 0.5 percent in 1978) caused by the tightening of monetary policy and a more restrictive fiscal policy. The government felt encouraged to reintroduce a hard DM peg and to revalue the schilling by 1.5 percent in September 1979. Between early September 1979 and the end of 1981, the schilling appreciated against

---

[193] *Jahrbuch der österreichischen Wirtschaft* 1976 (1977), Band 1, p. 14; Hochreiter and Winckler (1995, p. 92).

[194] Vranitzky (1993, p. 182).

[195] Androsch (1985, pp. 121–122), Androsch (1989, pp. 197–198). Androsch (1993, p. 200), Butschek (2001, p. 294).

the DM by almost 4.5 percent. In late 1981, the schilling was de facto fixed to the DM.[196]

The strategy worked only in the short term, however, and fell apart in the 1980s. In order to compensate for the negative effects of high interest rates, the government should have pursued a more expansionary fiscal policy. But further spending proved impossible because the deficits had already risen to a record level as a result of the unsustainable policies since 1975. In particular, debt service had become much higher than in the early 1970s.[197] As a result of this constraint, fiscal policy was contractionary from 1979 to 1981 and only slightly expansionary from 1981 to 1983 (see Table 6.4). The lack of room to maneuver and the inherited structural weaknesses led to an almost continuous rise in unemployment in the 1980s. Clearly, Austria had not found the golden way to navigate between inflation and unemployment but simply had postponed the hard choices.

In sum, the conventional explanation highlighting Austria's advantageous institutions fails to convince for four reasons. First, it excludes external constraints and opportunities that are central for understanding Austria's exchange-rate policy from a comparative perspective, namely, the favorable trade integration and the mobility of foreign workers. Second, it exaggerates the cooperative role of Austrian labor unions. As in most other small European countries, real wage increases were too high to be compatible with the DM peg. Austria maintained a strong currency despite the rise in unit labor costs and not because the unions were particularly flexible in adapting to the difficult economic environment after 1973. Third, it plays down the crucial role of the enormous amounts of subsidies the government gave to the exporting industries. And fourth, it ignores the fact that this policy of excessive subsidizing proved unsustainable, leading to a below-average employment record during the 1980s. It is thus fair to conclude that Austria's exceptional performance during the 1970s is not an exception confirming the rule but another example of the overwhelming influence of external constraints and opportunities on exchange-rate policies of small European states. Owing to its close ties with Germany and

---

[196] Hochreiter and Winckler (1995, p. 93).

[197] Lehner (1982, pp. 29 and 32): "*1978 entfielen von der Zunahme des Bruttodefizits bereits mehr als 70 Prozent auf den Finanschuldaufwand und die Steigerung des Nettodefizits war zu rund der Hälfte durch den zusätzlichen Zinsaufwand verursacht. Im Konjunkturabschwung 1981 war der Spielraum noch weiter verringert.*" Cf. Butschek (1985, pp. 169–170), and OECD, Austria, February 1984, p. 38: "The policy of active demand management has resulted ... in a relatively fast accumulation of government debt and rapid growth of interest payments."

Switzerland, Austria had little choice but to seek a strong schilling, and since real wages adjusted only slowly to the hard-currency policy, the business sector reduced the share of foreign workers and the government increased subsidies to avoid an increase in unemployment. Of course, domestic institutions and policy preferences played a role in this strategy but clearly were secondary to external constraints and opportunities.

SEVEN

The Swiss Exception

On Tuesday morning, 23 January 1973, shortly before the foreign-exchange market opened at 9.30 a.m., the Swiss National Bank announced that it would stop buying dollars at a fixed rate and let the franc float. It also explained that this measure was only temporary and would be reversed as soon as the markets had calmed down. Yet the temporary measure turned out to be a regime shift of historical proportions: Never before had a small European country permanently adopted a flexible-exchange-rate regime. As shown in Part 1 of this study, small European states only temporarily and half-heartedly let their currencies float during the interwar years, and after 1945, it was a small state outside of Europe, Canada, that adopted a flexible-exchange-rate regime (from 1952 to 1962 and from May 1970 onward).[1] Thus the Swiss decision to let the franc float was a new milestone in the monetary history of small European states.

From a comparative perspective, this episode raises two interesting questions: Why was Switzerland the only small European state shifting to a flexible-exchange-rate regime in 1973, and why was Switzerland's regime change not imitated by other small European countries before the European Monetary System (EMS) crisis of 1992–1993? It is striking that only in the 1990s did a flexible-exchange-rate regime became a vital option for Sweden (1993), Norway (1999), and Iceland (2001). As for the first question, I will argue that, as outlined in Chapter Five, the Swiss regime shift of 1973 was due to a unique combination of two factors: open financial markets and nonmembership in the European Community (EC). Like the Belgian franc and the Dutch guilder, the

---

[1] Bordo, Dib, and Schembri (2007).

Swiss franc was vulnerable because of open financial markets, but unlike the central banks of Belgium and the Netherlands, the Swiss National Bank did not have the option of revaluing the currency within the Snake to stop the outburst of inflation caused by capital inflows. The shift to a flexible exchange rate therefore was the only way to contain inflationary pressures in early 1973. This explanation, however, has not been elaborated on in great detail yet. The first section of this chapter therefore will try to fill this gap. A more precise account also will make it possible to compare the Swiss case with the regime shifts of Sweden and Norway in the wake of the EMS crisis of 1992, which will be treated in Chapter Eight.

As for the question why the Swiss regime shift of 1973 remained an isolated episode for 20 years, the historical narrative shows that there were no simple lessons to draw from Switzerland's experience with floating exchange rates. Even for Swiss policymakers, it remained unclear until the late 1970s whether or not the temporary regime change was to become permanent. The Swiss franc sometimes moved erratically owing to sudden changes in market sentiments, making policymakers hesitant to abandon the option of returning to a fixed exchange rate. In 1975, after a particularly severe currency crisis, the Swiss National Bank and the Swiss government were seriously exploring a participation in the Snake, and if France had not opposed it, Switzerland may have abandoned floating after a short period of little more than two years. In 1978, the Swiss National Bank temporarily shifted back to exchange-rate targeting by resorting to a massive intervention and by introducing an official exchange-rate ceiling vis-à-vis the deutsche mark (DM). In other words, the Swiss experience during the turbulent 1970s did not invalidate but rather confirmed the traditional notion that floating exchange rates were not suitable for small open economies. In the 1980s, while these turbulences were disappearing, it nevertheless remained difficult to draw a general lesson from Switzerland's flexible-exchange-rate regime. Ironically, the new problem was not volatility but extraordinary stability. The exchange rate moved within a narrow band of ±2 percent per year, which led many observers to conclude that the Swiss franc was informally pegged to the DM. Whether or not this observation corresponded with the real motivations of Swiss monetary policy was irrelevant. All that mattered was the conclusion that the exchange-rate regime of the Swiss franc was unique.

This chapter has four sections. The first section deals with the decision in January 1973 to let the franc float temporarily. The remaining three sections discuss Switzerland's experience from 1973 to 1992.

THE SHIFT TO FLOATING IN JANUARY 1973

Why was Switzerland in 1973 the only small European state to shift to a floating exchange rate? From a comparative perspective, it is sufficient to argue with the combination of two factors: a relatively high degree of financial openness and the lack of EC membership. Without further explanation, however, this reductionist formula is hardly comprehensible. It is therefore necessary to describe Switzerland's position in more detail, preferably in terms of the so-called trilemma, or impossible trinity. It states that policymakers can only pursue two of the three following goals, although all of them may be desirable: exchange-rate stability, free international capital mobility, and a monetary policy oriented toward domestic goals.[2] Thus, before proceeding to the comparative perspective, we have to explain why Swiss policymakers were not sacrificing financial openness and the goal of an independent monetary policy to save the fixed-exchange-rate regime.

As for the introduction of capital controls, narrative evidence suggests that policymakers were willing to go quite far. An urgent federal decree in October 1971 provided the government with the power to take a series of extraordinary measures against undesired capital inflows.[3] Based on this decree and in reaction to the sterling crisis of June 1972, the government used this authority and implemented these measures in late June and early July. It prohibited all investment by private companies and individuals in foreign funds, domestic securities, and real estate; it put a ban on payments of interest on nonresidents' Swiss franc deposits; it subjected borrowing abroad to license; it required that total foreign-exchange liabilities of banks equal the total of foreign-exchange assets by the end of the day; and it fixed minimum reserves.

Yet, at the same time, while these measures failed to solve the problem of capital inflows, policymakers also were aware of the fact that full-fledged exchange controls would have had too many negative consequences for the Swiss economy, especially for the financial sector. In the Report of the Federal Council to the Federal Assembly of August 1972, which justified the recent implementation of capital controls, the importance of the

---

[2] For an application of the trilemma to the monetary history of Europe, see Eichengreen (1992) and Obstfeld and Taylor (2004).

[3] In German: *Dringlicher Bundesbeschluss über den Schutz der Währung*. The parliament passed the decree on 8 October 1971, and the decree became effective on 15 October 1971. Swiss voters passed the bill on 4 June 1972, thus sanctioning the measures already taken by the government.

Table 7.1. *Foreign Assets of Domestic Banks (1970)*

	Foreign Assets of Banks (in Million USD)	Share in Total Foreign Assets Held by Domestic Banks (%)	Foreign Assets per Capita (in USD)
United Kingdom	37,128	25.1	762
Switzerland	16,199	10.9	2,584
United States	10,793	7.3	53
France	10,144	6.9	204
Japan	6,648	4.9	64

Source: IMF, International Financial Statistics, and author's calculations.

financial sector was explicitly mentioned.[4] The respect for the interests of the financial sector was understandable. By the early 1970s, Switzerland had become a major international financial center. Its share of international banking activity, as measured by banks' foreign assets, amounted to more than 10 percent, which put it in second place after the United Kingdom, and the per-capita figures were even more impressive[5] (Table 7.1). Of course, there were other reasons for this spectacular rise in world finance, among them political stability, neutrality, bank secrecy law, low inflation, sound government finances, geographic position, tourism, and multilingualism.[6] However, financial openness certainly was a necessary condition, so the introduction of tight capital controls would have seriously impaired the future development of the financial center.

Another reason for the reluctance of the Swiss government to impose tighter capital controls was that any interventionist measures "contradicted our traditional view of free trade and capital movement," as it wrote in the report cited earlier.[7] In fact, throughout the postwar period, Switzerland had been a champion of open capital markets and had maintained the

---

[4] *Bericht des Bundesrates an die Bundesversammlung betreffend Massnahmen zum Schutz der Währung* (16 August 1972), *Bundesblatt*, 1972, Vol. II, p. 385: "*Bei der Konzeption der Beschlüsse wurde darauf geachtet, die geschäftlichen Interessen des Bankgewerbes und die Funktionsfähigkeit des Finanzplatzes Schweiz so weit wie möglich zu wahren.*"

[5] Cassis (1995, p. 71). Cf. Schenk (2002, pp. 75–77).

[6] For an overview of the history of the Swiss banks and the Swiss financial center since World War I, see Iklé (1972), Bänziger (1986), Christensen (1986), Blackman (1989), Cassis (1991, 1994, 1995), Blattner (1992, 1993, 1996), Cassis and Tanner (1992, 1993), Körner (1993), Bauer and Blackman (1998), Guex (2000), and Straumann (2006).

[7] *Bericht des Bundesrates an die Bundesversammlung betreffend Massnahmen zum Schutz der Währung* (16 August 1972), *Bundesblatt*, 1972, Vol. II, p. 386.

convertibility of the Swiss franc, which contributed to the rise of the financial center.[8] One reason for this stance was that Switzerland had been spared from a German invasion during World War II, but as the Swedish example shows, it also was a matter of principle. Sweden equally survived the war without military occupation, but immediately after the war, the ruling Swedish Social Democrats sought to limit the power of the financial sector by putting the central bank under the control of the finance ministry and by introducing tight capital controls. In Switzerland, by contrast, the ruling center-right coalition stood for a more liberal economic order. As a result, Zurich and other Swiss cities became major international centers, whereas Stockholm did not play any role in world finance after 1945.[9]

From a comparative perspective, the reluctance to completely sacrifice the financial openness of the Swiss economy does not come as a surprise. Other European countries that also were advocates of liberal capital movements after 1945, such as Germany and the Netherlands, equally abstained from a complete reversal in the early 1970s.[10] Obviously, path dependence is an important factor in the development of financial regulation after 1945. Only during or immediately after World War II did governments in advanced economies dare to introduce tight capital controls, as the British and Swedish examples show.[11] The currency crises of the 1960s and 1970s, however, obviously were not regarded as a justification for a complete policy reversal.

In sum, there were at least two strong reasons that Swiss policymakers abstained from introducing tight capital controls in the early 1970s. Why, then, did they not sacrifice the goal of a monetary policy oriented toward domestic goals in order to save the fixed exchange rate? Again, it seems that such a move would have represented a major break with the traditionally liberal stance of Swiss economic policymaking and therefore was never considered to be a serious option. Throughout the whole of the twentieth century and especially since 1945, Switzerland had been renowned for its anti-inflationary stance and its independent central bank.[12] It was

---

[8] A strong currency is not a necessary condition for the rise of an international financial center, however. It depends on the structure of the financial center. In London, for example, the weak pound was positive for the emergence of the eurodollar market in the late 1950s. See Schenk (1998), Burn (1999), and Battilossi and Cassis (2002).

[9] Straumann (2006).

[10] See Bakker (1996) on the liberal principles of Germany and the Netherlands after 1945.

[11] See Straumann (2005) for the importance of path dependence of financial regulation in Germany, Luxembourg, Switzerland, and the United Kingdom.

[12] The Swiss National Bank had a reputation similar to that of the *Bundesbank*. Laubach and Posen (1997, p. 17).

Table 7.2. *External Positions of Reporting European Banks,*
December 1972 (in Million USD)

	US Dollars	Other Foreign Currencies					
		Deutsche Mark	Swiss Francs	Pound Sterling	Dutch Guilders	All Other Currencies	Total
Assets	98,000	20,400	7,780	2,180	720	2,760	33,840
Liabilities	96,730	19,540	8,810	2,210	1,360	3,280	35,200
Net position	12,70	860	−1,030	−30	−640	−520	−1,360

Source: BIS, Annual Report (1973–1974, p. 162).

particularly reassuring to international investors that during the 1960s
the Swiss National Bank had considered a rising liquidity overhang as the
main threat to the Bretton Woods system and not, as most other central
banks did, the shortage of liquidity. The Swiss preference for price stability
became particularly apparent when the Group of Ten discussed the creation of Special Drawing Rights (SDRs). Switzerland, though not a formal
member, was invited to participate in these negotiations and proposed an
extended gold exchange standard aimed at forcing more discipline on the
United States and other countries with a current-account deficit.[13] Because
of this good reputation, the Swiss franc has been one of the most important
international currencies since 1945. As Table 7.2 shows, the Swiss franc
was Europe's second most important reserve currency in December 1972.

Like other countries with strong currencies, Switzerland revalued the
franc in May and December 1971 by a total 13.9 percent against the US
dollar in order to avert future capital inflows and to contain the import
of inflation.[14] The Swiss National Bank had wanted to revalue the franc in
September 1969 when the German *Bundesbank* let the DM float, leading
to strong capital inflows into Switzerland. At that time, however, the Swiss
government declined to follow the advice of the central bank and kept the
exchange rate at its current level. An important reason was that the legal
framework did not allow for swift action. According to the Coinage Law
of 1952, the government was obliged to ask parliament when considering
a change in the parity of the Swiss franc. The decision also was subject
to an optional referendum, a process that would have taken months. In

[13] Ingold (2003).
[14] *Schweizerische Nationalbank* (1982, pp. 222–223), Bernholz (2007, pp. 164–165).

the context of speculative pressure, such a lengthy procedure was contraproductive.[15] This problem was soon to be resolved. Government and parliament revised the law in the following year, and in December 1970, the revision became effective. From then on, the government alone, in consultation with the Swiss National Bank, was entitled to change the parity of the franc.

Yet the basic problem remained. Swiss policymakers were determined to reduce inflation, and thanks to the high degree of central bank independence and the cooperation of labor unions, the institutional preconditions for such a strategy were given, whereas in many other European countries and the United States, the central bank was either not willing or not powerful enough to restore price stability, and labor unions were unilaterally pushing for maximum real wage increases.[16] Only if the Swiss National Bank had explained that it did not consider price stability a major goal of monetary policy would the demand for the Swiss franc have been stopped. But such a policy reversal was not only unthinkable but also not at all desirable. Accordingly, even after the Swiss franc had been revalued in May and December 1971, it remained a currency investors considered to be undervalued because the Swiss authorities showed they were resolute. In June 1972, the pound crisis shattered the European markets and led to the permanent exit of the British pound from the Snake.[17] Again, the Swiss franc came under pressure, and capital inflows inflated the domestic monetary stock. When the next crisis broke out in January 1973, the Swiss National Bank was not ready to accept a further wave of imported inflation. As the bank wrote in its Annual Report, continuing to buy dollars against francs "would have undermined the credibility of the efforts to fight inflation."[18]

The wave of capital inflows that led the Swiss National Bank to let the franc float was Italy's announcement on Sunday evening, 21 January, that it was introducing a two-tier exchange system.[19] By this measure, the Italian government hoped to contain capital flight. The governing board

---

[15] *Schweizerische Nationalbank* (1982, p. 221), Bernholz (2007, p. 163).
[16] See Chapter Five on central bank independence and the erosion of the postwar consensus in industrial relations.
[17] The Snake started to operate on 24 April 1972; the United Kingdom joined on 1 May and withdrew on 23 June. For a detailed analysis, see Chapter Five.
[18] Swiss National Bank, Annual Report, 1973 (66), p. 38: "*Weitere Interventionen hätten die Bemühungen zur Inflationsbekämpfung wegen der daraus resultierenden Notenbankgeldschöpfung unglaubwürdig gemacht.*"
[19] In a two-tier exchange system or dual exchange market, current-account transactions were controlled and settled at a fixed exchange rate, whereas capital-account transactions

of the Swiss National Bank, fearing that the Italian move would accelerate capital flight, expected a turbulent Monday and therefore invited the heads of the foreign-exchange departments of the three big banks to a meeting shortly before the market opened. At this meeting, the Swiss National Bank offered to buy US$105 million from the banks, a transaction it had planned for several weeks, to ease the market.[20]

The banks agreed, but they were not happy about the exchange rate offered by the Swiss National Bank. After some discussion, the banks succeeded in raising the rate slightly from 3.756 to 3.757 per US dollar. Since the bank made sure that the markets were promptly informed of its dollar purchases, the dollar appreciated slightly against the franc. Yet, at noon, this movement was reversed, and the dollar rate fell to the lower end of the band. According to the board, the depreciation was clearly due to Italian transactions, "presumably because Italian banks bought Swiss francs for debt redemption."[21] Since Italian banks had particularly high liabilities in Swiss francs, the extent of these transactions was considerable.

The reason why not only the Italian lira but also the US dollar came under pressure was the way Italian banks paid back their debts. First, they took out a loan in US dollars in the Euromarket. Then they bought Swiss francs with these dollars in order to pay back all their debts denominated in Swiss francs. The result of this transaction was that the Italian banks now had only dollar debts, whereas the banks that had sold Swiss francs to the Italian banks tried to sell the received dollars. As a result, there was a surplus of dollars and a shortage of Swiss francs, which triggered a sudden flight from the dollar to the franc. In this way, the transactions made by Italian banks led to a chain reaction and another currency crisis.

After the Swiss National Bank had acquired the agreed US$105 million from the three big Swiss banks, it bought another US$90 million from them to calm the market. The measure had only a temporary effect, though. At 2.30 p.m., Governor Leutwiler, one of the three members of the governing board and head of the department responsible for financial market operations, told the banks that from now on further dollar sales would lead to

were subject to exchange-rate fluctuations depending on the supply and demand of the currency. Cf. Bakker (1996, pp. 12 and 134–136).

[20] The following reconstruction of the major events is based on Archives Swiss National Bank, *Protokoll des Direktoriums*, 25 January 1973, pp. 120–127; *Bankausschuss*, 16 February 1973, pp. 35–42; *Bankrat*, 23 March 1973, pp. 266–270; *Amtliches stenographisches Bulletin, Ständerat*, 20 March 1973, pp. 247–250 (speech of Finance Minister Nello Celio); *Bericht des Bundesrates an die Bundesversammlung über Massnahmen zum Schutze der Währung* (18 April 1973), *Bundesblatt*, 1973, vol. 1, pp. 1381–1382.

[21] Archives Swiss National Bank, *Protokoll des Direktoriums*, 25 January 1973, p. 120.

blockage of the equivalent amount of funds in their accounts at the Swiss National Bank. After this measure was taken, the Swiss National Bank had to buy another US$72 million from the banks until the close of the market at 4 p.m. Altogether, the central bank bought US$276 million, corresponding to 1 billion Swiss francs on Monday, 22 January. Of this amount, one quarter – the additional US$72 million – was blocked.

However, the blocking had the undesired consequence that the market was split into two parts. While the central bank bought dollars at the rate of 3.7535 CHF per dollar, corresponding to the exchange rate at the lower end of the band, the commercial banks, namely, the Swiss Bank Corporation, could sell francs at an even lower dollar rate in the market because investors expected a devaluation of the dollar and a revaluation of the Swiss franc, respectively. The new market rate further accelerated the purchases of Swiss francs. Since the president of the governing board was on vacation in the Swiss Alps, it was another member of the board, Fritz Leutwiler, who urged the end of interventions.[22] After several consultations by phone between him, the convalescent President Stopper and Finance Minister Nello Celio in Berne, the Swiss National Bank informed the commercial banks on Tuesday morning, 23 January, shortly before the market opened, that it would not intervene in the market any more. It also issued a press release that ended with the following words: "It [the Swiss National Bank] will stay away from the market until the situation has become calmer."[23] In other words, the central bank regarded the measure as temporary.

The *Neue Zürcher Zeitung*, Switzerland's leading commercial newspaper, fully backed the decision of the central bank.[24] But some observers criticized it. Swiss banks and foreign-exchange traders in London could hardly understand why the bank had thrown in the towel after one day, given that the US dollar was about to recover.[25] And not surprisingly, the deputy manager of the International Monetary Fund (IMF), the

---

[22] Curiously enough, in Germany, the president of the central bank also was absent because of an illness when the decision to float was taken in March 1973. See the memoirs of Otmar Emminger, then vice president of the *Bundesbank*. Emminger (1986, p. 456).

[23] The press release had the following wording: "*Die Schweizerische Nationalbank teilt mit: Währungspolitische Massnahmen im Ausland haben am Montag eine starke, teilweise spekulative Nachfrage nach Schweizerfranken ausgelöst. Angesichts des Risikos neuer massiver Devisenzuflüsse, die mit einer entsprechenden Geldschöpfung verbunden wären, hat die Schweizerische Nationalbank im Einvernehmen mit dem Bundesrat heute darauf verzichtet, ihre Interventionen am Dollarmarkt aufzunehmen. Sie wird sich vom Markte fernhalten, bis eine Beruhigung eingetreten ist.*" Archives Swiss National Bank, *Protokoll des Direktoriums*, 25 January 1973, p. 123.

[24] *Neue Zürcher Zeitung*, 24 January, 1973.

[25] See Chapter Five for a detailed discussion of these reactions.

institution that was responsible for the stability of the Bretton Woods system, concluded that the "Swiss panicked."[26] Yet even Max Iklé, a former member of the governing board (until 1968), already cited for his conversation with Milton Friedman, criticized "the incredible carelessness and informality by which an international agreement was violated and the country was precipitated into an experiment whose consequences nobody could foresee."[27] Yet, with hindsight, it is hard see how the Swiss National Bank could have avoided the temporary floating of the franc. Given that the Nixon administration was not willing or able to reduce inflation, the US dollar was doomed to fall sooner or later, so the Swiss franc remained an attractive investment for international investors.

In sum, neither the introduction of tight capital controls nor a U-turn of economic policy was an option Swiss policymakers considered realistic or desirable in the early 1970s. Thus, according to the trilemma, the only way to resolve the problem was to let the franc float. From a comparative perspective, however, such an explanation is both too broad and too narrow. It is too broad because it was not special at the time for European countries to pursue a monetary policy oriented toward domestic goals. Switzerland was only special in that it was more averse to inflation than most other European countries and the United States. Yet the problem that domestic goals were hard to reconcile with fixed-exchange-rate stability also was imminent in countries whose policy stance was too expansionary. The same is true for Norway and Sweden in 1992. Of course, their currencies were overvalued and not undervalued, as was the Swiss franc in 1973, but the structural problem was similar: Domestic policies were not in synchronization with those of the EMS countries, notably Germany, so the peg lacked credibility and eventually had to be abandoned.[28]

Yet the explanation presented earlier is also too narrow because it does not take into account a third factor that proved highly relevant in the case of the Netherlands, which found itself in a position similar to Switzerland's but maintained the fixed-exchange-rate regime: EC membership.[29] Amsterdam had been an international financial center, the Dutch current account had been in surplus (for most of the time), total international reserves were increasing rapidly during the early 1970s,[30] and the Dutch

---

[26] Solomon (1982, p. 229).
[27] Iklé (1984, p. 139).
[28] See the discussion of Norway's and Sweden's regime shift in Chapter Eight.
[29] On the history of the relationship between the EC and Switzerland, see Grädel (2007) and Freiburghaus (2009).
[30] See Table 5.5.

guilder became a currency of some international importance, although to a lesser extent than the Swiss franc (see Table 7.2).

According to this similar structure, the Dutch central bank was confronted with similarly high amounts of capital inflows in the final weeks of Bretton Woods. As noted, the Swiss National Bank let the franc float after having purchased US$267 million on Monday, 22 January 1973. The *Nederlandsche Bank* was forced to purchase US$500 million from Dutch banks in the course of the dollar crisis in February 1973 to keep the Dutch guilder within the Snake and to defend the new exchange rate against the dollar.[31] And in the week from 5 February to 9 February, the *Nederlandsche Bank* bought US$400 million.[32] It is thus fair to conclude that if Switzerland had been a EC member at the time, it would have entered the Snake in April 1972, and the Swiss franc would have been revalued within the Snake in March 1973.

In sum, from a comparative perspective, it is sufficient to explain Switzerland's shift to floating with financial openness and the lack of EC membership. All other small European states either had tight capital controls (e.g., Austria, Norway, and Sweden) or were EC members and participated in the Snake (e.g., Belgium, Denmark, and the Netherlands), which provided them with the option of devaluing or revaluing their currencies within a fixed-exchange-rate system. Switzerland had neither tight capital controls nor was it an EC member. Accordingly, the decision to float was the only option and the right thing to do under the historical circumstances, although policymakers had not planned or foreseen such a regime shift. The comparative analysis also shows why Switzerland's regime shift was not imitated. It was the only small European country running out of options in the final years of the Bretton Woods system.

THE FIRST PHASE (1973–1975): SAYING NO, SAYING YES

Why was Switzerland' regime shift of 1973 not imitated by other small European countries before the EMS crisis of 1992–1993? As noted in the preceding two chapters, one reason was that Norway and Sweden did not start to liberalize their financial markets until the mid-1980s. Only then did it become theoretically possible to consider the option of floating. Before that date, a flexible-exchange-rate regime was out of question

---

[31] BIS, Annual Report, 1972–1973, p. 132.
[32] Solomon (1982, p. 230).

because tight capital controls allowed both Scandinavian countries to have a currency basket and to pursue a relatively independent monetary policy. The other reason why the Swiss regime shift of 1973 remained an isolated event for 20 years was that the success of its experiences with a floating exchange rate was inconclusive for other small European countries. During the turbulent 1970s, the enormous market volatility rather confirmed than invalidated the conventional wisdom implying that a flexible-exchange-rate regime was a bad option for a small, open economy because of expected negative effects on trade, investment, and monetary policy.[33] American economist James Tobin compared the vagaries of the Swiss franc to those of the prices of "rare coins, precious metals and baseball cards."[34] Then, during most of the 1980s, many observers ironically came to the opposite conclusion, namely, that the Swiss franc was too stable and therefore not a truly floating currency. The Swiss franc was rather seen as a satellite of the deutsche mark (DM) owing to the special relationship between the two central banks and the close integration of both economies.[35] This interpretation reinforced the impression that Switzerland was a special case.

To be sure, in the 1970s and 1980s, Switzerland's monetary policy was of great interest to central bankers across the world, especially in the United States and the United Kingdom. When, for example, the Thatcher government decided to adopt monetary targeting, it flew in Swiss advisors from the Swiss National Bank in Zurich.[36] Furthermore, Bernanke et al. (1999) have shown that Germany's and Switzerland's experiences with monetary targeting were important preconditions for the development of today's inflation targeting.[37] Yet, for small European states, Switzerland was not a model throughout the 1970s and 1980s. Only when New Zealand and Canada successfully adopted inflation targeting in 1990 and 1991 and the EMS crisis forced Sweden to abandon its unilateral peg to the European currency unit (ECU) was the conventional wisdom overturned.

The narrative evidence shows that for several years even the Swiss authorities themselves were unsure whether or not the temporary regime shift of 1973 was a viable option. On the basis of Figure 7.1, which plots the

---

[33] For the conventional view among policymakers, see Chapter Five.
[34] Tobin (1978, p. 524).
[35] See the debate between Genberg (1990) and Rich (1990a).
[36] Thatcher (1993, p. 515), refers to Fritz Leutwiler as "my old friend."
[37] See, for example, Bernanke et al. (1999), who view Germany and Switzerland as pioneers in the recent history of monetary policy.

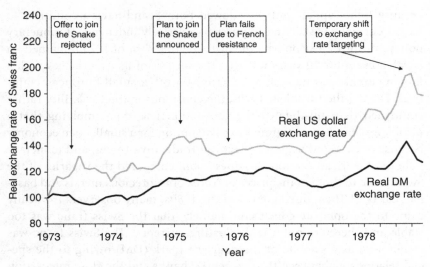

Figure 7.1. Chronology of major events and real exchange rates of USD/CHF and DM/CHF (monthly), 1973–1978 (1973 = 100). See text for chronology. (*Data from Swiss National Bank.*)

DM/CHF and USD/CHF rates and lists the most important events, we can divide the turbulent 1970s into two phases. The first phase, lasting from 1973 to 1975, was marked by the question of whether Switzerland should join the Snake or not. It ended in late 1975, when the Swiss realized that France would never welcome their strong currency being allied with the DM. It is true that the adoption of monetary targeting in late 1974 also fell into this phase and that this decision was a defining moment for the subsequent monetary history of Switzerland. Yet, at the time, it was far from clear whether this was a definite regime shift or not. If the French had agreed to let the Swiss franc in, history may have taken another course. The second phase was characterized by the search for an alternative way to stabilize the exchange rate after the Snake option had been buried in late 1975, and moderate foreign-exchange interventions and capital controls proved ineffective. The solution was found in autumn 1978 when the Swiss National Bank massively intervened and announced that it would keep the CHF/DM rate "clearly over the level of 80 francs per 100 DM." What ultimately made the regime shift to floating permanent was the turn of monetary policy in the United States following the appointment of Paul Volcker as the new chairman of the Federal Reserve and stabilization of the EMS currencies after 1983. This section treats the first phase, and the following section the second phase.

The years from 1973 to 1975 were characterized mainly by changing views toward the Snake.[38] First, in 1973, the Swiss were given the chance to enter but declined. Then, in 1975, the Swiss were seriously exploring the option of entering, but the French would not let them in. How can we explain this surprising development? The official offer to enter the Snake as an associate member came in March 1973, when the EC members decided to let the Snake float against all other currencies, notably the dollar and the yen.[39] The official reason for Switzerland's rejection of this offer was that both the Swiss National Bank and the Swiss government were afraid of making what they considered a premature decision. As long as the markets were uneasy, they reckoned, a fixed-exchange-rate regime would not be viable. On the morning of 15 March, the government issued a press release explaining that "in the light of the special monetary situation of Switzerland, further clarifications are needed." The government also instructed the Swiss National Bank "to follow the development and to discuss the open questions with foreign central banks."[40] The main concern was that a further inflow of capital would inflate the monetary base once Switzerland returned to a fixed exchange rate. The only element that was clear in the present situation was that the dollar would continue to float. With regard to the Snake, the Swiss National Bank concluded: "As long as there is no recession, the question arises whether we should help the export industry by joining the Snake. Besides the known benefits, there are also costs. There are two negative consequences: partial structural distortions, depending on the export market, and reinforcement of the inflationary pressure because of capital inflows."[41]

On 19 March, the day the Snake began to operate, Finance Minister Celio was asked in a session of the parliament if Switzerland was going to join the Snake in the near future. Celio repeated the official wait-and-see

---

[38] For a more detailed narrative of these changing views, see Bernholz (2007, pp. 170–182) and Halbeisen (2007).

[39] Gros and Thygesen (1998, p. 16).

[40] The press release had the following wording: "*Der Bundesrat hat in diesem Zusammenhang auch die Frage einer Mitwirkung der Schweiz an den Bestrebungen zur Stabilisierung der Wechselkurse zwischen einer Gruppe von europäischen Ländern einer ersten Prüfung unterzogen. Er misst dieser von der EWG ausgehenden Initiative grosse Bedeutung bei und bringt ihr Interesse entgegen. Angesichts der besonderen währungspolitischen Lage der Schweiz sind jedoch weitere Abklärungen unerlässlich. Der Bundesrat hat die Nationalbank beauftragt, die Entwicklung zu verfolgen und die noch offenen Fragen zusammen mit den beteiligten ausländischen Notenbanken zu erörtern.*" Neue Zürcher Zeitung, 15 March 1973, p. 9.

[41] Archives Swiss National Bank, 2260, *Währungspolitik, Allgemeines, 1973–1979, Währungskrise, Diverse Akten,* March 1973: "*Für die Sitzung mit dem Bundesrat*" (14 March 1973).

attitude: "In the present situation, it is not possible yet to make any commitments beyond the general goals of our exchange-rate policy. I was asked a precise question: Has Switzerland the intention to join or not? Switzerland cannot join today."[42] He also repeated the official reason for the Swiss policy: that the situation continued to be too fragile. With regard to Austria, Norway, and Sweden, which had entered the Snake, Celio explained that they were not threatened by speculative attacks and therefore would have no problems in maintaining a stable exchange rate.[43] The finance minister also saw a technical problem stemming from the fact that the market rate of the Swiss franc vis-à-vis the DM was too high at the time, and he argued that closer monetary cooperation would require a treaty to be ratified by the parliament and Swiss voters. Only a few months earlier, on 3 December, Switzerland had held a referendum on the Free Trade Agreement with the EC, and during the campaign, the government had always promised that a positive outcome would not entail closer cooperation with the EC apart from the trade issue.[44]

At the next meeting of the governing board with the Bank Council Committee, Governor Leutwiler explained the technical problem in more detail. In order to solve it, he argued, the Swiss franc would have to be revalued by 3 percent against the dollar, which would push the dollar rate "below today's rate, which is already substantially low." Since he believed that the exporting industry would not welcome a further strengthening of the franc, he concluded: "Confronted with these alternatives, floating our currency independently appears to be the lesser evil."[45] However, Leutwiler put less weight on the problem of ratification than Celio, probably because as a central banker he was concerned primarily about monetary, not

---

[42] *Amtliches stenographisches Bulletin, Nationalrat,* 19 March 1973, p. 328.

[43] For a detailed discussion of Austria, Norway, and Sweden, see Chapters Five and Six. Sweden, also outside the EC, accepted the invitation and joined the Snake on 19 March. Austria, equally not an EC member, declared on 29 March that it would peg the schilling to the Snake currencies and keep the fluctuation of the exchange rate within a band of ±2.25 percent without formally joining the Snake and thus participating in the system of intervention. Norway had joined the Snake before it held a referendum on EC membership in the autumn of 1972. Although Norwegian voters rejected EC membership, *Norges Bank* kept the krone within the Snake, arguing that it was only a technical matter.

[44] *Ibid.* See also the speech Celio gave in the Council of States. *Amtliches stenographisches Bulletin, Ständerat,* 20 March 1973, pp. 249–250.

[45] Appendix of the fourth meeting of the *Bankrat:* "*Bericht über die Währungslage: 1. Die gemeinsam flottierenden europäischen Währungen und das Floating des Schweizerfrankens (Herr Dr. F. Leutwiler),*" pp. 4–5. Cf. Report to the *Bankrat* on 23 March 1973, p. 272: "For the moment, it is premature to join the Snake. However, we have to leave this possibility open. For the time being, we need to wait for a more realistic exchange rate."

political matters.[46] Surprisingly, the possibility that Switzerland might be forced to weaken the banking secrecy law was never mentioned in the internal discussions of the Swiss National Bank or in the official documents of the Swiss government.

Whatever their exact arguments, the Swiss National Bank and the Swiss government were convinced that returning to a fixed exchange rate was premature and thus continued to wait for the return of international monetary stability. Interestingly, however, since this stability was at least partially restored in the course of 1973, neither the Swiss National Bank nor the government showed interest in ending the period of floating anymore. On the contrary, the rationale was adjusted: The international stability now became an important reason to wait even longer before returning to a fixed exchange rate. Leutwiler explained in September 1973: "Summarizing, we conclude that the development of the Snake must continue to be followed attentively, but that the time for a participation of Switzerland has not come yet. The exchange rate risks which we would have to accept are more severe than the advantage of having exchange rate stability vis-à-vis a relatively small circle of currencies, all the more so as this stability has largely been achieved de facto by the market."[47] In the same month, a high official of the finance ministry put forward the same argument: "Looking back at the joint floating during the last six months it can further be concluded that the exchange rate of the Swiss franc by and large followed the exchange rate movements of the jointly floating EC currencies so that Switzerland's participation in this system during this time would not have entailed any noteworthy advantages."[48]

From the summer of 1973 to the autumn of 1974, the Swiss National Bank in fact lived in the best of all worlds. The dollar rate fluctuated, but not excessively. The nominal and real CHF/DM rate also remained quite stable. Since foreign-exchange markets continued to be relatively calm

[46] Archives Swiss National Bank, 2260, *Währungspolitik: Allgemeines*, 1973–1979, *Währungskrise, Diverse Akten*, March 1973: "*Stichworte zum Block-Floaten*" (26.3.73), p. 3. Cf. Press release of the *Bankrat* on 23 March 1973.

[47] Archives Swiss National Bank, 2260, *Währungspolitik, Allgemeines*, 1973–1979, *Communiqué Vorort, Presse (inkl. Korrespondenz)*, 1973: Letter to the *Eidgenössisches Politisches Departement/Integrationsbüro*, 21 September 1973. The letter was sent because the office of integration sought an answer to an article published in the *Neue Zürcher Zeitung* in which two lecturers of the Hochschule St. Gallen (Mayrzedt and von Platen) demanded that Switzerland join the Snake and eventually the EEC. See *Neue Zürcher Zeitung*, 7 September 1973.

[48] Archives Swiss National Bank, 2260, *Währungspolitik, Allgemeines*, 1973–1979, *Communiqué Vorort, Presse (inkl. Korrespondenz)*, 1973. Letter of 26 September 1973, by the Deputy Director of the Finance Ministry (*stellvertretender Direktor Dr. B. Müller*).

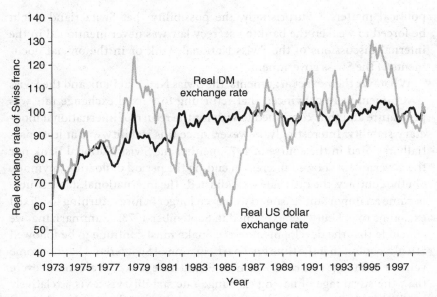

Figure 7.2. Real exchange rate of CHF against DM and USD, 1973–1998 (monthly, January 1999 = 100). (*Swiss National Bank.*)

throughout 1974, the Swiss National Bank also abstained from inter-vention – the last one had been in February 1973 – and the restrictions on capital inflows that had been implemented in the final period of the Bretton Woods system were dismantled. In addition, the bank developed and adopted monetary targeting as the new policy framework. At the beginning of 1975, the governing board announced that "an expansion by 6 percent of the money stock M1 … would be appropriate." It was a widely perceived step that enhanced the reputation of the Swiss National Bank.[49]

Yet, during the same period in which monetary targeting was being adopted, the Swiss franc fell victim to another severe currency crisis, and the Swiss National Bank had to readjust its rationale yet again. The cri-sis began in mid-November 1974, in the midst of the recession. In real terms, the Swiss franc appreciated sharply against both the dollar and the DM (Figure 7.2). Leutwiler, now president of the Swiss National Bank, was "startled" by these sudden upward movements and feared negative conse-quences for the Swiss exporting industry, as Otmar Emminger, then vice

---

[49] Swiss National Bank, Annual Report, 1975–1976, pp. 7–8. Because of its early shift to monetary targeting, Swiss monetary policy has been studied widely. See e.g., Rich (1997) and Bernanke et al. (1999).

president of the *Bundesbank,* wrote in his memoirs.[50] The Swiss National Bank took two measures. First, it reintroduced a ban on interest payments to nonresidents, which had been removed only a few months earlier.[51] Second, it intervened in the market in early January 1975.[52] These measures were not sufficient, however. Leutwiler therefore was glad to agree to the U.S. proposal to make a joint intervention. In the beginning of February 1975, Leutwiler met with Arthur Burns and the heads of the *Bundesbank* in London. In the following days, the three central banks intervened in the market and succeeded in correcting the misalignment of the dollar.[53]

In the course of the crisis, a great controversy broke out between executives of the Swiss exporting industry and of the commercial banks. The former were alarmed and warned of a contraction of the industrial sector. Companies of the chemical industry located in Basle publicly considered transferring their production facilities to foreign countries. The most outspoken sectors were the executives of the watch industry, who demanded introduction of a dual exchange market.[54] The advocates of the financial sector, by contrast, suggested that the exporting sectors, in particular, textile and watch makers, were mainly suffering from structural problems, not from the appreciation of the Swiss franc. They strongly rejected the idea of a dual exchange market, arguing that such a measure would damage the position of Switzerland as an international financial center.[55]

On 20 February 1975, the governing board of the Swiss National Bank discussed the issue of more central bank cooperation, namely, with the *Bundesbank,* for the first time since March 1973.[56] And a few days later, on 26 February, President Leutwiler told a surprised audience in Zurich that a Swiss participation in the Snake was to be seriously considered.[57] Two weeks later, at the meeting of the Bank for International Settlements (BIS)

[50] Emminger (1986, p. 311).
[51] Knapp (1977, p. 177), *Schweizerische Nationalbank* (1982, pp. 226 and 454*ff.*), Christensen (1986, pp. 34–36),
[52] *Schweizerische Nationalbank,* Annual Report, 1975–1976 (68), p. 11.
[53] Emminger (1986, pp. 311–312).
[54] For the definition of a dual exchange market, also called a two-tier exchange system, see footnote 19.
[55] *Schweizer Politik im Jahre,* 1975, pp. 71–72.
[56] Archives Swiss National Bank, *Protokoll des Direktoriums,* 20 February 1975, p. 316. The Swiss National Bank launched this initiative, not the government. See *Protokoll des Direktoriums,* 13 March 1975, p. 414.
[57] Archives Swiss National Bank, *Protokoll des Direktoriums,* 27 February 1975, p. 354.

in Basle on 7 March, Leutwiler explained the Swiss dilemma leading to the idea of joining the Snake:

The reasons for this interest [participating in the Snake] are likely to be known here: They lie in the fact that the rate of the Swiss franc, despite various defence measures and substantial interventions in the foreign exchange market, has reached a level which is creating serious problems, at least for certain branches of our export industry, especially for the watch industry and textile industry... Our announcement in respect of a possible participation of Switzerland in the 'serpent' [Snake] has been taken in good part both by the export industry and the press. We are now about to have things clarified at the technical level, the question as to the form in which this participation could be effected being in the foreground. I personally have in mind not so much the example of Austria but the Swedish and Norwegian model. As soon as an opinion thereon has been formed on our part, we shall have to ascertain in talks with our European colleagues whether a participation of Switzerland is at all considered as possible and desirable.[58]

Also at the BIS in Basle, Leutwiler held the announced special meeting with the central bank governors of the Snake countries, including Italy and France, which had left the Snake in February 1973 and January 1974, respectively. His words were well received, particularly by Klasen of Germany and Zijlstra of the Netherlands. However, Belgian Governor Cecil de Strycker and French Governor Bernard Clappier were skeptical. Clappier demanded that the Swiss join the EC before participating in the Snake, and de Strijcker wanted Switzerland to follow the Belgian example of introducing a dual market in order to bring capital movements under control. Leutwiler rejected both proposals as conditions for participation in the Snake.[59]

Despite ongoing French opposition, the Swiss National Bank continued to explore the Snake option because the initiative was supported by

[58] Archives Swiss National Bank, 3094, *Währungsschlange, diverse Akten: BIZ, Notizen*, 1975 (*Partizipation CH an Währungsschlange*). The meeting was held on Friday evening, 7 March 1975. On the exchange-rate policies of Austria, Norway, and Sweden, see Chapters Five and Six. With regard to Austria, see also Hellmann (1976, p. 73): "*Die österreichische Formel eines Mitziehens mit der Schlange aus eigenem autonomen, sonst niemand bindenden Entschluss, erschien für die Schweiz wenig geeignet. Der Schweizer Franken benötigte, um den Gleichschritt mit der Schlange glaubhaft und beständig erscheinen zu lassen, des gegenseitigen Interventionsversprechens. Allein konnte die Nationalbank keinen Schweizer Riegel gegen die stetige Selbstaufwertung des Frankens aufbauen.*"
[59] Archives Swiss National Bank, *Protokoll des Direktoriums*, 13 March 1975, pp. 414–415. The meeting was held on Tuesday, 11 March 1975. For a short version of the meeting with the Snake members, including France and Italy, see *Archives De Nederlandsche Bank* HA 2.3/70, 2.312.22/16/1, *wisselkoersenoverleg slang 1975, correspondentie en notities*, 13 March 1975: *Vergadering van Comité des Gouverneurs op 11 maart 1975.*

the major economic sectors, in particular, the exporting industries.[60] The Swiss National Bank was hoping that the *Bundesbank,* which supported the Swiss initiative, would help to overcome French resistance. And in fact, the French remained isolated within the EC, even after they reentered the Snake in July 1975. Nevertheless, the process remained blocked. France, though dropping the requirement that Switzerland join the EC before participating in the Snake, deliberately continued to set conditions that Switzerland never would be able or willing to fulfill.[61] For example, at the meeting of the Snake finance ministers on 22 September 1975, to which the Swiss Finance Minister Chevallaz and the President of the Swiss National Bank Leutwiler were invited, French Finance Minister Fourcade made a connection between the strength of the Swiss franc and Swiss banking secrecy that supposedly encouraged tax evasion.[62] Of course, Fourcade knew that Switzerland would never allow banking secrecy legislation to become an issue in the negotiations.

At a BIS meeting in October 1975, a German senior official hinted at a possible French veto.[63] In November, a few days before the summit at Rambouillet, Leutwiler met with the governor of the *Banque de France* in Paris and met strong opposition directed by the highest government level. The main reason, Leutwiler told his colleagues at the next board meeting, was the following: "In France, the franc is regarded as weak, but the Swiss franc as strong. Under these circumstances, the French fear that, if Switzerland joined, it could become difficult to keep the French franc within the Snake."[64] When French Finance Minister Fourcade repeated the reservations of this government after the summit in Rambouillet, the Swiss initiative began to lose momentum. On 21 November, Leutwiler emphasized in a public speech that "the doors were

---

[60] Archives Swiss National Bank, *Protokoll des Direktoriums,* 13 March 1975, p. 415; *Protokoll des Direktoriums,* 20 March 1975, pp. 479–480. See also the results of the consultation by the Swiss government. The exporting sectors welcomed the plan to join the Snake; banks and insurance companies were less enthusiastic but agreed in principle. See Archives Swiss National Bank, 3093: "*Composition et mandat de la délégation suisse invitée à participer à la réunion des ministres des finances des pays du serpent le 22 septembre 1975, à Bruxelles*" (Appendix 3: "*Réaction des principales associations professionelles et de quelques entreprises consultées sur l'opportunité pour la Suisse d'entrer dans le serpent monétaire Européen*").

[61] See, for example, the reports of the Swiss delegation of experts. Archives Swiss National Bank, *Protokoll des Direktoriums,* 2 October 1975, pp. 1564–1566; 9 October 1975, pp. 1612–1613.

[62] Archives Swiss National Bank, 3094: "*Finanzministertreffen der Schlangenländer in Brüssel am,*" 22 September 1975, p. 6.

[63] Archives Swiss National Bank, *Protokoll des Direktoriums,* 16 October 1975, p. 1651.

[64] Archives Swiss National Bank, *Protokoll des Direktoriums,* 17 November 1975, p. 1834.

not closed on both sides," but the German press was right in pointing out that the plan to join the Snake has been "silently buried."[65] The only result of these negotiations was that the Swiss National Bank was now invited into the system of daily exchange-rate consultations among Snake members.[66]

Switzerland's monetary history may have taken a different course in 1975 if the French had not vetoed its request to enter the Snake. Yet this counterfactual guessing is not the crucial point of this episode. More important, the seriousness of the Swiss initiative shows that the introduction of monetary targeting at the beginning of 1975 did not prevent the Swiss National Bank from exploring a return to a fixed-exchange-rate regime. Until the attempt to join the Snake failed definitely, the bank tried to maintain both options, a floating and a fixed exchange rate. The narrative evidence clearly shows that the historical process was more open than it may appear in retrospect.

THE SECOND PHASE (1975–1978): THE MAKING OF THE 1978 INTERVENTION

Since the option of joining the Snake had evaporated, the Swiss National Bank was forced to find other solutions to limit exchange-rate fluctuations. Business leaders, unions, and politicians representing the interests of the exporting sectors demanded that the Swiss National Bank become more active. The search for a new strategy culminated in a temporary shift to exchange-rate targeting in October 1978. The Swiss National Bank publicly announced that it sought to keep the CHF/DM rate "well over 80" and reached this goal by massive dollar interventions. This extraordinary measure was coupled with a dismantlement of capital controls introduced in the months before the decision to intervene was taken. Most important, it indicated that the question of which exchange-rate regime was most appropriate for a small, open economy was far from answered. In mid-December 1978, President Leutwiler explained in a meeting that the public announcement of an exchange-rate ceiling vis-à-vis the DM implied "a unilateral participation" in the EMS. Possibly, he added, this rapprochement would lead to a formal participation in the intervention

---

[65] Archives Swiss National Bank, 3093: Speech of Leutwiler ("*Geldpolitik in der Rezession*") and press articles. The citation is from the *Handelsblatt* (September 21, 1975). The *Frankfurter Allgemeine Zeitung* came to the same conclusion on 22 September ("*Schlange ohne Franken*").

[66] *Schweizerische Nationalbank* (1982, pp. 226–227).

mechanism – "the issue remains open."[67] Ultimately, a Swiss association was impossible because the EMS was tightly linked to the EC, whereas the Snake had been open to nonmembers. Moreover, the governing board also was aware of the fact that France still was strongly opposed to a Swiss association. The Élysée continued to fear that a currency bloc consisting of Germany, the Netherlands, and Switzerland would make the ECU too strong.[68] Nevertheless, the wording is striking: A fixed-exchange-rate regime, though informal and unilateral, was still an option considered by the Swiss National Bank.

Not surprisingly, the idea to announce an exchange-rate ceiling coupled with a massive intervention did not come immediately. According to Schiltknecht (1983), then chief economist of the Swiss National Bank, it took some time to realize that "[l]onger lasting deviations from the monetary target" were necessary to influence the exchange rate.[69] Until the autumn of 1978, the Swiss National Bank tried to reverse a sharp appreciation of the Swiss franc by enforcing capital controls and by making punctual interventions in the foreign-exchange market, but this strategy failed to change expectations. There were three episodes that taught the bank that it needed to intervene more decisively and that capital controls were rather useless because changing market sentiments, not massive capital inflows were the main reason for the sudden appreciation of the Swiss franc.

The first episode took place in late 1975, thus at the time when the idea of joining the Snake was finally buried. From the end of November 1975 to May 1976, the nominal effective exchange rate appreciated by 13.6 percent and the real exchange rate by almost 10 percent owing to depreciation of both the CHF/DM and CHF/USD rates.[70] The second episode began in the summer of 1977, after a calm period of 13 months. As in earlier cases, it was triggered by a policy shift in the United States. Although inflation was rising, the Carter administration tried to improve GDP growth by shifting to expansionary policies that weakened the dollar. The Swiss franc appreciated against the dollar but also dramatically against the DM.[71]

The third episode began in late May 1978. Again, the Swiss franc experienced strong upward pressures and appreciated not only against the dollar but also against the DM (see Figure 7.2). It was in the course of this crisis that

---

[67] Archives Swiss National Bank, *Bankausschuss*, 15 December 1978, p. 493.
[68] Archives Swiss National Bank, *Protokoll des Direktoriums*, 13 July 1978, pp. 821–822.
[69] Schiltknecht (1983, p. 77).
[70] *Schweizerische Nationalbank* (1982, p. 227).
[71] *Schweizerische Nationalbank* (1982, pp. 227–228).

the Swiss National Bank developed the idea of introducing an exchange-rate ceiling. Again, the dollar weakened because of expansionary policies in the United States,[72] and the depreciation of the DM was due mainly to the pledge to stimulate the domestic economy by fiscal measures that Germany had taken at the economic summit meeting held in Bonn in mid-July 1978. In addition, investors made forecasting errors, as Schiltknecht (1983) explains: "… [T]he market interpreted U.S. monetary policy in an unduly pessimistic manner, while at the same time viewing Switzerland as almost immune from any kind of economic ills. Such a biased view can lead to a situation where, for some time at least, expectations about exchange rate changes keep feeding on themselves, creating internal expectational dynamics preventing any effective counter-speculation."[73] The bias was so strong that even the massive joint interventions by various central banks could not stop the flight from the dollar. The main victim besides the Swiss franc was the yen. Moreover, the gold price began to rise.[74]

The governing board became increasingly concerned. At the beginning of August, the board decided to inject more liquidity in order to lower short-term interest rates. The measure had no lasting effect, however, as the board was forced to realize a week later.[75] Although short-term interest rates went down, the Swiss franc continued to appreciate. In mid-August, the board and the Swiss government discussed the situation and issued a press release.[76] It did not contain any substantial measures but tried to send a signal to the market that the current movement was not viewed as normal by the Swiss National Bank: "The loss of value of foreign currencies and the strong appreciation of the Swiss franc give rise to great concern. They are out of all proportions to the real economic conditions."[77] New economic data in fact suggested that the strong franc had slowed down economic growth.

Although the Swiss National Bank kept interest rates low and let the money supply grow by a higher rate than announced, the situation grew even worse in September. Some within the bank believed that a tightening of capital controls would be the only solution.[78] The list of proposals

---

[72] The era of stop-and-go ended only with the appointment of the new Fed Governor Paul Volcker in July 1979.

[73] Schiltknecht (1983, p. 77).

[74] *Schweizerische Nationalbank* (1982, p. 228). Cf. Discussion of the Governing Board, Archives Swiss National Bank, *Protokoll des Direktoriums*, 3 August 1978, p. 900.

[75] Archives Swiss National Bank, *Protokoll des Direktoriums*, 10 August 1978, pp. 914–920.

[76] Archives Swiss National Bank, *Bankausschuss*, 18 August 1978, pp. 118–130.

[77] *Neue Zürcher Zeitung*, 17 August 1978.

[78] Schiltknecht (1989, pp. 60–61).

contained measures such as increasing liquidity, lowering interest rates, purchasing and selling more actively in the foreign-exchange market, new legislation on foreign-exchange trading, promoting capital exports, and improving export financing.[79] On 26 September, the franc reached its highest peak: The CHF/DM rate was quoted at 75 and the CHF/USD rate at 1.45. Politicians and lobbyists of various exporting industries became more outspoken about the economic consequences of the strong franc, and the Swiss parliament announced that it would hold a debate in early October.[80] In this situation, as the crisis grew more severe, a strong signal became necessary. In this situation, the economists of the research department intervened, fearing that the governing board of the Swiss National Bank would be forced by the government to introduce tight foreign-exchange controls or a two-tier exchange system.[81] The economists proposed seeking a market solution by intervening massively in the foreign-exchange market and abandoning all regulating measures introduced in the course of 1978. The governing board welcomed the idea because it had received strong signals from the government that introduction of a two-tier exchange system was imminent: "The atmosphere in Berne is extremely nervous."[82]

On 1 October, the Swiss National Bank declared that the bank intended to raise the CHF/DM rate "well over 80" and intervened massively.[83] In the fourth quarter of 1978, it sold 10.6 billion Swiss francs all in all. As a result, M1 grew by 17.3 percent in 1978, whereas the target rate had been fixed at 5 percent (Figure 7.3). In the press release explaining the extraordinary intervention, the Swiss National Bank also made it clear that it was opposed to any further capital controls.[84] The strategy worked: The exchange rate depreciated, helped by the fact that the Carter administration began to change course toward a more restrictive policy from November 1978 on. In 1979, the situation eased further: The dollar appreciated, and the DM remained quite stable at the level of roughly 90 francs per 100 DM. Again, this improvement also was due to political developments in the United States. In August 1979, Paul Volcker became the new chairman of the Federal Reserve with the clear mandate to fight inflation by raising

[79] Archives Swiss National Bank, *Protokoll des Direktoriums*, 21 September 1978, pp. 1087–1089.

[80] Archives Swiss National Bank, *Protokoll des Direktoriums*, 29 September 1978, p. 1106.

[81] Bernholz (2007, p. 180).

[82] Archives Swiss National Bank, *Protokoll des Direktoriums*, 29 September, p. 1109.

[83] *Schweizerische Nationalbank* (1982, p. 228).

[84] The press release was drafted by the governing board at the meeting on 29 September. Archives Swiss National Bank, *Protokoll des Direktoriums*, 29 September 1978, pp. 1111–1114.

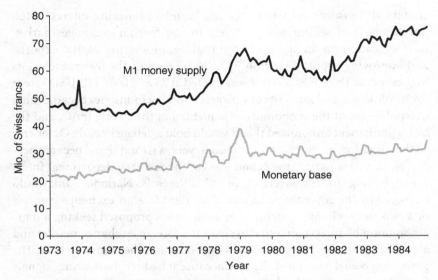

Figure 7.3. M0 and M1, in mio CHF (monthly). (*Swiss National Bank.*)

interest rates, which pushed the dollar upward. In this favorable situation, the Swiss National Bank could start to reduce the overhang of liquidity by selling the accumulated foreign-exchange reserves and returned to monetary targeting, but it abstained from a public announcement. At the end of 1979, an annual target for M0 was announced. The shift from M1 to M0 was justified by the observation that the money-multiplier forecasts had been deteriorating.[85]

Some contemporary observers and later President Leutwiler himself considered the 1978 intervention a mistake and believed that it had been the main cause for the inflationary surge in the early 1980s. Meanwhile, the architect of the intervention, chief economist Schiltknecht, maintains that not the intervention itself but rather the hesitant reduction of the monetary base was the real reason for the inflationary surge. His argument is that long-term interest rates did not rise after the intervention, indicating that asset holders saw no reason to demand higher interest rates because they were convinced that the steep increase in the monetary base was only temporary and soon to be reduced. In a recent article, Kugler and Rich (2002) support this interpretation.[86] This analysis does not prove, however, that the Swiss National Bank could have reduced the monetary

---

[85] *Schweizerische Nationalbank* (1982, p. 229).
[86] Schiltknecht (1983, p. 78), Rich (1997, p. 120), Rich and Kugler (2002, pp. 246–253).

overhang in a timely manner. Presumably, finding the right moment in a volatile environment, as in the late 1970s and early 1980s when interest rates and oil prices in the United States were skyrocking, was a difficult task. In any case, the 1978 intervention demonstrated that managing floating exchange rates remained a difficult task for the central bank of a small, open economy. In its annual report, the BIS devoted a long paragraph to the unusual operation of the Swiss National Bank, observing that the massive monetary expansion was undertaken "even at the risk of a resurgence of inflation."[87] Such comments made it clear that Switzerland was not a model for other small European countries.

THE 1980S: BACK TO EXCHANGE-RATE TARGETING?

In the 1980s, the situation became more comfortable for the Swiss National Bank because the CHF/DM rate never appreciated again beyond the limit of 80 francs per 100 DM (Figure 7.4). Russo and Tullio (1988) show on the basis of bilateral US dollar rates that from 1983 onward, the Swiss franc moved like a de facto member of the EMS.[88] Giavazzi and Giovannini (1989) observe that the Swiss franc closely followed the DM after

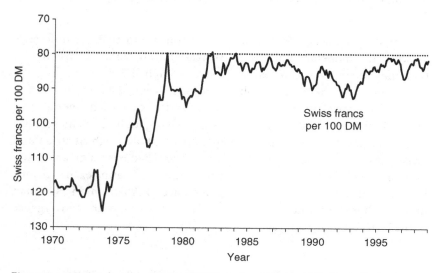

Figure 7.4. Nominal exchange rate of CHF against DM (monthly), 1970–1998. (*Swiss National Bank.*)

[87] BIS, Annual Report, 1979–1980, p. 61.
[88] Russo and Tullio (1988, p. 343).

1979.[89] Bayoumi and Eichengreen (1998) calculate that Switzerland displayed similarly low levels of volatility as Austria.[90] And according to Reinhart and Rogoff (2002), the nominal rate of the Swiss franc moved within a de facto moving band around the DM with a band width of ±2 percent on a yearly basis.[91]

Ironically, however, the stability of the Swiss franc was not seen as a sign that a small European country could manage a floating exchange rate successfully. On the contrary, many outside observers drew the conclusion that the Swiss franc was not a floating currency any more. For example, De Grauwe (1996) claimed that "since the early 1980s, ... the exchange rate policies of the Swiss authorities have been geared towards following the movements of the DM." Switzerland, he argued, has thus much in common with Austria:

Austria and Switzerland are two countries which have followed policies based on pegging their exchange rates to the DM. This policy used an implicit commitment, in the sense that it was well understood in the market that the authorities were committed to a particular range of the exchange rate with the DM. Whereas Austria has used such a policy since the start of floating exchange rates, Switzerland has only recently (since the early 1980s) embarked on such an exchange rate policy. In contrast to the EMS countries, however, there was no explicit international agreement.[92]

Similarly, Genberg (1990) came to the conclusion that the difference between the monetary policies of Austria and Switzerland was smaller than the different monetary policy strategies implied.[93]

In contrast to these outside observers, Swiss central bank officials and economists have claimed that there was no shift back to exchange-rate targeting. In his comment on Genberg's paper, Georg Rich, then chief economist of the Swiss National Bank, pointed out that although Austrian and Swiss policy experiences had been similar, there had been a greater room for maneuver afforded to the Swiss central bank by a floating exchange rate. His main argument was that the convergence of Austrian and German nominal short-term interest rates was clearly greater than the convergence of the Swiss and German rates[94] (Figure 7.5).

---

[89] Giavazzi and Giovannini (1989, pp. 133–144, especially tables on pp. 134 and 136).
[90] Bayoumi and Eichengreen (1998, p. 197, footnote 10).
[91] Reinhart and Rogoff (2002, p. 98).
[92] De Grauwe (1996, p. 215).
[93] Genberg (1990, pp. 216–217).
[94] Rich (1990a, pp. 221–223).

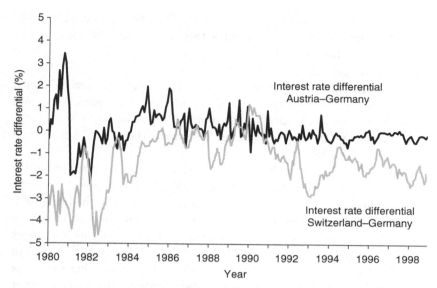

Figure 7.5. Interest-rate differentials Austria/Germany and Switzerland/Germany (Austria: money-market rate; Germany and Switzerland: LIBOR). (*IMF, International Financial Statistics.*)

Other Swiss economists have argued that a de facto band itself did not prove that the Swiss National Bank simply followed German monetary policy. Owing to a more stable international environment, they have pointed out, exchange-rate movements became less relevant in the 1980s, so there was little conflict between price stability and exchange-rate stability.[95] In fact, starting in the late 1970s, the United States and the United Kingdom reduced inflation and thereby ended the era of sudden flights out of the dollar and the pound. Similarly, most EC countries contributed to international exchange-rate stability by imposing more discipline on their domestic economic policies. In particular, the French government decided to change course.[96] Thanks to these changes abroad, the Swiss franc lost its attractiveness as a flight currency and became more stable.

There is also a technical reason endorsing the view that Switzerland maintained a flexible-exchange-rate system. The CHF/DM rate may never

---

[95] Jeitziner (1999) observes that after 1980, exchange-rate movements were less relevant for Swiss monetary policy than before the 1980s, and Cuche (2000) confirms this view for the 1980s and finds that inclusion of the exchange-rate element is necessary to depict the behavior of the Swiss National Bank after 1990.

[96] On the new consensus, see James (1996, pp. 409*ff.*), McNamara (1998), and Goodfriend (2007).

have climbed above the upper limit of 80 CHF per DM, but since the exchange-rate ceiling was not explicit throughout the 1980s and 1990s, the main condition for a floating regime was fulfilled, as Frankel (2003) argues: "The best classification scheme would define any managed floats as intermediate regimes if and only if there is an explicit target around which the central bank intervenes. Countries where the central bank intervenes in the foreign exchange market occasionally, but without any announced target, must be classified as floating; otherwise, there will be no actual countries in the latter category."[97]

On the other hand, the issue becomes less clear once we adopt a more flexible definition of exchange-rate targeting. A recent paper by Rathke and Straumann (2009) shows that from the mid-1960s to the late 1990s, the movement of the Swiss short-term interest rate was driven largely by the movement of the German short-term interest rate, whereas changes in the Swiss output gap and the Swiss inflation rate appear to have had only limited impact.[98] Second, narrative evidence shows that the Swiss National Bank intervened when the exchange rate approached the upper limit of 80 francs per 100 DM. The exchange-rate ceiling continued to be relevant for Swiss monetary policy (see Figure 7.4). In particular, there were two periods during the 1980s in which the CHF/DM rate approached the limit of 80 francs per 100 DM: in the first half of the 1980s and in 1986–1987.

As for the first period, the Swiss National Bank reacted in order to correct an earlier policy mistake, as Rich (1990b) observes with the benefit of hindsight.[99] In 1981, the bank had pursued a restrictive course in order to reduce inflation and to reverse depreciation of the franc, but the reaction turned out to be too restrictive. As a result, the CHF/DM rate underwent a rapid appreciation beginning in the second quarter of 1981 and passed the limit of 80 francs per 100 DM in November 1981. First, the Swiss National Bank intervened in the market, partially in cooperation with other central banks.[100] Then the bank relaxed monetary policy by announcing a monetary target of 3 percent.[101] This strategy proved successful, so the CHF/DM rate depreciated rapidly in 1982. But then the franc appreciated again in the course of 1983 and passed the upper limit once again, so the Swiss National Bank was forced to relax monetary conditions further and to

---

[97] Frankel (2003, p. 6).
[98] Rathke and Straumann (2009).
[99] Rich (1990b, p. 999).
[100] *Schweizerische Nationalbank,* Annual Report, 1981 (74), p. 27.
[101] *Schweizerische Nationalbank,* Annual Report, 1982 (75), p. 8.

intervene in the market together with other central banks.[102] After another rise above the limit of 80 francs per 100 DM in January 1984, the franc finally depreciated against the DM and stabilized at a lower level.

The second period in which the Swiss National Bank had to react to a sharp appreciation of the Swiss franc against the DM was in 1986. In the summer of that year, the franc approached the upper limit of 80 francs per 100 DM and remained at that level for a few weeks. In addition, the franc, together with other European currencies, had strongly appreciated against the dollar following the Plaza Agreement in 1985, which reversed the rise of the dollar or, more precisely, accelerated the depreciation of the dollar that had already begun. According to Rich (1992), the reasons for the strength of the Swiss franc were not clear because it did not reflect fundamentals. He assumes that the appreciation of the franc was due to a new market sentiment toward the DM in connection with the Louvre Accord in February 1987. Currency traders believed that the German *Bundesbank* was heading for a more expansionary policy and priced this new expectation into the exchange rate. In reality, the *Bundesbank* did not change course, yet the markets continued to make a distinction between the Swiss and German monetary authorities.[103] In reaction to the appreciation of the Swiss franc, the Swiss National Bank allowed the monetary base to grow at a higher rate than announced in the first half of 1987, the real interest rate fell considerably, and the Swiss franc depreciated against the DM.

Since the upward movement of the Swiss franc was reversed, the Swiss National Bank tightened monetary policy slightly in mid-1987, and since the *Bundesbank* also turned to a more restrictive course, the CHF/DM rate remained stable. Yet a series of events led to another dollar weakness that made the Swiss franc appreciate against the DM as well.[104] In late 1987, the real exchange rate vis-à-vis the DM climbed even higher than in 1986. With the Swiss National Bank injecting liquidity into the banking system following the stock market crash and lowering interest rates, the appreciation of the Swiss franc proved only temporary this time. In addition, the Swiss National Bank raised the monetary base target for 1988 from 2 to 3 percent. Unfortunately, however, the Swiss franc now unduly depreciated instead of returning to the equilibrium real exchange-rate level. Two financial innovations contributed to this outcome. The first innovation,

---

[102] *Schweizerische Nationalbank,* Annual Report, 1983 (76), p. 10.

[103] Rich (1992, p. 77).

[104] These events were the publication of new figures on the US trade deficit, the lack of restrictive fiscal measures of the US government to narrow the budget deficit, the injection of liquidity following the stock market crash in October 1987, and declarations by

which became effective in January 1988, modified bank cash reserve requirements, and the second one introduced a new electronic interbank payments system, called *Swiss Interbank Clearing* (SIC), that became fully operative in January 1988. Both innovations were expected to sharply reduce base-money demand, but it was very difficult to make any reliable forecast. The bank underestimated the extent to which the monetary base was reduced and did not react promptly, with the result that Swiss inflation got out of control in the late 1980s and early 1990s.[105]

Of course, neither the econometric evidence cited earlier nor the narrative account of these exchange-rate interventions proves that Switzerland abandoned the flexible-exchange-rate regime in the early 1980s. Yet they show that outside observers had good reasons to believe that management of the Swiss franc remained an exceptional experience based on a special relationship between Switzerland and Germany. Germany was by far the most important trading partner for Switzerland, and the central banks of both countries shared the same approach to monetary policy. Put differently, the stability of the Swiss franc during the 1980s did not invalidate the conventional wisdom that a flexible-exchange-rate system was not suited for a small European country. Only when two countries outside of Europe, New Zealand and Canada, adopted inflation targeting in 1990 and 1991, respectively, and the EMS crisis of 1992–1993 reshaped the European monetary scene did a shift to floating become a realistic alternative for the small countries outside the EMS.[106]

At a more general level, management of the floating Swiss franc has shown that the bipolar perspective, though correct from a bird's-eye view, underestimates the room for maneuvering in some special cases.[107] The space between an independent float and a very fixed-exchange-rate regime is not empty but filled with a surprising variety of solutions combining elements of both regimes. In the Swiss case, limiting exchange-rate volatility by some sort of exchange-rate target has been vital. Otherwise, we would have witnessed a return to a fixed-exchange-rate regime a long time ago. In this respect, Switzerland represented an early case of what has become quite popular recently among emerging markets in Asia and Latin

US officials that they wanted to have a weaker dollar. See Schweizerische Nationalbank, *Monatsbericht*, November 1987, p. 3.

[105] This version of events follows Rich (1992, pp. 77–78; 1997, pp. 120–125; 2003, pp. 33–38). Bernanke et al. (1999) also follow his argument. Many Swiss economists, however, have criticized the bank. See, for example, Capitelli and Buomberger (1990).

[106] On the regime shift of Canada and New Zealand, see Bernanke et al. (1999).

[107] For the bipolar view, see Eichengreen (1994), Summers (2000), and Fischer (2001).

America: floating with "hidden pegs."[108] The advantage of such a strategy was obvious: The Swiss National Bank could leave it open whether it wanted to intervene or not, thus minimizing the risk of speculative attacks. If the foreign-exchange markets had known with great certainty that the central bank would always intervene when the CHF/DM rate approached the limit of 80 francs per 100 DM, they would have had more incentives to enter into a game with the central bank. In this manner, the Swiss National Bank tried to reap some of the advantages of both pegging and floating. Of course, the Swiss case differed in many ways from today's Asian and Latin American cases. Most important, the strategy worked only because the Swiss National Bank enjoyed a high degree of credibility, and the Swiss government was able pay its debts in its own currency and therefore was not confronted with the problem of "original sin."[109]

---

[108] The seminal paper is Calvo and Reinhart (2002), who introduced the term "fear of floating." Genberg and Swoboda (2004, p. 6) speak of "fear of fixing" and Levy-Yeyati and Sturzenegger (2005) of "hidden pegs." Krugman (1989, p. 71) speaks of a "'covert' target zone."

[109] The expression was coined by Eichengreen and Hausmann (2004).

EIGHT

Floating in the North

For 20 years, Switzerland was the only small European country with a floating exchange rate, and in the early 1990s, it seemed very unlikely that this situation would change in the near future. In October 1990, the pound sterling joined the European Monetary System (EMS), and Norway unilaterally pegged its currency to the European currency unit (ECU), followed by Sweden and Finland in May 1991. But then, in late 1992, the EMS crisis forced Sweden and Norway to abandon their ECU link and to look for an alternative exchange-rate policy. In January 1993, the *Riksbank* officially adopted inflation targeting as a new monetary policy framework, and the krona has been a floating currency ever since. Norway, by contrast, experienced a more protracted regime shift but ended up with the same choice. In 2001, after having failed to keep the krone stable vis-à-vis the ECU for some time, the government announced inflation targeting. As a result of these regime changes, it has become more common for small European states to have a flexible exchange rate. Of course, small European states with a pegged exchange rate or the euro are still more numerous today, but the fact that Norway and Sweden, formerly staunch defenders of the fixed regime, shifted to floating in the 1990s is a clear indication that the era of "fixed ideas" ended in the late twentieth century.[1]

As in the chapter on the Swiss regime change (Chapter SEVEN), two questions are of particular interest. First, why and how did Sweden and Norway shift to a floating-exchange-rate regime? From close up, it seems that the differences between the regime changes of 1973 and 1992 matter more than the common features. First, one major reason why investors attacked the Swiss franc was that the currency was hugely undervalued.

---

[1] See Chapter FIVE for the importance of "fixed ideas" from the end of Bretton Woods to the EMS crisis of 1992.

Thus macroeconomic imbalances explain an important part of the story. In the case of the Norwegian krone and the Swedish krona, the story is more complicated. The latter was not undervalued but rather overvalued, so the defense of the ECU peg depended on the amount of foreign-exchange reserves, whereas the defense of the Swiss franc had been determined by the question of how much money creation and imported inflation were acceptable to the monetary authorities. Moreover, the Swedish krona was not as heavily overvalued as the Swiss franc was undervalued in 1973. Accordingly, not only macroeconomic imbalances but also the effect of contagion must have played a certain role. In the case of the Norwegian krone, contagion was even the major cause of the attack because the krone was only somewhat, if at all, overvalued in the autumn of 1992 when Norway was forced to abandon the ECU peg. Second, the transition to a flexible exchange-rate regime was different. Switzerland let the currency float from January 1973 on and officially adopted monetary targeting two years later. Sweden, by contrast, shifted to inflation targeting a few weeks after the krona had started to float. And Norway tried to avoid floating altogether for several years and only shifted to inflation targeting when exchange-rate targeting had evidently failed because of the strong fluctuation in oil prices.

However, from a bird's-eye view, the common features are more striking than the differences. First, the fact that all three countries had open financial markets that rendered their currencies vulnerable to speculative attacks was a more basic factor than the exact nature of the attacks. It is true that the regime transition was effected differently in the three countries, but owing to high capital mobility, the logic of transition toward a flexible exchange-rate regime was essentially the same. Second, all three countries had to give up the exchange-rate peg because, given their nonmembership in the European Community (EC), their commitment to the peg lacked the necessary credibility and strong support of domestic politics. Put differently, if Switzerland, Norway, and Sweden had been members of the EC at the time of the attacks, they would have opted for a readjustment of the exchange rate and not for a regime change.

The second question deals with the experiences that were gained with a flexible exchange rate. As noted in Chapter FIVE, Norwegian and Swedish policymakers had been particularly skeptical toward foreign-exchange markets. And Switzerland's experience during the 1970s only confirmed the conviction that small European states needed a fixed exchange rate. However, the Swiss case also has shown that the central bank has the power to enforce an implicit exchange-rate ceiling and therefore can manage a flexible exchange rate successfully. The most interesting question, therefore, is whether or not Sweden – Norway's regime shift is too recent – also needed to develop a special of form of managed floating.

The answer is no. The *Riksbank* has managed the floating exchange rate without introducing any implicit exchange-rate target. And the rejection of the euro in the referendum of September 2003 is a clear sign that Swedish voters support the central bank's policy. However, it is also interesting to note that the *Riksbank* could not abstain entirely from intervening in the market. Twice, in October 1998 and June 2001, it tried to reverse the depreciation trend of the krona by direct intervention. Obviously, even after abandoning the fixed exchange rate, Swedish policymakers continued to show less benign neglect toward fluctuations and misalignments than academic economists. Since these interventions evidently failed and have not been repeated since, it is also fair to conclude that they were rather symptoms of regime transition than essential elements of the Swedish monetary policy under a flexible exchange rate.

This chapter will address the experiences of Norway and Sweden in four steps. The first section discusses the causes of their regime shifts. The second and third sections deal with the transition to the new regimes. And the last section treats the market interventions of the *Riksbank* in October 1998 and June 2001.

THE EMS CRISIS IN 1992 AND THE END
OF THE ECU PEG

After a quiet period of more than five years, the EMS experienced a deep crisis in 1992–1993 that the Bank for Internationale Settlements (BIS) was to call "the most significant event in the international monetary system since the breakdown of the Bretton Woods arrangements" (BIS, 1993). Among the victims were – besides the currencies of the United Kingdom, Finland, Ireland, and the Southern European countries – the Norwegian krone and the Swedish krona (Table 8.1). Sweden abandoned the unilateral peg to the ECU on 19 November 1992; Norway took the same step on 10 December. Thus, once more, after exiting from the Snake in the late 1970s, both Scandinavian countries were forced to adopt an exchange-rate regime outside the monetary arrangement of the EC.

What were the reasons for this renewed exit? And were those reasons similar to those that caused Switzerland's regime shift in January 1973? In Chapter SEVEN I argued that three factors were crucial in the Swiss case: the high degree of financial openness, the undervaluation of the

Table 8.1. *Exchange-Rate Policies of Norway and Sweden (1990–2001)*

1990	
October 8	The pound sterling joins the EMS exchange-rate mechanism
October 19	**Norway unilaterally pegs krone to ecu (band width ±2.25%)**
1991	
May 17	**Sweden unilaterally pegs krone to ecu (band width ±1.5%)**
June 7	Finland unilaterally pegs markka to ecu (band width ±3%)
1992	
September 08	Finnish markka allowed to float
September 13	Italian lira devalued by 7%
September 16	Pound sterling and Italian lira "temporarily" leave EMS, Spanish peseta devalued by 5%
November 06	Finnish amendment to its Currency Act which legalizes float
November 19	**Swedish krone allowed to float**
November 22	Portuguese escudo and Spanish peseta devalued by 6%
December 10	**Norwegian krone allowed to float**
1993	
January 15	**Sweden adopts inflation targeting (target 2%, ±1%)**
January 30	Irish punt devalued by 10%
May 13	Portuguese escudo and Spanish peseta devalued by 6.5% and 8% respectively
Aug-02	EMS margins widened to ±15%
1994	
May 6	**Norway announces that "monetary policy to be conducted by Norges Bank shall be aimed at maintaining a stable krone exchange rate against European currencies"**
1996	
October 12	The Finnish markka joins the European exchange rate mechanism (ERM)
November 24	Italian lira reenters ERM
1999	
January 28	**Norges Bank de facto abandons exchange rate targeting**
2001	
March 29	**Norway adopts inflation targeting (target 2.5%, ±1%)**

Source: Moses (1995) and Gros and Thygesen (1998).

currency, and nonmembership in the EC.[2] The first two factors explain why the Swiss franc was vulnerable and came under attack, and the third factor explains why the Swiss National Bank was too weak to defend the fixed exchange rate of the franc. For had Switzerland been a member of the EC and thus participated in the Snake, the commitment to a fixed exchange rate would have been more credible, the *Bundesbank* and other European central banks would have come to the aid of the Swiss National Bank, and Switzerland could have revalued the franc in an orderly manner. Finally, all three factors together explain why Switzerland hesitated to enter the Snake in March 1973 when it was invited and was denied access in the autumn of 1975 when it wished to enter. In Chapter FIVE I also pointed out that during the 1970s, Switzerland was unique in that it combined open financial markets and nonmembership in the EC. All other small European states were either EC members or had tight capital controls.

The basic story was similar in Sweden and Norway. Financial markets had been liberalized in the course of the 1980s, which made both currencies potential targets for speculative attacks. And nonmembership in the EC made it difficult, if not impossible, to defend the exchange rate. The BIS wrote that in 1992 the daily turnover of foreign-exchange markets was roughly US$880 billion – a sum that easily surpassed the means of a central bank of a small country.[3] The comparison with Denmark is illustrative in this respect. The Danish krone came under enormous pressure, but thanks to interventions of the *Bundesbank* and other central banks, the krone could be defended at the current parity.[4]

Nonmembership in the EC also explains why it was difficult to return to a system of fixed exchange rates once the ECU link had been abandoned. As in Switzerland, the temporary shift became permanent as policymakers and the broader public realized that a flexible exchange rate was a viable long-term option. As a result, a majority of Swedish voters spoke out against adoption of the euro in September 2003, and in Norway, such a referendum has never been held, nor is it planned for the near future.[5] Finally, the claim that Switzerland was unique in that it combined financial openness with nonmembership in the EC also applied to Sweden and Norway in 1992. As noted, financial markets had been liberalized before the EMS crisis, and membership in the EC was only an explicit goal but was not yet

[2]   See also Chapter FIVE for the basic argument of why small EC states remained within the Snake during the 1970s, whereas large EC states were leaving.

[3]   BIS, Annual Report, 1993, p. 196.

[4]   Gros and Thygesen (1998, pp. 97–98).

[5]   For a comparative view, see the contributions in Miles (1996).

realized at the time of the attack. In sum, the regime shift of Sweden and Norway in 1992 was just as typical for small European states as the one by Switzerland 20 years earlier.

Yet, as far as the nature of the attacks are concerned, there were interesting differences between 1992 and 1973. The attack on the Swiss franc can be explained well by a so-called first-generation model highlighting the crucial role played by macroeconomic imbalances.[6] All speculators do is anticipate a change in the value of the currency that policymakers would be forced to make anyway at some point. The attack only forces them to take this step earlier than planned. In fact, in early 1973, selling dollars and buying francs was one of the surest bets in the history of postwar speculative attacks.

The attacks on the Swedish and Norwegian currencies, by contrast, were less conventional, as some economists have pointed out.[7] In particular Norway's macroeconomic fundamentals did not suggest that a devaluation was imminent. On the contrary, the economy had just begun to recover from the recession. Accordingly, there must have been a strong element of contagion.[8] And even in the case of Sweden, whose currency clearly was overvalued at the time of the attack, it would be wrong to exclude contagion altogether and to argue exclusively with a first-generation model. For, interestingly, when the Finnish markka was either devalued, as in November 1991, or forced to float, as in September 1992, speculators turned immediately against the Swedish krona, although Sweden's macroeconomic imbalances had been diminishing since 1990. Obviously, investors made no difference between Finland and Sweden.

Thus, certainly in the case of the Norwegian krone and to a lesser extent in the case of the Swedish krona the nature of the attacks resembled what economists have called the *second-generation model,* highlighting the self-fulfilling character of speculative attacks.[9] Even if macroeconomic fundamentals are in balance, speculators can find it attractive to attack a currency. By selling domestic assets at a high rate, they force policymakers to adopt more restrictive policies that may not be sustainable, in particular, during a recession. Speculators are also convinced that the authorities

---

[6] The seminal papers are Krugman (1979) and Flood and Garber (1994).

[7] Eichengreen and Wyplosz (1993).

[8] The systematic research on contagious currency crises has started only recently. See Eichengreen, Rose, and Wyplosz (1996), Glick and Rose (1998), and Kaminsky, Reinhart, and Vegh (2003).

[9] The seminal papers are Obstfeld (1986) and Obstfeld (1994). For a discussion of the new model, see Krugman (1996) and the comments by Obstfeld (1996), Eichengreen and Wyplosz (1993), and Gros and Thygesen (1998).

will relax their monetary policy once the devaluation has been made and thereby make the devaluation permanent.

In the remainder of this section I will try to give evidence to the claim that contagion played an important role. The next two sections will address the question how Sweden and Norway engineered their regime changes. As already indicated, the timing differed considerably from that of the Swiss in 1973. Switzerland let the currency float from January 1973 on and officially adopted monetary targeting two years later. Sweden shifted to inflation targeting only a few weeks after the krona had started to float. And Norway tried to avoid floating altogether for several years and shifted to inflation targeting only when exchange-rate targeting evidently had failed.

To understand the special nature of the 1992 attacks, it is necessary to review some macroeconomic indicators, as plotted in Table 8.2. It shows that Norway's macroeconomic fundamentals were pretty sound in 1992. It registered positive GDP growth, a positive current-account balance, a relatively small budget deficit, and a stable unemployment rate. Moreover, relative unit labor costs had been reduced since 1988, which was especially relevant for the strength of the ECU link. Sweden, by contrast, had a rather bad performance. In particular, relative unit labor costs increased until the early 1990s.[10] Comparative data on the banking crises that occurred in Finland, Norway, and Sweden during the early 1990s confirm this picture (Table 8.3): When the EMS crisis broke out in 1992, the Norwegian banking sector was already recovering, whereas profit losses of Finnish and Swedish banks peaked in that year.[11]

The main reason why Norway fared better was – once more – oil. It had at least two positive effects. First, increasing production in combination with rising prices from 1988 to 1990 stimulated the economy (Figure 8.1). In 1990, oil and gas extraction plus oil and gas-related services generated almost 50 percent of total export revenues.[12] According to Eika (1996), the Norwegian unemployment rate would have been at roughly 10 percent in 1993 instead of 6 percent.[13] The second positive effect was that the sharp drop in oil prices in 1986 and the ensuing recession cut the credit boom short – in Norway, the boom peaked in 1987–1988 and in Finland and

---

[10] Quarterly data show that Sweden's relative unit labor costs were highest in the last quarter of 1990. See Eichengreen and Wyplosz (1993, p. 70).

[11] For a comparative view of the depth of the northern banking crises, see Reinhart and Rogoff (2009).

[12] Statistics Norway, *Historical Statistics 1994*.

[13] Cited in Moses (2000, p. 163).

Table 8.2. *Crisis Indicators: Norway versus Sweden, Finland*

	1985	1986	1987	1988	1989	1990	1991	1992	1993	1994	1995
Real GDP (yearly growth rates)											
Norway	5.2	3.6	2	-0.1	0.9	2	3.1	**3.3**	2.7	5.5	3.8
Sweden	1.9	2.3	3.1	2.3	2.4	1.4	-1.1	**-1.4**	-2.2	3.3	3.9
Finland	3.3	2.4	4.1	4.9	5.7	0	-7.1	**-3.6**	-1.2	4.5	5.1
Current account balances as a percentage of GDP											
Norway	4.8	-6.2	-4.8	-4.1	-0.1	2.6	3.7	**3.5**	3	3	3.3
Sweden	-1	0	0	-0.3	-1.6	-2.6	-1.9	**-3**	-1.3	1.2	3.4
Finland	-1.5	-1	-1.9	-2.5	-5	-5.1	-5.4	**-4.7**	-1.3	1.1	4.1
Public-sector deficits as percentage of GDP: General government financial balances											
Norway	8.1	4.8	4	2.4	1.8	2.6	0.1	**-1.8**	-1.5	0.5	3.7
Sweden	-3.8	-1.2	4.2	3.5	5.4	4.2	-1.1	**-7.8**	-12.3	-10.3	-7.8
Finland	2.2	2.7	0.9	3.6	6	5.4	-1.5	**-5.9**	-8.4	-6.6	-5.7
Inflation (percentage change from previous period)											
Norway	5.7	7.2	8.7	6.7	4.6	4.1	3.4	**2.3**	2.3	1.4	2.5
Sweden	7.4	4.2	4.2	6.1	6.6	10.4	9.7	**2.6**	4.7	2.4	2.9
Finland	5.9	2.9	4.1	5.1	6.6	6.1	4.3	**2.9**	2.2	1.1	0.8
Relative unit labor costs in manufacturing, common currency (Index 1995 = 100)											
Norway	97	97	97	103	100	99	96	**95**	92	95	100
Sweden	130	130	129	136	142	145	151	**148**	107	102	100
Finland	142	135	132	136	141	148	144	**112**	86	88	100
Unemployment (percentage)											
Norway	2.6	2	2.1	3.2	4.9	5.2	5.5	**5.9**	6.0	5.4	4.9
Sweden	2.8	2.5	2.1	1.7	1.5	1.6	3	**5.3**	8.2	7.9	7.7
Finland	5	5.4	5.1	4.5	3.5	3.2	6.6	**11.7**	15.1	16.6	15.4

Source: Scharpf and Schmidt (2000a).

Sweden in 1990. Accordingly, the readjustment process of the Norwegian banking sector began and ended earlier than in Finland and Sweden.[14]

It is true that although the recovery had begun, the Norwegian economy still showed some weaknesses in 1992 when the krone was attacked. As

[14] Steigum (2004, pp. 69–70). For a comparative view of the Nordic banking crises, see Jonung, Söderström, and Stymne (1996), Drees and Pazarbasioglu (1998), and Sandal (2004). The most recent and most comprehensive study of the Norwegian banking crisis

Table 8.3. *Profit before Taxes of Banks (Percentage of Average Total Assets)*
in Finland, Norway, and Sweden

	1985	1986	1987	1988	1989	1990	1991	1992	1993	1994	1995
Finland											
Commercial banks	1.09	0.82	0.9	1.09	0.46	0.38	−0.73	−1.93	−1.76	−1.12	−0.55
Cooperative banks	0.75	0.67	0.73	0.96	0.6	0.78	0.76	0.03	−1.65	−1.17	−0.02
Savings banks	0.6	0.64	0.72	0.76	0.45	0.56	−0.41	−9.29	−4.94	−2.05	0.41
Norway											
Commercial banks	0.92	0.95	−0.04	−0.13	0.04	−1.17	−4.29	−1.25	0.58	1.21	2
Savings banks	0.86	0.94	0.63	−0.04	−0.3	−0.77	−1.21	0.04	2.03	1.28	1.87
Sweden											
Commercial banks	1.11	1.85	1.29	1.45	1.22	0.68	−0.5	−2.31	−1.22	0.98	1.33
Cooperative banks	1.1	1.56	1.21	1.47	1.57	1.06	−1.03	–	–	–	–
Savings banks	1.26	1.6	1.14	1.34	1.21	1.04	−1.79	−2.82	1.54	1.74	1.58

Source: Drees and Pazarbasioglu (1998, pp. 18–19).

noted earlier, the banking sector remained vulnerable despite successful rescue operations by the government. The mainland economy did not recover until the last quarter of 1992, and since the mainland sectors occupied the vast majority of Norwegian workers, the unemployment rate fell only after 1993. Yet it is still hard to make the case that the attack on the krone was fully justified by the state of the economy.[15] And interestingly, the markets seem to have been aware of the differences among the Nordic countries because they did not attack the Norwegian krone until July 1992.

is the volume edited by Moe, Solheim, and Vale (2004), in particular, the papers of Vale (2004), Steigum (2004), Schwierz (2004), and Wilse (2004). For a long-term view, see Knutsen and Ecklund (2000) and Gerdrup (2004), also in Moe, Solheim, and Vale (2004). On the Swedish banking crisis, see *Ekonomisk Debatt* (1998), Englund (1999), Englund and Vihriälä (2003), and Daltung (2004). For a long-term view, see Larsson (1995).

[15] Steigum (2004, p. 59): "It is quite possible that the basis for the attack was self-fulfilling expectations (Obstfeld, 1996)."

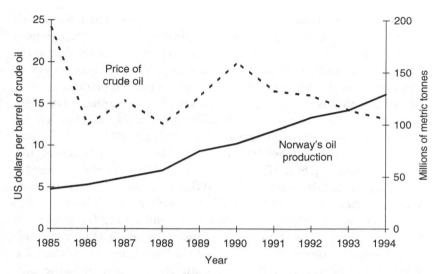

Figure 8.1. Price of crude oil and Norway's oil production. (*US Department of Energy and Norway statistics.*)

However, even in the case of Sweden, where the economy was in the midst of a recession in 1992, the data and the course of events suggest that macroeconomic imbalances don't explain the whole story. As noted earlier, two reasons suggest such an interpretation. First, as several scholars have argued, relative unit labor costs had been reduced since 1990.[16] Second, the attacks on the ECU peg of the Swedish currency *always* were preceded by attacks on the Finnish markka, although the crisis of the Finnish economy clearly was more serious than that of the Swedish economy. Finland's crisis, as measured by real GDP growth, was much deeper than Sweden's because of the collapse of trade with the Soviet Union.[17] Furthermore, the banking crisis was much more severe in Finland than in Sweden, especially because the Finnish savings banks registered losses equivalent to roughly 10 percent of total assets. Finally, Sweden's current account was not as negative as Finland's, although the devaluation of the markka had a direct negative

[16] Eichengreen and Wyplosz (1993, p. 69) and Hörngren and Lindberg (1994, p. 160). See also Rose and Svensson (1993), who find it difficult to find economically meaningful relationships between realignment expectations and macroeconomic variables. "There were few indications of poor ERM credibility before late August 1992; the dimensions of the currency crisis of September 1992 appear to have taken both policy-makers and private agents largely by surprise."

[17] In the mid-1980s, the Soviet Union had been Finland's most important trading partner. For Sweden, trade with the Soviet Union was negligible.

effect on Swedish trade because both countries competed against each other in certain sectors (e.g., timber and minerals).[18] Thus, although both countries were in a similar situation, it is hard to refute the thesis that the attacks on the Swedish krona also were due in part to contagionary effects stemming from the extreme vulnerability of the Finnish markka.

Of course, the discovery that contagionary effects were relevant does not come as a complete surprise given that Finland, Norway, and Sweden had pursued a similar exchange-rate policy since the early 1990s (see Table 8.1). Norway decided in October 1990 to replace the currency basket regime with a unilateral peg to the ECU. The band width remained unchanged at ±2.25 percent. The driving force behind this decision was the center-right Syse government, which hoped to facilitate greater EC participation and to enhance economic stability.[19] An important contributing factor was that the British government also had been considering an ECU link for some time. It took this step on 8 October, and the Norwegian government followed 11 days later. *Norges Bank,* by contrast, was opposed to the ECU link. Governor Herman Skånland explained that there was no good economic argument justifying this decision.[20]

Sweden and Finland followed a few months later. Sweden announced a unilateral peg to the ECU on 17 May 1991. The band width remained unchanged at ±1.5 percent. In the Swedish case, the driving force was the central bank.[21] The main rationale was to reduce inflation by strengthening the commitment to the fixed exchange rate. A clear signal to the markets and the social partners was necessary because the basket peg of the krona had increasingly lost credibility owing to a rising inflation-rate differential against Germany. The krona had been attacked twice, in February 1990 and in October 1990. *Riksbank* Governor Bengt Dennis was convinced that a stronger commitment was needed. The decision also was motivated by Sweden's decision in the autumn of 1990 to apply for EC membership. Monetary cooperation was seen as a first step toward the goal of full membership.[22]

---

[18] Sweden's exports to Finland amounted to roughly 4 percent in the early 1990s.

[19] Jan P. Syse's minority government ruled from 16 October 1989 to 3 November 1990. It consisted of the Conservative Party, the Christian Democratic Party, and the Centre Party. It was followed by the minority Labor government under Prime Minister Gro Harlem Brundtland's third government, ruling from 3 November 1990 to 25 October 1996.

[20] Moses (1995, pp. 361–372). Citation of Skånland on p. 367.

[21] In contrast to Norway, the Swedish *Riksbank* is exclusively responsible for conducting the exchange-rate policy and choosing the exchange-rate system.

[22] For the rationale of the *Riksbank,* see Hörngren and Lindberg (1994, pp. 133–164). For the decision-making process and the role of Governor Bengt Dennis, see Moses (1995, pp. 372–382) and Lindvall (2004, pp. 127–128).

Finland pegged the markka to the ECU on 7 June 1991, motivated by the same reasons and also against the background of increased market pressure.[23] For a moment, the trend toward fixed exchange rates looked unstoppable.

The first attack on the ECU peg of the krona in which there were elements of contagion took place in November 1991.[24] On 15 November, the Finnish markka had been devalued by 12.3 percent, and immediately, the Swedish krona came under heavy pressure. The *Riksbank* increased the overnight lending rate by 1 percent on 26 November, but this step did not stop capital outflows. On 6 December, the *Riksbank* raised the overnight lending rate by 6 percent to a record high of 17.5 percent, and this time the markets were impressed. Capital outflows ceased, and the *Riksbank* was able to reduce interest rates. Yet, after four months of relative calm, another attack took place at the beginning of April 1992 that, according to the BIS, was again a spillover of an attack against the markka.[25] The *Riksbank* sold foreign currency equivalent to 22 billion kronor (US$4 billion) during a single day and raised the overnight lending rate by 2 percent. Again, the defense was successful. Interest-rate differentials against Germany decreased, and capital flowed in.

When a further wave of attacks was triggered by the Danish rejection of the Maastricht Treaty in June 1992, markets aimed not only at the Swedish krona but also, for the first time, at the Norwegian krone. In the first half of July, the *Norges Bank* had to intervene heavily in support of its currency.[26] Obviously, contagion had spread from Sweden to Norway, and from the July crisis onward, markets always would attack both currencies. In late August, the next crisis broke out. Following the weakening of the Italian lira and the British pound, the Finnish markka and the Swedish krona were attacked again. Official interest rates were raised in Finland and Sweden. On 8 September, after the breakdown of a previously negotiated wage agreement, the Finnish government was forced to float the markka, and "the Swedish and Norwegian currencies also promptly came under pressure again," as the BIS wrote.[27] On 9 September, the *Riksbank* raised

---

[23] BIS, Annual Report, 1992, p. 153: Although markets expected a devaluation, Finland pegged the markka at the current parity (band width ± 3 percent) on 7 June 1992.

[24] Hörngren and Lindberg (1994, p. 151) conclude with respect to the attack in November 1991: "A priori, there seemed little reason for investors to draw parallels to Sweden as the differences between the Swedish and the Finnish economies were quite striking."

[25] According to the BIS, Annual Report, 1992, p. 153. Hörngren and Lindberg (1994, p. 152) conclude that it was "due to a shift in market sentiment of unclear origin."

[26] *Norges Bank*, Annual Report, 1992, p. 5.

[27] BIS, Annual Report, 1993, p. 186.

the overnight lending rate to 75 percent, and it was announced that Sweden would borrow roughly 15 billion ECUs (roughly US$20 billion) and would be prepared to borrow another 16 billion ECUs if necessary. The *Norges Bank* raised the overnight lending rate as well, but only by 1 percent to 11 percent, and also raised the sight-deposit rate from 9 to 11 percent.[28]

Owing to further attacks, the United Kingdom and Italy decided on 16 September 1992, on "Black Wednesday," to suspend further intervention in the foreign-exchange market.[29] The *Riksbank* increased the overnight lending rate to 500 percent, and the *Norges Bank* intervened heavily in the market and introduced a penalty rate of 40 percent above the overnight lending rate.[30] The *Riksbank* kept the rate at 500 percent for four days. The measure had the desired effect: Capital outflows stopped. Furthermore, the *Riksdag* passed a tough package of fiscal measures on 20 September. The *Riksbank* was able to lower the rate to 50 percent and in the following week to 40 percent. Since the markets remained unstable, the government and the opposition presented a second proposal that was supposed to improve the competitiveness of Swedish industry by cutting payroll taxes. The markets were convinced by these prompt measures, and the *Riksbank* could lower the overnight lending rate to 11.5 percent, corresponding to the level prior to the crisis.

As for the last round of attacks starting in mid-November, we can again observe how the weakness of the Swedish krona spilled over to Norway. The reason for the renewed weakness of the krona was the failure of the Swedish government to pass another fiscal austerity package.[31] The *Riksbank* first tried to stem capital outflows with sterilized intervention and, when this measure proved too weak, with higher interest rates. On 19 November, Swedish authorities threw in the towel and let the krona float. During the six days until this decision, capital outflow had amounted to US$26 billion, corresponding to roughly 11 percent of Sweden's GDP. Immediately, the Norwegian krone was attacked, as the *Norges Bank* wrote in its Annual Report: "When it was announced at 2.30 p.m. on 19 November that the Swedish krone would be allowed to float, this had an immediate impact on the Norwegian foreign exchange market."[32] Within

---

[28] *Norges Bank,* Annual Report, 1992, p. 6.
[29] For a detailed analysis of the exit of the British pound and the Italian lira, see Talani (2000).
[30] For the Swedish case, see the book *500 Percent* by *Riksbank* Governor Bengt Dennis (1998), as well as the inside report by Hamilton and Stuart (2003), in particular the useful chronology on p. 171. *Norges Bank,* Annual Report, 1992, pp. 6–7.
[31] BIS, Annual Report, 1993, pp. 188–189.
[32] *Norges Bank,* Annual Report, 1992, p. 7.

one hour, the central bank sold foreign exchange equivalent to more than US$2 billion. In the following days, the overnight lending rate was raised several times to the maximum level of 25 percent on 23 November, and the central bank intervened massively. Yet, following another attack on the krone and another series of interventions, the Norwegian authorities decided to follow Sweden, after yet another wave of large interventions in the foreign-exchange market, but without increasing interest rates. On 10 December, it was announced that the unilateral peg to the ECU was abandoned and that the krone was allowed to float.

In sum, Sweden's and Norway's regime changes were less predetermined than the Swiss change. The Norwegian krone was almost entirely a victim of contagion because there were only minor macroeconomic imbalances at the time of the attacks. And even in the case of the Swedish krona, which clearly was overvalued in 1991–1992, it is impossible to exclude contagion as a relevant factor altogether. The Swiss franc, by contrast, had been hugely undervalued for some time, so the attack in 1973 was fully justified by macroeconomic imbalances, whereas self-fulfilling expectations hardly played any role. All three regime shifts, however, resembled each other in that they occurred against the will of policymakers. They tried hard to defend the fixed exchange rate, but owing to the combination of financial openness and nonmembership in the EC, the defense was too weak. The unintended shift to a flexible exchange rate therefore was a big adventure. The next two sections take a look at how Sweden and Norway managed to cope with the new situation.

SWEDEN'S SHIFT TO INFLATION TARGETING

When Sweden and Norway were forced to abandon the peg to the ECU in late 1992, both countries were faced with the same problem. On the one hand, policymakers knew that there was no easy way back to a fixed exchange rate for the time being. On the other hand, they had no experience of how to manage a floating exchange rate. Interestingly, though confronted with the same problem, Sweden and Norway chose different approaches. Sweden swiftly adopted inflation targeting. On 15 January, 1993, the monetary authorities announced that, starting in 1995, the *Riksbank* would target an annual inflation rate (consumer price index) of 2 percent, with a margin of ±1 percent.

Norway, by contrast, tried to continue with some sort of exchange-rate targeting, first unofficially and then, in connection with the Revised National Budget for 1994, officially. The authorities explained that "the monetary policy to be conducted by *Norges Bank* shall be aimed at maintaining a stable krone exchange rate against European currencies, based on the range of the exchange rate maintained since the krone was floated on 10 December 1992."[33] Yet, eventually, Norway also adopted inflation targeting, de facto in early 1999 and *de jure* in March 2001. The inflation target was set slightly higher than Sweden's at 2.5 percent, with a margin of ±1 percent.[34]

How can we explain these different choices? Economically as well as in terms of foreign policy, both countries could have adopted floating at the same time. Sweden and Norway were not yet members of the European Union (EU), they were less open than the Benelux countries, and their trade structures by regions were more diversified than, for example, Austria's.[35] Norway with its oil business should have been even more interested in floating than Sweden. Finally, there was more "Euroskepticism" in Norway than in Sweden: On 13 November 1994, Sweden voted in favor of joining the EU; Norway rejected membership on 28 November.

Narrative evidence suggests that the depth of the economic and financial crisis determined the choices of policymakers. As for Sweden, we have seen that the recession was particularly severe. Real GDP growth was negative, the banking sector was near collapse, and fiscal deficits had risen dramatically. Accordingly, the Swedish authorities saw no possibility but to let the krona float. *Riksbank* Governor Dennis writes that "there was a consensus in the public debates" that a floating krona was "the only alternative."[36] Norway's policymakers, by contrast, believed that the relatively good condition of the economy allowed them to continue with exchange-rate targeting. This section looks more closely at the Swedish case, and the next section explores Norway's protracted path to inflation targeting.

---

[33] *Norges Bank,* Annual Report, 1994, p. 10: "The new regulation replaces Regulation no. 6 of 8 January 1993, and primarily contains a more precise formulation of what has been practised since 10 December 1992 (cf. Circular no. 5 of 6 May 1994)."

[34] I follow the interpretation by Steigum (2004, p. 26, footnote 6): "On March 29, 2001, *Norges Bank* received a new set of guidelines for monetary policy, involving an operational inflation target of 2.5 percent, but already in January 1999, *Norges Bank* began to set its interest rates in accordance with an inflation-targeting framework for monetary policy."

[35] For a more thorough discussion of the Nordic countries regarding openness, commodity concentration of exports, external shocks, and international correlation of output growth, see Gerlach (1997, pp. 244–251).

[36] Dennis (2003, p. 175): "*På sikt kunde återgang till fast kurs prövas men som läget såg ut den 19 november var flytande krona enda alternativet. Om det rådde enighet in den offentliga debatten.*"

Initially, Swedish officials were convinced that floating was only a temporary solution – just like the Swiss authorities 20 years earlier. When the krona started to float, politicians of both parties publicly stated that the European option continued to be the goal of Swedish monetary policy.[37] On 20 November, Prime Minister Carl Bildt told the *Financial Times* that "you cannot run an economy with a floating exchange rate." And Ingvar Carlsson, leader of the Social Democratic opposition, supported this statement by emphasizing that Sweden was different from Canada and New Zealand, two countries with a flexible exchange rate.[38]

Even when the Swedish authorities declared on 15 January 1993 that inflation targeting was the new monetary policy framework, there was still a general feeling that this regime shift was not supposed to be permanent. Only two weeks later, on 1 February 1993, Sweden started negotiations for accession to the EU, and the Bildt government explained its clear intention to become part of the European Monetary Union (EMU). According to Minister for Foreign Affairs Ulf Dinkelspiel, the only reservation the Swedish government had was that the decision about participation in the EMU would be taken at a later date – "in the light of future developments and in accordance with the provisions of the Treaty."[39] The goal of returning to a fixed exchange rate in due time also was repeated in the revised budget plan of April 1993.[40]

With the benefit of hindsight, we know that all these plans were premature. It turned out that the economic constraints proved to be too strong to allow a quick return to the old regime.[41] Swedish policymakers had no choice but to let the krona float, and they were forced to act rapidly in order to reassure markets that the inflationary pressure resulting from the fall of the krona would not remain unchecked. In addition, the *Riksbank* still was regarded as an institution with limited independence and credibility. And finally, the rising budget deficits and the banking crisis nurtured fears that the government could be tempted to resort to an overly expansionary monetary policy. In this respect, the *Riksbank* found itself in a more difficult situation than the Swiss central bank 20 years earlier. As noted, the Swiss National Bank had been an institution with a strong

---

[37] *Prop. 2000/01:100 Bilaga 5: Finans- och penningpolitiskt bokslut för 1990-talet*, p. 21.

[38] Citations in Dennis (2003, p. 174).

[39] *Regeringens proposition 1994/95:19: Sveriges medlemskap i Europeiska unionen (den 11 augusti 1994), Bilaga 1: Anförande av Europa- och utrikeshandelsminister Ulf Dinkelspiel vid öppnandet av Sveriges förhandlingar om EG-medlemskap den 1 februari 1993.*

[40] Dennis (2003, p. 174).

[41] *Propositionen 2000/01:100 Bilaga 5: Finans- och penningpolitiskt bokslut för 1990-talet*, p. 21.

anti-inflationary reputation. The fact that there was no fear of inflation had allowed the Swiss National Bank to wait and see until it communicated its new monetary framework in late 1974. Markets had attacked the franc because they knew that the franc was undervalued and would appreciate once it floated.

The *Riksbank* needed 10 days to prepare the regime change. On 19 November, the krona began to float, and on 1 December, the *Riksbank* sent a memorandum to the ministry of finance that included all important elements of the future monetary framework, and called for further budget consolidation that had begun in September 1992.[42]

How did the *Riksbank* proceed? Thanks to several personal records of key figures, we have a clear picture of the decision-making process.[43] The first step was to gather all information that was already available inside and outside the *Riksbank*.[44] For this reason, on Friday, 20 November, Governor Bengt Dennis urged that the *Riksbank* should convene a conference within two weeks and publish a volume on monetary policy under a flexible exchange-rate regime.[45] By this move, he hoped to accelerate the internal as well as the public discussion. The project was successful, and the volume appeared on 15 December.[46] The collection of articles included a piece about the experiences of New Zealand and Canada, which had pursued inflation targeting since 1990 and 1991, respectively.[47] The United Kingdom, by contrast, which had adopted inflation targeting in early October 1992, did not appear in any of the articles. And monetary targeting as practiced by Switzerland was seen as a framework involving too many problems: "In a world consisting of deregulated and well-developed financial markets, it is becoming increasingly difficult to direct monetary policy solely on the basis of growth in money supply as the intermediate goal."[48]

Parallel to the internal and public discussions, the *Riksbank* made direct contact with the Bank of Canada, whose monetary policy became the

---

[42] The memorandum is published in the appendix to Andersson (2003, pp. 271–276). This passage is on pp. 275–276.

[43] In November 2002, exactly 10 years after the fall of the krona, the major players met for a conference in Stockholm. Their contributions are published in Jonung (2003).

[44] Svensson (1995, p. 69) says that there was no contingency plan.

[45] Andersson (2003, pp. 247–250).

[46] *Sveriges Riksbank* (1992), "Monetary Policy with a Flexible Exchange Rate" (special edition of the Quarterly Review of the *Riksbank*).

[47] See Bernanke et al. (1999) for a brief review of inflation targeting in New Zealand and Canada.

[48] *Sveriges Riksbank* (1992, p. 53).

preferred model, possibly also for personal reasons: Krister Andersson, the chief economist of the *Riksbank*, had been familiar with Canadian monetary policy because he had worked at the International Monetary Fund (IMF) from 1987 to 1991. On Monday, 23 November, Andersson asked the Bank of Canada to send a delegation, and the bank responded immediately by sending a group of economists to Stockholm.[49] There were, of course, relevant differences between Sweden's and Canada's economies, especially with respect to the labor market. But the Canadian economists could teach the *Riksbank* economists how to interpret economic indicators under a regime of floating exchange rates. The IMF also sent a team to Stockholm shortly after 19 November to discuss the new situation with the *Riksbank*.[50]

The ministry of finance received the memorandum on 1 December. Now it was up to the *Riksbank* to convince the government. Initially, there was some resistance. On 11 December, *Riksbank* officials met with Finance Minister Anne Wibble, the daughter of Bertil Ohlin, to discuss the level of the inflation target and the phasing in of the new regime. Wibble was against a concrete price target, but the *Riksbank* prevailed: The inflation target was set at 2 percent (with a band of ±1 percent) to be realized from 1995 on.[51] The public accepted the new regime as a temporary solution without any major reservations. The only issue that encouraged opposition from politicians and economists alike was the high level of the interest rate.[52] The debate calmed down, however, because the *Riksbank* gradually lowered the key rate until the summer of 1994.

As in the Swiss case, it is hard to say when the temporary regime shift became a definite one. There seems to be a rule that once a regime change has taken place, it cannot be reversed unless another economic crisis forces policymakers to change course. Formally, Sweden's regime change had been temporary until the referendum in September 2003, when a clear majority voted against joining the EMU, thus giving strong endorsement to an independent monetary policy. However, it is more realistic to say that the defeat of the center-right government under Prime Minister Carl Bildt in the elections of September 1994 and the

[49] Dennis (2003, p. 173), Andersson (2003, pp. 241–242).

[50] Andersson (2003, pp. 242–243). The IMF again sent a team at the end of January: See International Monetary Fund, "Technical Assistance Mission to *Sveriges Riksbank*, January 25–29, 1993," Aide memoire.

[51] On the ambiguity of the declaration on 15 January 1993, see Bernanke et al. (1999, pp. 182–189).

[52] Dennis (2003, pp. 178–181 and 209–214).

close outcome of the EC referendum in November 1994 (52.3 percent yes) marked two important turning points.[53]

Another turning point was the successful consolidation of public finances by the Social Democratic Finance Minister Göran Persson. It contradicted the idea that Sweden would find the way back to sound economic policies only by joining the EMU. It thus was not surprising that the Social Democratic government decided in the spring of 1997 to remain outside the EMU at least until 2002. A final important milestone on the road to the definite adoption of inflation targeting was the passing of the *Riksbank* Act in November 1998. It made the Swedish central bank independent and facilitated the conduct of monetary policy. Thus, when Prime Minister Göran Persson announced in late 2002 that a referendum would be held in the following year, there was little enthusiasm among Swedish voters.[54] On 14 September 2003, 56 percent said no, and 42 percent said yes. Obviously, the regime shift of 1993 had been successful.

In conclusion, owing to the severe economic crisis, Sweden was forced to make a temporary regime change that has become permanent over the years – as in Switzerland during the 1970s. In January 1993, only a few weeks after abandoning the ECU peg, it shifted to inflation targeting and gradually optimized the new regime. Norway, by contrast, took another course. After abandoning the ECU peg, it continued to target the exchange rate. Eventually, though, it ended up with the same regime as Sweden, namely, inflation targeting. The next section explores Norway's choice and experience since December 1992.

NORWAY'S LONG ROAD TO INFLATION TARGETING

At 11 p.m. on 10 December 1992, the Norwegian ministry of finance suspended the central bank's obligation to buy and sell kroner and thereby abandoned the link to the ECU. The content of the statement was very similar to the one made by Swedish officials three weeks earlier. On 11 December, the ministry of finance explained to the Norwegian parliament: "In the period ahead, *Norges Bank* shall first aim at recovering a share of the foreign currency that flowed out of the country. Second, *Norges Bank* shall orient monetary policy with a view to establishing a new fixed exchange rate for the

---

[53] Bildt (2003, p. 86). As for the referendum on EU membership, 52.3 percent voted in favor, 46.8 percent voted against, and 0.9 percent registered blank votes. Turnout rate was high: 83 percent.

[54] *Economist*, 5 December 2002: "Sweden and the euro: Persson goes for a referendum."

krone as soon as international conditions permit."[55] Clearly, the suspension of the ECU link was seen as a temporary measure, just as in Sweden.

Apart from this similar content of the first statement, though, Norway chose a path that was very different from Sweden's. While the Swedish *Riksbank* adopted a new monetary policy framework in January 1993, the Norwegian authorities refused to make an official change and indicated that they wanted to keep the exchange rate as stable as possible. In the Revised National Budget for 1993, the government repeated its wish to return to a fixed-exchange-rate regime when international conditions would allow and that, for the time being, monetary policy would "be geared towards attaining stable conditions in the Norwegian foreign exchange market."[56]

It wasn't until May 1994 that the public got a better idea of what kind of monetary policy *Norges Bank* was pursuing exactly.[57] The Exchange Rate Regulation Act of 6 May 1994 stated that "the monetary policy to be conducted by *Norges Bank* shall be aimed at maintaining a stable krone exchange rate against European currencies, based on the range of the exchange rate maintained since the krone was floated on 10 December 1992." It also included an escape clause: "In the event of significant changes in the exchange rate, monetary policy instruments will be oriented with a view to returning the exchange rate over time to its initial range. No fluctuation margins are established, nor is there an appurtenant obligation on *Norges Bank* to intervene in the foreign exchange market."[58]

The plan to maintain a stable krone against European currencies did not last for a long time, however. In early 1999, the *Norges Bank* de facto adopted inflation targeting by disregarding the exchange rate when setting the interest rate. And on 29 March 2001, it was announced that from then on inflation targeting was the monetary policy framework of the *Norges Bank*. The inflation target (consumer price index) was set at 2.5 percent with a band width of ±1 percent.

Given that it is very hard for a small country heavily dependent on oil to maintain a stable exchange rate, it is not surprising that Norway was forced to adopt inflation targeting after a few years. The real surprise is why it took so long until policymakers realized that a flexible exchange rate was the only viable option. Why were the Norwegian authorities reluctant to take the same step as Sweden in early 1993? As noted in Chapter FIVE, the main reason was that policymakers of small

---

[55] *Norges Bank,* Annual Report, 1993, p. 5.
[56] *Ibid.*
[57] Nicolaisen and Qvigstad (1997, p. 102), Moses (2000, p. 186).
[58] *Norges Bank,* Annual Report, 1994, p. 10.

European states feared floating and therefore tried to maintain some sort of exchange-rate targeting as long as circumstances allowed. Since the Norwegian economy was in relatively good shape at the time of the EMS crisis – in contrast to the Swedish economy – policymakers were not forced to break with the past. Revenues from the oil sector had been rising since 1989, the peak of the banking crisis had been reached in 1991, and even the mainland economy had begun to recover in the last quarter of 1992.[59] Accordingly, the Norwegian government wanted to maintain as much continuity as possible.

The wish to save the old regime in the new environment also was motivated by an economic strategy called the "solidarity alternative" that had been developed in 1991. With this strategy, the authorities tried to preserve the competitiveness of the nonoil economy and to help smooth income and employment during and after the period of maximum oil exports. An important role was assigned to labor unions: They agreed to moderate wage increases in return for the government's commitment to orient monetary policy toward stabilizing the exchange rate and inflation. The role of fiscal policy was to regulate demand and to insulate the nonoil economy from developments in the oil sector by reinvesting a substantial part of the government's oil revenues abroad.[60] *Norges Bank* Governor Kjell Storvik explained the model in the following words:

In recent years economic policy in Norway has been based on three main pillars: Fiscal policy is oriented towards long-term balance in government finances, and it also bears the main responsibility for stabilizing the economy. Monetary policy is geared towards stabilizing the krone exchange rate, and thereby contributes to providing an anchor for income settlements and domestic price inflation. Incomes policy cooperation, which was formulated in the so-called 'Solidarity Alternative,' is responsible for maintaining the business sector's cost competitiveness through moderate wage growth.[61]

Because of the important role the exchange-rate policy played in this strategy, it is inaccurate to classify Norway's regime after 1992 as a managed float, as some scholars have suggested.[62] It is true that there was no

---

[59] Reinhart and Rogoff (2002, p. 89): "December 1992 does not register as a currency crash."

[60] Moses (2000, pp. 164–169).

[61] Annual address 1997 by Governor Kjell Storvik, Meeting of the Supervisory Council of *Norges Bank,* 6 February 1997.

[62] Qvigstad (2001, p. 17), Reinhart and Rogoff (2002, p. 89). *Norges Bank Watch of 2002* (published in September 2002), p. 29, also classifies Norway's exchange-rate regime after 1992 as managed floating. For a more accurate view, see Murray (1997, p. 134).

explicit target band that would have qualified the Norwegian regime as managed floating, but Norwegian politicians wanted anything but a floating exchange rate. The *Norges Bank* was assigned to keep the exchange rate as stable as possible, in sharp contrast to the Swedish *Riksbank*, which intervened only in what it considered to be emergencies.[63] Norway adopted managed floating only after its peculiar system of exchange-rate targeting failed.

Not surprisingly, the *Norges Bank* had been aware of the problems of the Exchange Rate Regulation of 1994 from the beginning. In a letter to the ministry of finance written two weeks before the regulation was passed, the bank made it clear that "if the economy is affected by serious disturbances or long-term and wide cyclical fluctuations, the intermediate exchange rate target ought to be adapted to the long-term objective of monetary policy."[64] This was a polite way to tell the government that this kind of flexible exchange-rate targeting would run into serious problems and that it would be better if the *Norges Bank* had the primary task of maintaining price stability, not exchange-rate stability. In retrospect, former *Norges Bank* Governor Hermod Skånland observed that "the system of 'flexible stability' of the exchange rate produces more flexibility than stability."[65]

The inconsistency of the Norwegian regime became visible when the krone started to experience large swings from 1996 onward, mainly owing to fluctuations in the oil price. Politicians gradually realized that they needed to make a choice between floating and a hard peg. The latter option was unrealistic because Norwegian voters had narrowly rejected joining the EU in November 1994 (52 percent no, 48 percent yes). Consequently, it was only a matter of time until exchange-rate targeting was abandoned altogether.

Figure 8.2 plots the oil price and exchange rate of the krone. We can distinguish two cycles. The first boom-and-bust cycle lasted three years from the spring of 1996 to December 1998. The oil price increased from US$13.68 to US$21.76 and then fell to US$8.03. While the reasons for

---

[63] Accordingly, Levy-Yeyati and Sturzenegger (2005) classify Norway as "Fix" and Sweden as a mixture of "Float, Intermediate, and Fix." More on Sweden's floating in the following section.

[64] Cited in *St prp nr 1 Tillegg nr 3, For Budsjetterminen 1998 (1997–1998), Om endring av St prp nr 1 om statsbudsjettet medregnet folketrygden 1998 Tilråding fra Finans- og tolldepartementet av 6. november 1997, godkjent i statsråd samme dag. Vedlegg 4: Brev fra norges bank til finansdepartementet 3. november 1997: Det økonomiske opplegget for 1998: 1.2.4 Penge- og valutapolitikken.*

[65] Skånland (1999, pp. 3–4).

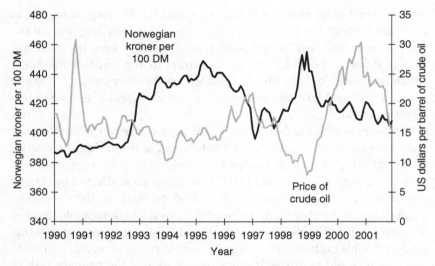

Figure 8.2. DM rate of Norwegian krone and price of crude oil. (*Norges Bank and US Department of Energy.*)

the strong surge in oil prices are somewhat unclear, the sharp fall can be explained well by the financial crisis starting in Asia in the summer of 1997 and spreading to Russia and Latin America in 1998. As a result of these swings in the oil price, the Norwegian krone first appreciated by 10 percent and then fell back to the level prior to the appreciation.

The second boom-and-bust cycle also lasted three years, extending from the end of 1998 until the end of 2001. The appreciation phase was even more dramatic than in 1996. The price almost quadrupled from US$8.03 (December 1998) to US$30.36 (November 2000). The appreciation of the krone that occurred in synchronization with the oil price rise was less pronounced than during the previous cycle, but it was still considerable: The exchange rate rose from about 450 to about 410 kroner per 100 DM, corresponding to an appreciation of almost 10 percent. And in contrast to the oil price, the krone continued to appreciate in 2001, although at a lower pace than in the previous two years.

As it became clear in the course of 1996 that exchange-rate stability was impossible to achieve, the *Norges Bank* began to hint at alternative exchange-rate regimes. In the traditional letter to the ministry of finance, written in autumn and containing the prospects of the economy in the following year, the bank explained that it could do little to maintain price stability because it was bound to lower interest rates in order to counteract appreciation of the krone. The bank also pointed out that fiscal and income policies were supposed to serve the function of dampening demand but obviously were unable to fulfill their task. In conclusion, the *Norges Bank* announced that it might reconsider the current monetary policy framework if the situation continued to worsen.[66]

The situation did worsen. On 10 January 1997, the *Norges Bank* decided to temporarily suspend intervention in the foreign-exchange markets. The pressure had become too strong. In 1996, the bank had made interventions equivalent to US$14 billion, and in the few days prior to 10 January, interventions amounted to US$4.7 billion. The *Norges Bank* took the decision on the basis of the escape clause of the Foreign Exchange Regulation. In the annual address, given in February 1997, Governor Kjell Storvik pointed out that the current regime was inconsistent: "There is little *Norges Bank* can do to address the latter problem [overheating of the Norwegian economy] as long as monetary policy is geared towards maintaining a stable exchange rate." And cautiously, he added: "An alternative approach could be to strike a balance between the aim of exchange rate stability and cyclical stability when formulating monetary policy. The aim would be to prevent monetary policy from amplifying cyclical fluctuations, so that the real economy and employment would be less prone to interest-rate shocks."[67] In a letter to the ministry of finance in the autumn of 1997, the *Norges Bank* repeated its concerns. It also explicitly mentioned inflation targeting as a possible alternative to the present regime.[68]

However, in its responses, the government rejected the proposal of the *Norges Bank,* and prevailed. Possibly, the lack of central bank independence was the main reason why Norway hesitated to adopt inflation targeting. As the preceding section has shown, the *Riksbank* was solely responsible for the choice of the exchange-rate regime. It only asked for the consent of the ministry of finance and the government in order to gain as much legitimacy as possible. Another, perhaps more plausible reason for the reluctance of the Norwegian government to change the exchange-rate regime

---

[66] *Brev til Finansdepartementet 22. november 1996;* cited in St prp nr 1 Tillegg nr 7 (1996–97) for Budsjetterminen 1997: Saldering av statsbudsjettet medregnet folketrygden 1997: Tilråding fra Finans- og tolldepartementet av 29. november 1996, godkjent i statsråd samme dag.

[67] Annual address 1997 by Governor Kjell Storvik, Meeting of the Supervisory Council of Norges Bank, 6 February 1997, pp. 3 and 12–13.

[68] St prp nr 1 Tillegg nr 3 for Budsjetterminen 1998 (1997–98): Om endring av St prp nr 1 om statsbudsjettet medregnet folketrygden 1998. Tilråding fra Finans- og tolldepartementet av 6. november 1997, godkjent i statsråd samme dag. Vedlegg 4: Brev fra norges bank til finansdepartementet 3. november 1997: Det økonomiske opplegget for 1998.

may have been that it was not forced to take this step. And finally, the government also was directly accountable for the functioning of the "solidarity alternative," so changing the exchange-rate regime meant abandoning the whole economic policy framework.[69]

In any case, the Swedish example has shown that regime change occurs only when the traditional regime is in deep crisis. In Norway, this was not the case yet. In November 1996, the government responded that a stable exchange rate was one of the main pillars of Norwegian economic policy. A regime change would hamper the competitiveness of the exporting sector and complicate wage bargaining.[70] One year later, the answer was essentially the same, although the situation had not improved.[71] The *Norges Bank* grew impatient in the face of the immobility of the government. In the annual address in February 1998, Governor Kjell Storvik reacted publicly to the answer of the Norwegian government: "This audience is probably aware that our political authorities and *Norges Bank* have somewhat different views on the question of how monetary policy should be oriented in the present situation. *Norges Bank* has not changed its view since last autumn, when the bank presented its assessment in a submission to the Ministry of Finance." However, in order to prevent an open conflict, the governor avoided further comments on the topic.[72]

In the letters to the ministry of finance in the spring and autumn of 1998, the *Norges Bank* once more insisted on adjusting the monetary policy framework.[73] The bank's call for a change was fully justified because Norway's economy continued its rollercoaster ride, but this time on a downward slope. In early 1997, the oil price had begun to decline, and with the outbreak of the Asian crisis in the second quarter of the year, this trend was reinforced: From the beginning of 1997 to the end of 1998, the price came down from US$21.76 to US$8.03 per barrel crude oil (see Figure 8.2). And because the *Norges Bank* had been forced to counteract the appreciation trend in 1997 by lowering interest rates, the krone depreciated rapidly.

[69] Nicolaisen and Qvigstad (1997, p. 128) make a similar argument.

[70] St prp nr 1 Tillegg nr 7 (1996–97): For Budsjetterminen 1997: Saldering av statsbudsjettet medregnet folketrygden 1997: Tilråding fra Finans- og tolldepartementet av 29. november 1996, godkjent i statsråd samme dag.

[71] St prp nr 1 Tillegg nr 3: For Budsjetterminen 1998 (1997–98): Om endring av St prp nr 1 om statsbudsjettet medregnet folketrygden 1998: Tilråding fra Finans- og tolldepartementet av 6. november 1997, godkjent i statsråd samme dag.

[72] Annual address by Governor Kjell Storvik, Meeting of the Supervisory Council of *Norges Bank*, 19 February 1998.

[73] Brev fra Norges Bank til Finansdepartementet 24. april 1998; Brev fra Norges Bank til Finansdepartementet 21 october 1998 (Det økonomiske opplegget for 1999).

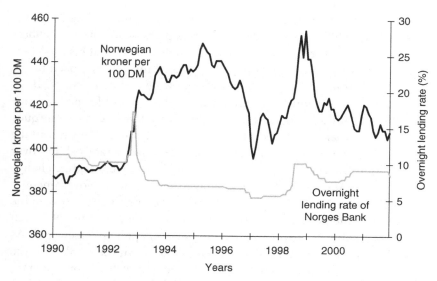

Figure 8.3. DM rate of Norwegian krone and key interest rate of *Norges Bank*. (*Norges Bank and US Department of Energy.*)

Once again, the *Norges Bank* was forced to pursue a pro-cyclic monetary policy to stabilize the exchange rate by increasing interest rates in the midst of a downturn. From early 1998 to summer 1998, the overnight lending rate was raised from 5.5 to 10 percent. (see Figure 8.3)

Given these experiences, the *Norges Bank* was running out of patience and began to search for ways to circumvent the current regime. It found a solution that was realized with the advent of new Governor Svein Gjedrem in January 1999. From then on, the governor began to apply a more flexible interpretation of the Exchange Rate Regulation of 1994 by invoking the escape clause more actively, and more important, he stretched the time period over which exchange-rate stability was supposed to be maintained. Thanks to this reinterpretation, the bank felt free to target inflation. At the first press conference during the first week of January, Gjedrem already hinted at the possibility of lowering interest rates despite a general weakness of the krone.[74]

A few weeks later, the *Norges Bank* did what its governor had hinted at. On 28 January 1999, the key rate (sight-deposit rate) was lowered by 0.5 percent to 7.5 percent, although the exchange rate had not yet recovered from the

---

[74] *Financial Times*, 8 January 1999.

deep fall in 1998.[75] On the same day, Governor Gjedrem presented the new approach in a public speech.[76] To avoid the impression that he was deliberately confronting the government, Gjedrem pointed out that his predecessor had advocated the same policy. He repeated the new approach in the annual address in February 1999. The crucial sentences were: "*Norges Bank* shall orient its instruments towards maintaining a stable krone exchange rate. We must not allow ourselves to be blinded by daily exchange rate quotations. The experience of recent years shows that *Norges Bank* must take into account the fundamental conditions for exchange rate stability over time."[77] In other words, *Norges Bank* had made a de facto regime change by early 1999. At the same time, it put more pressure on the government to follow up with a *de jure* change.[78] After some further exchange between the government and *Norges Bank,* the government announced on 29 March 2001 that inflation targeting was the new monetary policy framework.[79] As could be expected, the official statement played down the break with the past: "There are no changes to the constitutional framework for monetary policy. The Government remains responsible for overall economic policy, and sets guidelines for *Norges Bank*'s conduct of monetary policy."[80]

The statement shows that the government was not yet ready to give the *Norges Bank* more institutional and political independence. To this date, the act of 1985 has continued to be the main guideline for *Norges Bank,* in contrast to Sweden, where the central bank was made more independent in the *Riksbank* Act of 1998.[81] In *Norges Bank* Watch 2002, a team of renowned economists recommended comprehensive institutional reform. The ministry of finance took some steps in early 2003, but there has not

---

[75] Skånland (1999, p. 6): "The new understanding was applied already in January 1999 when *Norges Bank*'s signal rates were reduced in spite of the krone still being well below the desired level."

[76] Challenges to economic policy: Address by Central Bank Governor Svein Gjedrem, Gausdal, 28 January 1999, p. 8.

[77] Annual address by Governor Svein Gjedrem, Meeting of the Supervisory Council of *Norges Bank,* 18 February 1999.

[78] *St.meld. nr. 29 (2000–2001): Retningslinjer for den økonomiske politikken: Tilråding fra Finansdepartementet av 29. mars 2001, godkjent i statsråd samme dag: 3 Retningslinjer for pengepolitikken.* See also Skånland (1999, p. 5).

[79] *St.meld. nr. 29 (2000–2001): Retningslinjer for den økonomiske politikken: Tilråding fra Finansdepartementet av 29. mars 2001, godkjent i statsråd samme dag.*

[80] Regulation on Monetary Policy, established by Royal Decree of 29 March 2001 pursuant to Section 2, third paragraph, and Section 4, second paragraph, of the Act of 24 May 1985, no. 28, on *Norges Bank* and the Monetary System

[81] As for the *Riksbank,* the change was made unavoidable by Sweden's entry into the EU. The treaty required that national central banks were independent. Norway, not a member of the EU, has not been bound by this provision.

been a full-fledged reform yet.[82] Nevertheless, by the beginning of the new century, Norway had completed the protracted transition to a floating exchange rate. The conventional conviction that small European countries needed a fixed exchange rate was contradicted by another example.

THE INTERVENTIONS OF THE *RIKSBANK*

According to public statements, Sweden has had a floating exchange rate since November 1992 and has pursued inflation targeting since January 1993. How is this official classification related to actual country practice? The Swiss case has shown that during turbulent periods such as the 1970s, monetary policy under a flexible exchange-rate regime can be difficult for a small European state. In 1978, the Swiss National Bank announced an explicit exchange-rate ceiling against the deutsche mark (DM) and also prevented the franc from appreciating further against the euro from 2001 to 2003. It is therefore interesting to know whether Sweden has used similar instruments to stabilize the exchange rate.

So far Sweden has not introduced any implicit or explicit targets, and there is no sign that such a measure will ever be taken. Moreover, the exchange rate of the krona has fluctuated less than the Swiss franc did in the 1970s. Events such as the dramatic 1978 appreciation of the Swiss franc have not occurred in Swedish monetary history since 1993. One reason for this difference may be that Sweden has had a geographically more diversified trade structure than Switzerland (Table 8.4). Another reason may be that the period since 1993 has been calmer than the 1970s. And finally, the fact that the Swedish krona has not been considered a safe haven for nervous investors has perhaps helped to protect the exchange rate from dramatic fluctuations. In any case, management of the krona has been less "dirty" than the management of the Swiss franc during the 1970s.

According to Giavazzi and Mishkin (2006), however, the *Riksbank* did not abandon the exchange-rate target altogether after 1992. They observe that until 1996–1997 it was still an important factor in determining the level of the interest rate.[83] And it is interesting that even after 1997, the *Riksbank* could not fully abstain from intervening directly in the foreign-exchange

---

[82] *Ot.prp.nr.81 (2002–2003)* and *Innst.O.nr. 101 (2002–2003)*. See also *Norges Bank Watch 2003* (published in September 2003), p. 58, Appendix I: Implementation of *Norges Bank Watch 2002*. Not all economists share the opinion that the formal independence of *Norges Bank* needs to be strengthened. See, for example, *Norges Bank Watch 2005* (published in April 2005), p. 15.

[83] Giavazzi and Mishkin (2006, p. 50).

Table 8.4. *Major Trading Partners of Sweden and*
Switzerland at the Time of their Regime Change

	Imports		Exports	
	1973	1992	1973	1992
Sweden				
Denmark	8	8	10	7
France	4	5	5	6
West Germany	20	19	10	15
Netherlands	5	4	4	6
Norway	7	7	9	8
United Kingdom	12	9	15	10
United States	7	9	6	8
Switzerland				
Austria	5	4	6	4
France	14	12	9	10
West Germany	30	36	14	25
Italy	9	11	8	9
United Kingdom	6	6	8	7
United States	6	7	8	9

Source: Mitchell (2003).

market and undertook sterilized interventions in October 1998 and June 2001. Why? It is difficult to give a definite answer. Possibly, the decisions were accidental, owing to special individual preferences. But given that most small European states had long hesitated to adopt a flexible exchange-rate regime, my view is that the traditional mistrust of foreign-exchange markets still had some impact on the thinking of policymakers, especially among the older generation. In contrast to academic economists, who criticized the interventions as unnecessary and ill-timed measures, some senior *Riksbank* officials obviously were reluctant to regard exchange-rate fluctuations and misalignments with an attitude of benign neglect.[84] It is also clear, however, that owing to failure to have the desired effect, such interventions were a symptom of regime transition and not important elements of the Swedish monetary policy under a flexible exchange rate. In the remainder of this section I would like to illustrate this interpretation

---

[84] See, for example, Svensson (2000) for a textbook version of inflation targeting.

of the interventions by reconstructing the major arguments leading to the interventions of 1998 and 2001.

As for the first intervention of October 1998, the internal discussions leading to the intervention are not available.[85] Nevertheless, the statements made by top *Riksbank* officials in the aftermath of the intervention are clear enough to allow an interpretation. On the evening of 7 October, the day the intervention was made, *Riksbank* Governor Urban Bäckström indicated clearly that fear of erratic exchange-rate movements induced by "irrational" market sentiments had been an important reason: " The recent path of the Swedish krona is not consistent with the development of our economy's fundamentals. Under these circumstances the *Riksbank* has chosen to use currency interventions to underscore that the movements in the krona's exchange rate have been unduly abrupt and exaggerated."[86] One week later, on 14 October, Deputy Governor Lars Heikenstein described the dilemma Swedish policymakers were confronted with: "... the recent events illustrate that our vulnerability with a flexible exchange rate is considerable. The krona has fluctuated even though economic policy is basically focused on stability."[87]

Bäckström and Heikenstein were referring to the loss of confidence following the Asian crisis and its spread to Russia and Latin America. Until the second quarter of 1998, the krona, however, had not been hit by the crisis (Figure 8.4). The *Riksbank* wrote in its second inflation report of the year, released on 4 June, that the krona was supposed to appreciate in the next forecast period.[88] Accordingly, the repo rate was lowered from 4.35 to 4.10 percent with effect from 9 June. The forecast was based on good macroeconomic fundamentals. Also, the *Riksbank* was not suffering from credibility problems anymore, as in the first half of the 1990s.[89] The long-term (10-year) interest-rate differential vis-à-vis Germany had diminished from roughly 1.5 percent in July 1997 to 0.2 percent in June 1998.[90]

---

[85] The *Riksbank* started to publish the minutes in October 1999.

[86] Urban Bäckström: "The Swedish economy," Svenska Handelsbanken's seminar in New York, 7 October 1998.

[87] Lars Heikenstein: "Monetary policy," autumn conference arranged by the Centre for Business and Policy Studies, 10 October 1998.

[88] Inflation Report 2 (June), 1998, p. 19: "All in all, some appreciation of the TCW exchange rate is envisaged during the forecast period, giving an average level of just over 117 for the coming four quarters (1998:Q3–1999:Q2) and just over 116 for the four quarters after that (1999:Q3–2000:Q2). An important starting-point for this assessment is that the real exchange rate is currently weaker than the level associated with external and internal economic equilibrium in the long run."

[89] For the initial problems in gaining credibility, see Svensson (1995), Berg and Gröttheim (1997), and Bernanke et al. (1999).

[90] Inflation Report 3 (September), 1998, Annex, Figure 11.

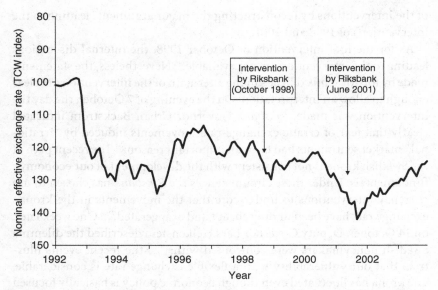

Figure 8.4. Nominal effective exchange rate of Swedish krona. (*Sveriges Riksbank.*)

But then, almost exactly on the day when the inflation report was released, the krona began to depreciate, and in August, the interest-rate differential vis-à-vis Germany began to increase again. Obviously, the krona became a currency that investors regarded as less secure than the DM or the Swiss franc. In mid-August 1998, the Russian government defaulted on its government debt, causing the Russian ruble to decline rapidly. In late September, the problems of the US hedge fund Long Term Capital Management (LTCM) became public. The krona continued to depreciate. However, in its third inflation report of the year, released on 28 September, the *Riksbank* still had good reasons to expect that the weakness of the krona was only a transitional phenomenon.[91]

Yet, a few days after the inflation report had been released, the *Riksbank* changed its opinion. Daily quotations of the krona suggest that the renewed decline by almost 4 percent from 30 September to 5 October triggered the intervention by the *Riksbank* on 7 October – by now, the depreciation since May 1998 amounted to 10 percent. Also, *Riksbank* Governor Bäckström explained three days after the intervention that the depreciation against the DM had been particularly alarming.[92] The exchange rate recovered in

---

[91] *Ibid.*, p. 16.
[92] Urban Bäckström, "The economic situation," Swedish Shareholders Association, 10 October 1998: "In a matter of days the exchange rate with the German mark declined by up to 5 per cent."

the second half of October, but the effect of the intervention was only temporary. In the second week of November, the krona fell back to the level at which the *Riksbank* had intervened. The main reason was an interest-rate cut that had become necessary owing to the deepening of the financial crisis that had led to new downward revisions by the IMF and Organisation of Economic Co-operation and Development (OECD).[93] Only when the international financial crisis subsided in 1999 did the Swedish currency recover permanently.

From the beginning, *Riksbank* officials were aware that their reaction to the depreciation of the krona meant a violation of the textbook version of inflation targeting. *Riksbank* Governor Bäckström explained three days after the intervention: "In that situation the *Riksbank* decided to intervene in the foreign exchange market, which nowadays is unusual. We did so to demonstrate that we considered the krona's fall excessive in relation to the fundamental state of the economy."[94] In the fourth inflation report, released on 3 December, the *Riksbank* repeated the rationale leading to the intervention: "A highly volatile exchange rate is liable to disturb resource allocation. Provided the inflation target is not jeopardised, there may therefore be grounds for the *Riksbank* to counter short-run instability in the foreign exchange market,"[95] Evidently, policymakers remained reluctant to accept the verdict of the market under all circumstances.

As for the second intervention in 2001, reconstruction of the decision-making process is easier because the minutes of the board are available. The intervention was of a different character than the one undertaken in 1998. While in the latter case the *Riksbank* had reacted to a dramatic short-term depreciation of the krona, it intervened in June 2001 because of a typical medium-term misalignment. Nevertheless, the rationale was the same: A majority of the executive board became increasingly unhappy with the gap between macroeconomic fundamentals and the weak exchange rate. Eventually, after another strong depreciation in late May and early June, it

---

[93] *Riksbank*, Annual Report, 1998, pp. 9–10. There were four interest-rate cuts: 3 November: repo rate from 4.10 to 3.85 percent with effect from 4 November; 12 November: deposit and lending rates in each case by 0.5 percent to 3.25 and 4.75 percent, respectively, with effect from 18 November; 24 November: repo rate from 3.85 to 3.60 percent with effect from 25 November. 15 December: repo rate from 3.60 to 3.40 percent with effect from 16 December.

[94] Urban Bäckström, "The Economic Situation," Swedish Shareholders Association, October 10, 1998: "In a matter of days the exchange rate with the German mark declined by up to 5 percent."

[95] Inflation Report 4 (December), 1998, p. 46. A similar phrasing was chosen in Annual Report, 1998, p. 10, published in April 1999.

decided that the *Riksbank* had to give a clear signal to the markets in order
to correct the imbalance.

It was in the inflation report of December 2000 that the *Riksbank*
for the first time highlighted possible risks stemming from the depreciation[96] From then on, this upside risk for inflation was thoroughly
discussed at every meeting, and there were signs of increasing impa-
tience with foreign-exchange markets. At the meeting on 26 March,
Deputy Governor Lars Heikenstein explained: "The current level [of
the exchange rate] cannot be explained in terms of Sweden's economic
fundamentals; it is not even close to being reasonable."[97] It also was at
this meeting that the option of an intervention was mentioned for the
first time.[98] The issue was not discussed further, however, neither in
March nor in the meetings held in late April and late May.[99] Yet, at the
latter meeting, one board member expressed great concern about the
exchange rate. However, given that the growth of the international economy was slowing down, he or she did not recommend an interest-rate
increase.[100]

The decision to intervene in the foreign-exchange market was taken on 14
June.[101] The meeting began with a statement by First Deputy Governor Lars
Heikenstein. He urged board members to discuss the consequences of the
weak exchange rate for future inflation and the question of a rate increase.
He also mentioned the option of an intervention. Against the background
of the continuous depreciation of the krona since the summer of 2000, its
renewed fall since the last inflation report was in fact extraordinary. From
29 May to 8 June, the exchange rate lost 3 percent. Yet Heikenstein's idea to

[96] Inflation Report 4 (December), 2000, p. 61, published on 20 December 2000.

[97] Separate minutes of the executive board meeting on 26 March, pp. 4–5.

[98] Separate minutes of the executive board meeting on 26 March, p. 7: "A member stated that
exchange market intervention is an instrument that is available to the *Riksbank* for supporting the krona."

[99] Separate minutes of the executive board meeting on 26 April 2001; No. 7, Separate minutes of the executive board meeting on 30 May 2001.

[100] Separate minutes of the executive board meeting on 30 May 2001, p. 8: "This member went
on to express concern over the exchange rate continuing to be weak. This can affect expectations and thereby pricing behaviour. The member considered that opinions about the
path of the krona have tended to shift towards the view that it may remain weak for some
time. Moreover, the monetary conditions are regarded as expansionary and a tightening of
fiscal policy is not foreseen. In this member's opinion, the main argument against raising
the interest rate is that the international economic trend may become appreciably weaker
in connection with a rapid adjustment of the dollar and the US current account. In such a
situation, prices would be more subdued."

[101] The minutes were not to be released until November 2001. Usually the period from the
meeting to publication had been two weeks.

intervene in the market was not welcomed by all board members. Two of them were strongly opposed, arguing that assessments of earlier interventions had shown that it was difficult to have a lasting effect on the exchange rate. And there was some criticism suggesting that more time and research were needed for such a far-reaching step as an intervention. Yet, despite these critical voices, a clear majority of the executive board followed the arguments of Heikenstein. It agreed to delegate "to the governor the right to decide, in consultation with the First Deputy Governor, on interventions in the foreign exchange market" Only one board member wanted his dissenting view to be put on record.[102]

In the afternoon after the meeting, held on a Thursday, the *Riksbank* published the wording of a speech Governor Bäckström was planning to give in the evening at a meeting of the Inter-Alpha's Steering Committee, a forum for discussions comprising a number of international banks.[103] The press release had the title, "Bäckström: Currency Interventions Cannot be Ruled Out." In this speech, Bäckström hinted at the possibility of an intervention. Early publication of the speech led to a marked appreciation of the krona and a rise in short-term interest rates.[104] The next morning at 9.00 a.m., a Friday, Deputy Governor Heikenstein gave a speech at the meeting of the Trevises Economic Club in Malmö. He drew the same conclusions as Bäckström: "The principal instrument for a central bank that targets inflation is the interest rate. But in a situation where the exchange rate deviates from a reasonable value and simultaneously constitutes a risk for inflation, currency-market interventions may be motivated."[105]

The *Riksbank* made the first intervention at 11.10 a.m., shortly after Heikenstein's speech, and issued another press release.[106] It was followed by two more interventions on the same day. Further interventions followed on Monday, 18 June and on Monday, 25 June. There was no lasting effect, however. By the end of June, the krona was at the same level as on the day before the first intervention was made. At the next meeting on 5 July, the board therefore decided to raise the repo rate by 0.25 percent to 4.25 percent. The decision was highly disputed.[107] Since there was a standoff, the

---

[102] Separate minutes of the executive board meeting on 14 June 2001, p. 4. The member was Villy Bergström.

[103] See www.riksbank.com under Press – Press releases – 2001 (Date 06/14/2001), Bäckström: Currency interventions cannot be ruled out.

[104] For a detailed chronology, see Separate minutes of the executive board meeting of 8 November 2001, pp. 2ff.

[105] See www.riksbank.com under Press – Press releases – 2001 (Date 6/15/2001): "Heikenstein: The krona has shifted the risk spectrum."

[106] Separate minutes of the executive board meeting on 8 November 2001, p. 2.

[107] Separate minutes of the executive board meeting on 5 July 2001, pp. 12–13.

vote of Governor Bäckström was crucial, favoring an interest-rate increase. The krona remained weak, however. Nevertheless, the board kept the repo rate unchanged at the meeting of 23 August.[108] After the terrorist attacks on 11 September, the krona depreciated even further. Yet, in view of the risks of a possible meltdown, the *Riksbank* lowered interest rates by 0.5 percent at the meeting of 17 September.[109] Now, under these special circumstances, the weak krona that had been the main concern for more than half a year was secondary for the conduct of monetary policy.

In conclusion, Sweden's experience with a flexible exchange-rate system clearly has been positive. The fears that had been expressed by most Swedish politicians during the 1970s and 1980s and even in the wake of the EMS crisis have not materialized. The Swedish economy, although small and open, has been able to cope successfully with the fluctuations of the krona. Otherwise, the referendum on the euro held in September 2003 would not have led to a negative outcome. Yet it is interesting to note that in two instances the *Riksbank* intervened in the market to stop excessive depreciation of the krona. My view is that these two interventions were partly inspired by the traditional mistrust of the irrational foreign-exchange market because the narrative evidence clearly shows that the decision to intervene was taken against the advice of academic economists. It is also evident, however, that these interventions were the relicts of a distant past and not important elements of the Swedish monetary policy framework because, after these two failed attempts to reverse the depreciation of the krona, the *Riksbank* seems to have completely abandoned the idea that the exchange rate of a small European country has to be protected against the moods of the market.

---

[108] Separate minutes of the executive board meeting on 23 August 2001.
[109] Separate minutes of the executive board meeting on 17 September 2001.

Conclusion

This study has attempted to answer the question of when, how, and why seven small and developed European states changed their exchange-rate regime during the twentieth century. The main results are as follows:

1. Basically, small European states made the same choices as large European states. They adopted the gold exchange standard during the interwar years, joined the Bretton Woods system, and later either introduced the euro or a floating-exchange-rate regime. Today, Austria and the Benelux countries have the euro – like France, Germany, and Italy – and Norway, Sweden, and Switzerland have a floating exchange rate – like the United Kingdom. Denmark has a fixed exchange rate against the euro.

2. However, despite sharing a common trend, small and large states pursued different paths during the interwar period and after Bretton Woods. During the interwar period, country size determined the timing of regime changes, that is, when countries adopted the gold exchange standard and when they abandoned it. In general, small states closely followed large states. After Bretton Woods, country size was relevant in two respects. First, small European states showed a stronger preference for fixed exchange rates than large European states (France, Germany, Italy, and the United Kingdom). The main reason was that in contrast with academic economists, small-state policymakers were convinced that it would be impossible to control inflation and have normal trade relations if their small, open economies were exposed to the highly volatile foreign-exchange markets. Second, country size mattered with respect to the causes of a regime shift from fixed to floating. In the case of the small states, the lack of European Community (EC) membership in combination with open financial markets played a crucial role, whereas large states were all EC members at the time they left the Snake and the European Monetary System (EMS), respectively. Accordingly, the causes of their regime shifts were different.

343

3. The differences between small European states mainly resulted from varying degrees of economic, financial, and political integration, not from divergent macroeconomic policies, the strength of the Left, or different institutional structures of the central bank and the wage bargaining system. During the interwar years, the crucial factors were the trade structure, the strength of the banking system, the amount of gold reserves, and the term structure of foreign debt. After the end of Bretton Woods, differences can be explained by EC (non)membership, trade structure, degree of financial openness, and dependence on oil and natural gas imports. Of course, in the long run, the degree of international integration and the structure of domestic economic and political institutions were linked to each other. For example, small states with strong Social Democratic parties had weak central banks and capital controls during the 1970s. However, since these differences were inherited and could not be changed in the short term, the constraints policymakers confronted directly with were related primarily to the kind of economic, financial, and political integration, not to domestic institutions or policy preferences.

In sum, the regime choices of small European states were inspired by a deep mistrust toward the foreign-exchange market and toward monetary experiments. Governments and central banks reacted only when they were forced to, and they tried to keep the changes as small as possible. In particular, small European states clung to the idea of achieving adjustments by making devaluations and revaluations and by negotiating wage agreements longer than France, Germany, Italy, or the United Kingdom did. Fearing that exchange-rate fluctuations under a flexible regime would hamper trade and investment, policymakers adhered to the idea that small, open economies needed a fixed exchange rate – hence the title "fixed ideas."

What are the implications of these findings? Since the main insight is that exchange-rate regime choices were shaped by a sense of vulnerability, it is obvious to make a connection to the work of Peter J. Katzenstein, who has come to a similar conclusion in his studies of the industrial policies of small European states. In a recent article, Katzenstein (2003) reiterated the main thesis with the following words:

I eventually convinced myself that an analysis that focused only on the objective data of economic openness missed the crux of the matter. Small size was a code for something more important, I learned from my interviews, readings and reflection that it was concealing an underlying and politically consequential causal connection. What really mattered politically was the perception of vulnerability, economic and otherwise. Perceived vulnerability generated an ideology of social partnership that had acted like a glue for the corporatist politics of the small European states.[1]

Apparently the perception of vulnerability not only inspired the choice of the exchange-rate regime but also enhanced the formation of corporatist institutions. The basic idea was the same in both policy areas, namely, that it was better to negotiate change than to let the markets alone determine the course of events. In this respect, the formation of corporatist institutions and the preference for fixed exchange rates were two sides of the same coin. Consequently, small-state policymakers preferred to devalue repeatedly – sometimes twice a year – over letting the currency float, and they tried to transform corporatism rather than abandon it altogether when it came under pressure during the 1970s.

However, as the fear of floating faded away in the course of the 1990s, it also has become clear that the sense of vulnerability is conditional. It still may be relevant in some policy areas, but it has lost its overwhelming influence on the choice of the exchange-rate regime. Norway and Sweden, once strong advocates of fixed exchange rates in combination with capital controls, have had overall positive experiences with inflation targeting and a flexible exchange rate. And, as noted in the Introduction, in September 2003, Swedish voters rejected adoption of the euro by a clear margin and thus confirmed the new monetary policy framework that had been introduced only 10 years prior to the referendum. It appears that, unexpectedly, corporatist institutions work just as well under a system of flexible exchange rates. Thus the 1990s clearly represent a major watershed in the history of economic policymaking of small European states. The main goal of this study was to make this recent change more visible and to explain how it came about.

[1]   Katzenstein (2003, p. 11).

Bibliography

1. Unpublished Sources

Austria

Oesterreichische Nationalbank (Vienna):
Protokoll der Sitzungen des Generalrats der Oesterreichischen Nationalbank, 1969–1971
Protokoll der ausserordentlichen Sitzungen des Generalrates der Oesterreichischen Nationalbank, 1969–1971
Besprechung der Mitglieder des Unterausschusses für Währungspolitik mit dem Präsidium und den Mitgliedern des Direktoriums am 5. Mai 1971 (25 B/II/1971)

Belgium

Banque Nationale de Belgique (Brussels):
Procès-verbal de l'assemblée générale des actionnaire du 25 février 1935 (A 006:3)

Denmark

Danmarks Nationalbank (Copenhagen):
Direktionsprotokol, 1918–1931

Netherlands

De Nederlandsche Bank (Amsterdam):
DNB Historisch Archief, DOOS 4, 1.832/208/1
DNB Historisch Archief, HA 01234, 2.312.22/65/1–2.312.22/76/1
DNB Historisch Archief, HA 01233, 2.312.22/147/1
DNB Historisch Archief, HA 2.3/70, 2.312.22/15/1–2.312.22/22/1
DNB Historisch Archief, HA 2.3/86, 2.312.22/44/1
DNB Historisch Archief, Press Archive
Algemeen Rijksarchief (Den Haag):
Sociaal-Economische Raad (SER), 1950–1979

Archief Ministerraad: Notulen van de Ministerraad, 1972
Archief Ministerraad: Notulen Raad Economische Adviseur (REA), 1972

Norway

Riksarkivet (Oslo):
Arkiv: Norges Bank, Direksjonsarkivet I, Arkivskaper: Serie A – Forhandlingsprotokoll for Direksjonen, 1918–1921 (A 0047)

Sweden

Sveriges Riksbank (Stockholm):
Särskilt protokol
Riksarkiv (Stockholm):
1920 Års Finanssakkunnigas: Protokoll och Handlingar (YK-no. 95/1 volume)

Switzerland

Schweizerische Nationalbank (Zurich):
Protokoll des Direktoriums
Beilage zum Direktionsprotokoll
Bankausschuss
Bankrat
Währungspolitik: Allgemeines, 1973–1979 (2.3/2260)
Währungsschlange (3.3/3092–3094)
Archiv für Zeitgeschichte (Zurich):
Protokolle des Vororts
Delegiertenversammlungen des Schweizerischen Handels- und Industrie-Vereins

2. Newspapers and Weekly Magazines

Aftenposten (Oslo)
Dagens Nyheter (Stockholm)
Der Spiegel (Hamburg)
Die Zeit (Hamburg)
Financial Times (London)
Frankfurter Allgemeine Zeitung (Frankfurt)
Handelsblad NRC (Amsterdam)
International Herald Tribune (New York and Paris)
Neue Zürcher Zeitung (Zurich)
The Economist (London)
Trouw (Amsterdam)
Wirtschaftsdienst (Hamburg)

3. Periodicals

Bank for International Settlements, Annual Reports, Basle

Banque Nationale de Belgique, Annual Report
Danmarks Nationalbank, Annual Report
De Nederlandsche Bank, Annual Report
Deutsche Bundesbank, Monthly Report, Frankfurt
Jahrbuch der österreichischen Wirtschaft, Vienna
Norges Bank Watch: An Independent Review of Monetary Policy and Institutions in Norway, Oslo
Norges Bank, Annual Report
Oesterreichische Nationalbank, Annual Report
Schweizerische Nationalbank, Annual Report
Schweizerische Nationalbank, Das schweizerische Bankenwesen im Jahre ... /Die Banken in der Schweiz, Zurich
Schweizerische Nationalbank, Monthly Report
Svenska Dagbladets Årsbok, Stockholm
Sveriges Riksbank, Annual Report

4. Published Sources

Austria

Stenographisches Protokoll der Sitzungen des Nationalrats
Pressedienst der Industrie, Wien
Jahrbuch der österreichischen Wirtschaft, Wien

Belgium

Procès-verbaux, Enquête parlementaire chargée de rechercher les responsabilités de la dévaluation du franc, 1935–1936
Documents parlementaires, Chambre, 1935–1936, rapport no. 231 du 20 avril 1936

Denmark

Valutakonferencens forhandlinger, Copenhagen, 1923
Valutakommissionens Betækning, Copenhagen, 1920.

Norway

Innstilling fra Valutakommisjonen, Oslo, 1926. (The document also can be found in *Stortingets Forhandlinger* 1926, Appendix to *Storting propositionen*, no. 62.)
Rigsdagstidende
Beretning om valutarådets virksomhet: 13de februar 1920–31te august 1921, Oslo, 1921

Sweden

Rikdagens protokoll (Förste Kammer, Andere Kammer)
Bihang till Riksdagens protokoll

Års Finanssakkunniga: Utlåtande angående frågan huruvida och i vad mån ett program för den närmaste framtiden för svensk finanspolitik må kunna åstadkommas. Avgivet den 6 Augusti 1920 av särskilda sakkunniga, Stockholm, 1920.

Switzerland

Bundesblatt
Amtliches stenographisches Bulletin, Nationalrat und Ständerat
Protokoll des Bundesrats vom 26. September 1936, in Diplomatische Dokumente der Schweiz 1848-1945, Vol. 11 (1934-1936), Bern, 1989, pp. 861-868.

5. Articles and Books

Abildgren, Kim (2004a), "A chronology of Denmark's exchange-rate policy 1875–2003," Danmarks Nationalbank Working Papers 12.

Abildgren, Kim (2004b), "Nominal and real effective krone rate indices for Denmark 1875–2002," Danmarks Nationalbank Working Papers 13.

Abildgren, Kim (2005), "A historical perspective on interest rates in Denmark 1875–2003," Danmarks Nationalbank Working Papers 24.

Åkerholm, Johnny (1990), "Comment," in Victor Argy and Paul De Grauwe (eds.), Choosing an Exchange Rate Regime: The Challenge for Smaller Industrial Countries. Washington, DC: International Monetary Fund, pp. 193–196.

Åkerholm, Johnny, and Alberto Giovannini (1994), "Introduction," in Johnny Åkerholm and Alberto Giovannini (eds.), Exchange Rate Policies in the Nordic Countries. London: CEPR, pp. 1–7.

Aldcroft, Derek H., and Michael J. Oliver (1998), Exchange Rate Regimes in the Twentieth Century. Cheltenham, England: Edward Elgar.

Alesina, Alberto (1989), "Politics and business cycles in industrial democracies," Economic Policy 8, pp. 55–98.

Alesina, Alberto, and Enrico Spolaore (2003), The Size of Nations. Cambridge, MA: MIT Press.

Aliber, Robert Z. (1962), "Speculation in the foreign exchanges: The European experience, 1919–1926," Yale Economic Essays 2, pp. 171–245.

Allgoewer, Elisabeth (2003), Gold Standard and Gold-Standard Mentality in Switzerland 1929–1936. Habilitationsschrift, University of St. Gallen.

Andersen, Torben M. (1994), "Disinflationary stabilization policy – Denmark in the 1980s," in Johnny Åkerholm and Alberto Giovannini (eds.), Exchange Rate Policies in the Nordic Countries. London: CEPR, pp. 100–132.

Andersen, Torben M., and Ole Risager (1990), "Wage formation in Denmark," in Lars Calmfors (ed.), Wage Formation and Macroeconomic Policy in the Nordic Countries. Stockholm: SNS Förlag, pp. 137–188.

Andersen, Torben M., Svend E. Hougaard Jensen, and Ole Risager (1999), "Macroeconomic perspectives on the Danish economy: Problems, policies and prospects," in Torben M. Andersen, Svend E. Hougaard Jensen, and Ole Risager (eds.), Macroeconomic Perspectives on the Danish Economy. London: Macmillan, pp. 1–39.

Andersson, Krister (2003), "Utformingen av inflationsmålet och den penningpolitiska analysramen," in Lars Jonung (ed.), *På jakt efter ett nytt ankare: Från fast kronkurs till inflationsmål*. Stockholm: SNS Förlag, pp. 223–280.

Andrews, David M. (ed.) (2006), *International Monetary Power*. Ithaca, NY: Cornell University Press.

Androsch, Hannes (1985), *Die politische Ökonomie der österreichischen Währung. Ein Überblick über die österreichische Währungspolitik von 1760–1984 vor dem Hintergrund der internationalen Entwicklung.* Wien: Orac.

Androsch, Hannes (1989), "Zwei Jahrzehnte wechselvoller Verbundenheit," in Werner Clement and Karl Socher (eds.), *Stephan Koren: Wirtschaftsforscher und Wirtschaftspolitiker in Österreich.* Wien: Orac, pp. 183–205.

Androsch, Hannes (1993), "10 Jahre danach – Versuch einer Bilanz: Hannes Androsch im Gespräch mit Fritz Weber," in Fritz Weber and Theodor Venus (eds.), *Austrokeynesianismus in Theorie und Praxis*. Wien: Jugend & Volk, pp. 189–206.

Argy, Victor (1900), "Choice of exchange rate regime for a smaller economy: A survey of some key issues," in Victor Argy and Paul De Grauwe (eds.), *Choosing an Exchange Rate Regime: The Challenge for Smaller Industrial Countries*. Washington, DC: International Monetary Fund, pp. 6–81.

Argy, Victor, and Paul De Grauwe (eds.) (1990), *Choosing an Exchange Rate Regime: The Challenge for Smaller Industrial Countries*. Washington, DC: International Monetary Fund.

Asselain, Jean-Charles (1993), "La dévaluation française de 1936: essai d'approche comparative du bloc-or," in Maurice Lévy-Leboyer et al. (eds.), *Du franc Poincaré à l'écu*. Paris: Comité pour l'histoire économique et financière de la France, pp. 239–268.

Bachinger, Karl (2001), "*Eine stabile Währung in einer instabilen Zeit – Der Schilling in der Ersten Republik*," in Karl Bachinger, Felix Butschek, Herbert Matis, and Dieter Stiefel (eds.), *Abschied vom Schilling: Eine österreichische Wirtschaftsgeschichte*. Köln: Styria, pp. 11–134.

Bäckström, Urban (2000), "The inflation targeting approach," *BIS Review* 50.

Baffi, Paolo (2003), *The Origins of Central Bank Cooperation: The Establishment of the Bank for International Settlements*. Rome: Editori Laterza.

Bagge, Gösta, Erik Lundberg, and Ingvar Svennilson (1933), *Wages in Sweden, 1860–1930*, 2 vols. Stockholm: Institute for Social Sciences, University of Stockholm.

Bairoch, Paul (1976), *Commerce extérieur et développement économique de l'Europe au XIXe siècle*. Paris: Mouton and Ecole des Hautes Etudes en Sciences Sociales.

Bakker, Age F. P. (1996), *The Liberalization of Capital Movements in Europe: The Monetary Committee and Financial Integration, 1958–1994*. Boston: Kluwer Academic Publishers.

Balderston, Theo (ed.) (2003), *The World Economy and National Economies in the Interwar Slump*. Basingstoke: Palgrave Macmillan.

Baltensperger, Ernst (1984), *Geldmengenpolitik und Inflationskontrolle*. Möglichkeiten, Kosten, flankierende Massnahmen, Diessenhofen: Rüegger.

Bänziger, Hugo (1985), "Vom Sparerschutz zum Gläubigerschutz – die Entstehung des Bankengesetzes im Jahre 1934," in Eidgenössische Bankenkommission (ed.), *50 Jahre eidgenössische Bankenaufsicht*. Zurich: Schulthess, pp. 3–81.

Bänziger, Hugo (1986), *Die Entwicklung der Bankenaufsicht in der Schweiz seit dem 19.* Stuttgart: Haupt.

Battilossi, Stefano (2002), "Introduction: International banking and the American challenge in historical perspective," in Stefano Battilossi and Youseff Cassis (eds.), *European Banks and the American Challenge: Competition and Cooperation in International Banking under Bretton Woods.* New York and Oxford: Oxford University Press, pp. 1–35.

Battilossi, Stefano, and Youssef Cassis (eds.) (2002), *European Banks and the American Challenge: Competition and Cooperation in International Banking under Bretton Woods.* New York and Oxford: Oxford University Press.

Baudhuin, Fernand (1936), *La dévaluation du franc belge – un an aprés.* Brussels: Edition Universelle.

Baudhuin, Fernand (1946a), *Histoire économique de la Belgique 1914–1939*, Vol. I. Brussels: Emile Bruylant.

Baudhuin, Fernand (1946b), *Histoire économique de la Belgique 1914–1939*, Vol. II. Brussels: Emile Bruylant.

Bauer, Hans, and Warren J. Blackman (1998), *Swiss Banking: An Analytical History.* London: Macmillan.

Baumann, Jan (2004), *Bundesinterventionen in der Bankenkrise 1931–1937: Eine vergleichende Studie am Beispiel der Schweizerischen Volksbank und der Schweizerischen Diskontbank.* Dissertation, University of Zurich.

Baumann, Jan, and Patrick Halbeisen (1999), *"Die Internationalisierung des Finanzplatzes Schweiz und ihre Folgen für die Währungspolitik: Konsens und Konflikte zwischen der Nationalbank und den Geschäftsbanken 1919–1939,"* mimeo.

Baxter, Marianne, and Alan C. Stockman (1989), "Business cycles and the exchange rate regime: Some international evidence," *Journal of Monetary Economics* 23, pp. 377–400.

Bayoumi, Tamim, and Barry Eichengreen (1998), "Exchange Rate Volatility and Intervention: Implications of theory of Optimum Currency Areas," *Journal of International Economics* 45, pp. 191–209.

Bean, Charles, and Nicholas Crafts (1996), "British economic growth since 1945: Relative economic decline ... and renaissance?" in Nicholas Crafts and Gianni Toniolo (eds.), *Economic Growth in Europe since 1945.* Cambridge and New York: Cambridge University Press, pp. 131–172.

Bébié, Rudolf (1939), *Die Abwertung des Schweizer Frankens. Ursachen, Durchführung und erste Auswirkungen.* Zurich: Verlag Waldgarten.

Begg, David, et al. (2003), *The Consequences of Saying No: An Independent Report into the Economic Consequences of the UK Saying No to the Euro.* London.

Bell, Geoffrey (1973), *The Euro-dollar Market and the International Financial System.* London: Macmillan.

Benner, Mats, and Torben Bundgaard Vad (2000), "Sweden and Denmark: Defending the welfare state," in Fritz W. Scharpf and Vivien A. Schmidt (eds.), *Welfare and Work in the Open Economy, Vol. II: Diverse Responses to Common Challenges.* New York and Oxford: Oxford University Press, pp. 399–466.

Berg, Claes, and Lars Jonung (1999), "Pioneering price level targeting: The Swedish experience 1931–1937," *Journal of Monetary Economics* 43, pp. 525–551.

Berg, Claes, and Richard Gröttheim (1997), "Monetary policy in Sweden since 1992," *BIS Policy Papers* 2, pp. 140–182.

Berger, Helge, and Ulrich Woitek (2005), "Does conservatism matter? A time-series approach to central bank behaviour," *Economic Journal* 115, pp. 745–766.

Bergman, Michael, Stefan Gerlach, and Lars Jonung (1993), "The rise and fall of the Scandinavian Currency Union, 1873–1920," *European Economic Review* 37, pp. 507–517.

Bergman, Michael, and Michael M. Hutchison (1999), "Economic expansions and fiscal contractions: International evidence and the 1982 Danish stabilization," in Torben M. Andersen, Svend E. Hougaard Jensen, and Ole Risager (eds.), *Macroeconomic Perspectives on the Danish Economy*. London: Macmillan, pp. 225–256.

Bergström, Asta (1995), *Åtstramning och Expansion: Den ekonomiska politiken I Sverige 1971–1982*. Lund: Lund University Press.

Bernanke, Ben S., and Harold James (1991), "The gold standard, deflation, and financial crisis in the Great Depression: An international comparison," in R. Glenn Hubbard (ed.), *Financial Markets and Financial Crises*. Chicago: The University of Chicago Press, pp. 33–68.

Bernanke, Ben S., Thomas Laubach, Frederic S. Mishkin, and Adam S. Posen (1999), *Inflation Targeting: Lessons from the International Experience*. Princeton, NJ: Princeton University Press.

Bernegger, Michael (1988), *Die Schweiz unter flexiblen Wechselkursen*. Stuttgart: Paul Haupt.

Bernholz, Peter (2007), "From 1945 to 1982: The transition from inward exchange controls to money supply management under floating exchange rates," in Swiss National Bank (ed.), *The Swiss National Bank 1907–2007*. Zurich: NZZ Libro, pp. 109–199.

Beveridge, William (1928), *British Food Control, Economic and Social History of the World War (Economic and Social History of the World War, British Series)*. London and New Haven, CT: Oxford University Press and Yale University Press.

Bie, Ronald van der (1995), *"Een doorlopende grosse roes": De economische ontwikkeling van Nederland, 1913–1921*. Amsterdam: Thesis Publishers.

Bildt, Carl (2003), *"Den stapplande vägen till reformer och till Europa,"* in Lars Jonung (ed.), *På jakt efter ett nytt ankare: Från fast kronkurs till inflationsmål*. Stockholm: SNS Förlag, pp. 51–88.

Birchler, Urs (1979), *Die Konjunkturpolitik in der Schweiz von 1950 bis 1975: unter besonderer Berücksichtigung der wirtschaftspolitischen Träger*. Dissertation, University of Zurich.

Blackman, Warren J. (1989), *Swiss Banking in an International Context*. London: Macmillan.

Blattner, Niklaus, Benedikt Gratzl, and Tilo Kaufmann (1996), *Das Vermögensverwaltungsgeschäft der Banken in der Schweiz*. Bern: Haupt.

Blattner, Niklaus, Hans Genberg, and Alexander Swoboda (eds.) (1992), *Competitiveness in Banking*. Heidelberg: Physica-Verlag.

Blattner, Niklaus, Hans Genberg, and Alexander Swoboda (eds.) (1993), *Banking in Switzerland*. Heidelberg: Physica-Verlag.

Bloemen, E. S. A. (1987), "The employers' associations," in Richard T. Griffiths (ed.), *The Netherlands and the Gold Standard, 1931–1936*. Amsterdam: Neha, pp. 30–46.

Bloemen, Erik (1993), "La politique monétaire et commerciale des Pays-Bas durant les années trente et la dévaluation du florin," in Maurice Lévy-Leboyer et al. (eds.), *Du franc Poincaré à l'écu*. Paris: Comité pour l'histoire économique et financière de la France, pp. 229–238.

Blustein, Paul (2005), *And the Money Came Rolling in (and Out): Wall Street, the IMF, and the Bankrupting of Argentina*. New York: Public Affairs.

Blyth, Mark (2001), "The transformation of the Swedish model: Economic ideas, distributional conflict, and institutional change," *World Politics* 54, pp. 1–26.

Bonoli, Giuliano, and André Mach (2000), "Switzerland: Adjustment politics within institutional constraints," in Fritz W. Scharpf and Vivien A. Schmidt (eds.), *Welfare and Work in the Open Economy, Vol. II: Diverse Responses to Common Challenges*. New York and Oxford: Oxford University Press, pp. 131–174.

Bordo, Michael (1993), "The Bretton Woods International Monetary System: An historical overview," in Michael Bordo and Barry Eichengreen (eds.), *A Retrospective on the Bretton Woods System: Lessons for International Monetary Reform*. Chicago: The University of Chicago Press, pp. 3–98.

Bordo, Michael (2003), "Exchange rate regime choice in historical perspective," *NBER Working Paper* 9654.

Bordo, Michael, and Harold James (2001), "The Adam Klug Memorial Lecture: Haberler versus Nurkse: The case for floating exchange rates as an alternative to Bretton Woods?" *NBER Working Paper* 8545.

Bordo, Michael, Thomas Helbling, and Harold James (2006), "Swiss exchange rate policy in the 1930s: Was the delay in devaluation too high a price to pay for conservatism?" *NBER Working Paper* 12491.

Bordo, Michael, and Harold James (2007), "The SNB 1907–1946: A happy childhood or a troubled adolescence?," in Swiss National Bank (ed.), *The Swiss National Bank, 1907–2007*. Zurich: NZZ Libro, pp. 29–108.

Bordo, Michael, and Lars Jonung (1999), "The future of EMU: What does the history of monetary unions tell us?" *NBER Working Paper* 7365.

Bordo, Michael, and Anna J. Schwartz (1999), "Monetary policy regimes and economic performance: The historical record," in John Taylor and Michael Woodford (eds.), *North Holland Handbook of Macroeconomics*. New York: Elsevier Science.

Bordo, Michael, and Marc Flandreau (2003), "Core, periphery, exchange rate regime and globalization," in Michael Bordo, Alan Taylor, and Jeffrey Williamson (eds.), *Globalization in Historical Perspective*. Chicago: The University of Chicago Press, pp. 417–468.

Bordo, Michael, Ali Dib, and Lawrence Schembri (2007), "Canada's pioneering experience with a flexible exchange rate in the 1950s: (Hard) lessons learned for monetary policy in a small open economy," *NBER Working Paper* 13605.

Bosman, Hans W. J. (1984). *Monetary Policy in the Netherlands in the Post-Smithsonian Era*. Société Universitaire Européenne de Recherches Financières (S.U.E.R.F.) Studies.

Bosshardt, Alfred (1970), *Aussenhandels-, und Integrations- und Währungspolitik aus schweizerischer Sicht*. Zurich: Schulthess.

Breuss, Fritz (1983), *Österreichs Aussenwirtschaft, 1945–1982*. Wien: Signum.

Broadberry, Stephen (1984), "The North European depression of the 1920s," *Scandinavian Economic History Review* 32, pp. 159–167.

Broder, Albert (1991), "Les mouvements de capitaux dans l'entre-deux-guerres: l'Allemagne, la France, les Etats-Unis, les Pays-Bas," *Economies et Sociétés* 16, pp. 7–38.

Brown, William Adams (1940), *The International Gold Standard Reinterpreted, 1914–1934*, 2 vols. New York: National Bureau of Economic Research (NBER).

Broz, J. Lawrence, and Jeffry A. Frieden (2006), "The political economy of exchange rates," in Barry R. Weingast and Donald Wittmann (eds.), *The Oxford Handbook of Political Economy*. New York and Oxford: Oxford University Press, pp. 587–597.

Bruno, Michael, and Jeffrey Sachs (1985), *Economics of Worldwide Stagflation*. Cambridge, MA: Harvard University Press.

Bucher, Bruno (1943), *Die Wirksamkeit der offiziellen Sätze der Schweizerischen Nationalbank*. Dissertation, University of Zurich.

Burn, Gary (1999), "The state, the city and the Euromarkets," *Review of International Political Economy* 6, pp. 225–261.

Burnham, Peter (2003), *Remaking the Postwar World Economy: Robot and British Policy in the 1950s*. London: Palgrave Macmillan.

Bussière, Éric (1993), "Les relations monétaires franco-belges de la stabilisation des années vingt à la dévaluation du Franc belge de mars 1935: histoire d'une rupture," in Maurice Lévy-Leboyer et al. (eds.), *Du franc Poincaré à l'écu*. Paris: Comité pour l'histoire économique et financière de la France, pp. 187–196.

Butschek, Felix (1985), *Die österreichische Wirtschaft im 20 Jahrhundert*, Wien: Österreichisches Institut für Wirtschaftsforschung.

Butschek, Felix (2001), "*Der Weg nach Europa – Vom Schilling zum Euro*," in Karl Bachinger, Felix Butschek, Herbert Matis, and Dieter Stiefel (eds.), *Abschied vom Schilling: Eine österreichische Wirtschaftsgeschichte*. Köln: Styria, pp. 287–343.

Cairncross, Alec, and Barry Eichengreen (1983), *Sterling in Decline: The Devaluations of 1931, 1949, and 1967*. Oxford, England: Basil Blackwell.

Calmfors, Lars (ed.) (1990), *Wage Formation and Macroeconomic Policy in the Nordic Countries*. Stockholm: SNS Förlag.

Calmfors, Lars, and Anders Forslund (1990), "Wage formation in Sweden," in Lars Calmfors (ed.), *Wage Formation and Macroeconomic Policy in the Nordic Countries*. Stockholm: SNS Förlag, pp. 63–136.

Calmfors, Lars, and John Driffil (1988), "Centralization of wage bargaining," *Economic Policy* 6, pp. 14–61.

Calomiris, Charles W. (2000), *U.S. Bank Deregulation in Historical Perspective*. New York: Cambridge University Press.

Calvo, Guillermo, and Carmen Reinhart (2002), "Fear of floating," *Quarterly Journal of Economics* 117, pp. 379–408.

Campillo, Marta, and Jeffrey A. Miron (1997), "Why does inflation differ across countries?" in Christina D. Romer and David H. Romer (eds.), *Reducing Inflation: Motivation and Strategy*. Chicago: The University of Chicago Press, pp. 335–357.

Capitelli, René, and Peter Buomberger (1990), "Zur Geldpolitik der achtziger Jahre: Einige grundsätzliche Überlegungen," *Schweizerische Zeitschrift für Volkswirtschaft und Statistik* 126, pp. 535–551.

Caramani, Daniele (2000), *Elections in Western Europe since 1815: Electoral Results by Constituencies*. London: Macmillan.

Carlson, Mark, and Kris James Mitchener (2006), "Branch banking, bank competition, and financial stability," *Journal of Money, Credit and Banking* 38, pp. 1293–1328.

Cassel, Gustav (1928), *Post-War Monetary Stabilization*. New York: Columbia University Press.

Cassiers, Isabelle (1989), *Croissance, crise et régulation en économie ouverte: La Belgique entre les deux guerres*. Brussels: De Boeck Université.

Cassiers, Isabelle (1995), "Managing the Franc in Belgium and France: The economic consequences of exchange-rate policies, 1925–1936," in Charles H. Feinstein (ed.), *Banking, Currency, and Finance in Europe Between the Wars*. New York and Oxford: Oxford University Press, pp. 214–236.

Cassiers, Isabelle, Philippe De Villé, and Peter Solar (1996), "Economic growth in postwar Belgium," in Nicholas Crafts and Gianni Toniolo (eds.), *Economic Growth in Europe Since 1945*. Cambridge and New York: Cambridge University Press, pp. 173–209.

Cassis, Youssef (1991), "L'histoire des banques suisses, aux XIXe et XXe siècles," *Schweizerische Zeitschrift für Geschichte* 41, pp. 512–520.

Cassis, Youssef (1994), "Switzerland/Liechtenstein," in Hans Pohl and Sabine Freitag (eds.), *Handbook on the History of European Banks*. Aldershot, England: Edward Elgar, pp. 1015–1133.

Cassis, Youssef (1995), "Commercial banks in 20th century Switzerland," in Youssef Cassis, Gerald Feldman, and Ulf Olsson (eds.), *The Evolution of Financial Institutions and Markets in Twentieth Century Europe*. Aldershot, England: Scolar Press, pp. 64–77.

Cassis, Youssef, and Jakob Tanner (1992), "Finance and financiers in Switzerland, 1880–1960," in Youssef Cassis (ed.), *Finance and Financiers in European History*, New York: Cambridge University Press, pp. 293–316.

Cassis, Youssef, und Jakob Tanner (eds.) (1993), *Banken und Kredit in der Schweiz (1850–1930)*. Zurich: Chronos.

Catterall, Ross E., and Derek Aldcroft (eds.) (2004), *Exchange Rates and Economic Policy in the 20th Century*. Aldershot, England: Ashgate.

Central Bureau voor de Statistiek (1987), *Macro-economische ontwikkelingen, 1921–1939 en 1969–1985: Een vergelijking op basis van herziene gegevens voor het interbellum*. Den Haag: CBS-Publikatie.

Cesarano, Filippo (2006), *Monetary Theory and Bretton Woods: The Construction of an International Monetary Order*. New York: Cambridge University Press.

Chang, Roberto (2005), "Financial crises and political crises," *NBER Working Paper* 11779.

Chlepner, Ben Serge (1943), *Belgian Banking and Banking Theory*. Washington, DC: Brookings Institution.

Christensen, Benedicte Vibe (1986), "Switzerland's role as an international financial center," *IMF Occasional Paper* 45.

Christiansen, Niels Finn, Karl Christian Lammers, and Henrik S. Nissen (1988), *Danmarks historie, Vol. 7: Tiden 1914–1945*. Copenhagen: Gyldendal.

Clarke, Stephen V. O. (1967), *Central Bank Cooperation 1924–1931*. New York: Federal Reserve Bank of New York.

Cohen, Benjamin J. (1996), "Phoenix risen: The resurrection of global finance," *World Politics* 48, pp. 268–296.

Cohn, Einar (1928), *Danmark under Den Store Krig: En Økonomisk Oversigt*. Copenhagen: G. E. C. Gads Forlag.

Cohn, Einar (1930), *Denmark in the World War*. New Haven, CT: Yale University Press.

Commission of Gold and Silver Inquiry United States Senate (1925), *Foreign Currency and Exchange Investigation*, Serial 9, Vol. II. Washington, DC: US Government Printing Office.

Cottrell, Philipp (1995), "The Bank of England and international central banking, 1694–1970," in Richard Roberts and David Kynaston (eds.), *The Bank of England: Money, Power and Influence*. New York and Oxford: Oxford University Press, pp. 125–156.

Crowe, Christopher, and Ellen E. Meade (2007), "The evolution of central bank governance around the world," *Journal of Economic Perspectives* 27, pp. 69–90.

Cuche, Nicolas A. (2000), *Monetary Policy Rules and Indicators: Empirical Evidence for Switzerland*, Bern: Studienzentrum Gerzensee.

Cukierman, Alex (1992), *Central Bank Strategy, Credibility, and Independence: Theory and Evidence*. Cambridge, MA: MIT Press.

Cukierman, Alex, and Francesco Lippi (1999), "Central bank independence, centralization of wage bargaining, inflation and unemployment: Theory and some evidence," *European Economic Review* 43, pp. 1395–1434.

Dahlfors, Gunnar (1991), "*Nationalekonomernas syn på växelkurspolitiken 1973–1985*," in Lars Jonung (ed.), *Devalveringen 1982 – Rivstart eller snedtändning? Perspektiv på svensk devalveringspolitik*. Stockholm: SNS Förlag, pp. 390–402.

Daltung, Sonia (2004), "The Swedish banking crisis," in Jack Reidhill (ed.), *Bank Failures in Mature Economies*. Basel: Bank for International Settlements, pp. 34–42.

De Grauwe, Paul (1996), *International Money: Postwar Trends and Theories*, 2nd ed. New York and Oxford: Oxford University Press.

De Grauwe, Paul (2003), *Economics of Monetary Union*, 5th ed. New York and Oxford: Oxford University Press.

De Grauwe, Paul, and Wim Vanhaverbeke (1990), "Exchange rate experiences of small EMS countries: Belgium, Denmark, and the Netherlands," in Victor Argy and Paul De Grauwe (eds.), *Choosing an Exchange Rate Regime: The Challenge for Smaller Industrial Countries*. Washington, DC: International Monetary Fund, pp. 135–155.

De Jong, A. M. (1957), "Uit de geschiedenis van 's rijks vlottende schuld," *Economist*, pp. 1–43 and 97–145.

DeLong, J. Bradford (1997), "America's peacetime inflation: The 1970s," in Christina Romer and David Romer (eds.), *Reducing Inflation: Motivation and Strategy*. Chicago: The University of Chicago Press, pp. 247–278.

De Ridder, Hugo (1991), *Le cas Martens*. Gembloux: Éditions Duculot.

De Rosa, Luigi (ed.) (2003), *International Banking and Financial Systems: Evolution and Stability*. Aldershot, England: Macmillan.

De Vries, Johan (1989), *Geschiedenis van de Nederlandsche Bank. Viijfde deel: De Nederlandsche Bank van 1914 tot 1948: Visserings tijdvak 1914–1931*. Amsterdam: NIBE.

De Vries, Johan (1994), *Geschiedenis van de Nederlandsche Bank. Viijfde deel: De Nederlandsche Bank van 1914 tot 1948: Trips tijdvak 1931–1948 onderbroken door de Tweede Wereldoorlog*. Amsterdam: NIBE.

De Vries, Margaret Garritsen (1985), *The International Monetary Fund, 1972–1978: Cooperation on Trial*. Washington, DC: International Monetary Fund.

Den Dunnen, Emile (1985), "Instruments of money market and foreign exchange market policy in the Netherlands," *De Nederlandsche Bank Monetary Monographs* 3.

Dennis, Bengt (1998), *500%*. Stockholm: Bokförlaget DN.

Dennis, Bengt (2003), "Första året med flytande krona," in Lars Jonung (ed.), *På jakt efter ett nytt ankare: Från fast kronkurs till inflationsmål*. Stockholm: SNS Förlag, pp. 173–222.

Deutsche Bundesbank (ed.) (1999), *Fifty years of the Deutsche Mark: Central Bank and the Currency in Germany since 1948*. New York and Oxford: Oxford University Press.

Drees, Burkhard, and Ceyla Pazarbasioglu (1998), "The Nordic banking crises: Pitfalls in financial liberalization?" *IMF Occasional Paper* 161.

Dyson, Kenneth, and Kevin Featherstone (1999), *The Road to Maastricht: Negotiating Economic and Monetary Union*. New York and Oxford: Oxford University Press.

Edison, Hali J., and Jan Tore Klovland (1987), "A quantitative reassessment of the purchasing power parity hypothesis: Evidence from Norway and the United Kingdom," *Journal of Applied Economics* 2, pp. 309–333.

Edison, Hali J., and Michael Melvin (1990), "The determinants and implications of the choice of an exchange rate system," in William S. Haraf and Thomas D. Willett (eds.), *Monetary Policy for a Volatile Global Economy*. Washinton, DC: AEI Press, pp. 1–44.

Edwards, Sebastian (2002), "The great exchange rate debate after Argentina," *NBER Working Paper* 9257.

Ehrsam, Paul (1985), "Die Bankenkrise der 30er Jahre in der Schweiz," in Eidgenössische Bankenkommission (ed.), *50 Jahre eidgenössische Bankenaufsicht*. Zurich: Schulthess, pp. 83–118.

Eichengreen, Barry (1992), *Golden Fetters: The Gold Standard and the Great Depression*. New York and Oxford: Oxford University Press.

Eichengreen, Barry (1994), *International Monetary Arrangements for the 21st Century*, Washington, DC: Brookings Institution.

Eichengreen, Barry (1996a), "Institutions and economic growth: Europe after World War II," in Nicholas Crafts and Gianni Toniolo (eds.), *Economic Growth in Europe since 1945*. Cambridge and New York: Cambridge University Press, pp. 38–72.

Eichengreen, Barry (1996b), *Globalizing Capital: A History of the International Monetary System*. Princeton, NJ: Princeton University Press.

Eichengreen, Barry (2000), "The EMS crisis in retrospect," *NBER Working Paper* 8035.

Eichengreen, Barry (2002), "Still fettered after all these years," *NBER Working Paper* 9276.

Eichengreen, Barry (2007), *The European Economy since 1945: Coordinated Capitalism and Beyond*. Princeton, NJ: Princeton University Press.

Eichengreen, Barry, and Beth A. Simmons (1995), "International economics and domestic politics: Notes on the 1920s," in Charles Feinstein (ed.), *Banking, Currency, and Finance in Europe Between the Wars*. New York and Oxford: Oxford University Press, pp. 131–147.

Eichengreen, Barry, and Charles Wyplosz (1993), "The unstable EMS," *Brookings Papers on Economic Activity*, pp. 51–144.

Eichengreen, Barry, and Jeffrey Sachs (1985), "Exchange rates and economic recovery in the 1930s," *Journal of Economic History* 45, pp. 925–946.

Eichengreen, Barry, and Olivier Jeanne (2000), "Currency crisis and unemployment: Sterling in 1931," in Paul Krugman (ed.), *Currency Crises*. Chicago: The University of Chicago Press, pp. 7–43.

Eichengreen, Barry, and Peter Temin (2000), "The Gold Standard and the Great Depression," *Contemporary European History* 9, pp. 183–207.

Eichengreen, Barry, and Peter Temin (2003), "'Afterword': Counterfactual histories of the Great Depression," in Theo Balderston (ed.), *The World Economy and National Economies in the Interwar Slump*. Basingstoke, England: Palgrave Macmillan, pp. 211–221.

Eichengreen, Barry, and Ricardo Hausmann (eds.) (2004), *Other People's Money: Debt Denomination and Financial Instability in Emerging Market Economies*. Chicago: The University of Chicago Press.

Eichengreen, Barry, and Richard Portes (1987), "The anatomy of financial crises," in Richard Portes and Alexander Swoboda (eds.), *Threats to International Financial Stability*. New York: Cambridge University Press, pp. 10–58.

Eichengreen, Barry, Andrew Rose, and Charles Wyplosz (1995), "Exchange market mayhem: The antecedents and aftermath of speculative attacks," *Economic Policy* 21, pp. 249–312.

Eichengreen, Barry, Andrew Rose, and Charles Wyplosz (1996), "Contagious currency crises: First tests," *Scandinavian Journal of Economics* 98, pp. 463–484.

Eichengreen, Barry, Paul Masson, Miguel Savastano, and Sunil Sharma (1999), "Transition strategies and nominal anchors on the road to greater exchange-rate flexibility," *Essays in International Finance* 213.

Eijffinger, Sylvester C. W., and Jakob De Haan (1996), "The political economy of central bank independence," *Princeton Studies in International Economics* 19.

Einzig, Paul (1932), *The Fight for Financial Supremacy*, 3rd ed. London: Macmillan.

Einzig, Paul (1970), *The Euro-Dollar System: Practice and Theory of International Interest Rates*, 4th ed. London: Macmillan.

Eitrheim, Øyvind, Jan Tore Klovland, and Jan F. Qvigstad (eds.) (2004), "Historical monetary statistics for Norway, 1819–2003," *Norges Bank Occasional Papers* 35.

Eitrheim, Øyvind, Karten Gerdrup, and Jan Tore Klovland (2004), "Credit, banking and monetary developments in Norway, 1819–2003," *Norges Bank Occasional Papers* 35, pp. 377–392.

Eklöf, Kurt (1990), "*Tre Valuta Kriser*," *Riksbank Occasional Paper* 8.

Emminger, Otmar (1986), *D-Mark, Dollar, Währungskrisen: Erinnerungen eines ehemaligen Bundesbankpräsidenten*. Stuttgart: Deutsche Verlags-Anstalt.

Englund, Peter (1999), "The Swedish banking crisis: Roots and consequences," *Oxford Review of Economic Policy* 15, pp. 80–97.

Englund, Peter, and Vesa Vihriälä (2003), "Financial crises in developed economies: The cases of Sweden and Finland," *Pellervo Economic Research Institute Working Papers* 63.

Ettlin, Franz, and Serge Gaillard (2002), "*Die lange Krise der 90er Jahre: Eine wettbewerbsfähige Wirtschaft braucht eine stabilisierende Geldpolitik*," *Schweizerischer Gewerkschaftsbund Dossier* 16.

Fase, M. M. G. (2000), *Tussen behoud en vernieuwing: Geschiedenis van de Nederlandsche Bank 1948–1973*. De Haag: Sdu Uitgevers.

Feinstein, Charles H. (ed.), *Banking, Currency, and Finance in Europe Between the Wars*. Oxford and New York: Oxford University Press, pp. 214–236.

Feinstein, Charles H., and Katherine Watson (1995), "Private international capital flows in Europe in the inter-war period," in Charles H. Feinstein (ed.), *Banking,*

Currency, and Finance in Europe Between the Wars. Oxford and New York: Oxford University Press, pp. 94–130.

Feinstein, Charles H., Gianni Toniolo, and Peter Temin (1997), *The European Economy Between the Wars.* Oxford and New York: Oxford University Press.

Feldman, Gerald D. (1998), "Current problems in the study of banking crises," in Clara Eugenia Núñez (ed.), *Finance and the Making of the Modern Capitalist World, 1750–1931, Proceedings of the Twelfth International Economic History Congress.* Sevilla, Spain: Secretariado de Publicaciones de la Universidad de Sevilla, pp. 53–61.

Feldt, Kjell-Olof (1991), *Alla dessa dagar ...: i regeringen 1982–1990.* Stockholm: Norstedts.

Ferguson, Thomas, and Peter Temin (2003), "Made in Germany: The German currency crisis of July 1931," *Research in Economic History* 21, pp. 1–53.

Ferguson, Thomas, and Peter Temin (2004), "Comment on 'The German twin crises of 1931,'" *Journal of Economic History* 64, pp. 872–876.

Ferrari, Luciano (1990), *Die Preisgabe fixer Wechselkurse durch die Schweizerische Nationalbank 1973: Ökonomische Bedingungen und theoretische Begründung.* Lizentiatsarbeit: Universität Zurich.

Ferrera, Maurizio, and Elisabetta Gualmini (2000), "Italy: Rescue from without?" in Fritz W. Scharpf and Vivien A. Schmidt (eds.), *Welfare and Work in the Open Economy, Vol. II: Diverse Responses to Common Challenges.* Oxford and New York: Oxford University Press, pp. 351–398.

Fior, Michel (2008), *Institution globale et marchés financiers: La Société des Nations face à la reconstruction de L'Europe, 1918–1931.* Bern: Peter Lang.

Fischer, Stanley (2001), "Exchange rate regimes: Is the bipolar view correct," *Journal of Economic Perspectives* 50, pp. 3–24.

Fisher, Irving (1933), "The debt-deflation theory of great derpessions," *Econometrica* 1, pp. 337–357.

Fisher, Irving (1934), *Stable Money.* New York: Adelphi Co.

Fitzmaurice, John (1996), *The Politics of Belgium.* London: Hurst.

Fleetwood, Erin E. (1947), *Sweden's Capital Imports and Exports.* Geneva: Journal de Genève.

Flood, Robert P., and Peter M. Garber, (1994), "Collapsing exchange rate regimes: Some linear examples," *Journal of International Economics* 17, pp. 1–17.

Flood, Robert P., and Andrew Rose (1995), "Fixing exchange rates: A virtual quest for fundamentals." *Journal of Monetary Economics* 36, pp. 3–37.

Fohlin, Caroline (2000), "Economic, political, and legal factors in the development of financial systems: International patterns in historical perspective," *California Institute of Technology Social Science Working Paper* 1089.

Forder, James (1996), "On the assessment and implementation of 'institutional' remedies," *Oxford Economic Papers* 48, pp. 39–51.

Forder, James (1998a), "The case for an independent European central bank: A reassessment of evidence and sources," *European Journal of Political Economy* 14, pp. 53–71.

Forder, James (1998b), "Central bank independence: Conceptual clarifications and interim assessment," *Oxford Economic Papers* 50, pp. 307–334.

Forsyth, Douglas J., and Daniel Verdier (2003), *The Origins of National Financial Systems: Alexander Gerschenkron Reconsidered.* London and New York: Routledge.

Frankel, Jeffrey A. (1999), "No single currency is right for all countries or at all times," *Princeton Essays in International Finance* 215.

Frankel, Jeffrey A. (2003), "Experience of and Lessons from Exchange Rate Regimes in Emerging Economies," NBER Working Paper 10032.

Franzese, J. Robert (2002), *Macroeconomic Policies of Developed Countries.* Cambridge and New York: Cambridge University Press.

Franzese, Robert, and Peter Hall (2000), "Institutional dimensions of coordinating wage bargaining and monetary policy," in Torben Iversen, Jonas Pontusson, and David Soskice (eds.), *Unions, Employers, and Central Banks: Macroeconomic Coordination and Institutional Change in Social Market Economies.* Cambridge and New York: Cambridge University Press, pp. 173–204.

Fregert, Klas (1994), *Wage Contracts, Policy Regimes and Business Cycles: A Contractual History of Sweden 1908–1990.* Lund: University of Lund.

Fregert, Klas, and Lars Jonung (2004), "Deflation dynamics in Sweden: Perceptions, expectations, and adjustment during the deflations of 1921–1923 and 1931–1933," in Richard C. K. Burdekin and Pierre L. Siklos (eds.), *Deflation: Current and Historical Perspectives.* Cambridge and New York: Cambridge University Press, pp. 91–128.

Freiburghaus, Dieter (2009), *Königsweg oder Sackgasse? Sechzig Jahre schweizerische Europapolitik.* Zürich: NZZ Libro.

Freitag, Markus (1999), *Politik und Währung: Ein internationaler Vergleich.* Bern, Stuttgart und Wien: Verlag Paul Haupt.

Frieden, Jeffry (1991), "Invested interests: The politics of national economic policies in a world of global finance," *International Organization* 45, pp. 425–451.

Frieden, Jeffry (2002), "Real sources of European currency policy: Sectoral interests and European monetary integration," *International Organization* 56, pp. 831–860.

Friedman, Milton (1953), "The case for flexible exchange rates," in Milton Friedman (ed.), *Essays in Positive Economics.* Chicago: The University of Chicago Press.

Friedman, Milton, and Anna J. Schwartz (1963), *A Monetary History of the United States, 1867–1960.* Princeton, NJ: Princeton University Press.

Fritschy, W., and P. E. Werkman (1987), "The trade unions," in Richard T. Griffiths (ed.), *The Netherlands and the Gold Standard, 1931–1936.* Amsterdam: Neha, pp. 63–83.

Froats, Daniel K. (1995), "'Sozialpartnerschaft and Hartwährungspolitik': Political prerequisites and effects of the Austrian hard currency policy, and implications for post-Maastricht monetary union in Europe," *Austrian National Bank Working Paper* 19, pp. 16–28.

Gäfvert, Björn (1979), *Kreuger, Riksbanken och Regeringen.* Dissertation, University of Stockholm.

Galenson, Walter (ed.) (1952), *Comparative Labor Movements.* New York: Prentice-Hall.

Garrett, Geoffrey (1998), *Partisan Politics in the Global Economy.* Cambridge and New York: Cambridge University Press.

Gautschi, Willi (1988), *Der Landesstreik 1918,* 3rd rev. ed. Zurich: Chronos Verlag.

Genberg, Hans (1990), "In the shadow of the mark: Exchange rate and monetary policy in Austria and Switzerland," in Victor Argy and Paul De Grauwe (eds.), *Choosing an Exchange Rate Regime: The Challenge for Smaller Industrial Countries.* Washington, DC: International Monetary Fund, pp. 197–219.

Genberg, Hans, and Alexander K. Swoboda (1985), *External Influences on the Swiss Economy under Fixed and Flexible Exchange Rates.* Grüsch: Verlag Rüegger.

Genberg, Hans, and Alexander K. Swoboda (2004), "Exchange rate regimes: Does what countries say matter?" *mimeo, Graduate Institute of International Studies, Geneva,* Switzerland.

Gerdrup, Karsten R. (2004), "Three booms and busts involving banking crises in Norway since the 1890s," in Thorvald G. Moe, Jon A. Solheim, and Bent Vale (eds.), *The Norwegian Banking Crisis, Norges Bank Occasional Papers* 33, pp. 145–178.

Gerlach, Stefan (1997), "Monetary policy issues in the Nordic countries after 1992," *BIS Policy Papers* 2, pp. 230–263.

Ghosh, Atish, Anne-Marie Gulde, and H. C. Wolf (2003), *Exchange Rate Regimes: Choices and Consequences.* Cambridge, MA: MIT Press.

Giavazzi, Francesco, and Alberto Giovannini (1989), *Limiting Exchange Rate Flexibility: The European Monetary System.* Cambridge, MA: MIT Press.

Giavazzi, Francesco, and Frederic S. Mishkin (2006), *An Evaluation of Swedish Monetary Policy between 1995 and 2005: A Report for the Riksdag Committee on Finance.* Stockholm: Riksdag.

Giscard d' Estaing, Valéry (1988), *Le pouvoir et la vie.* Paris: Compagnie 12.

Glete, Jan (1978), "The Kreuger Group and the crisis on the Swedish stock market," *Scandinavian Journal of History* 3, pp. 251–272.

Glete, Jan (1981), *Kreugerkoncernen och krisen på svensk aktiemarknad: studier om svenskt och internationellt riskkapital under mellankrigstiden.* Stockholm: A&W International.

Glick, Reuven, and Andrew Rose (1998), "Contagion and trade: Why are currency crises regional?" *NBER Working Paper* 6086.

Goldsmith, Raymond W. (1969), *Financial Structure and Development.* New Haven, CT: Yale University Press.

Goldstein, Morris (1995), *The Exchange Rate System and the IMF: A Modest Agenda.* Washington, DC: Institute for International Economics.

Goldthorpe, John H. (ed.) (1984), *Order and Conflict in Contemporary Capitalism.* Oxford: Clarendon Press.

Goodfriend, Marvin (2007), "How the world achieved consensus on monetary policy," *Journal of Economic Perspectives* 21, pp. 47–68.

Goodman, John B. (1992), *Monetary Sovereignty: The Politics of Central Banking in Western Europe.* Ithaca, NY and London: Cornell University Press.

Gourevitch, Peter (1986), *Politics in Hard Times: Comparative Responses to International Economic Crises.* Ithaca, NY and London: Cornell University Press.

Gourevitch, Peter, Andrew Martin, George Ross, Christopher Allen, Stephen Bornstein, and Andrei Markovits (1984), *Unions and Economic Crisis: Britain, West Germany and Sweden.* London: George Allen & Unwin.

Grädel, Markus (2007), *Vereint marschieren – getrennt schlagen! Die Schweiz, Norwegen, Österreich und Schweden zwischen EWR und Beitritt zur Europäischen Union.* Bern: Haupt.

Greef, Irene J. M. de, Paul L. C. Hilbers, and Lex H. Hoogduin (1998), "Moderate monetarism: A brief survey of Dutch monetary policy in the post-war period," *De Nederlandsche Bank Staff Reports* 28.

Griffiths, Richard T. (1987), "The policy makers," in Richard T. Griffiths (ed.), *The Netherlands and the Gold Standard, 1931–1936.* Amsterdam: Neha, pp. 165–192.

Griffiths, Richard T., and E. Schoorl (1987), "The single issue pressure groups," in Richard T. Griffiths (ed.), *The Netherlands and the Gold Standard, 1931–1936.* Amsterdam: Neha, pp. 139–164.

Griffiths, Richard T., and H. J. Langeveld (1987), "Economic and politics," in Richard T. Griffiths (ed.), *The Netherlands and the Gold Standard, 1931–1936.* Amsterdam: Neha, pp. 1–18.

Griffiths, Richard T., and M. E. de Vries (1987), "The agricultural lobby," in Richard T. Griffiths (ed.), *The Netherlands and the Gold Standard, 1931–1936.* Amsterdam: Neha, pp. 47–62.

Grilli, Vittorio, Donato Masciandaro, and Guido Tabellini (1991), "Political and monetary institutions and the public financial policies in the industrial countries," *Economic Policy* 13, pp. 341–392.

Grimm, Robert (1936), *Zur Wirtschafts- und Kreditkrise (Deflation and Abwertung).* Bern: Sozialdemokratische Partei der Schweiz.

Gros, Daniel (1990), "Comment," in Victor Argy and Paul De Grauwe (eds.), *Choosing an Exchange Rate Regime: The Challenge for Smaller Industrial Countries.* Washington, DC: International Monetary Fund, pp. 156–162.

Gros, Daniel, and Niels Thygesen (1998), *European Monetary Integration,* 2nd ed. Harlow, England: Longman.

Grossman, Richard S. (1994), "The shoe that didn't drop: Explaining banking stability during the Great Depression," *Journal of Economic History* 54, pp. 654–682.

Grytten, Ola Honningdal (1995), "The scale of Norwegian interwar unemployment in international perspective," *Scandinavian Economic History Review* 43, pp. 226–250.

Guex, Sébastien (1993), *La politique monétaire et financière de la Confédération Suisse, 1900–1920.* Lausanne: Editions Payot.

Guex, Sébastien (2000), "The origins of the Swiss banking secrecy law and its repercussions for Swiss federal policy," *Harvard Business History Review* 74, pp. 237–266.

Guex, Sébastien (2003), "*La politique de la Banque nationale suisse (1907–1939): modèles, références et spécificités,*" in Olivier Feiertag and Michel Margairaz (eds.), *Politiques et pratiques des banques d'émission en Europe (XVIIe-XXe siècle).* Paris: Albin Michel, pp. 549–568.

Guex, Sébastien (ed.) (1999), *La Suisse et les grandes puissances 1914–1945. Relations économiques avec les Etats-Unis, la Grande-Bretagne, l'Allemagne et la France.* Geneva: Droz.

Guger, Alois (1998), "Economic policy and social democracy: The Austrian experience," *Oxford Review Economic Policy* 14, pp. 40–58.

Gutt, Camille (1935), *Pourquoi le franc belge est tombé.* Brussels: Nouvelle Société d'Editions.

Gylfason, Thorvaldur (1990), "Exchange rate policy, inflation, and unemployment: The Nordic EFTA countries," in Victor Argy and Paul De Grauwe (eds.), *Choosing an Exchange Rate Regime: The Challenge for Smaller Industrial Countries.* Washington, DC: International Monetary Fund, pp. 163–192.

Haavisto, Tarmo, and Lars Jonung (1995), "Off gold and back again: Finnish and Swedish monetary policies, 1914–1925," in Charles H. Feinstein (ed.), *Banking, Currency, and Finance in Europe Between the Wars.* New York and Oxford: Oxford University Press, pp. 237–266.

Haavisto, Tarmo, and Lars Jonung (1999), "Central banking in Sweden and Finland in the twentieth century," in Carl-Ludwig Holtfrerich et al. (eds.), *The Emergence of Modern Central Banking from 1918 to the Present.* Aldershot, England: Macmillan, pp. 111–143.

Haberler, Gottfried (1982), "Austria's economic development after the two world wars: A mirror picture of the world economy," in Sven W. Arndt (ed.), *The Political Economy of Austria.* Washington, DC: American Enterprise Institute, pp. 61–75.

Hadenius, Stig (1990), *Schwedische Politik im 20. Jahrhundert.* Stockholm: Schwedisches Institut.

Halbeisen, Patrick (1998), "*Bankenkrise und Bankengesetzgebung in den 30er Jahren*," in Sébastien Guex et al. (eds.), *Krisen und Stabilisierung. Die Schweiz in der Zwischenkriegszeit.* Zurich: Chronos, pp. 61–79.

Halbeisen, Patrick (2005), "Goldstandard oder 'manipulierte Währung'? Partikularinteressen und Währungspolitik in den 1930er Jahren," *Traverse* 2005(1), pp. 168–176.

Halbeisen, Patrick (2007), "Cool lover? Switzerland and the road to European monetary union," in Piet Clement and J. C. Martinez Oliva (eds.), *European Central Banks and Monetary Cooperation after 1945.* Frankfurt am Main: European Association for Banking and Financial History, pp. 99–117.

Hamilton, Carl B., and Ulrika Stuart (2003), "*I stormens öga med strid på flera fronter*," in Jonung (ed.), *På jakt efter ett nytt ankare: Från fast kronkurs till inflationsmål,* Stockholm: SNS Förlag, pp. 89–172.

Hamilton, Malcolm B. (1989), *Democratic Socialism in Britain and Sweden.* New York: St. Martin's Press.

Handler, Heinz (1989), *Grundlagen der österreichischen Hartwährungspolitik: Geldwertstabilisierung, Phillipskurve, Unsicherheit.* Wien: Manzsche Verlags- und Universitätsbuchhandlung.

Handler, Heinz, and Eduard Hochreiter (1998), "Austria," in Erik Jones, Jeffry Frieden, and Franciso Torres (eds.), *Joining Europe's Monetary Club: The Challenges for Smaller Member States.* New York: St. Martin's Press, pp. 19–42.

Hanisch, Tore Jørgen (1979), "Om virkninger av paripolitikken: Et essay om norsk økonomi I 1920-årene," *Historisk Tidsskrift* 3, pp. 237–268.

Hanisch, Tore Jørgen, Espen Søilen, and Gunhild Ecklund (1999), *Norsk økonomisk politikk i det 20. århundre: Verdivalg I en åpen økonomi.* Kristiansand: Høyskoleforlaget.

Hansen, Per H. (1991), "From growth to crisis: The Danish banking system from 1850 to the interwar years," *Scandinavian Economic History Review* 39, pp. 20–40.

Hansen, Per H. (1994), "Production versus currency: The Danish central bank in the 1920s," in Alice Teichova, Terry Gourvish, and Agnes Pogána (eds.), *Universal Banking in the Twentieth Century: Finance, Industry and the State in North and Central Europe.* Aldershot, England: Edward Elgar, pp. 59–76.

Hansen, Per H. (1995), "Banking crises and lenders of last resort: Denmark in the 1920s and the 1990s," in Youssef Cassis, Gerald D. Feldman, and Ulf Olsson (eds.), *Evolution of Financial Institutions and Markets in Twentieth-Century Europe.* Aldershot, England: Scolar Press, pp. 20–46.

Hansen, Per H. (1996), *På glidebanen til den bitre ende*, Odense: Universitets-Forlag.

Hatton, T. J., and K. A. Chrystal (1991), "The budget and fiscal policy," in N. F. R. Crafts and N. Woodward (eds.), *The British Economy since 1945*. New York and Oxford: Oxford University Press.

Haupt, Paul H. (1927), "Die Einführung der Goldwährung in Dänemark," *Weltwirtschaftliches Archiv* 25, pp. 299–306.

Heath, Edward (1998), *The Course of My Life: My Autobiography*. London: Hodder & Stoughton.

Heckscher, Eli (1926), *Bidrag till Sveriges Ekonomiska och Sociala Historia under och efter Världkriget*. Stockholm and New Haven, CT: P. A. Norstedt & Söners Förlag and Yale University Press.

Heckscher, Eli (1930), *Sweden, Norway, Denmark and Iceland in the World War*. Oxford and New Haven, CT: Oxford University Press and Yale University Press.

Heikenstein, Lars (2003), "Bakom riksbankens tjocka väggar – hur inflationsmålpolitiken växte fram 1995–2003," in Lars Jonung (ed.), *På jakt efter ett nytt ankare: Från fast kronkurs till inflationsmål*. Stockholm: SNS Förlag, pp. 331–376.

Helleiner, Eric (1994), *States and the Reemergence of Global Finance: From Bretton Woods to the 1990s*. Ithaca, NY: Cornell University Press.

Heller, Robert H. (1978), "Determinants of exchange rate practices," *Journal of Money, Credit, and Banking* 10, pp. 308–321.

Hellmann, Rainer (1976), *Dollar, Gold und Schlange: Die letzten Jahre von Bretton Woods*, Baden-Baden: Nomos.

Hemerijck, Anton, Brigitte Unger, and Jelle Visser (2000), "How small countries negotiate change: Twenty-five years of policy adjustment in Austria, the Netherlands, and Belgium," in Fritz W. Scharpf and Vivien A. Schmidt (eds.), *Welfare and Work in the Open Economy, Vol. II: Diverse Responses to Common Challenges*. New York and Oxford: Oxford University Press, pp. 175–263.

Henrekson, Magnus (1990), "Did the devaluations of 1981 and 1982 induce a structural shift in the Swedish economy?" *Skandinaviska Enskilda Banken Quarterly Review* 4, pp. 90–98.

Henrekson, Magnus (1991), "*Devalveringarnas effekter på den svenska ekonomins struktur*," in Lars Jonung (ed.), *Devalveringen 1982 – rivstart eller snedtändning? Perspektiv på svensk devalveringspolitik*. Stockholm: SNS Förlag, pp. 44–83.

Henrekson, Magnus, Lars Jonung, and Joakim Stymne (1996), "Economic growth and the Swedish model," in Nicholas Crafts and Gianni Toniolo (eds.), *Economic Growth in Europe since 1945*. Cambridge and New York: Cambridge University Press, pp. 240–289.

Henriksen, Ingrid, and Niels Kaergård (1995), "The Scandinavian Currency Union, 1875–1914," in Jaime Reis (ed.), *International Monetary Systems in Historical Perspective*. London: Macmillan, pp. 91–112.

Hess, J. C. (1987), "The Social Democrats (SDAP)," in Richard T. Griffiths (ed.), *The Netherlands and the Gold Standard, 1931–1936*. Amsterdam: Neha, pp. 120–129.

Hey, Jeanne A. K. (ed.) (2003), *Small States in World Politics: Explaining Foreign Policy Behavior*. Boulder, CO: Lynne Rienner.

Hildebrand, Karl-Gustaf (1971), *Banking in a Growing Economy: Svenska Handelsbanken since 1871*. Stockholm: Svenska Handelsbanken.

Hochreiter, Eduard, and Adalbert Knöbl (1991), "Exchange rate policy of Austria and Finland: Two examples of a peg," *De Pecunia* 3, pp. 33–61.

Hochreiter, Eduard, and Georg Winckler (1995), "The advantages of tying Austria's hands: The success of the hard currency strategy," *European Journal of Political Economy* 11, pp. 83–111.

Hodne, Fritz (1983), *The Norwegian Economy, 1920–1980*. London: Croom Helm.

Hoffmeyer, Erik (1968), "Perioden 1931–1960," in Erling Olsen and Erik Hoffmeyer (eds.), *Dansk pengehistorie 1914–1960*. Copenhagen: Danmarks Nationalbank, pp. 155–331.

Hoffmeyer, Erik (1993), *Pengepolitiske Problemstillinger, 1965–1990*. Copenhagen: Danmarks Nationalbank.

Hogg, R. L. (1987), "Belgium, France and Switzerland and the end of the gold standard," in Richard T. Griffiths (ed.), *The Netherlands and the Gold Standard, 1931–1936*. Amsterdam: Neha, pp. 193–210.

Hohl, Marcela (1983), *Die wirtschaftspolitischen Vorstellungen von Max Weber (1897–1974) und sein Einfluss auf die Tätigkeit des Schweizerischen Gewerkschaftsbundes*. Zurich: Rüegger.

Holtrop, Marius (1970), "The balance-of-payments adjustment process, its asymmetry, and possible consequences for the international payments system," in Marius Holtrop (ed.), *Money in an Open Economy: Selected Papers on Monetary Policy, Monetary Analysis and Central Banking*. Leiden: Stenfert Kroese.

Honkapohja, Seppo, and Pentti Pikkarainen (1994), "Country characteristics and the choice of the exchange rate regime: Are mini-skirts followed by maxis?" in Johnny Åkerholm and Alberto Giovannini (eds.), *Exchange Rate Policies in the Nordic Countries*. London: CEPR, pp. 31–58.

Hörngren, Lars, and Hans Lindberg (1994), "The struggle to turn the Swedish krona into a hard currency," in Johnny Åkerholm and Alberto Giovannini (eds.), *Exchange Rate Policies in the Nordic Countries*. London: CEPR, pp. 133–172.

Houben, Aerdt C. F. J. (2000), *The Evolution of Monetary Policy Strategies in Europe*. Boston, Dordrecht, and London: Kluwer Academic Publishers.

Houwink ten Cate, Johannes (1989), "*Amsterdam als Finanzplatz Deutschlands (1919–1932)*," in Gerald D. Feldman et al. (eds.), *Konsequenzen der Inflation*. Berlin: Colloquium-Verlag, pp. 149–179.

Howson, Susan (2004), "Money and monetary policy since 1945," in Roderick Floud and Paul Johnson (eds.), *The Cambridge Economic History of Modern Britain, Vol. III: Structural Change and Growth, 1939–2000*. Cambridge and New York: Cambridge University Press, pp. 134–166.

Huberman, Michael, and Wayne Lewchuk (2003), "European economic integration and the labor compact, 1850–1913," *European Review of Economic History* 7, pp. 3–41.

Hug, Peter (2002), "*Steuerflucht und die Legende vom antinazistischen Ursprung des Bankgeheimnisses. Funktion und Risiko der moralischen Überhöhung des Finanzplatzes Schweiz*," in Jakob Tanner and Sigrid Weigel (eds.), *Gedächtnis, Geld und Gesetz. Vom Umgang mit der Vergangenheit des Zweiten Weltkriegs*. Zurich: Vdf Hochschulverlag, pp. 269–319.

Iklé, Max (1972), *Switzerland: An International Banking and Finance Center*. Stroudsburg, PA: Dowden, Hutchinson & Ross.

Iklé, Max (1984), *Erinnerungen*. Küsnacht.

Ingold, Evelyn (2003), "*Ungleichgewichte im Bretton-Woods-System: Die Mitwirkung der Schweiz an der internationalen Währungsreform in den 1960er Jahren*," in Hans-

Jörg Gilomen et al. (eds.), *Globalisierung – Chancen und Risiken. Die Schweiz in der Weltwirtschaft 18.-20. Jahrhundert.* Zurich: Chronos, pp. 297–316.

Iversen, Carl (1932), "Probleme der dänischen Währungspolitik," *Archiv für Sozialwissenschaft and Sozialpolitik* 67, pp. 641–669.

Iversen, Carl (1936a), "The importance of the international margin: Some lessons of recent Danish and Swedish monetary policy," in *Explorations in Economics: Notes and Essays Contributed in Honor of F. W. Taussig.* New York: McGraw-Hill, pp. 68–83.

Iversen, Carl (1936b), "Das Devalvationsproblem in Dänemark," *Weltwirtschaftliches Archiv* 43, pp. 29–61.

Iversen, Torben (1999), *Contested Economic Institutions: The Politics of Macroeconomics and Wage Bargaining in Advanced Democracies.* Cambridge and New York: Cambridge University Press.

Iversen, Torben (2000), "Decentralization, monetarism, and the Social Democratic welfare state," in Torben Iversen, Jonas Pontusson, and David Soskice (eds.), *Unions, Employers, and Central Banks: Macroeconomic Coordination and Institutional Change in Social Market Economies.* Cambridge and New York: Cambridge University Press, pp. 205–231.

Iversen, Torben, and Niels Thygesen (1998), "Denmark: From external to internal adjustment," in Erik Jones, Jeffry Frieden, and Franciso Torres (eds.), *Joining Europe's Monetary Club: The Challenges for Smaller Member States.* New York: St. Martin's Press, pp. 61–82.

Iversen, Torben, Jonas Pontusson, and David Soskice (eds.) (2000), *Unions, Employers, and Central Banks: Macroeconomic Coordination and Institutional Change in Social Market Economies.* Cambridge and New York: Cambridge University Press.

Jack, D. T. (1927), *The Restoration of European Currencies.* London: P. S. King & Son.

Jacobsen, Hans S. (1924), "Die norwegischen Bankkrisen in Verbindung mit der wirtschaftlichen Entwicklung Norwegens seit dem Kriege," *Weltwirtschaftliches Archiv* 20, pp. 41–61.

James, Harold (1991), "Introduction," in Harold James, Håkan Lindgren, and Alice Teichova (eds.), *The Role of Banks in the Interwar Economy.* Cambridge and New York: Cambridge University Press, pp. 1–12.

James, Harold (1992), "Financial flows across frontiers during the interwar depression," *Economic History Review* 45, pp. 594–613.

James, Harold (1996), *A History of International Monetary Cooperation since 1945.* New York and Oxford: Oxford University Press.

James, Harold (2001), *The End of Globalization: Lessons From the Great Depression.* Cambridge, MA and London: Harvard University Press.

James, Harold, Håkan Lindgren, and Alice Teichova (eds.) (1991), *The Role of Banks in the Interwar Economy.* Cambridge and New York: Cambridge University Press.

Janssens, Valery (1976), *Le franc belge: un siècle et demi d'histoire monétaire.* Brussels: Banque Nationale de Belgique.

Jeitziner, Bruno (1999), *Political Economy of the Swiss National Bank.* Heidelberg: Physica.

Johansen, Hans Christian (1987), *The Danish Economy in the Twentieth Century.* London and Sydney: Croom Helm.

Johnson, Harry G. (1969), "The Case for Flexible Exchange Rates," in Harry G. Johnson and John E. Nash (eds.), *UK and Floating Exchange Rates, London: The Institute of Economic Affairs*, pp. 9–37.

Johnson, Manuel H., and Robert E. Keleher (1996), *Monetary Policy: A Market Price Approach*. Westport, CT and London: Quorum Books.

Johnson, Peter A. (1998), *The Government of Money: Monetarism in Germany and the United States*. Ithaca, NY and London: Cornell University Press.

Johnston, R. B. (1982), *The Economics of the Euro-market: History, Theory and Policy*. New York: St. Martin's Press.

Jöhr, Walter Adolf (1956), *Die Schweizerische Kreditanstalt 1856-1956. Hundert Jahre im Dienste der schweizerischen Volkswirtschaft*. Zurich: Schweizerische Kreditanstalt.

Jones, Erik (1998a), "Belgium: Keeping up with the pack?" in Erik Jones, Jeffry Frieden, and Franciso Torres (eds.), *Joining Europe's Monetary Club: The Challenges for Smaller Member States*, New York: St. Martin's Press, pp. 43-60.

Jones, Erik (1998b), "The Netherlands: Top of the class," in Erik Jones, Jeffry Frieden, and Franciso Torres (eds.), *Joining Europe's Monetary Club: The Challenges for Smaller Member States*, New York: St. Martin's Press, pp. 149-170.

Jones, Erik (2008), *Economic Adjustment and Political Transformation in Small States*, New York and Oxford: Oxford University Press.

Jonker, Joost (1996), "Between private responsibility and public duty: The origins of bank monitoring in the Netherlands, 1860-1930," *Financial History Review* 3, pp. 139-152.

Jonker, Joost (1997), "The alternative road to modernity: Banking and currency, 1918-1914," in Marjolein 't Hart et al. (eds.), *A Financial History of The Netherlands*. Cambridge and New York: Cambridge University Press, pp. 94-123.

Jonker, Joost, and Jan Luiten van Zanden (1995), "Method in madness? Banking crises between the wars, and international comparison," in Charles H. Feinstein (ed.), *Banking, Currency, and Finance in Europe between the Wars*. New York and Oxford: Oxford University Press, pp. 77-93.

Jonung, Lars (1978), "En stabil stabiliseringspolitik," *Ekonomisk Debatt* 7 (1).

Jonung, Lars (1979a), "Knut Wicksell's norm of price level stabilization and Swedish monetary policy in the 1930s," *Journal of Monetary Economics* 5, pp. 459-496.

Jonung, Lars (1979b), "Cassel, Davidson and Heckscher on Swedish monetary policy: A confidential report to the Riksbank in 1931," *Economy and History* 22, pp. 85-101.

Jonung, Lars (1981), "The depression in Sweden and the United States: A comparison of causes and policies," in Karl Brunner (ed.), *The Great Depression Revisited*. Boston: Martinus Nijhoff, pp. 286-315.

Jonung, Lars (1992), "Swedish price-stabilization policy, 1931-1939: The *Riksbank* and Knut Wicksell's norm," in Sveriges Riksbank (ed.), *Monetary Policy with a Flexible Exchange Rate*. Stockholm: Riksbank, pp. 25-39.

Jonung, Lars (1999), *Med backspegeln som kompass - om stabiliseringspolitiken som läroprocess*. Stockholm: Finans-departementet.

Jonung, Lars (ed.) (1991), *Devalveringen 1982 - rivstart eller snedtändning? Perspektiv på svensk devalveringspolitik*, Stockholm: SNS Förlag.

Jonung, Lars (2007), "The political economy of monetary unification: The Swedish euro referendum of 2003," in Lars Jonung and Jürgen Nautz (eds.), *Conflict Potentials in Monetary Unions*. Stuttgart: Franz Steiner, pp. 157-178.

Jonung, Lars, and Eskil Wadensjö (1979), "Wages and prices in Sweden, 1912-1921," *Scandinavian Journal of Economics* 81, pp. 60-71.

Jonung, Lars, Hans Tson Söderström, and Joakim Stymne (1996), "Depression in the north: Boom and bust in Sweden and Finland, 1985–1993," *Finnish Economic Papers* 9, pp. 55–71.

Kaiser, Chantal (1999), *Bundesrat Jean-Marie Musy (1919–1934)*. Freiburg: Universitätsverlag.

Kaminsky, Graciela L., and Carmen M. Reinhart (1999), "The Twin Crises: The Causes of Banking and Balance-of-Payments Problems," *American Economic Review* 89, pp. 473–500.

Kaminsky, Graciela L., Carmen M. Reinhart, and Carlos Vegh (2003), "The unholy trinity of financial contagion," *NBER Working Paper* 10061.

Katzenstein, Peter J. (1984), *Corporatism and Change: Austria, Switzerland, and the Politics of Industry*. Ithaca, NY: Cornell University Press.

Katzenstein, Peter J. (1985), *Small States in World Markets: Industrial Policy in Europe*. Ithaca, NY and London: Cornell University Press.

Katzenstein, Peter J. (2003), "*Small States* and Small States Revisited," *New Political Economy* 8, pp. 9–30.

Keesing, F. A. G. (1947), *De conjuncturele ontwikkeling van Nederland en de evolutie van de economische overheidspolitiek, 1918–1939*. Utrecht and Antwerpen: Het Spectrum.

Keilhau, Wilhelm (1936), "Die faktische Schillingkrone Norwegens," *Weltwirtschaftliches Archiv* 43, pp. 62–81.

Keilhau, Wilhelm (1938), "*Volkswirtschaftspolitik und weltwirtschaftliche Stellung Norwegens*," *Kieler Vorträge* 54.

Keilhau, Wilhelm (1952), *Den norske pengehistorie*. Oslo: H. Aschehoug.

Keller, Theo (1955), *Leu & Co., 1755–1955, Denkschrift zum zweihundertjährigen Bestehen der Aktiengesellschaft Leu & Co Zürich*. Zurich: Leu & Co.

Kenen, Peter (1969), "The theory of optimum currency areas: An eclectic view," in Robert Mundell and Alexander Swoboda (eds.), *Monetary Problems of the International Economy*. Chicago: The University of Chicago Press, pp. 41–59.

Kennedy, James C. (1995), *Nieuw Babylon in Aanbouw: Nederland in De Jaren Zestig*. Amsterdam: Boom.

Keohane, Robert (1969), "Lilliputians dilemmas: Small states in international politics," *International Organization* 23, pp. 210–291.

Kerr, Ian M. (ed.) (1984), *A History of the Eurobond Market: The First 21 Years*. London: Euromoney Publications.

Kienzl, Heinz (1993), Gesamtstabilität, der Weg und das Ziel – Einkommenspolitik und Währungspolitik seit 1951, in Fritz Weber and Theodor Venus (eds.), *Austrokeynesianismus in Th eorie und Praxis*. Wien : Jugend & Volk , pp. 63–72.

Kindleberger, Charles P. (1934), "Competitive currency depreciation between Denmark and New Zealand," *Harvard Business Review* 12, pp. 416–426.

Kindleberger, Charles P. (1951), "Group behavior and international trade," *Journal of Political Economy* 59, pp. 30–46.

Kindleberger, Charles P. (1973), *The World in Depression, 1929–1939*. London: Allen Lane.

Kindleberger, Charles. P. (1974), "The formation of financial centers: A study in comparative economic history," *Princeton Studies in International Finance* 36.

Kindleberger, Charles P. (1989), *Manias, Panics and Crashes: A History of Financial Crises*. New York: Wiley.

Kitschelt, Herbert, Peter Lange, Gary Marks, and John D. Stephens (eds.) (1999), *Continuity and Change in Contemporary Capitalism*. Cambridge and New York: Cambridge University Press.

Kjellström, Erik (1934), *Managed Money: The Experience of Sweden*. New York: Columbia University Press.

Klein, Michael W., and Jay C. Shambaugh (2004), "Fixed exchange rates and trade," *NBER Working Paper* 10696.

Klein, Michael W., and Jay C. Shambaugh (2006), "The nature of exchange rate regimes," *NBER Working Paper* 12729.

Kleinewefers Lehner, Anne (1997), *Glaubwürdigkeitsaspekte der Geldpolitik in Deutschland, der Schweiz, den Niederlanden und Österreich*. Bern: Haupt.

Klemann, H. A. M. (1990), *Tussen Reich en Empire: De economische betrekkingen van Nederland met zijn belangrijkste handelspartners: Duitsland, Groot-Britainnië en België en de Nederlandse handelspolitiek, 1929-1936*. Dissertation, Vrije Universiteit te Amsterdam.

Klovland, Jan Tore (1998), "Monetary policy and business cycles in the interwar years: The Scandinavian experience," *European Review of Economic History* 2, pp. 309-344.

Klovland, Jan Tore (2004a), "Historical exchange rate data, 1819-2003," *Norges Bank Occasional Papers* 35, pp. 289-328.

Klovland, Jan Tore (2004b), "Monetary aggregates in Norway, 1819-2003," *Norges Bank Occasional Papers* 35, pp. 181-240.

Knapp, Oscar (1977), *Die schweizerische Wechselkurspolitik in der Zeit von 1968-1975: Analyse und Ausblick*. Dissertation, Hochschule St. Gallen.

Kneschaurek, Francesco (1952), *Der schweizerische Konjunkturverlauf und seine Bestimmungsfaktoren dargestellt auf Grund der Periode von 1929 bis 1939*. Zurich: Polygraphischer Verlag.

Knutsen, Sverre (1991), "From expansion to panic and crash: The Norwegian banking system and its customers, 1913-1924," *Scandinavian Economic History Review* 39, pp. 41-71.

Knutsen, Sverre (1994), "Norwegian banks and the legacy of the interwar years," in Alice Teichova, Terry Gourvish, and Agnes Pogána (eds.), *Universal Banking in the Twentieth Century: Finance, Industry and the State in North and Central Europe*, Aldershot, England: Edward Elgar, pp. 77-95.

Knutsen, Sverre (1995), "Phases in the development of the Norwegian banking system, 1880-1980," in Youssef Cassis, Gerald D. Feldman, and Ulf Olsson (eds.), *Evolution of Financial Institutions and Markets in Twentieth-Century Europe*. Aldershot, England: Scolar Press, pp. 78-121.

Knutsen, Sverre (2001), "Financial fragility or information asymmetry? The interwar banking crisis in Norway," Mimeo.

Knutsen, Sverre, and Gunhild J. Ecklund (2000), *Vern mot Kriser? Norsk finanstilsyn gjennom 100 år*. Bergen: Fagbokforlaget.

Kock, Karin (1931), "Hur Sverige tvingades att överge guldmyntfoten," in Gunnar Myrdal (ed.), *Sveriges väg genom penningkrisen*. Stockholm: Bokförlaget Natur och Kultur, pp. 141-160.

Kock, Karin (1933), "Paper currency and monetary policy in Sweden," in *Economic Essays in Honour of Gustav Cassel, October 20th, 1933*. London: Allen and Urwin, pp. 343-356.

Körner, Martin (1993), *"Schweiz,"* in Hans Pohl (ed.), *Europäische Bankengeschichte*. Frankfurt am Main: Fritz Knapp Verlag, pp. 279–285, 415–418, 551–560.

Krugman, Paul (1979), "A model of balance-of-payments crises," *Journal of Money, Credit and Banking* 11, pp. 311–325.

Krugman, Paul (1989), "The case for stabilizing exchange rates," *Oxford Review of Economic Policy* 5, pp. 61–72.

Krugman, Paul (1996), "Are currency crises self-fulfilling?" in Ben S. Bernanke and Julio J. Rotemberg (eds.), *NBER Macroeconomics Annual 1996*. Cambridge, MA: MIT Press, pp. 345–378.

Kruse, D. C. (1980), *Monetary Integration in Western Europe: EMU, EMS and Beyond*. London: Butterworths.

Kugler, Peter, and Georg Rich (2002), "Monetary policy under low interest rates: The experience of Switzerland in the late 1970s," *Schweizerische Zeitschrift für Volkswirtschaft und Statistik* 138, pp. 241–269.

Kugler, Peter, and Beatrice Weder (2002), "The puzzle of the Swiss interest rate island: Stylized facts and a new interpretation," *Aussenwirtschaft* 57, pp. 49–63.

Kuipers, S. K., J. Muysken, and J. van Sinderen (1979), "The vintage approach to output and employment growth in the Netherlands, 1921–1976," *Weltwirtschaftliches Archiv* 115, pp. 485–506.

Kunz, Diane B. (1987), *The Battle for Britain's Gold Standard in 1931*. London: Croom Helm.

Kurgan-van Hentenryk, Ginette (1992), "Finance and financiers in Belgium, 1880–1940," in Youssef Cassis (ed.), *Finance and Financiers in European History, 1880–1960*. Cambridge and New York: Cambridge University Press, pp. 317–335.

Kurz, Hermann, and Gottlieb Bachmann (1928), *Die schweizerischen Grossbanken, ihre Geschäftstätigkeit und ihre wirtschaftliche Bedeutung*. Zurich and Leipzig: Orell Füssli.

Kurzer, Paulette (1993), *Business and Banking: Political Change and Economic Integration in Western Europe*. Ithaca, NY and London: Cornell University Press.

Lafferty, William M. (1971), *Economic Development and the Response of Labor in Scandinavia: A Multi-Level Analysis*. Oslo, Bergen, Tromsö: Universitetsforlaget.

Landmann, Julius (1916), "Der schweizerische Kapitalexport," *Zeitschrift für Schweizerische Statistik und Volkswirtschaft* 52, pp. 389–415.

Landsorganizationen i Sverige (1986), *De centrala överrenskommelserna mellan LO och SAF 1952–1987*. Stockholm: Tidens Förlag.

Lane, Philipp R. (1995), "Inflation in open economies," mimeo, Columbia University.

Langeveld, H. J. (1987), "The political parties," in Richard T. Griffiths (ed.), *The Netherlands and the Gold Standard, 1931–1936*. Amsterdam: Neha, pp. 84–138.

Larsson, Mats (1991), "State, banks and industry in Sweden, with some reference to the Scandinavian countries," in Harold James, Håkan Lindgren, and Alice Teichova (eds.), *The Role of Banks in the Interwar Economy*. Cambridge and New York: Cambridge University Press, pp. 80–103.

Larsson, Mats (1993), "Scandinavia," in Hans Pohl (ed.), *Europäische Bankengeschichte*. Frankfurt am Main: Fritz Knapp Verlag, pp. 333–342.

Larsson, Mats (1995), "Overcoming institutional barriers: Financial networks in Sweden, 1910–1990," in Youssef Cassis, Gerald Feldman, and Ulf Olsson (eds.), *The Evolution of Financial Institutions and Markets in Twentieth Century Europe*. Aldershot, England: Scolar Press, pp. 122–142.

Laubach, Thomas, and Adam S. Posen (1997), "Disciplined discretion: The German and Swiss monetary targeting frameworks in operation," *Federal Reserve Bank of New York Research Paper* 9707.

League of Nations (1920), *International Financial Conference (1920: Brussels)*. London: Harrison & Sons.

League of Nations (1922), *Memorandum on Central Banks, 1913, 1918–1921*. Geneva.

League of Nations (1925), *Memorandum on Balance of Payments and Foreign Trade Balances, 1910–1924*. Geneva.

League of Nations (1931), *Memorandum on Commercial Banks, 1913–1929*. Geneva.

Lehner, Gerhard (1982), "'Deficit-spending' in Österreich," *Wirtschaftspolitische Blätter* 29, pp. 24–35.

Lester, Richard A. (1939), *Monetary Experiments: Early American and Recent Scandinavian*. Princeton, NJ: Princeton University Press.

Levy, Jonah D. (2000), "France: Directing adjustment?" in Fritz W. Scharpf and Vivien A. Schmidt (eds.), *Welfare and Work in the Open Economy, Vol. II: Diverse Responses to Common Challenges*. New York and Oxford: Oxford University Press, pp. 308–350.

Levy-Yeyati, Eduardo, and Federico Sturzenegger (2005), "Classifying exchange rate regimes: Deeds vs. words," *European Economic Review* 49, pp. 1603–1635.

Lindahl, Erik (1936), "Der Übergang zur Papierwährung in Schweden 1931," *Weltwirtschaftliches Archiv* 43, pp. 82–96.

Lindbeck, Assar (1997), *The Swedish Experiment*. Stockholm: SNS Förlag.

Lindgren, Håkan (1982), "The Kreuger crash of 1932: In memory of a financial genius, or was he a simple swindler?" *Scandinavian Economic History Review* 30, pp. 189–206.

Lindgren, Håkan (1988), *Bank, investmentbolag, bankirfirma: Stockholms enskilda bank 1924–1945*. Stockholm: Almqvist & Wiksell.

Lindgren, Håkan (1991), "Swedish historical research on banking during the 1980s: Tradition and renewal," *Scandinavian Economic History Review* 39, pp. 5–19.

Lindgren, Håkan (1997), "The influence of banking on the development of capitalism in the Scandinavian countries," in Alice Teichova, Ginette Kurgan- van Hentenryk, and Dieter Ziegler (eds.), *Banking, Trade and Industry: Europe, America and Asia from the Thirteenth to the Twentieth Century*. Cambridge and New York: Cambridge University Press, pp. 191–213.

Lindvall, Johannes (2004), *The Politics of Purpose: Swedish Macroeconomic Policy after the Golden Age*, PhD dissertation, Gothenburg University.

Loriaux, Michael (1991), *France after Hegemony: International Change and Financial Reform*. Ithaca, NY and London: Cornell University Press.

Ludlow, Peter (1982), *The Making of the European Monetary System*. London: Butterworth.

Lundberg, Erik (1957), *Business Cycles and Economic Policy*. London: George Allen & Unwin.

Lundberg, Erik (1996), *The Development of Swedish and Keynesian Macroeconomic Theory and its Impact on Economic Policy*. Cambridge and New York: Cambridge University Press.

Lutz, Friedrich A. (1954), "The case for flexible exchange rates," *Banca Nazionale del Lavoro Quarterly Review*, pp. 175–185.

Luykx, Theo, and Marc Platel (1985), *Politieke geschiedenis van België van 1789 to heden. Volume 1: 1789–1944.* Antwerpen: Kluwer rechtswetenschappen.

Maddison, Angus (1991), *Dynamic Forces in Capitalist Development: A Long-Run Comparative View.* Oxford and New York: Oxford University Press.

Maddison, Angus (2001), *The World Economy: A Millenial Perspective.* Paris: OECD.

Maes, Ivo (2002), *Economic Thought and the Making of European Monetary Union.* Cheltenham, England: Edward Elgar.

Maes, Ivo, and Amy Verdun (2005), "Small states and the creation of EMU: Belgium and the Netherlands, pace-setters and gate-keepers," *Journal of Common Market Studies* 43, pp. 327–348.

Magnusson, Lars (2000), *An Economic History of Sweden.* London: Routledge.

Manow, Philip, and Eric Seils (2000), "Adjusting badly: The German welfare states, structural change, and the open economy," in Fritz W. Scharpf and Vivien A. Schmidt (eds.), *Welfare and Work in the Open Economy, Vol. II: Diverse Responses to Common Challenges.* Oxford and New York: Oxford University Press, pp. 264–307.

Martens, Wilfried (1985), *Parole donnée: Autoportrait.* Bruxelles: Didier Hatier.

Masson, Paul R. (2001), "Exchange rate regime transitions," *Journal of Development Economics* 64, pp. 571–586.

Mast, Hans J. (1971), "Geldpolitik und Schweizer Banken," *Schweizerische Zeitschrift für Volkswirtschaft und Statistik* 107, pp. 291–300.

McKeown, Timothy J. (1999), "The global economy, post-Fordism, and trade policy in advanced capitalist states," in Herbert Kitschelt, Peter Lange, Gary Marks, and John D. Stephens (eds.), *Continuity and Change in Contemporary Capitalism.* Cambridge and New York: Cambridge University Press, pp. 11–35.

McKinnon, Ronald (1963), "Optimum currency areas," *American Economic Review* 53, pp. 717–724.

McNamara, Kathleen R. (1998), *The Currency of Ideas: Monetary Politics in the European Union.* Ithaca, NY and London: Cornell University Press.

Meade, James (1955), "The case for variable exchange rates," *Three Banks Review* 27, pp. 3–27.

Meese, Richard A., and Kenneth Rogoff (1983), "Empirical exchange rate models of the seventies: Do they fit out of sample?" *Journal of International Economics* 14, pp. 3–24.

Melvin, M. (1985), "The choice of an exchange rate system and macroeconomic stability," *Journal of Money, Credit and Banking* 17, pp. 467–478.

Menzel, Ulrich (1988), *Auswege aus der Abhängigkeit: Die entwicklungspolitische Aktualität Europas.* Frankfurt am Main: Suhrkamp.

Mikkelsen, Flemming (1992), *Arbeijdskonflikter in Skandinavien 1848–1980.* Odense: Universitetsforlag.

Mikkelsen, Richard (1993), *Dansk Pengehistorie, 1960–1990.* Copenhagen: Danmarks Nationalbank.

Miles, Lee (ed.) (1996), *The European Union and the Nordic Countries.* London: Routledge.

Miles, Lee (1997), *Sweden and European Integration.* Aldershot, England: Ashgate.

Miles, Lee (2005), *Fusing with Europe? Sweden in the European Union.* Aldershot, England: Ashgate.

Mishkin, Frederic S. (1991), "Asymmetric information and financial crises: A historical perspective," in R. Glenn Hubbard (ed.), *Financial Markets and Financial Crises*. Chicago and London: The University of Chicago Press, pp. 69–108.

Mitchell, B. R. (2003), *International historical statistics: Europe, 1750–2000*. Basingstoke: Palgrave Macmillan.

Mjøset, Lars (1987), "Nordic economic policies in the 1970s and 1980s," *International Organization* 41, pp. 403–456.

Moe, Thorvald G., Jon A. Solheim, and Bent Vale (eds.) (2004), "The Norwegian banking crisis," *Norges Bank Occasional Papers* 33.

Mommen, André (1994), *The Belgian Economy in the Twentieth Century*. London: Routledge.

Montgomery, Arthur (1955), "Economic fluctuations in Sweden in 1919–1921," *Scandinavian Economic History Review* 3, pp. 203–238.

Mooij, Joke, and H. M. Prast (2002), "A brief history of the institutional design of banking supervision in the Netherlands," *Research Memorandum Nederlandsche Bank*, October.

Moravcsik, Andrew (1999), *The Choice for Europe: Social Purpose and State Power from Messina to Maastricht*. London: UCL Press.

Moses, Jonathon W. (1995), *Devalued Priorities: The Politics of Nordic Exchange Rate Regimes Compared*, Ph.D. Dissertation, University of California, Los Angeles.

Moses, Jonathon W. (1998), "Sweden and EMU," in Erik Jones, Jeffry Frieden, and Franciso Torres (eds.), *Joining Europe's Monetary Club: The Challenges for Smaller Member States*, New York: St. Martin's Press, pp. 203–224.

Moses, Jonathon W. (2000), *Open States in the Global Economy: The Political Economy of Small-State Macroeconomic Management*. Basingstoke, England: Macmillan.

Mouré, Kenneth (1991), *Managing the Franc Poincaré: Economic Understanding and Political Constraint in French Monetary Policy, 1928–1936*. Cambridge and New York: Cambridge University Press.

Mouré, Kenneth (2002), *The Gold Standard Illusion: France, the Bank of France, and the International Gold Standard, 1914–1939*. New York and Oxford: Oxford University Press.

Müller, Margrit (2002), "Coping with barriers to trade: Internationalisation strategies of Swiss firms in the interwar period," in Hubert Bonin et al. (eds.), *Transnational Companies, 19th-20th Centuries*. Paris: PLAGE, pp. 239–254.

Muller, Patrice, and Robert W. R. Price (1984), "Structural Budget Deficit and Fiscal Stance," OECD Monetary and Fiscal Policy Division Working Paper 15.

Müller, Philipp (2001), *La bataille pour le franc: La Suisse entre déflation et dévaluation (1931–1936)*. Lizentiatsarbeit: Universität Lausanne.

Mundell, Robert (1961), "The theory of optimum currency areas," *American Economic Review* 53, pp. 717–724.

Murray, John (1997), "Comments on 'Monetary policy in Norway – Experience since 1992' (Nicolaisen and Qvigstad 1997)," *BIS Policy Papers* 2, pp. 133–139.

Myhrman, Johan (1978), "Dags för omprövning av svensk penningpolitik," *Skandinaviska Enskilda Bankens Kvartalsskrift* ½.

Nannestad, Peter (1991), *Danish Design or British Disease? Danish Economic Policy 1974–1979 in Comparative Perspective*. Aarhus: Aarhus University Press.

Nelson, Edward (2005), "The great inflation of the seventies: What really happened?" *Advances in Macroeconomics* 5, pp. 1–48.

Neumann, Manfred J. M. (1999), "Monetary stability: Threat and proven response," in Deutsche Bundesbank (ed.), *Fifty Years of the Deutsche Mark: Central Bank and the Currency in Germany since 1948*. New York and Oxford: Oxford University Press, pp. 269–306.

Nicolaisen, Jon, and Jan F. Qvigstad (1997), "Monetary policy in Norway: Experience since 1992," *BIS Policy Papers* 2, pp. 101–132.

Nielsen, Peter Erling (1994), "Monetary policy in Denmark in the last 10 years," in Johnny Åkerholm and Alberto Giovannini (eds.), *Exchange Rate Policies in the Nordic Countries*. London: CEPR, pp. 59–99.

Nordvik, Helge W. (1992), "Bankkrise, bankstruktur og bankpolitikk i Norge i mellomkrigstiden," *Historisk Tidsskrift* 71, pp. 170–192.

Nordvik, Helge W. (1993), "The banking system, industrialization and economic growth in Norway, 1850–1914," *Scandinavian Economic History Review* 41, pp. 51–72.

Nordvik, Helge W. (1995), "Norwegian banking in the inter-war period: A Scandinavian perspective," in Charles H. Feinstein (ed.), *Banking, Currency, and Finance in Europe between the Wars*. New York and Oxford: Oxford University Press, pp. 434–457.

Notermans, Ton (2000), *Money, Markets, and the State: Social Democratic Economic Policies since 1918*. Cambridge and New York: Cambridge University Press.

Núñez, Clara Eugenia (ed.) (1998), *Finance and the Making of the Modern Capitalist World, 1750–1931, Proceedings of the Twelfth International Economic History Congress*. Sevilla: Secretariado de Publicaciones de la Universidad de Sevilla.

Nurkse, Ragnar (1944), *International Currency Experiences*. Geneva: League of Nations.

Nützenadel, Alexander (2005), *Stunde der Ökonomen. Wissenschaft, Expertenkultur und Politik in der Bundesrepublik 1949–1974*, Göttingen: Vandenhoeck & Ruprecht.

Obstfeld, Maurice (1986), "Rational and self-fulfilling balance of payments crises," *American Economic Review* 76, pp. 72–81.

Obstfeld, Maurice (1994), "The logic of currency crises," *Cahiers Economiques et Monétaires* 43, pp. 189–213.

Obstfeld, Maurice (1996), "Comment," in Ben S. Bernanke and Julio J. Rotemberg (eds.), *NBER Macroeconomics Annual 1996*. Cambridge, MA: MIT Press, pp. 393–403.

Obstfeld, Maurice, and Alan M. Taylor (2004), *Global Capital Markets: Integration, Crisis, and Growth*. Cambridge and New York: Cambridge University Press.

OECD (1988), *Why Economic Policies Change Course: Eleven Case Studies*. Paris: OECD.

Olsen, Erling (1968), "Perioden 1914–1931," in Erling Olsen and Erik Hoffmeyer (eds.), *Dansk pengehistorie 1914–1960*. Copenhagen: Danmarks Nationalbank, pp. 11–152.

Olsson, Ulf (1991), "Comparing the interwar banking history of five small countries in North-west Europe," in Harold James, Håkan Lindgren, and Alice Teichova (eds.), *The Role of Banks in the Interwar Economy*. Cambridge and New York: Cambridge University Press, pp. 26–34.

Östlind, Anders (1945), *Svensk Samhällsekonomi, 1914–1922: Mer särskild hänsyn till industri, banker och penningväsen.* Stockholm: Svenska Bankföreningen.

Pedersen, Jørgen (1931), *Economic Conditions in Denmark after 1922.* Copenhagen: Institute of Economics and History.

Pedersen, Peder J. (1996a), "Postwar growth of the Danish economy," in Nicholas Crafts and Gianni Toniolo (eds.), *Economic Growth in Europe since 1945.* Cambridge and New York: Cambridge University Press, pp. 541–575.

Pedersen, Thomas (1996b), "Denmark and the European Union," in Lee Miles (ed.), *The European Union and the Nordic Countries.* London and New York: Routledge, pp. 81–100.

Perrenoud, Marc (2000), "Aspects de la politique financière et du mouvement ouvrier en Suisse dans les années 1930," *Etudes et Sources* 26, pp. 83–121.

Perrenoud, Marc, Rodrigo López, Florian Adank, Jan Baumann, Alain Cortat, and Suzanne Peters (2002), "*La place financière et les banques suisses à l'époque du national-socialisme: Les relations des grandes banques avec l'Allemagne (1931–1946), Veröffentlichungen der Unabhängigen Expertenkommission Schweiz – Zweiter Weltkrieg,* Vol. 13. Zurich: Chronos.

Posen, Adam (1995), "Declarations are not enough: Financial sector sources of central bank independence," in Ben S. Bernanke and J. Rotemberg (eds.), *NBER Macroeconomics Annual 1995.* Cambridge, MA and London: MIT Press, pp. 253–274.

Posen, Adam (1998), "Central bank independence and disinflationary credibility: A missing link?" *Oxford Economic Papers* 50, pp. 335–339.

Prader, Gaudenz (1981), *50 Jahre schweizerische Stabilisierungspolitik: Lernprozesse in Theorie und Politik am Beispiel der Finanz- und Beschäftigungspolitik des Bundes.* Zurich: Schulthess.

Qvigstad, Jan F. (2001), "Monetary policy in real time," *Norges Bank Working Paper* 1/2001.

Rathke, Alexander, and Tobias Straumann (2009), "*Estimating a Swiss Monetary Policy Rule,*" mimeo, University of Zurich.

Reinhart, Eberhard (1971), "Wechselkurspolitik und Bankapparat," in *Verstehen und Gestalten der Wirtschaft. Festgabe für Friedrich A. Lutz.,* Tübingen: Mohr, pp. 295–313.

Reinhart, Carmen, and Kenneth Rogoff (2002), "A modern history of exchange rate arrangements: A reinterpretation," *NBER Working Paper* 8963.

Reinhart, Carmen, and Kenneth Rogoff (2004), "The modern history of exchange rate arrangements: A reinterpretation," *Quarterly Journal of Economics* 119, pp. 1–48.

Reinhart, Carmen, and Kenneth Rogoff (2009), "The aftermath of financial crises," *NBER Working Paper* 14656.

Renou, René (1939), *La dévaluation du franc suisse: Ses causes, ses effects, son enseignement.* Bordeaux: Librarie Delmas.

Rich, Georg (1990a), "Comment," in Victor Argy and Paul De Grauwe (eds.), *Choosing an Exchange Rate Regime: The Challenge for Smaller Industrial Countries.* Washington, DC: International Monetary Fund, pp. 220–223.

Rich, Georg (1990b), "Exchange-rate management under floating exchange rates: A skeptical Swiss view," *Journal of Banking and Finance* 14, pp. 993–1021.

Rich, Georg (1992), "Die schweizerische Teuerung: Lehren für die Nationalbank," *Quartalsheft SNB* 1/1992, pp. 73–88.

Rich, Georg (1997), "Monetary targets as a policy rule: Lessons from the Swiss experience," *Journal of Monetary Economics* 39, pp. 113–141.

Rich, Georg (2003), "Swiss Monetary Targeting 1974–1996: The Role of Internal Policy Analysis," ECB Working Paper 236.

Ritzmann, Franz (1973), *Die Schweizer Banken. Geschichte, Theorie, Statistik.* Bern: Haupt.

Roberts, Richard, and David Kynaston (eds.) (1995), *The Bank of England: Money, Power and Influence 1694–1994.* Oxford and New York: Oxford University Press.

Rødseth, Asbjørn, and Steinar Holden (1990), "Wage formation in Norway," in Lars Calmfors (ed.), *Wage Formation and Macroeconomic Policy in the Nordic Countries.* Stockholm: SNS Förlag, pp. 237–286.

Roger, Charles (1936), "Die Währungsabwertung und die Politik des wirtschaftlichen Wiederaufbaus in Belgien," *Weltwirtschaftliches Archiv* 43, pp. 255–289.

Rogoff, Kenneth, Aasim M. Husain, Ashoka Mody, Robin Brooks, and Nienke Oomes (2003), "Evolution and performance of exchange rate regimes," *IMF Working Paper* 243.

Romer, Christina D., and David H. Romer (2004), "A new measure of monetary shocks: Derivation and implications," *American Economic Review* 94, pp. 1055–1084.

Romer, David (1993), "Openness and inflation: Theory and evidence," *Quarterly Journal of Economics* 108, pp. 870–903.

Rose, Andrew (2000), "One money, one market: The effect of common currencies on trade," *Economic Policy* 30.

Rose, Andrew (2007), "A stable international monetary system emerges: Inflation targeting is Bretton Woods, reversed," *Journal of International Money and Finance* 26, pp. 663–681.

Rose, Andrew, and Lars E. O. Svensson (1993), "European exchange rate credibility before the fall," *NBER Working Paper* 4495.

Rossi, Nicola, and Gianni Toniolo (1996), "Italy," in Nicholas Crafts and Gianni Toniolo (eds.), *Economic Growth in Europe since 1945.* Cambridge and New York: Cambridge University Press, pp. 427–454.

Rothstein, Robert L. (1968), *Alliances and Small Powers.* New York: Columbia University Press.

Ruin, Olof (1990), *Tage Erlander: Serving the Welfare State, 1946–1969.* Pittsburgh, PA: University of Pittsburgh Press.

Ruoss, Eveline (1992), *Die Geldpolitik der Schweizerischen Nationalbank 1907–1929: Grundlagen, Ziele und Instrumente.* Dissertation, University of Zurich.

Russo, Massimo, and Giuseppe Tullio (1988), "Monetary policy coordination within the European Monetary System: Is there a rule?" in Francesco Giavazzi, Stefano Micossi, and Marcus Miller (eds.), *The European Monetary System.* Cambridge and New York: Cambridge University Press, pp. 292–366.

Rutz, Wilfried (1970), *Die schweizerische Volkswirtschaft zwischen Währungs- und Beschäftigungspolitik in der Weltwirtschaftskrise – wirtschaftspolitische Analyse der Bewältigung eines Zielkonflikts.* Dissertation, Hochschule St. Gallen, Zurich and St. Gallen: Polygraphischer Verlag AG.

Rygg, Nicolai (1950), *Norges Bank i mellomkrigstiden.* Oslo: Gyldendal Norsk Forlag.

Rygg, Nicolai (1954), *Norges banks historie.* Kristiania.

Sandal, Knut (2004), "The Nordic banking crises in the early 1990s: Resolution methods and fiscal costs," in Thorvald G. Moe, Jon A. Solheim, and Bent Vale (eds.), *The Norwegian Banking Crisis, Norges Bank Occasional Papers* 33, pp. 77–115.

Sayers, R. S. (1976), *The Bank of England, 1891-1944.* Cambridge and New York: Cambridge University Press.

Scharpf, Fritz W. (1991), *Crisis and Choice in European Social Democracy.* Ithaca, NY and London: Cornell University Press.

Scharpf, Fritz W. (2000), "Economic changes, vulnerabilities, and institutional capabilities," in Fritz W. Scharpf and Vivien A. Schmidt (eds.), *Welfare and Work in the Open Economy, Vol. I: From Vulnerability to Competitiveness.* Oxford and New York: Oxford University Press, pp. 21–124.

Scharpf, Fritz W., and Vivien A. Schmidt (eds.) (2000a), *Welfare and Work in the Open Economy, Vol. I: From Vulnerability to Competitiveness.* Oxford and New York: Oxford University Press.

Scharpf, Fritz W., and Vivien A. Schmidt (eds.) (2000b), *Welfare and Work in the Open Economy, Vol. II: Diverse Responses to Common Challenges.* Oxford and New York: Oxford University Press.

Schenk, Catherine R. (1998), "The origins of the Eurodollar market in London: 1955–1963," *Explorations in Economic History* 35, pp. 221–238.

Schenk, Catherine R. (2002), "International financial centres, 1958-1971: Competitiveness and complementarity," in Stefano Battilossi and Youssef Cassis (eds.), *European Banks and the American Challenge: Competition and Cooperation in International Banking under Bretton Woods.* New York and Oxford: Oxford University Press, pp. 36–52.

Schiltknecht, Kurt (1983), "Switzerland: The pursuit of monetary objectives," in Paul Meek (ed.), *Central Bank Views on Monetary Targeting.* New York: Federal Reserve Bank, pp. 72–79.

Schiltknecht, Kurt (1989), "*Geldmengenpolitik und Wechselkurs – der Schweizerische Weg*," in Norbert Bub, Dieter Duwendag, and Rudolf Richter (eds.), *Geldwertsicherung und Wirtschaftsstabilität. Festschrift für Helmut Schlesinger zum 65. Geburtstag,* Frankfurt am Main: F. Knapp, pp. 243–257.

Schnabel, Isabel (2004a), "The German twin crisis of 1931," *Journal of Economic History* 64, pp. 822–871.

Schnabel, Isabel (2004b), "Reply to Thomas Ferguson and Peter Temin's Comment on 'The German twin crisis of 1930,'" *Journal of Economic History* 64, pp. 877–878.

Schön, Lennart (2000), *En modern svensk ekonomisk historia. Tillväxt och omvandling under två sekel.* Stockholm: SNS Förlag.

Schoorl, E. (1987), "The economists' debate," in Richard T. Griffiths (ed.), *The Netherlands and the Gold Standard, 1931-1936.* Amsterdam: Neha, pp. 19–29.

Schubert, Aurel (1991), *The Credit-Anstalt Crisis of 1931.* Cambridge and New York: Cambridge University Press.

Schwartz, Anna J. (2003), "Comment," in Michael Bordo, Alan Taylor, and Jeffrey Williamson (eds.), *Globalization in Historical Perspective.* Chicago: The University of Chicago Press, pp. 468–472.

Schwarz, Herbert (1937), "Geld- und güterwirtschaftliche Probleme Hollands und der Schweiz nach einem Jahr Währungsabwertung," *Schweizerische Zeitschrift für Volkswirtschaft und Statistik* 74, pp. 376–393.

Schweizerische Nationalbank (1932), *Schweizerische Nationalbank, 1907 bis 1932.* Zurich: Schweizerische Nationalbank.

Schweizerische Nationalbank (1957), *Schweizerische Nationalbank 1907–1957.* Zurich: Schweizerische Nationalbank.

Schweizerische Nationalbank (1982), *75 Jahre Schweizerische Nationalbank: Die Zeit von 1957 bis 1982.* Zurich: Verlag Neue Zürcher Zeitung.

Schwierz, Christoph (2004), "Economic costs associated with the Nordic banking crises," Thorvald G. Moe, Jon A. Solheim, and Bent Vale (eds.), *The Norwegian Banking Crisis, Norges Bank Occasional Papers* 33, pp. 117–144.

Seidel, Hans (1982), "The Austrian economy: An overview," in Sven W. Arndt (ed.), *The Political Economy of Austria.* Washington, DC and London: American Enterprise Institute, pp. 7–21.

Sejersted, Francis (1973), *Ideal, teori og virkelighet. Nicolai Rygg og pengepolitikken i 1920-årene.* Oslo: Cappelen.

Shepherd, Henry L. (1936), *The Monetary Experience of Belgium, 1914–1936*, Princeton, NJ: Princeton University Press.

Siebrand, J. C. and N. Van der Windt (1983), "Economic crisis and economic policy in the thirties and the seventies," *De Economist* 131, pp. 517–547.

Siklos, Pierre L. (2002), *The Changing Face of Central Banking: Evolutionary Trends since World War II.* Cambridge and New York: Cambridge University Press.

Simmons, Beth (1994), *Who Adjusts? Domestic Sources of Foreign Economic Policy during the Interwar Years.* Princeton, NJ: Princeton University Press.

Simmons, Beth (1996), "Rulers of the game: Central bank independence during the interwar years," *International Organization* 50, pp. 407–443.

Simmons, Beth (1999), "The internationalization of capital," in Herbert Kitschelt, Peter Lange, Gary Marks, and John D. Stephens (eds.), *Continuity and Change in Contemporary Capitalism.* Cambridge and New York: Cambridge University Press, pp. 36–69.

Sjögren, Hans (1991), "The financial contracts of large firms: A longitudinal study of Swedish firms and commercial banks, 1919–1947," *Scandinavian Economic History Review* 39, pp. 72–94.

Skånland, Hermod (1999), "Norway and the euro," *Norwegian School of Management, Centre of Monetary Economics, Working Papers* 8/1999.

Söderlund, Ernst (1978), *Skandinaviska banken i det svenska bankväsendets historia 1914–1939.* Stockholm: Almqvist & Wiksell.

Sohmen, Egon (1961), *Flexible Exchange Rates.* Chicago: The University of Chicago Press.

Solomon, Robert (1982), *The International Monetary System, 1945–1981.* New York: Harper & Row.

Somary, Felix (1929), *Wandlungen der Weltwirtschaft seit dem Kriege.* Tübingen: Mohr.

Somary, Felix (1986), *The Raven of Zurich. The Memoirs of Felix Somary.* London and New York: C. Hurst & Company, St. Martin's Press.

Soskice, David (2000), "Macroeconomic analysis and the political economy of unemployment," in Torben Iversen, Jonas Pontusson, and David Soskice (eds.), *Unions, Employers, and Central Banks: Macroeconomic Coordination and Institutional Change in Social Market Economies.* Cambridge and New York: Cambridge University Press, pp. 38–74.

Sozialdemokratische Partei der Schweiz (ed.), *Zur Währungsfrage: Diskussionsbeitrag.* Bern: Sozialdemokratische Partei der Schweiz, 1936.

Steigum, Erling (2004), "Financial deregulation with a fixed exchange rate: Lessons from Norway's boom-bust cycle and banking crisis," in Thorvald G. Moe, Jon A. Solheim, and Bent Vale (eds.), *The Norwegian Banking Crisis, Norges Bank Occasional Papers* 33, pp. 23–76.

Stiefel, Dieter (1988), *Die grosse Krise in einem kleinen Land: Österreichische Finanz- und Wirtschaftspolitik, 1929–1938.* Wien: Böhlau.

Straumann, Tobias (2005), "Finanzplatz und Pfadabhängigkeit. *Die Bundesrepublik, die Schweiz und die Vertreibung der Euromärkte (1955–1980),*" in Christoph Maria Merki (ed.), *Europas Finanzzentren – Geschichte und Bedeutung im 20. Jahrhundert.* Frankfurt am Main: Campus, pp. 245–268.

Straumann, Tobias (2006), "Der kleine Gigant: Der Aufstieg Zürichs zu einem internationalen Finanzplatz," in Hans Pohl (ed.), *Europäische Finanzplätze im Wettbewerb.* Frankfurt am Main: Knapp Verlag.

Straumann, Tobias, and Ulrich Woitek (2009), "A pioneer of a new monetary policy? Sweden's price level targeting of the 1930s revisited," *European Review of Economic History* 13, pp. 251–282.

Summers, Lawrence H. (2000), "International financial crises: Causes, prevention, and cures," *American Economic Review, Papers and Proceedings* 90, pp. 1–16.

Sutherland, Alan (1994), "Discussion," in Johnny Åkerholm and Alberto Giovannini (eds.), *Exchange Rate Policies in the Nordic Countries.* London: CEPR, pp. 56–58.

Svensson, Lars E. O. (1995), "The Swedish experience of an inflation target," *NBER Working Paper* 4985.

Svensson, Lars E. O. (2000), "Open-economy inflation targeting," *NBER Working Paper* 6545.

Sveriges Riksbank (1992), *Monetary Policy with a Flexible Exchange Rate.* Stockholm: Riksbank.

Swenson, Peter, and Jonas Pontusson (2000), "The Swedish employer offensive against centralized bargaining," in Torben Iversen, Jonas Pontusson, and David Soskice (eds.), *Unions, Employers, and Central Banks: Macroeconomic Coordination and Institutional Change in Social Market Economies.* Cambridge and New York: Cambridge University Press, pp. 77–106.

Sylla, Richard, Richard Tilly, and Gabriel Tortella (eds.) (1999), *The State, the Financial System and Economic Modernization.* Cambridge and New York: Cambridge University Press.

Szász, André (1981), "Het wisselkoersdebat," in E. den Dunnen, M. M. G. Fase, and A. Szász (eds.), *Zoeklicht op beleid: Opstellen aangeboden aan Prof. Dr. G.A. Kessler naar aanleiding van zijn uittreden als directeur van de Nederlandsche Bank per 1 mei 1981.* Leiden and Antwerpen: H. E. Stenfert Kroese B.V., pp. 303–323.

Szász, André (1988), *Monetaire Diplomatie: Nederlands Internationale Monetaire Politiek, 1958–1987.* Leiden and Antwerpen: H. E. Stenfert Kroese B.V.

Szász, André (1999), *The Road to European Monetary Union.* London: Macmillan.

Sœter, Martin (1996), "Norway and the European Union: Domestic debate versus external reality," in Lee Miles (ed.), *The European Union and the Nordic Countries.* London and New York: Routledge, pp. 133–149.

't Hart, Marjolein C., Joost Jonker, and Jan Luiten van Zanden (eds.) (1997), *A Financial History of the Netherlands*. Cambridge and New York: Cambridge University Press.

Talani, Leila Simona (2000), *Betting For and Against EMU: Who Wins and Who Loses in Italy and in the UK from the Process of European Monetary Integration*. Aldershot, England: Ashgate.

Talani, Leila Simona (2004), *European Political Economy: Political Science Perspectives*. Aldershot, England: Ashgate.

Tanner, Jakob (1997), "Die internationalen Finanzbeziehungen der Schweiz zwischen 1931 und 1950," *Schweizerische Zeitschrift für Geschichte* 47, pp. 492–519.

Tanner, Jakob (2000), "Goldparität im Gotthardstaat: Nationale Mythen und die Stabilität des Schweizer Frankens in den 1930er und 1940er Jahren," *Studien und Quellen* 26, pp. 45–85.

Temin, Peter (1989), *Lessons from the Great Depression*. Cambridge, MA: MIT Press.

Temin, Peter (2008), "The German crisis of 1931: Evidence and tradition," *Cliometrica* 2, pp. 5–17.

Thatcher, Margaret (1993), *The Downing Street Years*. London: HarperCollins.

Therborn, Göran (1986), *Why Some People Are More Unemployed than Others*. London: Verso.

Thielemans, Marie-Rose (1980), *La grande crise et le gouvernement des banquiers: Essai*. Brussels: Institut de Science politique.

Thomas, Brinley (1936), *Monetary Policy and Crises*. London: Routledge.

Thygesen, Niels (1979), "Exchange rate experiences and policies of small countries: Some European examples of the 1970s," *Essays in International Finance* 136.

Tobin, James (1978), "A proposal for monetary reform," *Eastern Economic Journal* 29/2003, pp. 519–526.

Toniolo, Gianni (2005), *Central Bank Cooperation at the Bank for International Settlements, 1930–1973*. Cambridge and New York: Cambridge University Press.

Traxler, Franz (1997), "European transformation and institution building in east and west: The performance of and preconditions for neocorporatism," in Randall W. Kindley and David F. Good (eds.), *The Challenge of Globalization and Institution Building: Lessons from Small European States*. Boulder, CO: Westview Press, pp. 145–178.

Tsoukalis, Loukas (1977), *The Politics and Economics of European Monetary Integration*. London: George Allen & Unwin.

Unabhängige Expertenkommission Schweiz – Zweiter Weltkrieg (2002), *Die Schweiz und die Goldtransaktionen im Zweiten Weltkrieg*. Veröffentlichungen der Unabhängigen Expertenkommission Schweiz – Zweiter Weltkrieg, Vol. 16. Zurich: Chronos.

Unabhängige Expertenkommission Schweiz – Zweiter Weltkrieg (2002), *Die Schweiz, der Nationalsozialismus und der Zweite Weltkrieg. Schlussbericht*. Zurich: Pendo.

Ungerer, Horst (1997), *A Concise History of European Monetary Integration: From EPU to EMU*. Westport, CT and London: Quorum Books.

Union Bank of Switzerland (ed.) (1987), *The Swiss Economy 1946–1986: Data, Facts, Analyses*. Zurich: Union Bank of Switzerland.

Vale, Bent (2004), "The Norweigan banking crisis," in Thorvald G. Moe, Jon A. Solheim, and Bent Vale (eds.), *The Norwegian Banking Crisis, Norges Bank Occasional Papers* 33, pp. 1–21.

Van Ark, Bart, Jakob de Haan, and Herman J. de Jong (1996), "Characteristics of economic growth in the Netherlands during the postwar period," in Nicholas Crafts and Gianni Toniolo (eds.), *Economic Growth in Europe since 1945*. Cambridge and New York: Cambridge University Press, pp. 290–328.

Van der Wee, Herman, and K. Tavernier (1975), *La Banque Nationale de Belgique et l'histoire monétaire entre les deux guerres mondiales*. Brussels: Banque Nationale de Belgique.

Van Zanden, Jan Luiten (1988), "De dans om de gouden standaard. Economische beleid in de depressie van de jaren dertig," in Jan Luiten van Zanden (ed.), *The Economic Development of The Netherlands since 1870*. Cheltenham, England and Brookfield: Edward Elgar, pp. 120–136.

Van Zanden, Jan Luiten (1997), "Old rules, new conditions, 1914–1940," in Marjolein 't Hart et al. (eds.), *A Financial History of The Netherlands*. Cambridge and New York: Cambridge University Press, pp. 124–151.

Van Zanden, Jan Luiten (1998), *The Economic History of the Netherlands, 1914–1995: A Small Open Economy in the "Long" Twentieth Century*, London: Routledge.

Van Zanden, Jan Luiten, and Richard T. Griffiths (1989), *Economische geschiedenis van Nederland in de 20e eeuw*. Utrecht: Het Spectrum.

Vandeputte, Robert (1985), *Economische Geschiedenis van Belgie 1944–1984*. Tielt: Lannoo.

Vanthemsche, Guy (1980), "L'élaboration de l'arrêté royal sur le contrôle bancaire (1935)," *Revue Belge d'Histoire Contemporaine* 11, pp. 389–435.

Vanthemsche, Guy (1997), "The bank from 1934 to date," in Herman Van der Wee (ed.), *The Generale Bank 1822–1997*. Tielt: Lannoo, pp. 287–531.

Visser, Jelle, and Anton Hemerijck (1997), *A Dutch Miracle: Job Growth, Welfare Reform and Corporatism in the Netherlands*. Amsterdam: Amsterdam University Press.

Vissering, G., and J. Westerman Holstijn (1928), *The Effect of the War upon Banking and Currency*. New Haven, CT: Yale University Press.

Vogler, Robert Urs (2000), "Das Bankgeheimnis – seine Genese im politisch-wirtschaftlichen Umfeld," *Schweizerische Monatshefte* 80, pp. 37–43.

Von Dosenrode, Sören Z. (1993), *Westeuropäische Kleinstaaten in der EG und EPZ*. Zurich: Rüegger.

von Hagen, Jürgen (1999), "A new approach to monetary policy," in Deutsche Bundesbank (ed.), *Fifty Years of the Deutsche Mark: Central Bank and the Currency in Germany since 1948*. New York and Oxford: Oxford University Press, pp. 403–438.

Vranitzky, Franz (1993), "10 Jahre danach – Versuch einer Bilanz: Franz Vranitzky im Gespräch mit Fritz Weber," in Fritz Weber and Theodor Venus (eds.), *Austrokeynesianismus in Theorie und Praxis*. Wien: Jugend & Volk, pp. 179–188.

Wallerstein, Michael, and Miriam Golden (2000), "Postwar wage setting in the Nordic countries," in Torben Iversen, Jonas Pontusson, and David Soskice (eds.), *Unions, Employers, and Central Banks: Macroeconomic Coordination and Institutional Change in Social Market Economies*. Cambridge and New York: Cambridge University Press, pp. 107–137.

Walsh, James I. (2000), *European Monetary Integration and Domestic Politics*. Boulder, CO: Lynne Rienner.

Wandschneider, Kirsten (2008) "The Stability of the Interwar Gold Exchange Standard: Did Politics Matter?", *Journal of Economic History* 68, pp. 151–181.

Wellink, Nout (1994), "The economic and monetary relation between Germany and the Netherlands," in Age Bakker, Henk Boot, Olaf Sleijpen, and Wim Vanthoor (eds.), *Monetary Stability through International Cooperation: Essays in Honour of André Szász.* Amsterdam: De Nederlandsche Bank, pp. 67–84.

Werin, Lars, Peter Englund, Lars Jonung, and Clas Wihlborg (1993), *Från räntereglering till inflationsnorm: Det finansiella systemet och riskbankens politik 1945–1990.* Stockholm: SNS Förlag.

Wetter, Ernst (1918), *Bankkrisen und Bankkatastrophen der letzten Jahre in der Schweiz (1910–1914).* Zurich: Orell Füssli.

Williamson, Philip (1992), *National Crisis and National Government: British Politics, the Economy and Empire, 1926–1932.* Cambridge and New York: Cambridge University Press.

Wilse, Hans Peter (2004), "Management of the banking crisis and state ownership of commercial banks," in Thorvald G. Moe, Jon A. Solheim, and Bent Vale (eds.), *The Norwegian Banking Crisis, Norges Bank Occasional Papers* 33, pp. 179–207.

Windmuller, John Philip (1969), *Labor Relations in the Netherlands.* Ithaca, NY and London: Cornell University Press.

Wolf, Nikolaus (2008), "Scylla and Charybdis: Explaining Europe's exit from gold, January 1928-December 1936", *Explorations in Economic History* 45, pp. 383–401.

Wright, C. M. (1939), *Economic Adaptation to a Changing World Market.* Copenhagen: Munksgaard.

Wyplosz, Charles (1994), "Discussion," in Johnny Åkerholm and Alberto Giovannini (eds.), *Exchange Rate Policies in the Nordic Countries.* London: CEPR, pp. 129–132.

Zijlstra, Jelle (1992), *Per slot van rekening – Memoires.* Amsterdam: Uitgeverij Contact.

Zis, George (2004), "The elusive case for flexible exchange rates," in Ross E. Catterall and Derek Aldroft (eds.), *Exchange Rates and Economic Policy in the 20th Century.* Aldershot, England: Ashgate, pp. 254–295.

Zurlinden, Mathias (2003), "Gold standard, deflation and depression: The Swiss economy during the Great Depression," *Swiss National Bank Quarterly Bulletin* 2/2003, pp. 86–116.

Index